PACIFIC LATIN AMERICA
IN PREHISTORY

PACIFIC LATIN AMERICA IN PREHISTORY

The Evolution of Archaic and Formative Cultures

Edited by Michael Blake

Washington State University Press
Pullman, Washington

Washington State University Press
PO Box 645910
Pullman, WA 99164-5910
Phone 800-354-7360; FAX 509-335-8568

Library of Congress Cataloging-in-Publication Data

Pacific Latin America in prehistory : the evolution of archaic and
    formative cultures / edited by Michael Blake.
        p.   cm.
    Includes bibliographical references.
    ISBN 0-87422-166-8 (pbk. : alk. paper)
    1. Paleo-Indians—Latin America—Pacific Coast.   2. Pacific Coast
(Latin America)—Antiquities.   I. Blake, Michael, 1953-   .
E65.P12 1999
911'.8'091823—dc21   98-43834
                                                                CIP

Preface

Circum-Pacific Prehistory Volumes

This volume is the second in a Washington State University Press series focusing on the prehistory of the vast Pacific Basin area. The first volume was *Pacific Northeast Asia in Prehistory, Hunter-Fisher-Gatherers, Farmers, and Socio-political Elites* edited by C. Melvin Aikens and Song Nai Rhee and published in 1992. This new volume, *Pacific Latin America in Prehistory,* focuses on the opposite side of the Pacific. A proposed third volume, edited by Robert E. Ackerman, will discuss the earliest occupation of the Pacific Coast from Siberia through Alaska to as far south as Chile in South America. Therefore, much of the rich prehistoric heritage of the Pacific Basin region is being closely examined as an overall unit for the first time in this WSU Press series.

Drafts of the papers in this volume originally were presented at the Circum-Pacific Prehistory Conference in two major sessions on Pacific Latin America chaired by the editor, Michael Blake, on August 1-6, 1989, in Seattle, Washington. The conference was held in conjunction with the Washington State Centennial celebration. It provided a format for over 200 scholars and indigenous peoples from around the Pacific Basin to present perspectives on the events that have shaped human heritage throughout the Pacific Basin. Following the conference, the section editors have worked closely with authors to revise, cross-reference, and edit their materials to form updated, cohesive volumes.

This publication represents the first synthesis of Pacific Latin American prehistory in one volume. Of all the archaeological regions of the Pacific (e.g., South Pacific, Southeast Asia, Northwest Asia, Northwest Coast of America), one that is rarely studied as a contiguous whole is the Mesoamerican and South American Pacific area. Possibly, this is one of the most important contributions of this volume—a look at this archaeological region from a Pacific Coast perspective. Michael Blake has brilliantly synthesized the works of specialists who have explored this area in terms of archaic period adaptations, the development and spread of agriculture, the beginnings of sedentism, the formative periods of civilizations, and the origins of socio-political inequality. This first ever synthesis provides an up-to-date cross-section of current work in this region. It illustrates the considerable potential of Pacific Latin American archaeology as a whole and its possible contribution to answering basic questions important to world prehistory.

Pacific Latin America in Prehistory explores the Pacific Coast of west and southeastern Mexico, Guatemala, Panama, Ecuador, Peru, and Chile, in a time span ranging from the Archaic through the Formative period, prior to the emergence of advanced states. One of the intentions of the Circum-Pacific Prehistory Conference was to encourage an ongoing exchange of research and scholarship in the years after the meeting. This and other volumes will help to accomplish that aim.

Dale R. Croes
Series Editor
Circum-Pacific Prehistory Volumes
October 1996

Acknowledgments

The appearance of this volume is due, in no small part, to all of the individuals and corporate and institutional sponsors who helped make the Circum-Pacific Prehistory Conference a success. These people and organizations were recognized in the first volume of the WSU Press series, but recognition of their contributions is warranted again.

An initial Centennial planning grant provided by the M.J. Murdock Charitable Trust made the conference possible. Other particularly noteworthy supporters were Washington State University, the 1989 Washington Centennial Commission, the City of Seattle, and the Pacific Northwest Archaeological Society. The Washington State University Press contributed to the conference by producing and distributing posters, programs, registration packets, and printed abstracts.

Ray and Jean Auel assisted in supporting initial coordination of the volume series.

Members of the Pacific Northeast Planning Committee who organized the original conference and now serve as planners and editors of this series include: Dr. Robert E. Ackerman, Washington State University; Dr. C. Melvin Aikens, University of Oregon; Dr. William Ayres, University of Oregon; Dr. Stephen Dow Beckham, Lewis and Clark College; Dr. Michael Blake, University of British Columbia; Ms. Pat Britz, Resource System Analysis; Dr. Dale R. Croes, Washington State University; Dr. James Haggarty, Royal British Columbia Museum; Ms. Bonnie Hardenbrook, Pacific Northwest Archaeological Society; Dr. Chuan Kun Ho; Dr. Grover Krantz, Washington State University; Ms. Lynn Larson, Larson Anthropological/Archaeological Services (LAAS); Dr. Astrida R. Blukis Onat, BOAS; Dr. Song Nai Rhee, Northwest Christian College; Dr. David Rice, U.S. Army Corps of Engineers; Dr. Richard Ross, Oregon State University; Dr. Mark Stoneking, The Pennsylvania State University; Dr. Robert Wenke, University of Washington; Mr. Bernie Whitebear, United Indians of All Tribes Foundation; and Dr. Robert Whitlam, Washington Office of Archaeology and Historic Preservation.

The Pacific Northwest Archaeological Society members who volunteered hundreds of hours of their time supporting the original conference include: Ruth Bobbit, Betty Crews, Claudia Estes, Gerald and Rebecca Fritts, Rebecca Gilford, Bonnie Hardenbrook, Jackie Hendrick, Jeff Mangel, Bob and Elsie Slagle, Connie Suagee, Nancy L. Thomas, Larry M. Tradelender, and Charlotte Turner-Zila.

The original conference sponsorship that provided the means for bringing participants together include Alaska Airlines, Jean and Ray Auel, Continental Airlines, Delta Airlines, the Federal Executive Board, G.T.E., Ivars, Inc., the Museum of History and Industry, the Oregon Historical Society, the Pacific Summit and Symposia, San Juan Air, the Seattle District U.S. Army Corps of Engineers, the L.J. Skaggs and Mary C. Skaggs Foundation, Glenn Terrell, Tillicum Village and Tours, United Airlines, the University of Washington Burke Museum, US West Communications, the Washington Commission for the Humanities, Washington State University Computer Services Center, Western Greyhound Lines, and Edith Williams.

These sponsors, the authors, the conference participants, and many previous researchers have shared in making the Pacific Basin human heritage project possible.

D. R. C.
1996

Contents

Preface v

Acknowledgments vii

Introduction
1. Introduction to the Archaeology of Pacific Latin America
    by Michael Blake 3

Part I: Mesoamerica
2. The Marismas Nacionales Project, Sinaloa and Nayarit, Mexico
    by Stuart D. Scott 13

3. On the Origin, Evolution, and Dispersal of Maize
    by Bruce F. Benz 25

4. Late Archaic Period Coastal Collectors in Southern Mesoamerica:
    The Chantuto People Revisited
    by George H. Michaels and Barbara Voorhies 39

5. The Emergence of Hereditary Inequality: The Case of Pacific Coastal Chiapas, Mexico
    by Michael Blake and John E. Clark 55

6. Early Formative Societies in Guatemala and El Salvador
    by Mary E. Pye, Arthur A. Demarest, and Barbara Arroyo 75

7. Economic Patterns in the Development of Complex Society in Pacific Guatemala
    by Michael W. Love 89

Part II: Central America
8. Precolumbian Fishing on the Pacific Coast of Panama
    by Richard G. Cooke and Anthony J. Ranere 103

9. The Origins and Development of Food Production in Pacific Panama
    by Dolores R. Piperno 123

Part III: South America
10. Wetlands as Resource Concentrations in Southwestern Ecuador
    by Alfred H. Siemens 137

11. Early Formative Societies in the Tropical Lowlands of Western Ecuador:
    a View from the Valdivia Valley
    by J. Scott Raymond 149

12. Agricultural Evolution and the Emergence of Formative Societies in Ecuador
    by Deborah M. Pearsall 161

13. Andean Coastal Adaptations: Uniformitarianism and Multilinear Evolution
     by Michael E. Moseley 171

14. The Development of Agriculture and the Emergence of Formative Civilization
    in the Central Andes
     by Thomas C. Patterson 181

15. Archaic Period Maritime Adaptations in Peru
     by Karen Wise 189

16. Archaic Adaptation on the South-Central Andean Coast
     by Lautaro Núñez. 199

17. The Late Preceramic-Early Formative Transition on the South-Central Andean Littoral
     by Mark S. Aldenderfer 213

    Contributors 223

INTRODUCTION

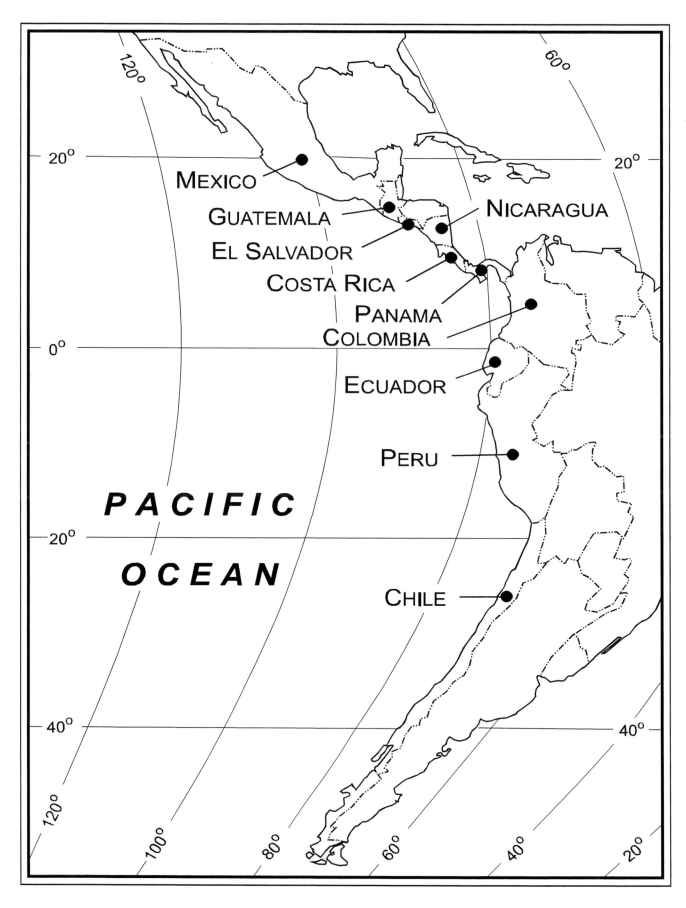

MEXICO

GUATEMALA

NICARAGUA

EL SALVADOR

COSTA RICA

PANAMA

COLOMBIA

ECUADOR

PERU

PACIFIC

OCEAN

CHILE

Figure 1. Pacific Latin America.

1

Introduction to the Archaeology
of Pacific Latin America

Michael Blake

When first asked to organize a session about Pacific coastal Latin American archaeology for Washington State's 1989 Centennial Circum-Pacific Prehistory Conference, my initial response was: "...okay, but why?" I had usually considered Latin American archaeology from the perspective of the traditional culture areas, such as Mesoamerica, Lower Central America, the Coastal Andean region, and so on. I could not, initially at least, see what was to be gained by cross-cutting those areas with a focus on the Pacific Coast. However, after participating in the conference, reading all of the papers, and discussing shared topics with other participants, it became clear that there were a number of themes that could be profitably examined with such a geographic focus. I am now convinced that there are many insights to be gained by such an approach, as the papers in this volume demonstrate. When the region is looked at as a whole, there are some similarities, but mostly many differences between the various cultures that existed along the Pacific Coast of Latin America. Understanding these similarities and differences can help us in our search for answers to one of the central questions in archaeology: How do civilizations arise?

The papers collected in this volume do not present an exhaustive summary of the current research into the origins and evolution of cultures in Pacific coastal Latin America, but they do give the reader an overview of the range of ancient societies and the diversity of environments and economies that flourished along the Pacific Coast.[1] The examples presented here range from as far north as the Marismas region of coastal West Mexico, to the north coast of Chile (Figure 1). Along the way we will look at archaeological work in southern Mexico, Guatemala, Panama, Ecuador, and Peru. These examples, when looked at in unison with some of the other Circum-Pacific regions discussed in other volumes in this series, show that the ancient peoples of the Pacific region were an extremely varied lot indeed. To what extent were these variations caused by different historical traditions, environmental conditions, and interactions with neighboring cultures? The authors of the different chapters in this volume do not, of course, present a unified answer to these questions, but they do present evidence which allows the reader to examine a number of common themes running through these diverse cultures and times.

One of the first of these themes is the nature of Archaic period adaptations. Unfortunately, with a few notable exceptions, we still know very little about the earliest inhabitants of Pacific Latin America. However, by about 5000 B.C., a growing number of people and cultures occupied the coastal regions and, from that period on, there was a trend towards increasing numbers and types of archaeological sites present along the coast. Another theme is the trend towards increasing sedentism. What is the evidence for the transition from relatively mobile Archaic period peoples to increasing numbers of sedentary communities? This trend is complex and began at different times along the Pacific Coast. However, by between 2500 and 1500 B.C. almost all Pacific coastal cultures had adopted a pattern of sedentism and we see an enormous expansion in the numbers and sizes of ancient communities.

An ongoing and still unresolved set of questions in Latin American archaeology is why, when, and how did the practice of agriculture come into being? Much of the initial evidence for early agriculture comes from the highland or inland regions of Latin America and not from coastal zones. But, with the onset of sedentism, there is increasing evidence that coastal peoples were developing their own sets of cultivated plant species as well as adopting and adapting plants that originated in highland or inland regions. This theme is an important one for understanding the processes whereby civilizations emerged, because by 1000 B.C. all coastal cultures from Mexico to Chile were certainly engaged in agricultural pursuits.

Another important question to come out of the archaeological research along the Pacific shores of Latin America is to what extent were people reliant on fishing and how did this reliance change as agricultural production evolved and improved over the course of three to four millennia? The variation in fishing strategies is in itself remarkable. Some fishing peoples engaged in open sea fishing, others focused on river and estuary systems, and still others concentrated on fresh and brackish water swamp systems in the littoral zone. One overriding similarity in all of these strategies and regions is the highly productive nature of the fisheries. The prime case is to be found along the coast of Peru where huge complex societies developed during the Late Archaic and Formative periods (Moseley 1992), but there are many other cases where sedentary and semi-sedentary communities evolved with a strong economic reliance on aquatic resources.

A final theme that threads its way through some of the papers in this volume is the question of how societies evolved socially and politically? There is a broad consensus in the field of Latin American archaeology that before about 2000 B.C. most societies, whether mobile hunter-fisher-gatherers, or sedentary part-time farmers, were organized along the lines of small-scale egalitarian communities. It is also clear that by A.D. 500 and earlier in most regions, societies were organized into large-scale states with complex social and political hierarchies and most of the trappings of complex civilization. The transitions in social and political life that took place after 2000 B.C. left their mark on the archaeological record and can be clearly traced through the centuries and millennia. What is not so clear though is why and how these transitions took place. In the papers presented here we are not able to answer all these questions, but we show how some of these transitions began and present some of the recent evidence for the social and political changes that can be inferred.

Archaic Period Adaptations

The term "Archaic" is used throughout Latin America to denote a number of aspects of ancient cultures. They were generally mobile peoples who made their living by hunting, fishing, and gathering. They left behind archaeological sites which illustrate many characteristics of this life-way: they were small in size, they had few, if any, permanent buildings or features, they had tools that were light-weight and portable, and they contain plant and animal remains from species that could be collected or caught rather than produced agriculturally. However, in most areas, Archaic peoples developed strategies of interacting with plants that could be categorized as "domesticatory," (Pearsall, Chapter 12) and it was these Archaic period patterns of plant use that generated the cornucopia of plant products grown in later periods. Traditionally, the societies that produced these sites are thought of as having been small-scale and socially and politically egalitarian. There is usually little or no evidence of hereditary status differences and the social distinctions that did exist can most often be understood in terms of age, gender, and skill differences.

Coastal archaeological sites provide evidence of a great deal of variation in this traditional pattern and suggest that the Archaic adaptations were much more complex than elsewhere in Latin America. Furthermore, the papers in this volume and other recent publications show that there were significant differences in Archaic period societies along the Pacific Coast of Latin America. For some Archaic peoples marine fishing became the mainstay of their economy, while for others fishing and hunting in coastal estuaries and swamps prevailed. Hunting and gathering remained important in some areas but was replaced by a combination of fishing and cultivation in other areas. There is no over-arching economic, social or political pattern that characterizes Pacific coastal Latin America.

Beginning in the northern portion of the Pacific Coast, Stuart Scott (Chapter 2) discusses the interesting, if enigmatic, case of El Calón in the Marismas region of Sinaloa and Nayarit, in western Mexico. There, Archaic period peoples lived, as did later peoples, in estuaries along the Pacific Ocean shore. The site of El Calón is known for its huge mound, one which Scott argues may have been the largest monumental construction in Archaic period Mesoamerica. There have been few recent publications summarizing the archaeology of western Mexico, and those that do have relatively little to say about the Archaic and Formative period coastal populations (e.g., Foster and Weigand 1985). The work in the Marismas region suggests that it would be profitable to re-examine this coastal region in search of the cultural antecedents of later peoples who flourished along the west Mexican coast.

George Michaels and Barbara Voorhies document, in Chapter 4, recent work on the only well-known Pacific coastal Archaic period culture in Mexico—the Chantuto people of Chiapas (Voorhies 1976). They discuss the archaeological findings from a series of large shell mound sites dating from about 3000 to 2000 B.C. Additional discoveries by John Clark and colleagues from the nearby shell mound site of Cerro de las Conchas extends the Chantuto dates back to about 4000 B.C. (Blake et al. 1995). The Chantuto people who occupied these sites subsisted by shell-fish collecting, fishing, hunting, and perhaps shrimping. Michaels and Voorhies suggest that the coastal estuary and swampland sites represent only one portion of the overall settlement pattern and that future investigations may well discover inland sites that were part of a more complex seasonal settlement and subsistence round. One of the fascinating discoveries at the shell mound site of Tlacuachero is a deeply buried clay floor. The floor preserved a posthole pattern of a large apsidally-shaped structure and some of its associated artifacts (Voorhies et al. 1991). This is one of the few known Archaic structures in Mesoamerica, and one of the only ones from a coastal setting.

Farther to the south, along the Pacific Coast of Panama, Richard Cooke and Anthony Ranere (Chapter 8) show that the faunal assemblages in sites dating between ca. 5000 and 3000 B.C. were dominated by a wide range of fish remains.

They compare these ancient fish remains with those collected at a more recent site, dating from about A.D. 1 to A.D. 400, and find that were some significant changes between the Archaic period and later period fishing practices. One of their conclusions is that the importance of watercraft and gillnets increased through time. This ensured that fishing provided an abundant and reliable food source over several millennia and was instrumental in emergence of later complex societies (Cooke and Ranere 1992).

In Chapter 9, Dolores Piperno argues that along the central Pacific watershed of Panama the process of plant cultivation was under way before 5000 B.C. Remains such as phytoliths from several genera of plants, including *Maranta* sp., *Calathea* sp., and *Dioscorea* sp., have been recovered from Archaic period sites outside their natural ranges. Piperno also discusses the early presence of maize cultivation in Panama, dating from about 5000 B.C., and suggests that non-local cultigens such as maize and perhaps squash, were introduced into an ancient pre-existing agricultural system. Her analyses suggest that our models of the Archaic period must include detailed knowledge of plant communities that were used in complex ways leading up to the full-blown adoption of agriculture. This pattern is in line with Flannery's recent study of Archaic people at Guilá Naquitz in Highland Oaxaca where he documents a rich and complex pattern of plant use beginning at least 10,000 years ago (Flannery 1986). However, recent dating of early maize is leading to a re-evaluation of its antiquity, a point we will return to below.

Not much is yet known of the Archaic period of Ecuador, but in Chapter 12, Deborah Pearsall summarizes the Las Vegas phase patterns originally described by Stothert (1985). Between 8000 and 4600 B.C., these Archaic period peoples exploited a mix of terrestrial fauna, plants, and fish. There is phytolith evidence that maize was present by Late Las Vegas times (6000-4600 B.C.) and continued in use throughout the subsequent periods.

Alfred Siemens' provocative chapter (10) reports on the wetlands and their associated landforms in the Arenillas Lowlands of southwestern Ecuador. Although his study is geomorphological and not archaeological, he argues that several of these wetland formations could have provided Archaic hunter-gatherer-fishers as well as later agriculturalists with seasonal concentrations of resources. In recent decades, archaeologists have found that the ancient use and manipulation of wetlands along lake, river, and swamp margins was much more important and frequent an activity than previously suspected. Archaeologists are finally beginning to pay more attention to the sorts of wetland features that Siemens describes in coastal Ecuador, and are finding, throughout the New World, that they are often rich in archaeological remains (Siemens 1983).

Archaic period adaptations along the coast of Peru and northern Chile provide some of the most striking patterns of variation in Pacific coastal Latin America. Chapters by Michael Moseley, Thomas Patterson, Karen Wise, Lautaro Núñez, and Mark Aldenderfer all show that not only does this region differ from zones further north along the coast, but there is also remarkable variation within the region. Michael Moseley (Chapter 13) argues that these differences as well as differences between the coastal regions and the adjacent highlands should be viewed as a product of differing ecological relationships and evolutionary trajectories. For example, along the central coast of Peru, late Archaic peoples developed sedentary communities where the primary subsistence resources came from the sea. They cultivated plants such as cotton for the production of fibers used in making fishing nets rather than cultivating subsistence items such as maize. Moseley points out that the emergence, at the end of the Archaic period, of large-scale, corporately organized communities without archaeological evidence of hereditary rulers, indicates that our traditional unilinear models of cultural evolution do not work along the Peruvian coast.

Thomas Patterson, in Chapter 14, makes the case that there were significant changes in the organization of production along the central coast of Peru beginning during the Archaic period, and corresponding to the shifts seen from Paloma to Conchas to La Florida society. All of these societies were organized communally, in contrast to the subsequent state-based societies after about 400 B.C. Patterson's chapter details some of the patterns that Moseley touched on earlier, and shows how the gradual development of food-producing economies and the development of a truly agrarian economy transformed the communal social and political structures that originated during the Archaic period. I will return later to the themes raised by both Moseley and Patterson.

Further to the south, Wise (Chapter 15) and Núñez (Chapter 16) show that Archaic coastal peoples initially made use of a wide range of marine resources and then, through time, concentrated on a narrower range of species. Wise examines a model of intensification of the use of marine resources on the south-central Andean coast. These marine resources were dispersed, stable, abundant, and predictable, in contrast to the much sparser terrestrial resources found on the desert coast. Wise postulates that Archaic people initially diversified their use of marine resources, until about 5000 B.P. when there is evidence that they began to specialize and intensify their fishing and hunting activities. These changes in resource use correlate with increasing sedentism, settlement aggregation, and perhaps, sparked the process of increasing social and political complexity in the region.

Núñez shows that for north coastal Chile the pattern was somewhat more variable than for southern Peru. He takes us from the earliest Archaic periods about 10,000 to 8000 B.P. through to the beginning of the Early Formative period (3200-1800 B.P.). One of the most fascinating developments of this era is the Chinchorro stage, during the Late Archaic period. Anatomical evidence suggests that the

Chinchorro people may have had occupational specializations with, for example, some individuals specializing in deep sea diving. This is also the period when complex mummification practices were used in mortuary rituals.

Finally, Mark Aldenderfer, in Chapter 17, presents a model of Late Archaic (Late Preceramic) economic and social organization that explores the relationship between "regional packing" and "ecological complementarity" of populations in the south-central Andes. He discusses evidence for the increase in the number of groups from two to three around 5000 B.P. These groups occupied three different neighboring habitats: the littoral, the mid-valley, and the high sierra/puna zones. At the same time, these groups began to increase the frequency of exchanges and range of goods traded among themselves. With the added shift to increased food production, the pattern was set for the high degree of ecological complementarity that characterized the region during the Early Formative and later periods.

Origins and Spread of Agriculture

It has already become evident that most of the papers in this volume address, either directly or peripherally, the question of the origins of agriculture and show that there were many and diverse paths along this evolutionary sequence. In particular, when, where, and how *maize* developed as one of the most important staple food crops in the New World is one of the central questions in studies about agricultural origins, as a series of recent books and articles make clear (e.g., Gebauer and Price 1992; Johannessen and Hastorf 1994; Cowan and Watson 1992). Taking up this theme, Bruce Benz (Chapter 3) examines the origins and spread of maize, summarizing the genetic basis for arguments that maize evolved from tesosinte. After reviewing current ideas about the origin of maize as well as the new radiocarbon dates for early samples of maize (Long et al. 1989), he proposes a model for its origin, dispersal, and diversification. Using a cladistic analysis of maize chromosome knobs from 110 populations in Mexico, Benz is able to outline the biogeography of the various races of maize. His analysis suggests that maize originated in Pacific basin river valleys such as the Río Balsas, and then diversified as it spread into other environments to the north and south. He stresses that a systematic analysis of existing and new archaeological assemblages of maize is necessary in order to test the model (Benz 1994).

Along the Pacific Coast of Chiapas, Mexico, Blake and Clark (Chapter 5) present a brief summary of the evidence for agriculture and maize use among the Early Formative villages dating between 1600 and 1100 B.C. They show that even in the earliest deposits of these villages the charred remains of maize, beans, and avocados were the most ubiquitous plant materials recovered. However, even though maize was the most common plant remain in the paleo-botanical assemblages, its dietary importance is questioned. Stable carbon isotope analyses of human bone samples suggest either these early villagers did not eat much maize, or that it was consumed infrequently, perhaps on a seasonal basis. They suggest that maize may have been imported into tropical lowland environments, such as those along the Pacific Coast of Chiapas, for its early importance in the production of alcoholic beverages, and not as a staple food crop. The current isotope data do suggest that maize had become an important dietary staple by Middle Formative times. However, more isotopic analyses are under way and as data from other regions and time periods accumulate, it should be possible to resolve the question of Early Formative period maize use.

Returning for a moment to Dolores Piperno's discussion (Chapter 9) of the Archaic period origins of agriculture in Panama where a number of plants, in addition to maize, were cultivated, perhaps beginning as early as 5000 B.C., we should reconsider the data in light of the new radiocarbon dates that Benz mentions for the Tehuacán maize (Long et al. 1989). As already discussed above, Piperno relies on both plant phytolith and macrobotanical remains to document the development and spread of agriculture in early Panama. With respect to maize, her data and interpretations contrast with Benz and his colleagues, who argue that the early domesticated maize at the Coxcatlán and San Marcos caves in the Tehuacán Valley, Mexico would date to 2745 B.C. at the earliest—at least 1500 years younger than previously thought. This apparent contradiction suggests a number of possibilities. It may mean that teosinte and not maize was being widely used in Mesoamerica and beyond before the third millennium B.C. Or it may mean that there were initially several independent loci of early teosinte/maize domestication, and that later, perhaps by the second millennium B.C., new strains of maize, ones that had developed in Mexico, later spread to other regions of the continent.

The pattern that is emerging is that the early use of maize or its ancestor was widespread in Pacific Latin America, but the nature of that use is different, or certainly more variable, than we had previously thought. Until about 1000 B.C. or later, maize may have been a marginal or supplemental plant produced not as a subsistence staple, but rather as a specialty product consumed seasonally, and perhaps for its ability to be converted into alcoholic beverages. These patterns and questions illustrate that we need build a corpus of direct radiocarbon dates on early samples of teosinte and maize from other parts of the New World if we are to describe and explain the origin and spread of systems of maize agriculture.

For example, returning to Pearsall's work in Chapter 12, where she summarizes the evidence for plant use at sites in the Valdivia region of Ecuador, she notes that maize use began there by about 6000 B.C. and other plants such as squash, either cultivated or wild, were in use much earlier. During the Formative period, the evidence for maize comes from phytolith samples and charred kernels. At the site of

Real Alto only a few maize phytoliths were found in Valdivia I and II samples (dating as early as 3200-2300 B.C.), but by Valdivia III times (after 2300 B.C.) maize phytoliths were ubiquitous in the samples. Charred maize kernels, jack beans, and other remains were recovered from deposits at Loma Alta as early as Valdivia I times. This would make the earliest Valdivia maize some five centuries earlier than the Coxcatlán maize. This striking pattern implies that there may have been many origins for agricultural production beginning early in the Archaic period. Different plants had different time-lines and likely different processes for their domestication and spread. Coastal populations adapted agricultural plants, some of which may have originated inland and in the highland regions, in addition to domesticating their own assemblages of lowland plant species. The particular mix depended on the natural plant availability and the degree of productivity and reliability of other foods.

As a point of comparison with the Pacific coastal lowlands let me briefly mention the recent research in the coastal lowlands of Belize where evidence is accumulating for forest clearing and cultivation of crops such as maize as early as 2500-2000 B.C. (Pohl 1990; Jones 1994). As in Panama, and Ecuador, the discovery of maize and manioc pollen, and increasing evidence of disturbance vegetation and particulate carbon, taken together suggest that peoples in the humid coastal lowlands of Mesoamerica were actively involved in forest clearing and planting even before the advent of settled villages. Much more work remains to be done in order to document the precise geographical distribution and timing of agriculture and early village life in these regions.

In the more arid regions of the Pacific coast, quite different patterns are emerging. A recently published study of botanical remains from El Paraíso in Peru shows that this huge Late Preceramic site with enormous monumental architecture was built and supported without subsistence agriculture food crops. Quilter et al. (1991) argue that it may have been a center of cotton production which, along with other plants, was grown for exchange purposes. Fishing was extremely important in the food production system of the central coast of Peru and remained so throughout most periods. As mentioned earlier, both Moseley's and Patterson's chapters (Chapters 13 and 14) examine the implications of the relationship between marine resource and agricultural food production.

The examples discussed in this volume show that there was a great diversity in the timing of agriculture's introduction as well as the mix of agricultural production and naturally available food resources. In summary, by 2000 to 1500 B.C. agriculture was important in most areas of Pacific Latin America, but the degree of reliance on maize, the crop that was to become the cornerstone of all later Latin American civilizations, varied considerably from region to region. It was probably not until much later, perhaps after 1000 B.C., that maize became the dominant

staple in most regions of the Pacific Coast.

Origins of Sedentism and the Formative Period

The origins of sedentism along the Pacific Coast also defy a clear-cut and uniform explanation. In Mesoamerica the first sedentary communities appeared to be ceramic-using and like some of their Archaic period ancestors, they practiced agriculture. Blake and Clark (Chapter 5) and Mary Pye, Arthur Demarest, and Barbara Arroyo (Chapter 6) discuss some of the first sedentary communities along the Pacific Coast of Chiapas, Mexico and neighboring Guatemala. By about 1600 B.C. these Early Formative period societies had settled in permanent villages with the full range of material culture that characterized village life in Mesoamerica for the next three and one half thousand years. As with the people of coastal Panama, these Early Formative villagers had a modified Archaic subsistence pattern, relying to a large extent on estuary net-fishing for the bulk of their protein and supplementing their diet with gathered and cultivated plants and hunting.

Sixteen centuries earlier, along the coast of Ecuador, the Valdivian culture settled in small villages with houses, communal buildings, ceramic technology, and agriculture. In Chapter 11, Scott Raymond analyses the changing settlement patterns of the Valdivian people, showing how they lived along rivers in close proximity to well-watered, arable land. He describes the settlement data from the Valdivia River valley, and, using settlement pattern maps for each period, illustrates the continual growth in the number and sizes of settlements through time. As previously mentioned, in Chapter 12, Deborah Pearsall argues that these early sedentary societies were growing a number of crops which were becoming increasingly important during the long Valdivia sequence. She hypothesizes that it was not until the Terminal Valdivia period (VII-VIII, ca. 1600 B.C.) that subsistence systems underwent a significant transformation. People may have become so reliant on agriculture that they began colonizing areas away from the main river valleys and clearing and modifying the landscape in order to expand the zones of agricultural production. Pearsall suggests that the settlement and botanical data may indicate a shift from the domesticatory stage of production to the agricultural stage by around 1600 B.C.

Farther to the south, sedentism began during the Archaic period and by the late Preceramic period people began building huge monuments. Michael Moseley (Chapter 13) describes the transition from Archaic to Preceramic society and provides summaries of key examples of these communities. Sites like Paloma in Peru, dating to about 4500 to 3000 B.C., preserve evidence of the first sedentary houses along the coast. The striking thing about this site is the discovery of hundreds of well-preserved burials. Analyses of the remains shows that these early villagers relied primarily on a diet of small net-caught fish such as anchovies and sardines, mollusks, large fish, sea birds, sea mammals, and wild plants. Some cultivated plants were also found, including squash, beans, and gourds. There is some indication of emerging social inequity between households at the site, and the inequities were bolstered, in part, by the elaborate treatment and preservation, including the salting, of important ancestors.

Patterson (Chapter 14) describes the transformation to permanently sedentary communities by Conchas times (ca. 3000 B.C.). He argues that this transition was enabled, in part, by a new territorial organization of production. The emergence of economically specialized farming and fishing communities generated a greater degree of inter-regional interdependence. It may have been the efficiency of such an economic system that allowed and even encouraged the growth in community size later during the Preceramic period.

The unprecedented growth of larger communities during the Late Preceramic, such as Aspero and El Paraíso, included the construction of enormous platform mounds, the most visible features at these sites. Although we still do not know much about the structure of the communities responsible for the construction and maintenance of these buildings, most researchers agree that they were fully sedentary. This sedentary economy continued to be based on fishing as the primary source of protein—with little evidence of maize agriculture (Quilter et al. 1991).

Along the coast of south-central Peru and extending south into northern Chile, fully sedentary communities were in place by about 1500-1000 B.C. according Núñez (Chapter 16) and Aldenderfer (Chapter 17). Here, sedentary villages grew in regions with both fishing and farming potential, but they did not build the gigantic platform mounds found to the north (Núñez 1983; Aldenderfer 1989; 1993).

Origins of Socio-Political Inequality

One of the most intriguing yet difficult questions to answer is: how and why social inequality and political complexity arose? Researchers often have difficulty identifying evidence for this transition in prehistory simply because it is so ill-defined, both empirically and in terms of our theoretical models and perspectives. Contributing to the problem is the common occurrence of layer upon layer of the remains of later civilizations covering the remnants of their earlier ancestors. An excellent recent volume examines some of the current theoretical approaches to the emergence of socio-political inequality, providing summaries of the wide range of processes and mechanisms that archaeologists consider important in the transition (Price and Feinman 1995). Unfortunately, though, none of the case studies in the volume include examples from Pacific coastal Latin America, an area where the emergence of complex society is both relatively clear and varied. Several papers in our volume address this question, either directly or indirectly, and illustrate some of the different paths to socio-political inequality in each part of Pacific coastal Latin America.

Three chapters examine the archaeological evidence for this transition along the southeastern Pacific Coast of Mesoamerica: Blake and Clark (Chapter 5), Pye, Demarest, and Arroyo (Chapter 6), and Love (Chapter 7). Blake and Clark examine the case of the Mokaya tradition villagers in Chiapas, Mexico, proposing that the initial emergence of hereditary inequality could take place only while the mechanisms that maintained social egalitarianism were being actively broken down. They label this process "transegalitarian" and go on to suggest how it might be monitored archaeologically. The Early Formative Mokaya case illustrates the transegalitarian process using archaeological evidence from recent excavation and regional survey in the Mazatán region of coastal Chiapas. Blake and Clark show that between about 1600 and 1100 B.C., as egalitarian society was beginning to break down, signs of hereditary inequality were coming into play. These changes are examined using settlement patterns, population estimates, craft production, food production, and material symbols of status and prestige.

Pye et al. (Chapter 6) describe the distribution of closely related Early Formative villages extending southeast from the Mexico-Guatemala border to El Salvador. Showing examples of the ceramics and other artifacts and features, they illustrate the wide distribution of the Mokaya tradition over several hundred kilometers of coastline. They caution, however, that we do not yet know exactly what social, economic, or political processes are responsible for this distribution and that more testing is necessary in order to understand the similarities and differences in the Early Formative material record.

It was not until the Middle Formative Conchas phase, beginning perhaps as early as 900 B.C., when large-scale monumental construction began and more solid evidence of social ranking, hereditary inequality, and political complexity appeared. Michael Love (Chapter 7) argues that stylistic variation in ceramics during the Conchas phase of Pacific coastal Guatemala represents the symbolism of elites and that, by this period, a clear-cut hereditary status differentiation had emerged. While this pattern may have resulted from the linkage of coastal communities into larger pan-Mesoamerican networks of elite interaction (e.g., Demarest 1989), Love argues that the development of large political centers such as La Blanca resulted from the playing out of long-term local processes. His discussion outlines the need to reconsider the role of Olmec styles and symbols across Mesoamerica and in the context of developing local traditions (Sharer and Grove 1989).

This volume contains no examples of increasing complexity from other parts of Mesoamerica and Central America but we pick up the theme again in Pacific coastal South America. Raymond, in Chapter 12, briefly outlines the evidence for social differentiation in the Formative cultures of coastal Ecuador. In the Chanduy Valley, the site of Real Alto appears to have been an important center, perhaps with specialized political and religious functions. Its dominant position in the settlement hierarchy is suggested by the presence of a formalized ceremonial plaza which was in use by Middle Valdivia times (ca. 2300 B.C.). By contrast, in the Valdivia Valley there was no indication of social or political hierarchy until much later during the Middle Formative period (ca. 1200 B.C.). Raymond suggests that we need to look at settlement patterns on a multi-valley scale in order to monitor the sequence of changes in population size, settlement differentiation, and the emergence of social and political hierarchies.

In Chapter 13, Michael Moseley discusses how unilinear models of cultural evolution have traditionally constrained our thinking about the origins of civilization. The central Peruvian Coast is one of several cases where complex society arose based on the harvesting of marine resources and without staple grain crop production. He argues that the correspondence of Preceramic period platform mound construction with the high natural productivity of the anchovy fishery is more than simply a casual relationship. However, there is little evidence to suggest that, during the Preceramic period, this economy produced a political or social system of hereditary leadership. Moseley suggests that governance may have been based on organizational systems found in egalitarian societies, such as the "Cargo" system of rotating office-holding. It may not have been until after 500 B.C. that hereditary, or descent-based rulers such as *curacas*, came into being.

In a similar vein, Thomas Patterson (Chapter 14) makes the case that Preceramic societies developed communal modes of production and that there is no evidence for anything but community-based production and kin, age, and gender-based social differentiation. Even large sites with monumental architecture such as Aspero and El Paraíso had no evidence for hereditary status differentiation, or class-stratification.

In many ways this pattern contrasts with the south coast of Peru and Chile where there are early signs of descent-based social differentiation (Wise, Chapter 15; Núñez, Chapter 16). However, the southern region lacked the large-scale monumental constructions that appeared farther north along the coast.

Summary

This volume by no means provides an exhaustive discussion of the Archaic and Formative period societies along the Pacific Coast of Latin America. It does, however, represent a reasonably up-to-date cross-section of current perspectives and themes that have engaged archaeologists working in the region during the past decade. Work is progressing: since the writing of most of these papers all of the volume's participants along with dozens of other scientists have conducted many more seasons of fieldwork, adding to the

discoveries, models, and theories discussed here. The works presented in this volume illustrate the potential of the Pacific Coast region in contributing to our general understanding of the economic, political, social and ideological transformations faced by most of the world's cultures during the past 10,000 years. Cultural evolution along the Pacific Coast illustrates the varied interplay of peoples and their environments, subsistence practices, social interactions, technologies, trade practices, and many other factors in shaping the trajectories of emerging civilizations.

Note

1. The Circum-Pacific Prehistory Conference took place in Seattle, Washington, during August, 1989. These papers were, for the most part, written during 1989 and revised during 1989 and 1990. They were all sent out for review and comments, after which further revisions were made. Unfortunately, though, funding only became available to publish volume one in the series: *Pacific Northeast Asia in Prehistory: Hunter-Fisher-Gatherers, Farmers, and Sociopolitical Elites*, edited by C. Melvin Aikens and Song Nai Rhee (1992), and Washington State University Press decided not to publish the other volumes. While we were looking for another publisher for this volume, WSU Press acquired new printing technology that made the reproduction of the volume economically feasible, and so decided to go ahead with publication in 1996. Unfortunately, this means that during the intervening years, there have been new developments in the archaeology of each region discussed in this volume: but the papers have not all been revised accordingly. The authors have all tried to include, where possible, an endnote that lists a small selection of the most recent publications in each area and that we hope will help the reader find the most current sources on each topic.

I would like to thank both Dale Croes, the Series editor, and Glen Lindeman, of WSU Press, for ensuring that this volume was finally produced.

References Cited

Aikens, C. M., and S. N. Rhee (editors)
1992   *Pacific Northeast Asia in Prehistory: Hunter-Fisher-Gatherers, Farmers, and Sociopolitical Elites*. WSU Press, Pullman.

Aldenderfer, M.
1989   The Archaic Period in the South-central Andes. *Journal of World Prehistory* 3(2):117-158.

Aldenderfer, M. (editor)
1993   *Domestic Architecture, Ethnicity, and Ecological Complementarity in the South-Central Andes*. University of Iowa Press, Iowa City.

Benz, B.
1994   Reconstructing the Racial Phylogeny of Mexican Maize: Where Do We Stand? In *Corn and Culture in the Prehistoric New World*, edited by S. Johan-

nessen and C. A Hastorf, pp. 157-179. Westview Press, Boulder.

Blake, M., J. E. Clark, V. Voorhies, G. Michaels, M. W. Love, M. E. Pye, A. A. Demarest, and B. Arroyo
1995   Radiocarbon Chronology for the Late Archaic and Formative Periods on the Pacific Coast of Southeastern Mesoamerica. *Ancient Mesoamerica* 6:161-183.

Cooke, R. G., and A. J. Ranere
1992b   The Origin of Wealth and Hierarchy in the Central Region of Panama (12,000-2,000 B.P.). In, *Wealth and Hierarchy in the Intermediate Area*, edited by F. W. Lange, pp. 243-316. Dumbarton Oaks, Washington, D.C.

Cowan, C. W., and P. J. Watson (editors)
1992   *The Origins of Agriculture: an International Perspective*. Smithsonian Institution Press, Washington.

Demarest, A. A.
1989   The Olmec and the Rise of Civilization in Eastern Mesoamerica. In *Regional Perspectives on the Olmec*, edited by R. J Sharer and D. C. Grove, pp. 303-344. School of American Research Advanced Seminar Series, J. Haas, general editor. Cambridge University Press, Cambridge.

Flannery, K. V. (editor)
1986   *Guilá Naquitz: Archaic Foraging and Agriculture in Oaxaca, Mexico*. Academic Press, Orlando.

Foster, M., and P. Weigand (editors)
1985   *The Archaeology of West and Northwest Mesoamerica*. Westview Press, Boulder.

Gebauer, A. B., and T. D. Price (editors)
1992   *Transitions to Agriculture in Prehistory*. Monographs in World Archaeology No. 4. Prehistory Press, Madison.

Johannessen, S., and C. A. Hastorf (editors)
1994   Corn and Culture in the Prehistoric New World. Westview Press, Boulder.

Jones, J.
1994   Pollen Evidence for Early Settlement and Agriculture in Northern Belize. *Palynology* 18:205-211.

Long, A., B. Benz, D. Donahue, A. Jull, and L. Toolin
1989   First Direct AMS Dates on Early Maize from Tehuacán, Mexico. *Radiocarbon* 30:130-135.

Moseley, M.
1992   *The Inca and their Ancestors*. Thames and Hudson, London.

Núñez, L.
1983   Paleoindian and Archaic Cultural Periods in the Arid and Semiarid Regions of Northern Chile. In *Advances in World Archaeology*, vol. 2, edited by F. Wendorf and A. Close, pp. 161-203. Academic Press, New York.

Pohl, M. (editor)
1990   *Ancient Maya Wetland Agriculture: Excavations on Albion Island, Northern Belize*. University of Minnesota Publications in Anthropology and Westview Press, Boulder.

Price, T. D., and G. M. Feinman (editors)
1995   *Foundations of Social Inequality*. Plenum Press, New York.

Quilter, J., E. B. Ojeda, and D. M. Pearsall
1991   Subsistence Economy of El Paraíso, an Early Peruvian Site. *Science* 251:277-83.

Sharer, R. J., and D. C. Grove (editors)
1989   *Regional Perspectives on the Olmec*. School of American Research Advanced Seminar Series, J. Haas, general editor. Cambridge University Press, Cambridge.

Siemens, A. H.
1983   Wetland Agriculture in Pre-hispanic Mesoamerica. *Geographical Review* 73(2):166-181.

Stothert, K. E.
1985   The Preceramic Las Vegas Culture of Coastal Ecuador. *American Antiquity* 50(3):613-637.

Voorhies, B.
1976   *The Chantuto People: An Archaic Period Society of the Chiapas Littoral, Mexico*. Papers of the New World Archaeological Foundation No. 41. Brigham Young University, Provo.

Voorhies, B., G. H. Michaels, and G. M. Riser
1991   Ancient Shrimp Fishery. *National Geographic Research & Exploration* 7(1):20-35.

Part I
MESOAMERICA

2

The Marismas Nacionales
Project, Sinaloa and Nayarit, Mexico

Stuart D. Scott

In the late 1960s, the State University of New York launched a program of estuarine studies on the Nayarit-Sinaloa coastal plain. The publication of the first volume of the *Handbook of Middle American Indians* (West 1964) was, in several ways, a primary incentive for the Marismas study, particularly for its focus on the major configurations of Mexico's environments. My review of that volume (Scott 1965) opened a dialogue with John Vann who had just recently completed a geographic reconnaissance of the

Sinaloa and Nayarit coasts for the Office of Naval Research (Vann 1972). A physical geographer, Vann's familiarity with the Pacific coastal lowlands included his observations of the substantial traces of prehistoric human activity to be found there. The work of Sauer and Brand (1932) and Curray and others (Curray and Moore 1964a, 1964b; Curray et al. 1969) also called my attention to the abundant archaeological remains scattered along the lower river valleys and flood plains. Accordingly, a State University

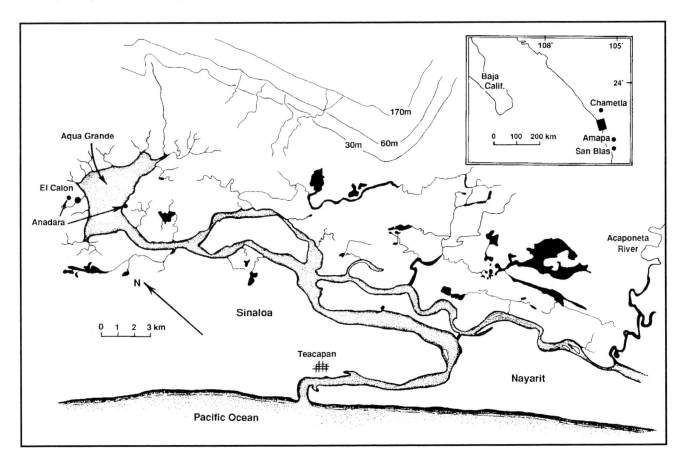

Figure 1. The West Mexican Coastal Plain, Showing Location of the Marismas Nacionales.

program was established with headquarters at Teacapan, Sinaloa, a rural west Mexican commercial and agricultural village of about 2,500 inhabitants. "Modestly holistic" may be a grammatical contradiction but it the best way to describe our approach which was to bring a number of disciplines to the Marismas to examine changes in the regional geography, geology and prehistory so as to better understand both past and modern human occupation of this coastal environment. Using fieldwork data from soil stratigraphy, mangrove ecology, pollen and faunal analysis, archaeology, ethnohistory, human osteology and burial practices, the collective aim was to provide an objective view of the natural world of the Marismas Nacionales, to examine the record of human occupation there, and to the extent that the data might support them, to examine the implications for human social organization in this specific environmental setting.

The West Mexican coastal plain (Figure 1) is a distinct physiographic province (Connally 1977) about 200 km long and 4 to 35 km wide. North of Mazatlán in Sinaloa and south of San Blas in Nayarit, rise the foothills and rocky slopes of the Sierra Madre Occidental. These rugged mountains, which reach altitudes of 3000 m or more, form the eastern border and backdrop for the coastal plain. Most of the arable land lies on emergent beach ridges between Mazatlán and the village of Teacapan, 90 km to the south, or on the alluvial plain between San Blas and the San Pedro River, 40 km to the north. The rest of the coastal plain comprises the Marismas Nacionales—a complex of interlacing waterways, salt pans, and mangrove forests. This low relief flood plain was pictured in the Ortelius Atlas (1579 edition) as being of equal size to Lake Chapala (Figure 2). Although this sixteenth century view may be distorted by showing its highest volumetric content during a flood season, the Marismas Nacionales zone is nevertheless one of Mexico's largest compound deltaic estuaries. The Marismas Nacionales can be assigned to the second of Odum's (1974:599) three major "first order" classes of ecosystems: the subsidized solar-powered ecosystem, or one in which there are utilizable sources of energy other than the direct

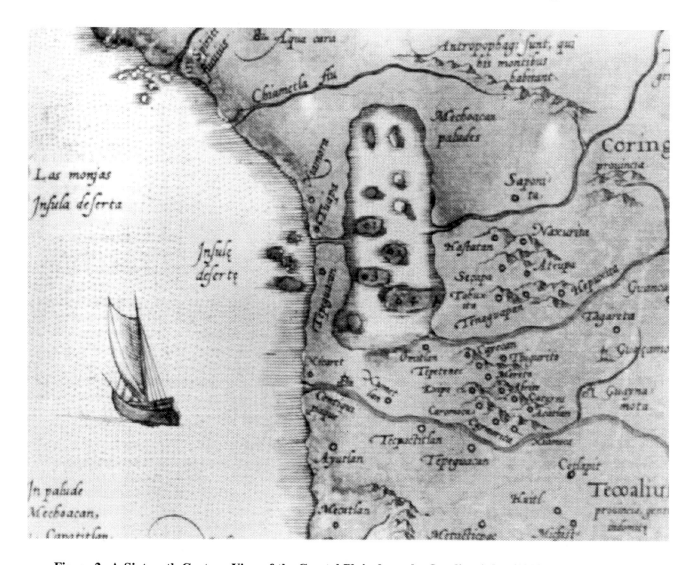

Figure 2. **A Sixteenth Century View of the Coastal Plain from the Ortelius Atlas (1579). The Marismas Nacionales Appear as a Vast Embayment with Islands.**

rays of the sun. In such an ecological system, tides and rainfall are two auxiliary energy sources affecting food transport, mineral cycling, and waste disposal. Man himself may provide other energy subsidies, as in the case of agriculture or marine and estuary subsistence.

A number of sources provide summary information about various classes of environmental and cultural data pertaining to the Marismas (Connally 1984; Foster 1974; Gill 1969, 1971, 1974, 1977, 1985; Pool, Snedaker, and Lugo 1977; Scott 1974, 1985; Sweetman 1974). The final volume of our research results will present unpublished data from natural, social and physical science field studies in the Marismas between 1968 and 1978. The scope of the present paper, however, is restricted to (1) summary descriptions of the basic chronology and natural and cultural structure of the Marismas setting and (2) the possible implications of research findings for comparison with other maritime cultures of the Americas.

The Accretional Coastal Plain

The larger chronological framework is based on the mapping of stratigraphic soil units and air photo interpretation of landforms and relationships between geomorphic groupings (Allen and Connally 1977). As a consequence of the creation of major landforms during episodes of emergence and submergence of the coastal plain, we have an improved picture of the relationship between the cultural and natural environments during their coevolution. The sequence (Figure 3a-d) of large scale paleogeographic

reconstructions is a schematic and highly simplified tracing of the principal features associated with four shoreline positions in the region's late Quaternary and Holocene history. In Figure 3a we see the study area prior to construction of the coastal plain. This view probably prevailed for several thousand years up to about 7000 years ago. Two reference points are to be noted: the present fishing village of Teacapan, and one of the archaeological sites, El Calón. At the point in time shown, both sites are, as it were, out to sea. They are shown for reference in the next several views. If we assume that the scene we are looking at represents 7000 years B.P., then this was a time when eustatic sea level hesitated in its transgressive rise, and, given the abundance of sediment available, set the stage for progradation and the first phase of coastal plain construction. So, from this point on, sediments consisting of sand, silt and clay would be dumped seaward and initiate a time of regression of the sea, despite a general rise in world-wide sea level. The offshore area was a shallow continental terrace serving as the basement on which future sediments would be deposited.

Figure 3b depicts the shoreline of the Marismas as it might have looked approximately 4000 years ago. In a fluvial regime of low relief and the interplay of the longshore current and fluctuating supply of sediment, the pace of this alluvial phase must have changed many times. The general picture, though, is one of rivers, large and small, delivering their sediment to the sea, constructing small deltas, flood plains, fans, swamps and distributaries and pushing the sea back as interdistributary lagoons were formed. We believe that at this time the longshore current

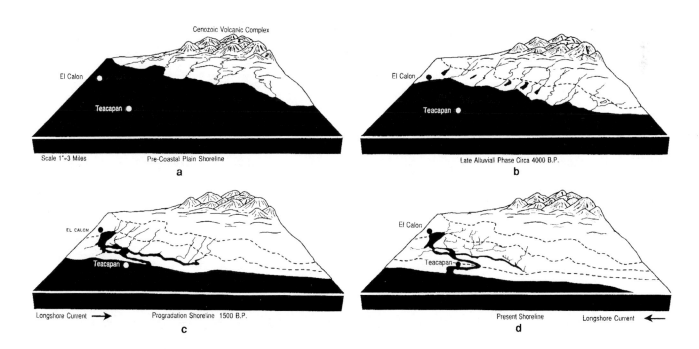

Figure 3. **Schematic View of Coastal Progradation Showing** (*a*) **Pre-Coastal Plain Shoreline,** (*b*) **Late Alluvial Phase, ca. 4000 B.P.,** (*c*) **Progradation Shoreline ca. 1500 B.P., and** (*d*) **Present-Day Shoreline.**

was flowing northerly most of the time, bringing a more moderate and temperate climate. Such a climatic change may have been a factor in attracting human occupation. In any case, the El Calón mound was constructed about 2000 B.C., at or close to the existing shoreline.

The next view approximates the shoreline at about 1500 years ago. A shift in longshore current to south-flowing resulted in a rapid progradation as a regressive phase, extending the coastal plain seaward as a series of sub-parallel beach ridges. More than 280 such sand beach ridges are present in the Marismas today. Thus coastal plain construction took on a new look, with marine processes dominating fluvial processes. Rivers persisted in pushing through the beach ridges, building flood plains but being forced to adopt a sinuous passage through the beach ridges. These beach ridges exhibit duning, and on the average include a 50 m spacing from one ridge to the other. It was at this time—1500 years ago (Figure 3c)—that the change in longshore current coincides with the appearance of new archaeological sites on the then partly constructed

Teacapan peninsula.

The final view (Figure 3d) represents the shoreline of the Marismas as it looks today. The longshore current has reversed again, bringing about the construction of the present new peninsula that enclosed the Estuary of Teacapan. This peninsula is still growing northward, and sub-parallel beach ridges are still being added as the progradational regressive phase continues. El Calón, once on the seacoast, is now well inland. The village of Teacapan, with time, will also be well inland. The Marismas are still growing, adding more land for human occupation that once belonged to the sea.

As we have seen, the sequential growth of this alluvial plain was punctuated by periods of submergence, one of which, occurring during Middle Beach progradation, accounts for the gap in which no material culture remains or other signs of human occupation were found. The overriding fact would seem to be that other than the El Calón mound, and possibly two other nearby low, surface *Anadara* shell mounds, archaeological data for the earliest occupation

Figure 4. A Lens of Estero Phase Pottery and Shell Beneath an Overbank of Flood-Deposited Silt.

episode are either buried or submerged and are not readily available for examination.

As another indication of how the area's culture history occurred concurrently with landform development, we have another hiatus of about 200-300 years, based on evidence both from local geologic processes and ceramics. One example of this is a buried mixed lens of shell and Estero phase pottery beneath an over-bank of alluvial silts with the Los Angeles Soil development on the upper surface (Figure 4). A similar pattern was found by excavators at Amapa where there is also physical and cultural evidence of a clearly-evident break in occupation (Grosscup 1964). In the original Amapa sequence, Tuxpan was a hypothetical phase to account for missing connections between early and late (Figure 5). It agrees well with our evidence of an assumed abandonment at the same time. Meighan (1976) also recognizes the interruption but places it earlier, based on obsidian hydration dating (Figure 5). The possibility of other unseen cultural horizons buried by flood-deposited silts raises the question of how many other times, beyond our two recognized periods of abandonment, the coastal plain may have been depopulated because of flooding.

Culture History

The Marismas sequence comprises at least three distinct occupational phases, separated by periods of abandonment due to marine intrusion of the landscape (Figure 5). The

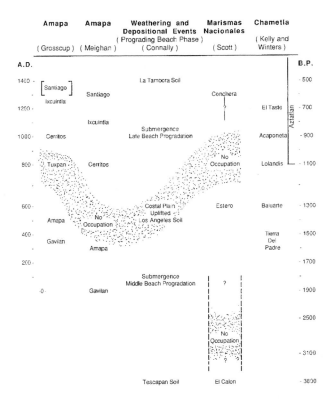

Figure 5. Selected Cultural Sequences for the Sinaloa-Nayarit Region.

latest phase, called Conchera, is Postclassic, approximately 1000 A.D. to Spanish contact, and correlates stylistically and temporally with Ixcuintla and Santiago phases at Amapa to the south (Meighan 1976) and the El Taste phase of Chametla to the north (Kelly and Winters 1960). As the name suggests, Conchera marks a phase of oyster midden accumulation. The oyster middens are the most numerous among several shellmound types. In the course of our survey over 500 discrete shell middens were located and measured (Shenkel 1971). They range in size from surface lenses of about 3 m in diameter to rather symmetrical mounds up to 60 m in length and 6 m high. They are generally distributed throughout most of the final meanders of the Teacapan Estuary and contain abundant artifacts, including potsherds, obsidian, and ground stone tools.

Estero phase is the name we have given to the cultural occupation on the Los Angeles Soil that developed on Middle Beach ridges between 1500 and 1100 years ago. This pre-oyster midden horizon, Classic in time period, produces pottery that correlates with the Amapa phase at the Amapa site and the Baluarte phase of the Chametla sequence. A corpus of nearly two dozen radiocarbon dates supports the assignment of Estero/Conchera earth and shellmounds to the latter (Classic and Postclassic) part of the chronology (Foster 1989).

Regarding issues in the sociocultural evolution of Marismas coastal societies, during the Classic and Postclassic periods, there is little reason to doubt Meighan's (1971:755) characterization of this region as one with no dominating capital, but rather a series of small city-states, each with its own political center, tributary towns, and villages such as are described in the earliest historic documents. This kind of political organization explains a feature of the region's archaeology—the fact that in delta, estuary, and flood plain regions, the sites appear to go on for miles.

In terms of general subsistence economy, the presence of metates and manos, carbonized maize kernels, and cultigens in the pollen record point to agriculture as a common, if not the dominant, method of food procurement for both Estero and Conchera phase peoples. In spite of the considerable amount of shell refuse, we suspect that the oysters were probably no more than a dietary supplement to what would otherwise be a typical Precolumbian agrarian subsistence.

Earliest in the Marismas record of occupation is the El Calón phase which takes its name from the presence of a single large shellmound, one of the three sites located near, or adjacent to, the northernmost meander of the Teacapan Estuary where it broadens into the Laguna de Agua Grande (Figure 1). The El Calón mound, situated 13 km inland, is a unique archaeological feature, remarkable for its size, height and apparent articulated shells of the large marine pelecypod, *Anadara grandis*. From three preliminary power auger holes surrounding the site, Cottrell (1973:100) concluded that "El Calón rests upon an older alluvial surface." Subsequently, Connally (1984) probed the entire vicinity and reached the same conclusion, namely, that a

Table 1. Radiocarbon Dates for El Calón.

Lab No.	Sample Shell Species	Radiocarbon Age B.P. (1950)	Date B.C.	Corrected Date B.C.[a]	Corrected Range B.C.[a]	Corrected Range B.C.[b]
SI-1540	*Anadara*	3235 ± 110	1285	1591 ± 172	1763-1419	1755-1355
SI-1541	*Anadara*	3265 ± 75	1315	1638 ± 150	1788-1488	1860-1385
SI-1542	*Anadara*	3845 ± 85	1895	2399 ± 175	2574-2224	2640-2090
SI-2729	*Tivela*	4050 ± 80	2100	2660 ± 177	2837-2483	2900-2325
ANU-1611	*Anadara*	4320 ± 60	2370	1960[c]		

[a](Damon et al. 1974).
[b](Klein et al. 1982).
[c]Recalculated to Smithsonian standard (Polach, personal communication, 1976).

compact shell layer at 1 to 1.25 m below the present surface, appearing in all cores, served to identify the surface on which El Calón was constructed.

No excavations have been undertaken at El Calón but extensive observations and surface collections on the mound were made during each of four succeeding field seasons following its discovery. Each of the hundreds of other shellmounds observed in the Marismas were formed more or less amorphously as the discard products of shellfish harvesting, though many were probably used as living surfaces. In contrast, Cerro El Calón was built by the purposeful raising of a steep-sided, semi-pyramidal platform mound, using live mollusks as a construction medium. Its summit was finished as a semi-squared and leveled plateau that measures approximately 7 m by 10 m.

Shell samples for radiocarbon dating were taken from cleaned profiles within erosional gullies on the mound's sloping surfaces (Connally 1989). In all such profiles the deposition of shell appeared to be very clean without soil or organic accumulation that would be expected in a midden. Although there are no apparent strata within the mound, suggesting therefore a single construction period, future excavation might discover different occupations or construction phases.

As to when construction may have occurred, we have six radiocarbon dates on three different materials from two laboratories. The first was an organic carbon date of about 4600 B.P. from a segment of a pollen core. The sample came from a depth of about one meter in the substrate and within 10 m of the base of the mound. Although such an early date could be thought of as setting an outside limit, I would eliminate the pollen core from consideration in the age of El Calón since it was not in direct association with the mound. That leaves us with five shell dates that average out to about 3700 radiocarbon years, or about 1750 B.C.

(Table 1).

Can we consider this a secure chronological placement for El Calón, in view of the problem of variations in marine shell ^{14}C values (Berger, Taylor and Libby 1966; Taylor and Berger 1967; Taylor 1987)? In a regime with regular influxes of freshwater, shells are known to incorporate quantities of older dissolved carbonates—the sort of error that increases the radiocarbon age. While contamination is a serious problem with shell, the problem can be circumvented by choosing only well-preserved shell samples and pre-treating them by careful leaching with dilute acid to remove the outer surfaces of the shell. All such precautions were observed for the El Calón series.

One possible explanation for the early average age would be the prehistoric use of older shell beds for the source material. This would be an attractive explanation for those who feel that a temple-like, public works structure in the Marismas at such an early time is unlikely. However, in view of the number of whole, closed shells, I would suggest that fresh shells were used. When a pelecypod mollusk dies in nature, its valves quickly become separated as it is scavenged and wave-washed, although some number of shells of a mudflat species might stay closed by remaining buried in the mud after death.

Species diversity and habitat/sub-habitat are other factors in the emerging environmental picture of El Calón. *Anadara grandis* appears to be the primary constituent but other shells used in construction were obtained from a variety of ecological regimes (Shenkel 1989). The Anadara ribbed clam is a mangrove swamp and sandbar species and it is only one of the molluskan species that is presently found in the Laguna de Agua Grande (Wing 1968:97), although its population densities are low (Snedaker 1971:16). *A. subrugosa* is a saline mud-flat inhabitant; *M. nigritus* is a carnivorous conch that lives on reefs and sandy beaches.

The oyster is a mangrove species but it requires a greater salinity than present in the Laguna de Agua Grande. *C. gnidia* is found in bays and offshore to depths of 18 fathoms (Keen 1958:144). *A. tuberculosa* is a low salinity mangrove flat dweller. *M. patula* and *H. brassica* both inhabit intertidal beaches and sand flats to ten meters. *T. byronesis* is an intertidal sand and mud flat species. In summary, the environments represented by the shells of El Calón include mangrove swamp, intertidal sand and mud flats, reefs, saline bays as well as offshore habitats. As shown (Figure 1), the present topography places the Gulf of California 13 km distant overland; 5 km of this is mangrove forest. The closest oyster habitat is 28 km downstream, nearer the mouth of the estuary. Besides the lack of shells in the immediate environment to provide the raw materials for construction, Snedaker (1971:15-18) points to the inhospitable character of the mangrove environment and the buried or subsided lower portion of the mound itself in his argument that a far different micro-environmental regime existed at the time of mound construction. The suggested dating for El Calón, though not entirely useful for understanding the use dates of the mound, nevertheless allows for the very considerable time required for a change in the hydrostatic head of the estuary and the formation of barrier land between the site and the Gulf shoreline.

Sirkin (1974) initiated palynological studies on the West Mexican coastal plain to develop a biostratigraphic framework for the geologic and archaeological research. Sirkin (1989) presents the description and analysis of the fossil pollen spectra from depositional basins, miscellaneous soils, and archaeological samples, together with a survey of the expected taxa from various coastal plant associations, e.g., thorn forest, cropland, savanna, marshland and so on. From Sirkin's interpretive summary, the following data are pertinent to the developing picture of El Calón.

Systematic probes found the thickest accumulation of estuarine sediments along the western and southwestern margins of the mangrove within 10 m of the El Calon shellmound. Here, core thicknesses ranged from 6.0 m to approximately 7.5 m—the depth attributed to a buried channel that follows the general curve of the mound, then trends westward toward the ocean. All the El Calón cores (four) penetrate the basal clastics (clay and sandy alluvium), above which the sediments are dominantly lagoonal silts with scattered shell fragments, very finely macerated organic debris, microfossil tests, of which foraminifera are common, and occasional thin (1-3 cm) bands of brown peat.

Analysis of the cores at both 25 cm and 10 cm intervals has revealed microfossils that vary in taxa and in pollen sums. The first pollen occur at 6.25-6.50 m where Gramineae (grass) and Compositae (composites) comprise 15 out of 22 specimens, along with three of *Rhizopora* (red mangrove), and one each of *Alnus* (alder) and *Urtica*. Sirkin (1989) speculates that the counts reflect low pollen influx, owing possibly to the oxidation of organics in an arid, terrestrial environment at that time. Higher in the El

Calón pollen profile, mangrove becomes more abundant. At 6 m, their total of 55 percent of the sum includes red mangrove (11 percent), *Avicennia* (white mangrove, 25 percent) with the *Terminalia*-type pollen included, and *Laguncularia* (black mangrove, 3 percent), as well as additional taxa in the Verbenaceae (16 percent). Pollen of representative species associated with the lowland forests, such as *Caesalpina*, Sapotaceae, Myrtaceae (cf. Eucalyptus), and Palmae are common but upland and marsh species are rare at this level.

The assemblages in higher stratigraphic zones show increases in upland species, *Pinus* (pine) and *Quercus* (oak), with red, black and white mangrove in changing orders of dominance. Sirkin (1989) notes the first probable specimen of a cultigen, a possible pollen grain of melon appears at 2.25 m and pollen of *Cucurbita* (squash) and *Agave* occur at 1.75 m. Squash and melon reappear at 0.50 m and in the surface sample *Zea* (maize) and the Solanaceae are abundant. In summary, the floral history suggests a fluctuating coastal plain with advances and retreats of several mangrove species, pine, oak, grasses, sedges and so on. It seems probable that the builders of El Calón were agriculturalists but this is by no means confirmed.

El Calón: Cultural Context

El Calón is set off as a unique feature of the coast as much by its natural as by its cultural attributes. Earlier in this paper I proposed the El Calón mound as the main referent for a phase of the same name. Realistically, the evidence from El Calón may be too fragmentary for a phase designation if, for defining a site phase, we look for the usual archaeological criteria, namely an artifact complex, sensitive to change and perhaps other data categories that correlate with related sequences. The only other sites found in the region of the northernmost meander of the estuary are two broad, flat accumulations of Anadara valves (disarticulated), one at 1/2 km northwest of El Calón and the other located at the entrance to the Laguna de Agua Grande (Figure 1). No artifacts were found at either locations and no radiocarbon samples were collected. If only as an occupation "marker" then, rather than a phase, El Calón nevertheless does incorporate some cultural distinctions. First and most obviously El Calón calls attention to itself by its size and appearance—features which offer little toward an understanding of the mound's history and function, but do serve at least to point up the peculiarity of a temple-like mound with a summit plateau. There can be little doubt that a 25 m high platform mound using unopened *Anadara grandis* as a construction medium was not just a heap of shell but rather an artifact of some localized social, political, and/or religious activity. Unfortunately, by the time documentary evidence becomes available, particularly several enticing references to places sacred in the worship of the Totorame pantheon (Scott 1989), El Calón had been subject to nearly three thousand years of changing physical landscape. Thus by the beginning of the Historic period, El Calón was no longer on or near the seaboard but instead was sequestered by forest and alluvium many kilometers from the coastline. Of course the inshore position of El Calón would not preclude its later reuse as a focal point for religious associations, e.g., as a repository for offerings. As if to further the idea that El Calón served as a place of worship, at least at some period, only a single artifact class—clay figurines—was found in association with the mound. The total figurine collection consists of 17 pieces with torso and limb fragments predominating, with one head and one almost-whole figure (Figure 6). Although no excavation of El Calón was attempted, the figurines were found buried in shell at the summit of the mound—an inadvertent discovery from a workman's casual turning up of shells while resting at the top of the mound. The most diagnostic pieces were thus found at the southern edge of the crown of the mound at a depth of 8-10 cm. During a revisit the following year, the remaining fragments were found in the erosional scree down the south facing slope of the mound. No sherds or other artifacts were seen.

Apart from the occurrence of a solitary artifact class, little can be said about such a small and fragmented sample. The pieces are solid and appear to be hand-molded. The paste is heavily granular giving the figurines the initial appearance of stone. Owing possibly to excessive leaching or weathering, there is very little detail in the modeling beyond gross shape and size. The two pieces with faces have similar bulbous noses and the head fragment has elongated blobs for ears and engraved slashes for eyes and mouth. The extremely grainy paste is uncharacteristic of other figurine assemblages described for neighboring complexes of West Mexico, all of which date to the Classic and Postclassic periods (e.g., Grosscup 1964; Kelly 1938; Meighan 1971, 1976). From his examination of the El Calón figurines, Warren Barbour notes that the granular paste, the proportions, and the technique for making the eye all point to the figurines having been made in the Middle to Late Formative periods. Formative figurines from Guerrero and Oaxaca exhibit similar coarseness. The beige grey paste color is reminiscent of the Middle and Late Formative figurines from the highland sites. The eye treatment is a common technique on the south coast and in the highlands during this period. Barbour suggests that they are not comparable to the Gulf coast Olmec due to differences in style and paste characteristics. He also notes that the treatment of the noses of the El Calón figurines is distinctive, appearing as large projecting noses rather than representing prognathic faces (Warren Barbour, personal communication 1984).

From his own examination of the photographs, Malcomb Webb concurs in the probability of a Formative period date for these figurines. He notes that a crude, solid clay figurine is dated as early as 2300 B.C. at Zohapilco, Tlapacoya in the Mexican basin (Neiderberger 1976), but that figurines in general become relatively common throughout southern

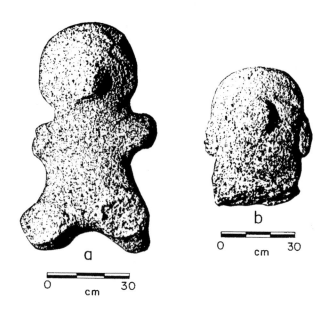

Figure 6. Figurines from El Calón.

Mesoamerica by 1500 B.C. (Ford 1969; Malcomb Webb, personal communication 1984). Although the general resemblance of the figurines to early types would help to support the suggested Formative age of El Calón, they can also be seen to bear some resemblance to the figurines styles that appear in the early part of the Chametla sequence. Kelly's solid "Bullethead" figurines (1938: plate 15i-l) of rough granular clay, without polish, have cylindrical heads; eyes and mouth are marked by horizontal grooves and ears are represented in relief, but never in detail (Kelly 1938:54-57).

There are, therefore, demonstrable trait affinities with both Formative and early Classic period styles. However, no chronological association can be assigned with confidence since such artifacts could have been deposited long after mound construction. On the other hand, the pieces found on the summit were buried at a depth of up to 10 cm which might indicate contemporaneity with at least the latest phase of mound construction.

There is a third possibility. Kelly (1938:53-54) describes the Chametla figurine inventory in terms of discrete groupings:

Chametla figurines fall with surprising precision into the groups outlined below. Naturally there are numbers of straggling oddments, small fragments, which cannot be placed anywhere. But by and large, the classification below is adequate. Moreover, the distribution breaks nicely into sequences with relatively little overlapping.

Her Red-face crested, Bullethead, and other distinctive figurines that are restricted to the Tierra Del Padre phase could be carryover types from a yet undefined West Mexican Formative figurine horizon style. If so, there would be no contradiction between a Formative figurine complex at

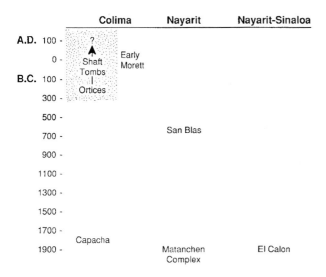

	Colima	Nayarit	Nayarit-Sinaloa
A.D. 100 -	?		
0 -	Shaft	Early	
B.C. 100 -	Tombs	Morett	
300 -	Ortices		
500 -			
700 -		San Blas	
900 -			
1100 -			
1300 -			
1500 -			
1700 -	Capacha		
1900 -		Matanchen Complex	El Calon

Figure 7. **Formative Chronology of the West Mexican Littoral.**

El Calón that bears considerable similarity to early Classic types from Chametla. The El Calón sample is small and the dating context tenuous but it may yet be important in some future regionalization of early styles. This is one of many specific empirical problems in West Mexican prehistory—one that calls for a major critical review and catalog of West Mexican figurine typology. Though it is too small a sample to bear reliable comparison, the occurrence of figurines is none the less interesting in that by the uniqueness of their appearance as an exclusive artifact class, they give the site a cultural "separateness." As we've seen, the same could be said for the mound itself, which in its height and configuration can be interpreted as an isolated case of public (civic or religious?) architecture.

Conclusion

Clearly, archaeology lies at a very early starting point in its understanding of the development of hunting-fishing-gathering societies on the West Mexican coast. The earliest available evidence from the coast dates to the Formative period, broadly characterized by Mountjoy (1989) as a time of regional adaptation by people who, in contrast to the hunter-collectors of the Archaic, lived in permanent settlements and depended to a significant extent on the cultivation of domestic plants. Within the 3,000 km range from Guaymas to Guatemala, the low, wide coastal plains of Nayarit, Sinaloa and Sonora and those of the Gulf of Tehuantepec correspond to the major inshore fisheries of Pacific Mexico today. Extrapolating into the Prehispanic past, those tidal marshes and estuaries offered perhaps the most productive of coastal habitation zones. In the intermediate area of Jalisco, Colima and Michoacán, the coastal strip is narrower and more mountainous. Without the large tracts of marshes, estuaries, and adjoining wetlands, we

might expect adaptive strategies among prehistoric populations to have been different than in other kinds of shoreline locations. The close proximity of higher ground fringing the coastal zone would have influenced mobility and subsistence as well as other social and economic strategies. As common sense dictates, transportation would have followed the mountain river courses. In Colima, for example, Kelly's archaeological zones coincide with the major drainage systems while "the coastal strip of Colima seems, during certain phases, a thing apart" (Kelly 1980:3).

Nearest in time to the early Marismas shellmounds is Mountjoy's Matanchén, the earliest of five major archaeological complexes (Figure 7) on the south-central coast of Nayarit (Mountjoy 1970, Mountjoy et al. 1972). Located only 140 km to the south, the Matanchén coast dwellers would have had access to generally the same plants and animals as would have people at El Calón, yet on present evidence, the archaeological pattern of coastal land use is different. The Matanchén complex is known from a 3 m thick shell deposit situated near the base of a volcanic hill at about 5-10 m above sea level but close to estuaries, a fresh water drainage channel, and the ocean. This early coastal midden lacks pottery and instead consists of shellfish exploited for food as well as other items of domestic refuse, e.g., fish, turtle, and bird bones, stone flakes and cobble implements.

The location of the Matanchén mound on higher ground would account for the continued accessibility of its deposits whereas it would appear that the location of El Calón made it subject to flooding and alluviation. As noted, these processes may have submerged the occupational debris near El Calón and may account for the site's eventual abandonment. Characterizing the Matanchén complex as the product of a "decidedly one-dimensional adaptive orientation" with possible seasonal movement, Mountjoy (1970) draws a picture of an Early Formative, preceramic population, attracted to the West Mexican coast, at least partially for the abundance of its aquatic resources. Contending that Matanchén adds another link to a chain of Early Formative, preceramic shellmound deposits from California to Panama, Mountjoy et al. (1972:1243) remind us of an unresolved but essential aspect of aboriginal coastal studies. They ask to what extent these early shell-midden deposits represent parallel, independent adaptations to similar ecological settings or alternatively, a unified and specialized coastal adaptation by historically related peoples; two postulates, with broad assumptions, that will obviously require far more baseline data on human use of coastal zones for an answer. To that end, can we expect archaeological data from the Marismas to contribute to such an inquiry?

Evidence of developing maritime societies, in the West Mexican coastal sub-region, though often highly provisional and even impressionistic, does nevertheless suggest a number of individual evolutionary forms—responses to both biophysical and perhaps social environments. From the early cultural time range within the natural region of the

21

Marismas we find today a low density of small mounds and a single 25 m high platform mound. The immediate archaeological problems associated with El Calón are the fundamental ones of stratigraphy and context. Until more basic information is available, the reconstitution of Early Formative life in the Marismas can only be guessed at by posing the questions raised by El Calón. Were the El Calón builders transient visitors to the coast? If not, and instead they were permanent settlers, as the finding of cultigen grains suggests, would the community pattern be substantially different than that of other Formative period shoreline dwellers or later coastal occupants?

As with other littoral sites from an early time range, the best evidence may lie buried by cycles of mixed fluvial-marine deposits. The history of the Marismas alluvial plain was punctuated by periods of submergence, one of which, Middle Beach progradation, accounts for the gap during which no material remains or other signs of human occupation have been found. Sometime following the building of the El Calón shellmound, it became the victim of that long interval of environmental instability, the immediate consequence of which was the rupture of whatever coastal tradition the El Calón phase people had evolved.

If, as suggested before, the figurines were cached in a later, post-construction period of its history, El Calón, like Matanchén, may also be an artifact of a preceramic horizon. Assuming though that they are of approximate equal age, a more visible record from the Marismas may someday reveal a similar maintenance strategy as well as other common factors in coastal adaptation between El Calón and Matanchén.

At the risk of over-stressing the uniqueness of El Calón, that mound does constitute a novel factor that contrasts sharply with other coastal scenarios. It represents the consumptive use of shell but not in any way comparable to the exploitation and disposition of oysters or other shellfish elsewhere on the West Mexican coast. Nor does it appear to bear any relationship in cultural terms, to other sites even within the Marismas locality. And what of its associative/symbolic importance? To identify behavior as ritualistic or to infer socio-political organization is risky, even on the basis of much fuller archaeological information. A long-held idea is that the natural beneficence of certain coastline environments was recognized very early by aboriginal populations—people who adapted themselves, either as permanent strandloopers or as seasonal tenants only, with restricted maritime/coastal economies. We assume further that they were more or less culturally homogeneous, with unstructured, egalitarian access to the vast array of aquatic resources of coastal Mexico. Could the appearance and practice of a horticultural economy on the northwest coast of Mexico coincide with any new order change, visible in the archaeological record? In that connection, one assumption that might underlie continuing investigations of El Calón is the notion that public structures are not common in egalitarian society. If, conjectur-

ally, El Calón served as an important Formative center for ceremonial activities, we can only point to its size and special circumstances as implying an "institutionalized" expression not reported elsewhere on the Pacific coastal lowlands.

References Cited

Allen, B. L., and G. G. Connally
1977 Soil and Soil Stratigraphic Units of the West Mexican Coastal Plain. *Geological Society of America Abstracts with Programs*, Vol. 9, Boulder.

Berger, R., R. E. Taylor, and W. F. Libby
1966 Radiocarbon Content of Marine Shells from the California and Mexican West Coast. *Science* 153:864-866.

Connally, G. G.
1977 The West Mexican Coastal Plain: Physiographic Definition. *Geological Society of America Abstracts with Programs*, Vol. 5, Boulder.
1984 Soil Stratigraphy and Inferred Tectonic History of the West Mexican Coastal Plain. In *Neotectonics and Sea Level Variations in the Gulf of California Area, A Symposium*, edited by V. Malpica-Cruz, S. Celis-Gutiérrez, J. Guerrero-García, and L. Ortlieb, pp. 56-73. Universidad Nacional Autónoma de México, Instituto Geología, México, D.F.
1989 Age and Origin of the Teacapan Peninsula and Surrounding Areas of the Marismas Nacionales, West Mexico. In *The Marismas Nacionales: Human Settlement Systems and Their Interrelationship with the Age and Origin of the Coastal Plain, Western Mexico*, edited by S. D. Scott. Ms. on file, Department of Anthropology, State University of New York, Buffalo.

Cottrell, D. J.
1973 Some Geomorphological Aspects of the Marismas Nacionales. In *The Marismas Nacionales of Mexico: Report on Continuing Investigations of the Archaeology and Related Natural Science Studies*. West Mexican Prehistory, Part 6. Ms. on file, Department of Geology, State University of New York, Buffalo.

Curray, J. R., and D. G. Moore
1964a Pleistocene Deltaic Progradation of the Continental Terrace, Costa de Nayarit, Mexico. In *Marine Geology of the Gulf of California, A Symposium*, edited by T. H. van Andel, and G. G. Shor, pp. 193-215. Memoir 3. American Association of Petroleum Geologists.
1964b Holocene Regressive Littoral Sand, Costa de Nayarit, Mexico. In *Deltaic and Shallow Marine Deposits*, edited by I. M. J. U. van Straaten, pp. 76-82. Elsavier, Amsterdam.

Curray, J. R., F. J. Emmel, and P. J. S. Crampton
1969 Holocene History of a Strand Plain, Lagoonal

Coast, Nayarit, Mexico. Paper presented at United Nations Symposium: Lagunas Costeras, UNAM-UNESCO, Nov. 28-30, 1967, México, D.F.

Damon, P. E., W. W. Ferguson, A. Long, and E. I. Wallick
1974 Dendrochronologic calibration of the radiocarbon time scale. *American Antiquity* 39:350-66.

Ford, J.
1969 *A Comparison of Formative Cultures in the Americas.* Smithsonian Institution Press, Washington, D. C.

Foster, M.
1974 *Excavations in Mound C, Venadillo, Sinaloa, Mexico.* Unpublished M.A. thesis, Department of Anthropology, University of Colorado, Boulder.
1989 Subsistence Patterns at Venadillo, Sinaloa. In *The Marismas Nacionales: Human Settlement Systems and Their Interrelationship with the Age and Origin of the Coastal Plain, Western Mexico,* edited by S. D. Scott. Ms. on file, Dept. of Anthropology, State University of New York, Buffalo.

Gill, G.
1969 Human Skeletal Remains: Chalpa and Tecualilla Sites. In *Archaeological Reconnaissance and Excavations in the Marismas Nacionales, Sinaloa and Nayarit, Mexico.* West Mexican Prehistory, Part 3, edited by S. D. Scott, pp. 112-132. Ms. on file, Department of Anthropology, State University of New York, Buffalo.
1971 *The Prehistoric Inhabitants of Northern Coastal Nayarit: Skeletal Analysis and Description of Burials.* Unpublished Ph.D. dissertation, Department of Anthropology, University of Kansas.
1974 Toltec Period Burial Customs Within the Marismas Nacionales of Northwestern Mexico. In *The Archaeology of West Mexico,* edited by B. Bell, pp.83-105. Sociedad de Estudios Avanzados del Occidente de México, Ajijic, Jalisco.
1977 Manifestations of a Conceptual Artistic Ideal within a Prehistoric Culture. *American Antiquity* 42(1):101-110.
1985 Cultural Implications of Artificially Modified Human Remains from Northwestern Mexico. In *The Archaeology of West and Northwest Mesoamerica,* edited by M. Foster and P. Weigand, pp. 193-215. Westview Press, Boulder.

Grosscup, G.
1964 *The Ceramics of West Mexico.* Unpublished Ph.D. dissertation, Department of Anthropology, University of California, Los Angeles.

Keen, M. A.
1958 *Seashells of Tropical West America.* Stanford University Press, Stanford.

Kelley, J. C., and H. D. Winters
1960 A Revision of the Archaeological Sequence in Sinaloa, Mexico. *American Antiquity* 25(4):547-561.

Kelly, I.
1938 *Excavations at Chametla, Sinaloa.* Ibero-Americana No. 14. Univ. of California Press, Berkeley.
1980 *Ceramic Sequence in Colima: Capacha, An Early Phase.* Anthropological Papers No. 37. University of Arizona, Tucson.

Klein, J., J. C. Lerman, P. E. Damon, and E. K. Ralph
1982 Calibration of Radiocarbon Dates: Tables Based on the Consensus Data of the Workshop on Calibrating the Radiocarbon Time Scale. *Radiocarbon* 24:103-150.

Meighan, C.
1971 Archaeology of Sinaloa. In *Archaeology of Northern Mesoamerica,* edited by G. Ekholm and I. Bernal, pp. 754-767. Handbook of Middle American Indians, Vol. 11, R. Wauchope, general editor. University of Texas Press, Austin.
1976 *The Archaeology of Amapa, Nayarit.* Monumenta Archaeologica, 2. Institute of Archaeology, University of California, Los Angeles.

Mountjoy, J. B.
1970 *Prehispanic Culture History and Cultural Contact on the Southern Coast of Nayarit, Mexico.* Unpublished Ph.D. dissertation, Southern Illinois University, Carbondale.
1989 Algunas Observaciones Sobre el Desarrollo del Preclásico en la Llanura Costera del Occidente. In *El Preclásico o Formativo: Avances y Perspectivas,* edited by M. C. Macías, pp. 11-26. Museo Nacional de Antropología and Instituto Nacional de Antropología e Historia, México, D. F.

Mountjoy, J., R. E. Taylor, and L. Feldman
1972 Matanchén Complex: New Radiocarbon Dates on Early Coastal Adaptation in West Mexico. *Science* 175:1242-1243.

Neiderberger, C.
1976 *Zohapilco: Cinco Milenos de Ocupación Humana en un Sitio Lacustre de la Cuenca de México.* Colección Científica 30. Instituto Nacional de Antropología e Historia, México D.F.

Odum, E. P.
1974 Halophytes, Energetics and Ecosystems. In *Ecology of Halophytes,* edited by R. J. Queen and W. H. Queen, pp. 599-602. Academic Press, New York.

Ortelius, A.
1579 *Theatrum Orbis Terrarvm.* Antwerp, Christopher Plantin. Nova Hispania, Folio 6.

Pool, D. J., S. C. Snedaker, and A. E. Lugo
1977 Structure of Mangrove Forests in Florida, Puerto Rico, Mexico, and Costa Rica. *Biotropica* 9(3):195-212.

Sauer, C. O., and D. D. Brand
1932 *Aztatlan: Prehistoric Mexican Frontier on the Pacific Coast.* Ibero-Americana No. 1. University of California Press, Berkeley.

Scott, P. K.
1989 The Marismas Nacionales: An Historical View of the Conquest and Early Post-Conquest Periods. In *The Marismas Nacionales: Human Settlement Systems and Their Interrelationship with the Age and Origin of the Coastal Plain, Western Mexico*, edited by S. D. Scott. Ms. on file, Department of Anthropology, State University of New York, Buffalo.

Scott, S. D.
1965 Review of *Natural Environment and Early Cultures*, edited by R. West. Handbook of Middle American Indians, Vol. 1, R. Wauchope, general editor. *Ethnohistory* 12(4):380-382.

1974 Archaeology and the Estuary: Researching Prehistory and Paleoecology in the Marismas Nacionales, Sinaloa and Nayarit, Mexico. In *The Archaeology of West Mexico*, edited by B. Bell, pp. 51-56. Sociedad de Estudios Avanzados del Occidente de México, Ajijic, Jalisco.

1985 Core Versus Marginal Mesoamerica: A Coastal West Mexican Perspective. In *The Archaeology of West and Northwest Mesoamerica*, edited by M. Foster and P. Weigand, pp. 181-191. Westview Press, Boulder.

Shenkel, J. R.
1971 *Cultural Adaptation to the Mollusk: A Methodological Survey of Shellmound Archaeology and a Consideration of the Shellmounds of the Marismas Nacionales, Mexico.* Unpublished Ph.D. dissertation, Department of Anthropology, State University of New York, Buffalo.

1989 Shellmounds of the Marismas Nacionales. In *The Marismas Nacionales: Human Settlement Systems and Their Interrelationship with the Age and Origin of the Coastal Plain, Western Mexico*, edited by S. D. Scott. Ms. on file, Department of Anthropology, State University of New York, Buffalo.

Sirkin, L.
1974 A Palynologic Model for Reconstructing Vegetation and Environments in the Marismas Nacionales, Sinaloa, Mexico. In *The Marismas Nacionales of Mexico: Report on Continuing Investigations of the Archaeology and Related Natural Science Studies.* West Mexican Prehistory, Part 8. Ms. on file, Department of Anthropology, State University of New York, Buffalo.

1989 The Marismas Nacionales: Palynological Studies. In *The Marismas Nacionales: Human Settlement Systems and Their Interrelationship with the Age and Origin of the Coastal Plain, Western Mexico*, edited by S. D. Scott. Ms. on file, Department of Anthropology, State University of New York, Buffalo.

Snedaker, S. C.
1971 The Calón Shellmound: An Ecological Anachronism. In *Archaeological Reconnaissance and Excavations in the Marismas Nacionales, Sinaloa and Nayarit, Mexico.* West Mexican Prehistory, Part 5. Ms. on file, Department of Anthropology, State University of New York, Buffalo.

Sweetman, R.
1974 Prehistoric Pottery from Coastal Sinaloa and Nayarit. In *The Archaeology of West Mexico*, edited by B. Bell, pp. 68-82. Sociedad de Estudios Avanzados del Occidente de México, Ajijic, Jalisco.

Taylor, R. E., and R. Berger
1967 Radiocarbon Content of Marine Shells from the Pacific Coasts of Central and South America. *Science* 158:1180-1182.

Taylor, R. E.
1987 *Radiocarbon Dating: An Archaeological Perspective.* Academic Press, Orlando.

Vann, J. H.
1972 *Physical Geography of the Pacific Coastal Lowland of Sinaloa and Nayarit, Mexico.* Submitted to the Office of Naval Research, Project NR 388-028, Contract NONR 4501(00). Copies available from O.N.R., Washington, D.C.

West, R. C. (editor)
1964 *Natural Environment and Early Cultures.* Handbook of Middle American Indians, Vol. 1, R. Wauchope, general editor. University of Texas Press, Austin.

Wing, E. S.
1968 Preliminary Note on the Faunal Remains Excavated from Several Sites in Sinaloa and Nayarit, Mexico. In *Archaeological Reconnaissance and Excavations in the Marismas Nacionales, Sinaloa and Nayarit, Mexico.* West Mexican Prehistory, Part 2. Ms. on file, Department of Anthropology, State University of New York, Buffalo.

3

On the Origin, Evolution, and Dispersal of Maize

Bruce F. Benz

Introduction

The Occident of Mexico (narrowly defined as Sinaloa, Nayarit, Aguascalientes, Jalisco, Colima and Michoacán), has been the subject of archaeological and ethnohistoric research for over five decades. Though never having received the attention of large-scale lengthy research efforts like those of the Petén or northern Yucatán, the Valley of Oaxaca or the Tehuacán Valley, substantial and noteworthy effort has been directed at deciphering its prehistory. Had we known earlier what we know now about the evolution of maize, it seems likely that the prehistory of the Occident of Mexico would be much more well-studied than it is today.

Much of the early work in the Occident of Mexico focused on the more recent prehistoric periods, especially the contact and Postclassic periods. Subsequent work provided general comprehension of the entire chronological sequence, calling particular attention to the Classic and Preclassic periods (Bell 1971; Foster and Wiegand 1985; Kelly 1945, 1949, 1980; Lister 1971). The so-called shaft and tomb burial complex so notable for this area has received considerable attention, as has the topic of pre-hispanic intercontinental contact (Kelly 1980). While much of this work has focused on chronology building (Meighan 1974), or salvage operations (Mountjoy 1982), a substantial amount of problem-oriented research has informed us of coastal adaptations (Mountjoy et al. 1972; Scott 1985, Chapter 2, this volume), and the evolution of cultural complexity in the region (Wiegand 1985).

Our knowledge of the preceramic era in this region is limited. Apart from a few isolated finds of Paleoindian and Archaic period projectile points (Wiegand 1985), we know next to nothing of the duration or extent of this early stage. This, of course, makes it difficult to discuss the beginnings of maize agriculture on the Pacific slope of Mexico. At present, all the archaeological evidence purportedly documenting the beginnings of these biocultural events and processes comes not from the Pacific slope but from sites situated on continental divides (Tehuacán and Guilá Naquitz) or in areas actually much closer to the Gulf coast (Ocampo Canyon, Infernillo Valley, and Tamaulipas). Furthermore, the maize recovered at the majority of these sites is only now being analyzed in the detailed fashion it deserves (see Flannery 1986; Mangelsdorf et al. 1967a, 1967b). To establish a temporal and evolutionary context for future studies on the Pacific coast some of this early archaeological material will be discussed here though it is only relevant temporally, not geographically, to the topic of this volume.

Following a short discussion of the most ancient Mexican maize a brief review of research dealing with present-day maize races and maize's putative ancestor teosinte (Benz 1987; Bretting and Goodman 1989; Doebley et al. 1984, 1985, 1987; McClintock et al. 1981) will be presented in order to provide a biogeographical context for current and future archaeological studies of maize's origin, early evolution, and racial diversification. In summarizing these data the region of maize's origin, the manner, mode and direction of dispersal, and the patterns of diversification will be discussed in hope of developing a testable framework for future research on the Pacific Slope of Mesoamerica.[1]

Historical Antecedents

Maize's origin and evolution have been the subject of debate since Harshberger postulated a century ago that its origin should be sought in the mid-elevation dry forests of south-central Mexico (Harshberger 1893). Arguments and hypotheses presented over the past century have stimulated research but only recently have the critical questions been framed that will elucidate the processes of maize's origin and the beginnings of maize agriculture.

Critical analyses of the wider taxonomic relationships between the obligate cultigen maize (*Zea mays* L. subsp. *mays*) and its closest relatives, teosinte (*Zea* spp.), and *Tripsacum* spp., are finally providing the data to focus on the biogeographic context of maize's origin. The archaeological maize collections, that purportedly resolved the debate of maize's origin and evolution, have been re-evaluated allowing greater resolution of the timing of certain morphological changes associated with the domestication. Re-evaluation of the archaeological material has cast doubt on many of the previous conclusions.

Research on how the maize ear originated and evolved continues (Doebley et al. 1990; Iltis 1983, 1987), and proves to be a controversial topic of discussion. Botanical insights and genetic information have shed light on how the maize ear originated as botanists and geneticists (Doebley et al. 1984, 1987; Sundberg 1990) apply new technologies to this century old question. Nevertheless, until archaeologists uncover the requisite archaeo-botanical materials, the theory and hypotheses, the botanical and genetic data on how teosinte gave rise to maize, as well as the temporal dimension of this process, will remain uncorroborated.

Theories of maize's racial evolution in the New World have generally been rather speculative due to a paucity of data. However, research has produced a veritable wealth of data that offer new and testable hypotheses (see Benz 1986; Bretting and Goodman 1989; Doebley et al. 1985; Hanson 1984; McClintock et al. 1981) which, if pursued with the same vehemence as the maize ear controversy, may eventually elucidate maize's migration and diffusion and aid in understanding Mesoamerica's culture history (Anderson 1943).

While a detailed treatment of the aforementioned topics is not possible here, I will briefly consider some of these controversies because maize's origin and racial diversification have direct bearing on the prehistory of the Pacific Basin.

Teosinte and *Tripsacum*: Direct and Indirect Ancestors

The long recognized morphological similarity between maize, teosinte and *Tripsacum* leaves little doubt that maize originated and evolved in the Americas (see Iltis and Doebley 1984:fig. 4). The role attributed to *Tripsacum*, or to teosinte, in maize's origin, as well as in the origin of diversity of maize races has, to a large extent, determined the geographic focus of the question (Iltis 1993). For example, Mangelsdorf (Mangelsdorf and Reeves 1939) considered teosinte to be a descendant and not an ancestor of maize. This belief, in concert with the formidable racial diversity of maize in South America, initially led him to hypothesize that South America was the continent where maize originated. Later, Mangelsdorf maintained that Guatemala was an equally likely site of origin due to the large number of "tripsacoid" races present there (Mangelsdorf and Cameron 1942). Following the subsequent discoveries of maize, teosinte and *Tripsacum* in the cave deposits of the Infernillo valley of Tamaulipas, and the maize in the caves of the Tehuacán Valley, he again revised

his thesis, to hypothesize Mexico as maize's homeland (Mangelsdorf et al. 1967a, 1967b).

The eco-geographic distribution of teosinte has, for some, carried more weight in the interpretation of maize's origin (Doebley 1990; Iltis 1983, 1985, 1987; see also Wilkes 1967, 1989). Following the line of reasoning adopted by Vavilov and later by Harlan and associates (the concept of centers of origin of domesticated plants), Iltis (1987), for example, argued that the biogeographic evidence would place maize's origin in the region of sympatry of the cultigen maize, particularly its primitive races, and its closest relative, teosinte.

The center of diversity of the genus *Tripsacum* also occurs in the region of sympatry of primitive maize races and teosinte (Wilkes 1972). While *Tripsacum* has nothing whatever to do with the origin of maize, the distribution of its species diversity suggests that the genus *Zea* did evolve in Mesoamerica. While *Tripsacum* species have a history very much distinct from *Zea*, a recently discovered sexual mutant producing pistillate organs in otherwise staminate "flowers" appears to support Iltis' Catastrophic Sexual Transmutation Theory (CSTT, Iltis 1983, 1987) on maize's origin from teosinte (see DeWald et al. 1987).

Teosinte: Biogeographical, Ecological and Ethnobotanical Considerations

The Pacific slope of Mesoamerica is very likely the region in which maize evolved from teosinte (Doebley et al. 1984, 1987; Doebley 1990; Iltis and Doebley 1984; see also Harshberger 1893). The wild species of *Zea* are distributed in isolated pockets, though frequently as dominant elements of the local vegetation, from Nicaragua, Honduras, and Guatemala (Iltis et al. 1985), to the Mexican state of Chihuahua (Sanchez and Ordaz 1987). These taxa are distributed almost exclusively in the hydrologic basins that drain to the Pacific Ocean. Only populations of the two Guatemalan taxa, *Zea luxurians* (Durieu) Bird and *Zea mays* subsp. *huehuetenangensis* (Iltis and Doebley) Doebley, are found in Atlantic watersheds, the former in the headwaters of the Motagua River, and the latter in the headwaters of the Usumacinta River.

The largest and most extensive populations of teosinte occur in Mexico in the Balsas or Lerma River basins, both of which drain into the Pacific. A large number of small populations are scattered across Mexico in the small river drainages of Chihuahua, Durango, Jalisco, and Oaxaca. Because of teosinte's recognized usefulness (Wilkes 1977; Benz et al. 1990) there should be little doubt that teosinte may have been more widespread sometime in the past (Ford 1976; Mangelsdorf et al. 1967a; Smith 1981). Humans may have been partially responsible for the distribution of teosinte, but we can only speculate about their influence on its overall range. Archaeological investigation may shed considerable light on this topic.

Biochemical investigations of taxonomic (using isoenzymes) and phylogenetic (using chloroplast DNA) relationships between wild *Zea* and maize demonstrate that the populations of *Zea mays* subsp. *parviglumis* (Iltis and Doebley) of northern Guerrero, southern Mexico and eastern Michoacán are the most similar to maize, and therefore ancestral to it (Doebley et al. 1984, 1987; Doebley 1990).

Concrete archaeological evidence is still lacking which shows how the maize ear evolved from teosinte. Morphological study of *Zea* spp. inflorescences suggest several relationships between the two (Benz 1986, 1987; Benz and Iltis 1991; Doebley et al. 1990). However, while experiments with sex-changing hormones, and study the ontogentic relationships of *Zea* inflorescences (Sundberg and Orr 1986, 1989) will provide hypotheses of the biological mechanics of the ear's origin, the best test will come from archaeological material of impeccable context. Furthermore, the immediate post-domestication events are also inadequately known (Benz and Iltis 1991; Benz 1994) because there is so very little archaeobotanical material representing these events and because this material has not been critically examined. Even less is known of the processes related to the diffusion or adaptive radiation of maize following domestication, processes responsible for the diversity of forms and adaptation so evident in maize today. Without doubt, the transport of seed and the migration of people along the Pacific coast of Mexico, Central America, and South America has been partially responsible for much of the diversity (and similarity) of forms and adaptation.

The Archaeological Evidence, or Lack Thereof

MacNeish's archaeological research in Tamaulipas, although bringing to light the association of maize, teosinte and *Tripsacum*, did not provide evidence relevant to maize's origin (Mangelsdorf et al. 1967a). While the earliest suggested dates imply preceramic maize, the maize specimens themselves are so strongly reminiscent of extant races (in size and form) that their great antiquity is equivocal. A reanalysis of this assemblage and its chronological placement is certainly needed.

The sequence recorded in the Valley of Mexico, at Zohapilco (Neiderberger 1976, 1979) apparently demonstrates a clear association of *Zea* and preceramic human occupation. While an increase in pollen size of *Zea* is suggested, the macrobotanical evidence is scarce and of questionable authenticity (e.g., 5000 year old non-carbonized fruitcases; Lorenzo and Gonzalez 1970; Wilkes 1989; Hernandez X. 1993). Here, the question of exactly when the human-*Zea* symbiosis began appears to be well-documented; concerns of how and why maize evolved remain unaddressed.

Flannery's (1986) work in Oaxaca also provides little direct evidence of how and why maize evolved. Schoenwetter's (Schoenwetter 1974; Schoenwetter and Smith 1986) analysis of pollen from the preceramic horizons suggest that the human-*Zea* association dates at least as early as 5000

B.C. Authentic remains of maize exhibiting what might be evidence of hybridization with teosinte, or the early stages of domestication are present there. These specimens were recovered from an undated ash horizon attributable to either preceramic or Preclassic occupations.

For the past 20 years the archaeological remains from Tehuacán, Puebla have assumed the greatest import in regard to maize's origin. They were initially, and continue to be (MacNeish 1981; Mangelsdorf 1986) cast as wild maize; that is, remains of a now extinct, naturally-occurring, self-sowing species apparently native to the deserts of the Tehuacán Valley. The remains found in the domestic refuse deposits of two caves have been at the center of debate concerning whether or not they are the remains of a wild species. Their small size, morphological uniformity, and great antiquity (ca. 6000-4500 B. C.) suggested that they are (Mangelsdorf et al. 1967b).

Mexico's National Institute of Anthropology and History permitted study of the material and destructive dating of some specimens (Long et al. 1989; Benz 1995, 1992). The first series of tandem accelerator mass spectrometer (TAMS) dates of six specimens from Coxcatlán Cave and four from San Marcos Cave indicated that the specimens from Coxcatlán Phase deposits are at least 1500 years younger than the average age designated for the Coxcatlán Phase (cf. Long et al. 1989; Johnson and MacNeish 1972); that is, they are no older than 3550 B.C. This has obvious implications for the morphological character of the material itself—how "wild" or primitive might we expect such material to be?

Morphological study of these specimens casts further doubt on earlier conclusions. These cobs are typical of extant maize in most respects, only their minute size and an occasional distichous (2-ranked, 4-rowed) fragment are worthy of note by comparison (Benz and Iltis 1990). Indeed, because they so closely resemble modern maize, there should have been some doubt of their being wild maize.

Mangelsdorf and associates argued that the grains were readily shed and naturally disarticulating from their spikelets. Moreover, they indicated that the cobs themselves readily disarticulated. To have unearthed articulated fragments of "naturally disarticulating" inflorescences still intact after 5500 years of burial is puzzling. In addition, the "disarticulated," or more appropriately, digested and highly eroded specimens, show no consistent pattern of disarticulation, and particularly not in a manner consistent with that of the 80 or more genera of grasses classified in the same tribe as maize (Andropogoneae). In none of maize's relatives does the grain naturally disarticulate from the spikelet, the inflorescence disarticulates, each spikelet being dispersed containing the grain.

Morphological comparison of the earliest Tehuacán maize remains with a race of cultivated maize presently grown in South America (Benz and Iltis 1990) demonstrates the two to be statistically indistinguishable. While the

Table 1. T-test Comparison of the "Wild Maize" from San Marcos and Coxcatlán Caves in the Tehuacán Valley.

Characteristic	t value
Row Number	1.30 [a]
Cupule Aperture Length	0.11 [a]
Cupule Wing Length	0.08 [a]
Rachid Length	0.85 [a]
Cupule Aperture Depth	0.95 [a]
Interstice Length	0.06 [a]
Rachis Diameter	3.49 [b]
Pith Diameter	6.12 [c]
Cob Diameter	5.04 [c]
Cupule Width	2.85 [b]
Cupule Aperture Width	2.62 [b]
Cupule Wing Width	3.00 [b]

Note: Without adjusting degrees of freedom for repeated tests on the same population, the tests presented above violate the rules of the test. They are shown here merely to suggest that differences apparently exist between two assemblages of what Mangelsdorf et al. (1967b) identified as "wild maize."

[a] n.s.

[b] $p < 0.01$

[c] $p < 0.001$

archaeological material from Tehuacán represents an obligate cultigen resembling an extant race, it does exhibit numerous primitive characteristics (e.g., distichous ears, shallow or almost flat cupules, and thin cupules and rachis).

The extreme variability exhibited by this material (Benz 1992), suggests that the Tehuacán Valley material represents a stage of the domestication process following an adaptive shift from natural to human dispersal. The selection pressure at this stage would be focused at the pistillate inflorescence and thus indirectly at attendant structures such as the inflorescence-bearing branch, the leaves of this branch, and the atavistic staminate inflorescence at its apex. Rindos (1984:178ff.) characterizes this stage as transitional between an r-selected to a k-selected ecological regime. This transition is apparent when the early specimens from San Marcos and Coxcatlán caves are compared. Temporal differences between the earliest specimens from San Marcos and Coxcatlán is at least 600 years (Long et al. 1989), a period sufficiently long enough under human selection for differences to be manifest.

The two collections show little morphological difference when longitudinal dimensions of the cob are considered (Table 1), but cob and rachis diameters as well as width measures show considerable differences. The Coxcatlán

specimens exhibit significantly larger diameters and widths. These differences may be the result of a more focused selection for the grain production, with greater diameter and width measures indicating increasing space on the rachis for more and/or larger seeds as well as a greater efficiency in packing later in time. Larger seeds might have been sought as a means of increasing production (human selection), or, possibly, in a more developed agroecology, due to a need for greater competitive ability (natural selection).

In sum, the archaeological evidence documenting the early stages of evolution of maize from teosinte is scarce, perhaps because archaeo-botanical investigations have not been conducted in the right place (Iltis and Doebley 1984; Doebley 1990; Doebley et al. 1987). The archaeological data for Tehuacán provides only a flavor of what will be found for the earliest stages.

Our understanding of ancient, or even recent, processes of racial evolution is still very incomplete (see Benz 1994). Although a considerable quantity of material has been unearthed, the carbonized and non-carbonized maize cob fragments either never reach the laboratory or are never placed under an analyst's microscope. Given the vast regional diversity of extant Mexican maize races (Benz 1986, 1987; Bretting and Goodman 1989; Doebley et al. 1985; Wellhausen et al. 1952), and the appreciable local diversity which apparently results from a local traditional diversified agricultural strategy (Hernandez X. 1993), Mexican archaeological maize has been very poorly characterized. For that reason, the processes giving rise to such differentiation that otherwise might help us to understand local agricultural adaptations, diffusion, contacts between cultures, migration and the like, are also poorly understood.

The remainder of this essay offers a hypothetical reconstruction of the racial phylogeny of Mexican maize. While the countless fragments of archaeological maize available in museums and storage facilities might provide the most temporally and geographically appropriate base for developing such a reconstruction, collections sufficient in number to cover Mesoamerica have not yet been amassed. Morphological and genetic descriptions of extant races and species have thus been employed here in an attempt to reconstruct the origin and racial diversification processes of maize on the Pacific slopes of Mexico. It must be stressed that the results presented here are only a first approximation; races of maize from the highlands of Mexico, as well as the Mexican Gulf Coast have not yet been so treated.

Origin, Dispersal and Diversification: General Considerations

Maize probably descended from populations of annual teosinte in the Balsas River Basin (Doebley et al. 1984, 1987), but whether the actual transition from teosinte to maize occurred there or elsewhere is still speculation. Various authors have suggested that allopatric speciation was most likely due to the genetic effects of swamping by the ancestor's pollen (Mangelsdorf 1974). Similarly the direction and speed of the dispersal of maize immediately following speciation is not well known.

Many authors have recognized the utility of a crop for illuminating human history, particularly migration, economic and social interaction and especially the consequent cultural changes (Anderson 1943; de Candolle 1886), though only a few have taken up this line of investigation (Bird 1984; Hanson 1984). A general lack of hard data regarding the biological bases of racial differences, the complexities resulting from maize's dispersal solely by humans and the maintenance of differences, however slight, by this single dominant force of selection, complicated by stochastic historical factors and interactions of cultural systems make it difficult to fully comprehend the mechanisms of racial diversification. Phenetic classification has provided the most consistent basis for generalizing about the racial phylogeny of maize but even this has its limits, particularly when dealing with prehistoric material.

Current distributional patterns help to identify relationships between species (Mayr 1981:600) but when combined with a temporal dimension, phenetic similarity can be misleading. For example, though progenitor species x, is absent in the area today, it is possible that it might have been present 500 years earlier. A race of maize that may have existed in Oaxaca 3000 years ago, may still exist in Yucatán today though it might be expected to have undergone at least minor genetic changes (Wellhausen et al. 1952). Whether such changes are sufficient to distinguish Yucatán maize from that in Oaxaca depends on the criteria used to make racial distinctions and the researcher's concept of "species." A local race may evolve in isolation and leave no descendants, or it may produce one or a few descendants with local or regional competitive advantage. The diversification process can be attributed to one or to numerous factors, hence each race will undoubtedly have its own unique evolutionary history.

In addition, few direct comparisons of extant races with the elements of prehistoric assemblages have been made in a rigorous fashion (Benz 1994). For example, of the seven races identified in the Tehuacán cave assemblages, no comparative data describing the prehistoric cobs were presented (Mangelsdorf et al. 1967b), yet all the cobs were classified to race!

Even during the earliest evolutionary stages, maize may have had the wide ecological tolerances that characterize it today. It seems probable that it was a species whose novelty and adaptability led it into new areas where humans had created and were maintaining its habitat. If maize possessed such ecological tolerances initially, the distribution of the species could have expanded like waves along a front with the limits of dispersal determined by transhumant settlement systems of the hunters-gatherers-gardeners who incorporated it into their subsistence regime. At this stage

Table 2. Mexican Maize Race Populations Employed in the Phylogenetic Analysis.

Race[a]	State	Collection Number[b]
Maize Ancho	Guerrero	221, 222, 225, 228
	Morelos	3, 27, 60, 79, 93
	Puebla	196
Pepitilla	Guerrero	3, 4, 6, 8, 9, 77
	Jalisco	99, 211
	Michoacán	78, 79
	Morelos	13, 14, 15 17, 18
	Puebla	200
Tabloncillo	Jalisco	24, 239, 263
	Sinaloa	1
Reventador	Guerrero	99, 106
	Jalisco	161, 163
	Michoacán	17, 157, 166
	Nayarit	15, 39
	Sonora	23
Jala	Nayarit	72
Harinoso de Ocho	Nayarit	4, 59
	Sinaloa	7
	Sonora	1
Olotillo	Chiapas	237
	Guerrero	60
Bolita	Oaxaca	28, 40, 60, 63, 66, 74
Dzit Bacal	Quintana Roo	1
	Yucatán	37
Conejo	Guerrero	17, 100, 121, 168, 174, 177
Chapalote	Sinaloa	2, 6
	Sonora	27, 55
Zapalote	Chiapas	104, 110, 113, 223, 236
	Oaxaca	48, 50, 51, 52, 54, 57, 70, 175, 179
Nal Tel	Yucatán	7, 36, 43, 75, 102, 129, 146, 148
	Chiapas	139, 144
	Oaxaca	148 171
Balsas Teosinte		
Huetamo	Guerrero	45, 46, 47, 48, 49
Luvianos	Guerrero	32, 33, 34, 35, 36, 37
Teloloapan	Guerrero	8, 9, 10, 11

[a] Classification according to Benz (1986, 1987).

[b] Collection number, or map number following McClintock et al. (1981).

maize was probably still a plant whose seed-bearing inflorescence was still lax and disarticulated naturally (i.e., disarticulation of the rachis, grains surrounded by the spikelets' glumes, lemmas etc., and falling with a segment of the rachis).

Estimating its rate of diffusion is difficult but is probably a function of, (1) the regional and local development of a suitable agroecology (Rindos 1984:164), (2) the geographical range of the bands, (3) the frequency of interaction with neighboring human populations, as well as (4) the bands' seasonal migratory habits (e.g., which vegetational zones were frequented during which seasons). We might suspect that bands whose seasonal permanence in any one locality might have been quite short, extra-local contacts brief, or with a large seasonal foraging range, would not have been among those who accepted and dispersed maize because the development of a suitable agro-ecological niche would not be expected to develop under such conditions in spite of maize's suspected wide ecological tolerance and because such gatherers would not effectively disperse it.

Maize dispersal patterns might be expected to be similar to those established for other organisms whose habitat is created by a wide-ranging forager. One such pattern is a broad and expanding wave of colonization characteristic of newly evolved ecotypes or introduced organisms (e.g., many New World weeds of European or Asiatic origin) that rapidly colonize widely distributed available habitats. A second pattern is characteristic of widespread but only locally common organisms that are highly vagile though very habitat specific. One or both patterns of dispersal probably occurred during maize's diffusion and consequent race formation. Maize's dispersal in the early evolutionary stages might resemble that of a moving front that colonized and covered a fairly large area rapidly. The colonization area most likely was sharply delineated by suitable environmental conditions at first (for example, moderate altitude and highly seasonal precipitation), as well as by the patterns of environmental modification encountered along this front as discussed above. The dispersal pattern exemplified by highly vagile organisms probably occurred also but only after a fairly stable agroecosystem had become established. Long distance migration or travel, by land or sea, of

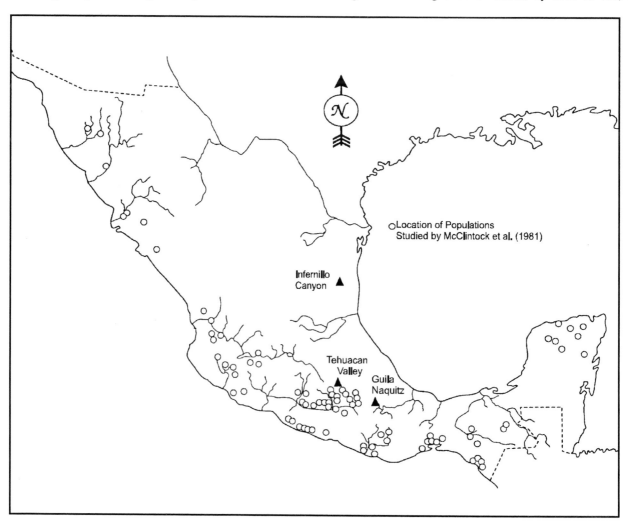

Figure 1. Location of Maize and Teosinte Populations Studied by McClintock et al. (1981), and Used in this Study to Reconstruct the Evolution and Diversification of Mexican Maize Races.

foraging groups or agriculturalists, was undoubtedly responsible for the dispersal of this cultigen.

Dispersal patterns are interrelated with racial diversification. Interaction on a regional scale that enhanced interchange of propagules might provide for increased opportunities of hybridization. This might slow or halt the diversification process. On the other hand, regional or local isolation would promote race formation and lead to diversification that might be detectable on a regional scale (Bretting et al. 1987). The following analysis integrates this theory with existing data.

The Data and Method

A cladistic approach has been adopted to reconstruct, if only partially, the evolution and diversification of maize in

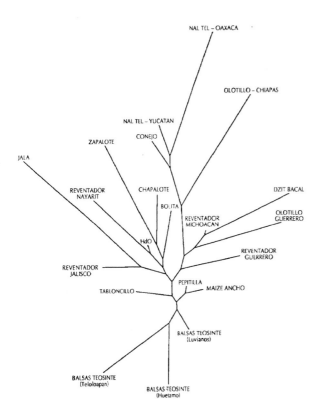

Figure 2. Phylogenetic Tree Generated from Chromosome Knob Frequency Data Using Felsenstein's Restricted Maximum Likelihood Estimate. The branches pointing downward (the "root" of the tree) are three teosinte populations used here to represent the ancestral populations. Branch length indicates degree of evolutionary diver-gence. The first three branches to diverge, the races Tabloncillo, Pepitilla and Maíz Ancho represent the origin and initial radiation of maize. Subsequent branching is interpreted as diversification and continued radiation.

Mexico. Phylogenetic relationships of twelve morphologically primitive maize races and three populations of Balsas teosinte are analyzed. These races, the majority of which occur in drainages of the Pacific Basin, were chosen principally because prior research (Benz 1986, 1987; Benz and Iltis 1991) indicate that they are the most closely allied to teosinte and very likely the most ancient races of maize. The teosinte populations used here to root the tree are herein believed to be representative of those occurring in the region considered by Doebley (Doebley et al. 1984; 1987) to be where maize originated.

Data on occurrence and size of 21 chromosome knobs provided by McClintock et al. (1981) were transformed to frequencies and populations assigned to race, following, for the most part, the designation provided by these authors (Table 2). Both morphological and geographical considerations suggest that some populations are geographically isolated and hence could be considered distinct races. Various populations, grouped into races by McClintock et al. (1981) are herein maintained as distinct entities because they appear to be geographically isolated. Racial means of knob size frequencies of 110 populations were analyzed by cladistic methods. Only Nal Tel and Dzit Bacal, both from Yucatán, are presumed to be non-indigenous to Pacific Basin watersheds (Figure 1).

Analysis of knob size frequencies seek to evaluate phylogenetic relationships between races, patterns of evolutionary diversification, and biogeographic routes of dispersal. Although a Restricted Maximum Likelihood Estimate (Felsenstein 1981, 1988) approach was employed to take advantage of the frequency data, Wagner Parsimony was also applied to a data set transformed to presence/absence of each knob size. The Restricted Maximum Likelihood Estimate algorithm (Felsenstein 1981) constructs a phylogenetic tree depicting relationships that represent time or genetic differentiation assuming pure random genetic drift. This model is assumed to accurately represent the principal force(s) that cause racial diversification, though in small founder populations extreme differentiation might be confused with lengthy separation times. Such discrepancies will be examined in detail below. Patterns of migration and dispersal are hypothesized from the phylogenetic tree and the extant distribution of the races.

It must be stressed that the tree presented here is the shortest thus far obtained (over 11,000 were examined) but it may not be the best tree. The occurrence of interior tree segments of potentially zero length suggest that alternative trees may need to be considered (Felsenstein 1988).

The Origin of Maize

Maize probably evolved from teosinte fairly rapidly. The hypothesized relationships (Figure 2) suggest that maize diversified little initially. During this early period, maize may have been dispersed only throughout the Balsas Basin and onto the mid-elevation plains, plateaus and valleys of

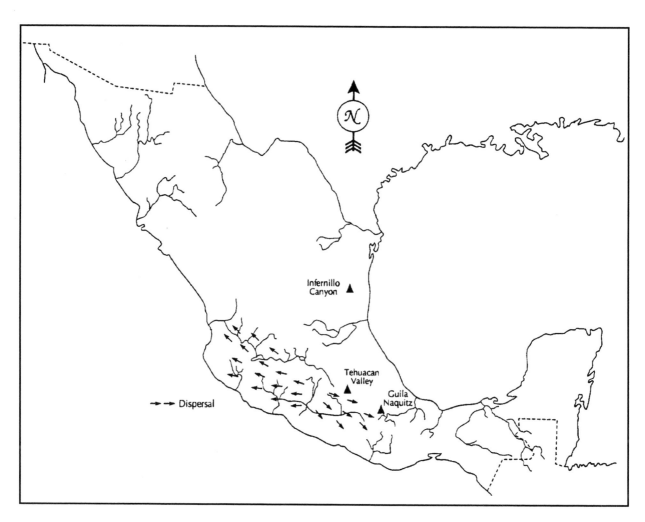

Figure 3. Using the Present-day Geographic Locations of the Maize Populations Herein Analyzed and the Phylogenetic Relations Depicted in Figure 2. This Figure Depicts the Hypothetical First Stage of Maize's Evolution—the Origin and Initial Radiation of Maize.

western Mexico via the Tepalcatepec River basin (Figure 3). This short early stage is represented in the phylogenetic tree by the short lower branches (terminating with Tabloncillo, Maize Ancho and Pepitilla). Tabloncillo is encountered throughout south-central Jalisco and Colima between 600 m and 1500 m elevation. Pepitilla and Maize Ancho are mid-elevation races (700-1700 m) found principally in Guerrero, México, Michoacán, Morelos, and Puebla. Few collections of these races are available due to difficult access so it is not known whether these races may have, at one time, formed a more continuous range across Michoacán. During the early evolutionary stages, when the maize ear was probably achieving consolidation, its distribution across southwestern Mexico was probably localized but may have been more or less continuous (Figure 3).[2]

Dispersal and Diversification

Subsequently, maize was dispersed very widely and diversification appears to have occurred in situ (Figure 4).

Maize appears to have diversified into two apparently distinct lineages. The first originated from populations dispersed early into Jalisco-Colima, which then made its way on to the coastal plain of Nayarit and from there moved up the Pacific coast of Mexico and presumably into the American Southwest. This lineage comprises the races depicted on the left side of Figure 2 and includes Reventador (from both Jalisco and Nayarit), the race Jala from Nayarit, and Chapalote from Sinaloa and Sonora. This lineage also seems to have given rise to two races in Oaxaca, viz., Zapalote, from the south coast of the Isthmus of Tehuantepec, and Bolita, from the central valleys. Inclusion of the two latter races in this lineage presents some difficulty in ascertaining location and direction of dispersal. Bolita was presumably a fairly early descendent of the lineage diversifying in western Mexico since it terminates a relatively short branch following the split of two earlier clades geographically centered in Jalisco-Nayarit (Figure 2), suggesting dispersal by sea or across the coastal plain from Jalisco-Nayarit to Oaxaca (possibly from where the Río Santiago empties into the Pacific to the mouth of the Río Verde), and from there into the interior valleys.

Zapalote presents a similar pattern of dispersal from the western to the southern coast but it lies at the end of a very long branch of the lineage containing the race Chapalote. Although dispersal by sea or along the coastal plain could be hypothesized, the long branch indicates either ancient dispersal, the dispersal of very small population (a founder population), or its passage through an evolutionary bottle-neck that would have appreciably narrowed the genetic variation present in the ancestral population.

The long branch terminating with Jala suggests historical conditions similar to that of Zapalote. Although extreme environmental or even human selection have been hypothe-sized as the cause for its genetic and morphological distinc-tiveness (Benz 1986), early dispersal and long isolation might be equally tenable propositions that could be tested archaeologically in the valley to which it appears to be endemic.

The second racial lineage (appearing at the right of Figure 2) models, as did the first lineage, both in situ diversification and long distance dispersal. The latter process apparently occurred toward the south and east. The first race to diverge was Reventador (the population from Guerrero); divergence apparently taking place in the Balsas River basin. Subsequent diversification produced two clades, one diversifying first in situ, or very nearby (Reventador from Michoacán, Olotillo from Guerrero) and from which evolved Dzit Bacal, a race encountered princi-pally in the northern part of the Yucatán Peninsula.

The long branches terminating in Dzit Bacal and Olotillo-Guerrero merit discussion. Dzit Bacal appears to differ substantially from its progenitor populations, possibly resulting from isolation following long distance dispersal and perhaps partly confounded by temporal isolation. It is also possible that a small founder population was dispersed into Yucatán which subsequently rapidly increased in size. Olotillo from Guerrero resembles both Tabloncillo and Olotillo from Chiapas, perhaps because the latter was dispersed from Jalisco to Chiapas, possibly with the

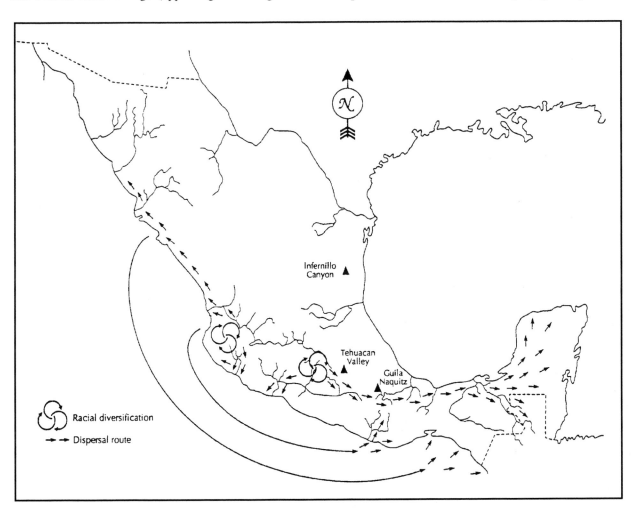

Figure 4. Based on the Present-day Geographic Locations of the Maize Populations Herein Analyzed and the Phylogenetic Relations Depicted in Figure 2. This Figure Depicts the Directions and Mode (by Sea or by Land) of Dispersal During Secondary Radiation and Subsequent Racial Diversification.

Chiapanec (Benz 1986, 1987). Olotillo from Guerrero should exhibit greater genetic similarity to Tabloncillo if the Chiapanec migration hypothesis is correct, but it is possible that the race ancestral to Tabloncillo and to Olotillo-Guerrero may have covered the area from Guerrero through Jalisco. Archaeological evidence from Jalisco-Colima, Guerrero and Chiapas would be useful for testing this hypothesis.

With the exception of Olotillo from Chiapas discussed above, the three remaining races are low elevation races. The close relationship between Conejo, from coastal Guerrero, and Nal Tel from Yucatán suggests that their common ancestor was indigenous to the Balsas Basin or to coastal Guerrero. The Oaxacan populations of Nal Tel, found today near the border with Guerrero, are related to the Yucatán populations, and to the coastal populations of Conejo. The long branch segment terminating in Nal Tel from Oaxaca may represent a founder population, whose ancestral population may have been originally in the Maya area.

Discussion

The process of racial diversification is complex and involves long distance dispersal, isolation, founder effects, and both cultural and environmental selection. These evolutionary phenomena might increase or decrease the variation present in ancestral populations. The model presented here provides greater resolution of inter-racial relationships than have phenetic studies of the same genetic data where populations were not segregated ecogeographically (Bretting and Goodman 1989). The results of this study are supported generally by morphological data (Benz 1986) and by isoenzyme data (Doebley et al. 1985). The results suggest that the Balsas-West Mexican and Isthmian Alliances (Benz 1987), based upon morphology, are polyphyletic. However, they do corroborate an earlier designation of races in the Balsas-West Mexican Alliance to be the more primitive (Benz and Iltis 1991) and suggest that the races Nal Tel and Chapalote are not among the races believed to be primitive by others (Mangelsdorf et al. 1967b; Mangelsdorf 1974; Miksicek et al. 1981; Wellhausen et al. 1952). These findings support earlier suggestions (cf. Doebley et al. 1984; Iltis and Doebley 1984; Benz 1986, 1987) that maize's early evolution might be archaeologically documented in the Balsas River valley. Western Mexico should not be ignored, however, because here too, very early evolution and racial diversification appears to have taken place and the center from which apparently all of the races herein-analyzed (with the exception of Pepitilla and Maize Ancho) diversified. On the other hand, while Maize Ancho and Pepitilla appear to be evolutionary "dead ends" from the results presented here, it is possible that they are branches that form the lineage which populated the central highlands of Mexico. The biochemical evidence suggest that maize's origin occurred in the Balsas River

Valley and the chromosome knob data suggest that maize arrived and diversified very early in western Mexico.

Early diversification seems to have occurred in the area of Colima-Jalisco-Nayarit and in Guerrero. Dispersal from these "centers" apparently moved to the north and south from the western center, and to the south and east from the Guerrero center. Racial evolution resulted from dispersal into new geographic areas which exposed the founding populations to different environmental and cultural conditions. In some cases, early dispersal may have played an more important role in the evolution of quite divergent genotypes (Zapalote or Jala), while in some cases long distance dispersal may have played an equally important role (e.g., Olotillo from Chiapas, Nal Tel from Oaxaca).

Summary

The archaeological record does not yet provide a clear picture of the maize's initial evolutionary stages. The Tehuacán collection provides a sample probably representative of the stages preceding the diversification of lineages but long after maize's speciation. It gives only a general picture that needs confirmation through procurement and study of other such collections. Undoubtedly the Tehuacán collection's later material could provide a very clear picture of the local diversification process(es) if analyses were to be conducted in a more quantitative fashion that allowed more objective hypothesis testing.

The processes of racial diversification appear to have proceeded in somewhat different ways in each of the two geographic centers described above. In the western center, populations were dispersed along both a northerly, presumably coastal, route as well as a southerly route, also along the Pacific coast. Maize in the Guerrero center, on the other hand, appears to have diversified in situ such as in the western center, but seems to have been dispersed in an exclusively southern and easterly direction.

We cannot yet offer hypotheses regarding the temporal dimensions of the various stages presented above and depicted in Figure 2. At the present time, we can only speculate that diversification probably did not precede the Tehuacán assemblage's earliest maize (ca. 3500 B.C.; Long et al. 1989).

Acknowledgments

This work was supported by a Fulbright Research Fellowship. P. Bretting offered useful suggestions and greatly improved the prose; G. Wilkes commented on an earlier draft. Their help is gratefully acknowledged.

Notes

1. Since this manuscript was submitted, a number of very relevant developments have come to light in the area of molecular genetics. Doebley's analysis of the genetic

differences between maize and two species of Mexican annual teosinte suggest that five restricted regions of the genome account for most of the differences in inflorescence morphology (Doebley 1994 and references cited therein). In addition, Goloubinoff et al. (1993) obtained intact DNA fragments from three specimens of archaeological maize. Efforts to clone and sequence the major genes responsible for differences between maize and teosinte will allow future application of ancient DNA technology to prehistoric specimens that will permit archaeologists to characterize the timing and cultural context of prehistoric genetic changes in teosinte and maize. Developments in the archaeological arena have not kept pace. The significance of the AMS dates obtained on the Tehuacán maize have only recently entered mainstream archaeological thought (Fritz 1994, 1995; McLung de Tapia 1992; Pearsall 1995). The critical evidence to resolve this long-standing debate will have to come from archaeology and the time to pursue it has arrived.

2. Unfortunately, chromosomal knob frequency data are not available for the annual populations of *Z. mays* subsp. *parviglumis* in Jalisco-Colima. I suspect that once these are closely studied, they will be seen to be range extensions of the Balsas populations that are directly ancestral to maize. Their presence in Jalisco-Colima may be due to their having followed maize into western Mexico after maize's domestication and early dispersal.

References Cited

Anderson, E.
1943   Races of Maize II: A General Survey of the Problem. *Acta Americana* 1:58-68.

Bell, B.
1971   Archaeology of Nayarit, Jalisco, and Colima. In *Archaeology of Northern Mesoamerica*, edited by Gordon Ekholm and Ignacio Bernal, pp. 694-753. Handbook of Middle American Indians, Vol. 11, Robert Wauchope, general editor. University of Texas Press, Austin.

Benz, B.
1986   *Taxonomy and Evolution of Mexican Maize.* Unpublished Ph.D. dissertation, Department of Botany, University of Wisconsin, Madison.
1987   Racial Systematics and the Evolution of Mexican Maize. In *Studies in the Neolithic and Urban Revolutions: the V. Gordon Childe Colloquium, Mexico, 1986*, edited by L. Manzanilla, pp. 121-136. B.A.R. International Series 349, British Archaeological Reports, Oxford.
1992a   Studies in Archaeological Maize II: Morphological Variation of the Earliest Archaeological Maize from the Tehuacán Valley. Ms. on File, Laboratorio Natural Las Joyas, Universidad de Guadalajara, México.

1994   Reconstructing the Racial Phylogeny of Mexican Maize: Where Do We Stand? In *Corn and Culture in the Prehistoric New World*, edited by S. Johannessen and C. A Hastorf, pp. 157-179. Westview Press, Boulder.
1995   El Maíz Silvestre de Tehuacán Revisitado. In *Investigaciones Recientes en Paleobotánica y Palinología*, edited by M. Montufa, pp. 45-54. Colección Cientifica No. 294. Instituto Nacional de Antropología e Historia, México.

Benz, B. F., and H. H. Iltis
1990   Studies in Archaeological Maize I: The "Wild Maize" from San Marcos Restudied. *American Antiquity* 55:500-511.
1991   Evolution of Female Sexuality in the Maize Ear (*Zea mays* L. subsp. *mays*, Gramineae). *Economic Botany* 46:212-222.

Benz, B. F., L. R. Sanchez-Velazquez, and F. J. Santana M.
1990   Ecology and Ethnobotany of *Zea diploperennis*: Preliminary Investigations. *Maydica* 35:85-94.

Bird, R. McK.
1984   South American Maize in Central America. In *Pre-Columbian Plant Migration*, edited by D. Stone, pp. 43-65. Papers of the Peabody Museum of Archaeology and Ethnology, vol. 76. Cambridge.

Bretting, P., and M. Goodman
1989   Karyotypic Variation in Mesoamerican Races of Maize and its Systematic Significance. *Economic Botany* 43:107-124.

Bretting, P., M. Goodman, and C. Stuber
1987   Karyological and Isozyme Variation in West Indian and Allied American Mainland Races of Maize. *American Journal of Botany* 74:1601-1613.

de Candolle, A. L. P. P.
1886   *Origin of Cultivated Plants.* Hafner Publishing Co., New York.

DeWald, C. L., B. L. Burson, J. M. J. DeWet, and J. R. Harlan.
1987   Morphology, Inheritance and Evolutionary Significance of Sex Reversal in *Tripsacum dactyloides*. *American Journal of Botany* 74:1055-1059.

Doebley, J. F.
1990   Molecular Systematics of *Zea*. *Maydica* 35:143-150.
1994   Genetics and Morphological Evolution of Maize. In *The Maize Handbook*, edited by M. Feeling and V. Walbot, pp. 61-66. Springer-Verlag, New York.

Doebley, J. F., M. M. Goodman, and C. W. Stuber
1984   Isozyme Variation in *Zea* (Gramineae). *Systematic Botany* 9:203-218.
1985   Isozyme Variation in the Races of Maize from Mexico. *American Journal of Botany* 72:629-639.

Doebley, J. F., W. Renfroe, and A. Blanton
1987   Restriction Site Variation in the *Zea* Chloroplast Genome. *Genetics* 117:139-147.

Doebley, J. F., A. Stec, J. Wendel, and M. Edwards.
1990   Genetic and Morphological Analysis of a Maize-teosinte F_2 Population: Implications for the Origin of Maize. *Proceedings of the National Academy of Science* 87:9888-9892. Washington, D.C.

Felsenstein, J.
1981   Evolutionary Trees from Gene Frequencies and Quantitative Characters: Finding Maximum Likelihood Estimates. *Evolution* 35:1229-1242.
1988   Phylogenies and Quantitative Characters. *Annual Review of Ecology and Systematics* 19:445-471.

Flannery, K. V. (editor)
1986   *Guilá Naquitz: Archaic Foraging and Early Agriculture in Oaxaca, Mexico.* Academic Press, Orlando.

Ford, R. I.
1976   Appendix XIII. Carbonized Plant Remains. In *Fábrica San José and Middle Formative Society in the Valley of Oaxaca*, by R. D. Drennan, pp. 261-268. Memoirs No. 8. Museum of Anthropology, University of Michigan, Ann Arbor.

Foster, M., and P. Wiegand (editors)
1985   *The Archaeology of West and Northwest Meso-america.* Westview Press, Boulder.

Fritz, G. J.
1994   Are the First American Farmers Getting Younger? *Current Anthropology* 35:305-309.

Fritz, G. J.
1995   New Dates and Data on Early Agriculture: the Legacy of Complex Hunter-gatherers. *Annals of the Missouri Botanical Garden* 82:3-15.

Goloubinoff, P., S. Pääbo, and A. C. Wilson
1993   Evolution of Maize Inferred from Sequence Diversity of an *Adh2* Gene Segment from Archaeological Specimens. *Proceedings of the National Academy of Science* 90:1997-2001.

Hanson, W. D.
1984   Intergradation among Latin American Maize Based on an Analysis of Chromosome Knob Frequencies. *Theoretical and Applied Genetics* 68:347-354.

Harshberger, J. W.
1893   Maize, a Botanical and Economic Study. *Contributions to the Botanical Laboratory of the University of Pennsylvania* 1:75-202. Philadelphia.

Hernandez X., E.
1993   La Agricultura Tradicional Como una Forma de Conservar el Germoplasma de Cultivos in situ. In *Biología, Ecología y Conservación del Género Zea*, compiled by B. Benz, pp. 31-32. Universidad de Guadalajara, Guadalajara, Jalisco.

Iltis, H. H.
1983   From Teosinte to Maize: the Catastrophic Sexual Transmutation. *Science* 222:886-894.
1985   *The Maize Mystique—A Reappraisal of the Origin of Corn.* Contributions to the University of Wisconsin Herbarium No. 5. Madison.
1987   Maize Evolution and Agricultural Origins. In *Grass Systematics and Evolution*, edited by T. Soderstrom, K. Hilu, C. Campbell, and M. Barkworth, pp. 195-213. Smithsonian Institution Press, Washington.
1993   La Taxonomía del *Zea* desde una Perspectiva Histórica. In *Biología, Ecología y Conservación del Género Zea*, compiled by B. Benz, pp. 1-25. Universidad de Guadalajara, Guadalajara, Jalisco.

Iltis, H. H., and J. F. Doebley
1984   *Zea*—A Biosystematical Odyssey. In *Plant Biosystematics*, edited by W. F. Grant, pp. 587-616. Academic Press, Montreal.

Iltis, H. H., D. A. Kolterman, and B. F. Benz
1985   Accurate Documentation of Germplasm: the Lost Guatemalan Teosintes (*Zea*, Gramineae). *Economic Botany* 40:69-77.

Johnson, F., and R. S. MacNeish
1972   Chronometric Dating. In *The Prehistory of the Tehuacán Valley, Vol. 4: Chronology and Irrigation*, edited by F. Johnson, pp. 3-55. University of Texas Press, Austin.

Kelly, I.
1945   *Archaeology of the Autlan-Tuxcacuesco Area of Jalisco. I: The Autlan Zone.* Ibero-Americana No. 26. University of California Press, Berkeley.
1949   *Archaeology of the Autlan-Tuxcacuesco Area of Jalisco. II: The Tuxcacuesco-Zapotitlán zone.* Ibero-Americana No. 27. University of California Press, Berkeley.
1980   *Ceramic Sequence in Colima: Capacha, an Early Phase.* Anthropological Papers No. 37. University of Arizona, Tucson.

Lister, R. H.
1971   Archaeological Synthesis of Guerrero. In *Archaeology of Northern Mesoamerica*, edited by Gordon Ekholm and Ignacio Bernal, pp. 619-631. Handbook of Middle American Indians, Vol. 11, Robert Wauchope, general editor. University of Texas Press, Austin.

Long, A., B. Benz, D. Donahue, A. Jull, and L. Toolin
1989   First Direct AMS Dates on Early Maize from Tehuacán, Mexico. *Radiocarbon* 30:130-135.

Lorenzo, J. L., and L. Gonzalez
1970   *El Más Antiguo Teosinte.* Boletín del Instituto Nacional de Antropología e Historia No. 42. México.

MacNeish, R. S.
1981   Tehuacán's Accomplishments. In *Supplement to the Handbook of Middle American Indians*, vol. 1, edited by J. Sabloff, pp. 31-47. V. R. Bricker, general editor. University of Texas Press, Austin.

Mangelsdorf, P. C.

1974 *Corn: Its Origin, Evolution, and Improvement.* Harvard University Press, Cambridge.

1986 The Origin of Corn. *Scientific American* 255(2): 80-86.

Mangelsdorf, P. C., and J. W. Cameron

1942 Western Guatemala: A Secondary Center of Origin of Cultivated Maize Varieties. *Botanical Museum Leaflets, Harvard University* 10:217-254.

Mangelsdorf, P. C., and R. G. Reeves.

1939 *The Origin of Indian Corn and its Relatives.* Texas Agricultural Experiment Station, Bulletin No. 574.

Mangelsdorf, P. C., R. S. MacNeish, and W. Galinat

1967a Prehistoric Maize, Teosinte and Tripsacum from Tamaulipas, Mexico. *Botanical Museum Leaflets, Harvard University* 22:33-63.

1967b Prehistoric Wild and Cultivated Maize. In *The Prehistory of the Tehuacán Valley, Vol. 1: Environment and Subsistence*, edited by Douglas S. Byers, pp. 178-200. University of Texas Press, Austin.

Mayr, E.

1981 *The Growth of Biological Thought.* Harvard University Press, Cambridge.

McClintock, B., T. A. Kato Y., and A. Blumenshein

1981 *Chromosome Constitution of Races of Maize.* Colégio de Postgraduados, Chapingo.

Meighan, C.

1974 Prehistory of West Mexico. *Science* 184:1254-1261.

Miksicek, C. H., R. Mck. Bird, B. Pickersgill, S. Donaghey, J. Cartwright, and N. Hammond

1981 Preclassic Lowland Maize from Cuello, Belize. *Nature* 289:56-59.

Mountjoy, J.B.

1982 *El Proyecto Tomatlán de Salvamento Arqueológico Fondo Etnohistórico y Arqueológico, Desarrollo del Proyecto, Estudios de la Superficie.* Colección Científica: Arqueología 122. Instituto Nacional de Antropología e Historia, México D. F.

Mountjoy, J. B., R. E. Taylor, and L. Feldman

1972 Matanchén Complex: New Radiocarbon Dates on Early Coastal Adaptation in West Mexico. *Science* 175:1242-1243

Neiderberger, C.

1976 *Zohapilco: Cinco Milenos de Ocupación Humana en un Sitio Lacustre de la Cuenca de México.* Colección Científica 30. Instituto Nacional de Antropología e Historia, México D.F.

1979 Early Sedentary Economy in the Basin of Mexico. *Science* 203:131-142.

Pearsall, D.

1995 Domestication and Agriculture in the New World Tropics. In *Last Hunters first Farmers*, edited by T. Douglas Price and Anne Birgitte Gebauer, pp.

157-192. School of American Research Press, Santa Fe.

Rindos, D.

1984 *The Origins of Agriculture: An Evolutionary Perspective.* Academic Press, San Diego.

Sanchez G., J. J., and L. Ordaz S.

1987 *El Teocintle en México.* Systematic and Ecogeographic Studies on Crop Genepools No. 2. IBPGR, Rome.

Schoenwetter, J.

1974 Pollen Records of Guilá Naquitz Cave. *American Antiquity* 39:292-303.

Schoenwetter, J. and L. D. Smith

1986 Pollen Analysis of the Oaxaca Archaic. In *Guilá Naquitz, Archaic Foraging and Early Agriculture in Oaxaca, Mexico*, edited by K. V. Flannery, pp. 179-237. Academic Press, Orlando.

Scott, S. D.

1985 Core Versus Marginal Mesoamerica: a Coastal West Mexican Perspective. In *The Archaeology of West and Northwest Mesoamerica*, edited by Michael Foster and Phil Weigand, pp. 181-193. Westview Press, Boulder.

Smith, J. E.

1981 Appendix IX. Formative Botanical Remains at Tomaltepec. In *Excavations at Santo Domingo Tomaltepec: Evolution of a Formative Community in the Valley of Oaxaca, Mexico*, by M. Whalen, pp. 186-194. Memoirs No. 12. Museum of Anthropology, University of Michigan, Ann Arbor.

Smith, C. E. Jr., and P. Tolstoy

1981 Vegetation and Man in the Basin of Mexico. *Economic Botany* 35:415-433.

Sundberg, M. D.

1990 Inflorescence in *Zea diploperennis* in Relation to Other *Zea* Species. *Maydica* 35:119-133.

Sundberg, M. D., and A. R. Orr

1986 Early Inflorescence and Floral Development in *Zea diploperennis*, Diploperennial Teosinte. *American Journal of Botany* 77:141-152.

1990 Inflorescence Development in Two Annual Teosintes: *Zea mays* subsp. *mexicana* and *Zea mays* subsp. *parviglumis*. *American Journal of Botany* 77:141-152

Weigand, P.

1985 Evidence for Complex Societies During the Western Mesoamerican Classic Period. In *The Archaeology of West and Northwest Mesoamerica*, edited by M. Foster and P. Weigand, pp. 47-92. Westview Press, Boulder.

Weigand, P and M. Foster

1985 Introduction. In *The Archaeology of West and Northwest Mesoamerica*, edited by Michael Foster and Phil Weigand, pp. 1-8. Westview Press, Boulder.

Wellhausen, E. J., L. M. Roberts, and E. Hernandez X.

1952 *Races of Maize in Mexico.* Bussey Institution, Harvard University, Cambridge.

Wilkes, H. G.

1967 *Teosinte: The Closest Relative of Maize.* Bussey Institution, Harvard University, Cambridge.

1972 Maize and its Wild Relatives. *Science* 177:1071-1077.

1977 Hybridization of Maize and Teosinte in Mexico and Guatemala and the Improvement of Maize. *Economic Botany* 31:254-293.

1989 Maize: Domestication, Racial Evolution, and Spread. In *Foraging and Farming: The Evolution of Plant Exploitation*, edited by D. R. Harris and G. C. Hillman, pp. 440-453. Unwin and Hyman, London.

4

Late Archaic Period Coastal Collectors in Southern Mesoamerica: the Chantuto People Revisited

George H. Michaels and Barbara Voorhies

The purpose of this paper is to reconstruct the probable lifeways of an ancient people who lived on the Pacific coastal plain of southern Mesoamerica during the time immediately prior to the development of settled village farming. The known archaeological signatures of these ancient people are several large island-sites in an estuary of southern Chiapas, Mexico (Figure 1). These substantial features are accretionary deposits that consist almost entirely of shells of a small brackish water clam. We argue here that these shell heap sites represent only one component of the total settlement pattern of the people responsible for their deposition and that other sites formed by these same people have yet to be discovered by archaeologists (cf. Lowe 1978:346). Moreover, we think that the sites functioned primarily as specialized procurement and processing locations, for fish, clams, and possibly shrimp.

Islona de Chantuto was the first of these sites investi-

gated by archaeologists. During a brief visit in 1947, Philip Drucker (1948) determined that under an upper layer of pottery-bearing soil there was a deposit that consisted entirely of clam shells in which there were stone tools but absolutely no pottery. At that time this was only the second known site in Mesoamerica where aceramic and ceramic deposits occurred in the same stratigraphic section. Drucker considered his discovery to be very significant for understanding the transition from a preceramic to an early ceramic horizon (Drucker 1948:166).

Subsequently, four similar sites were found in the immediate vicinity of the Chantuto site. Campón (CAP-6) was discovered by José Luis Lorenzo (1955) who mapped the site, as well as Chantuto (CAP-3). El Chorro (CAP-4) and Tlacuachero (CAP-7) were found by Carlos Navarrete (1969), who mapped and tested the first mentioned site. Voorhies (1976) found Zapotillo (CAP-8). The locations of

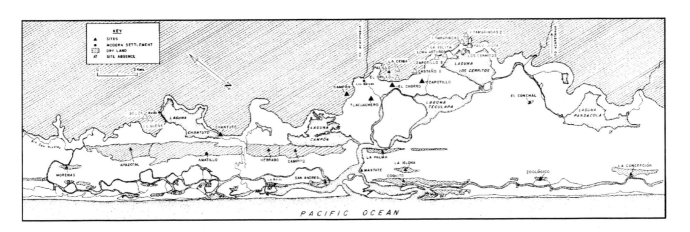

Figure 1. Map of the Acapetahua Estuary Showing Locations of Archaeological Sites. Large Black Triangles—Sites with Known Archaic Components. Large White Triangles—Sites with Possible Archaic Components. Small Black Triangles—Sites of Other Ages.

these sites are shown in Figure 1.

The first problem-oriented research at these sites was conducted by Voorhies in 1973. Working at three of the five known sites, she used an excavation strategy designed to expose deep stratigraphic sections in order to address diachronic issues. This research resulted in the recovery of stone tools and both invertebrate and vertebrate animal remains, providing information about the ancient economy of the region from 3000 to 2000 B.C. Voorhies concluded that no significant changes in the stone tool assemblages nor in the use of resources were discernible in the excavated deposits.

One of the reasons we returned to Tlacuachero in 1988 was to collect data that would allow us to develop a more comprehensive model of Chantuto society.[1] This endeavor seemed to us to be particularly deserving of study in view of the dearth of information available about how coastal people organized their societies immediately prior to the development of settled village farming life in Mesoamerica. In this paper we present the model that we are currently testing by means of various ongoing analyses of material recovered during the 1988 season.

Only a relatively few Mesoamericanists have taken an interest in studying the Archaic period occupations of the coasts (cf. Voorhies 1978). On the Atlantic seaboard there are two significant studies (Figure 2). One was carried out by Jeffrey Wilkerson (1973, 1975) at two sites in the vicinity of the Río Tecolutla in southern Veracruz, and the other study was directed by Richard S. MacNeish (1986) who surveyed the coast of Belize. The final detailed reports of these two studies are pending but they have produced some information about ancient human behavior that will be summarized in our concluding section. On the Pacific coast there are three studies in addition to the work by various investigators on the Chantuto sites. John E. Clark and colleagues (Clark et al. 1987) excavated Cerro de las Conchas, a short distance southeast of Chantuto and situated at the edge of the same wetland formation as those sites. Joseph Mountjoy (1971, 1974, 1989) excavated several sites on the coast of Nayarit, and in the 1970s, Stuart Scott and colleagues (1985, and this volume) discovered and excavated at sites, some of which may be Archaic, in the Marismas Nacionales region of Sinaloa-Nayarit. In addition, Charles Brush (1965, 1969) excavated a small volume of material at Puerto Marquéz, near Acapulco, Guerrero. For a variety of reasons these investigators have not yet attempted formulations of subsistence and settlement models for the ancient people responsible for the archaeological remains. Accordingly, at present there are no comprehensive models, generated directly from field studies, for the transition of coastal peoples from a hunting-gathering to an agricultural way of life.

This unsatisfactory situation pertains to the Mesoamerican coastal lowlands only; in the highlands a much clearer picture has emerged as a result of a great investment in archaeological research in two key upland valleys. We refer

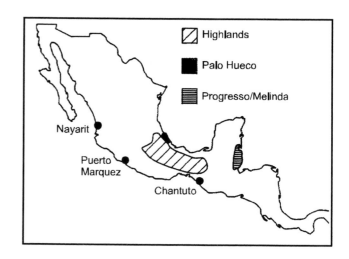

Figure 2. **Map of Mesoamerica Showing Areas with Archaic Period Studies. (Adapted from MacNeish 1986: Fig. 2.5)**

to the studies by MacNeish and colleagues (e.g., MacNeish et al. 1972) in the Tehuacán Valley and that of Flannery (1983, 1986) and his associates in the Valley of Oaxaca.

One model that may help in understanding the evolution of Archaic period economy and society in the Chantuto region is the Forager-Collector Model proposed recently by Binford (1980). He initially made the distinction between foragers and collectors to characterize two basic mobility patterns observed in the ethnographic record of hunter-gatherers. At one extreme, foragers shift their residences among a series of resource patches primarily in accord with the seasonality of the preferred resources. Food is typically not stored but is gathered daily, so Binford describes the food-getting strategy as one of "mapping onto" resources. In the ideal model, the archaeological sites expected to be produced are the residential base, which is the hub of subsistence activities, and the location, a place where extractive activities are carried out exclusively. In Binford's forager model the latter type of site is used briefly and produces only limited quantities of archaeological remains. He (Binford 1980:9) refers to them as "low bulk" procurement sites.

Collectors, at the other extreme, manifest a greater degree of specialization in that specially organized task groups concentrate on the procurement of specific resources. That is, the procurement strategy emphasizes the deployment of some members of the group to procure a particular type of food for the group as a whole, so Binford refers to this strategy of food-getting as "logistical." Collectors often depend more on food storage than do foragers. Binford (1980:10) identifies five site types as being typically produced by collectors: field camps, stations, caches, residential bases and locations. Field camps are temporary operation centers used by a task group while it is away from its residential base. Stations in Binford's terminology are information gathering places such as hunting stands.

Caches are places where bulk items are temporarily stockpiled by specialized task groups for larger consuming groups. The residential bases of collectors are similar to those of foragers in that a wide range of activities are carried out there. The locations of collectors, however, typically differ from locations of foragers in that they have much more archaeological debris due to the fact that task groups in collecting societies are seeking products for social groups far larger than themselves. As Binford (1980:10) puts it:

> Such large and highly visible sites are...the result of logistically organized groups, who frequently seek goods in very large quantities to serve as stores for consumption over considerable periods of time.

In the sections that follow, we will attempt to show that the Chantuto sites are best interpreted as locations produced by specialized task groups who were logistically organized. In the concluding section we shall suggest how other known late Archaic period sites from Mesoamerican coastal settings might fit into the collector model as well.

The Chantuto Sites and their Settings

The biomes in the Chantuto region today are similar to those of the Late Archaic period. At present, evidence for this similarity derives exclusively from the faunal remains found in the archaeological deposits: all of the archaeological bones and shells are from species that are present today in the vicinity of the sites. Since an analogous study of palaeobotanic remains has not yet been completed, we lack a second data set by which we can evaluate our initial interpretation.

We emphasize that by assuming the ancient presence of the same biomes in the past as in the present we are not asserting that they had the same actual distributions as today. In fact, the dynamic nature of estuaries, as well as evidence that this specific coastline has been prograding in recent geological time, strongly suggest that the mosaic of biomes during the Chantuto phase must have been different from that of today.

The Chantuto Sites

In simple terms, the sites are massive piles of tiny shells capped with a mantle of soil. Shaped basically like trun-

Table 1. Dimensions of the Chantuto Phase Sites.

Site name	Number	Height (m)	Area (ha)
Chantuto	CAP-3	4.5	0.46
El Chorro	CAP-4	5.5	0.41
Campón	CAP-6	6.0	0.83
Tlacuachero	CAP-7	7.0	2.12
Zapotillo	CAP-8	11.0	1.06

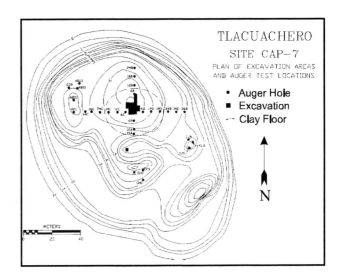

Figure 3. Map of Tlacuachero Showing Locations of Excavation Units and Auger Holes.

cated cones, they form islands within the mangrove forest swamp in which they are situated. A map of one of these sites, Tlacuachero, is shown in Figure 3. The dimensions of these five islands are given in Table 1.

Today all of the islands occur on the landward side of the network of shallow, brackish water lagoons that are the habitat for marsh clams, the major constituent of the shellmounds. Except for Chantuto, the mounds are not situated at the edge of any of these lagoons but we presume that they were so located at the time of their formation. In fact, we speculate that they mark the former inland edge of the lagoons. There are two lines of reasoning for this idea.

First, this interpretation is consistent with the apparent depositional process of the sites. Clams were likely used close to the procurement site because they are a relatively heavy resource. Furthermore, Waselkov (1987:115) has empirically found that traditional shellfish gatherers process shellfish close to the procurement location. Given this assumption we note that the shellmounds are linearly aligned with one another, as would occur if they bordered a lagoon. Moreover, the circular outlines of the mounds indicate that they accumulated under environmental constraints, such as within an aquatic environment (c.f. Waselkov 1987: 115-117), rather than along linear features such as banks or shorelines where shellmounds with elongated plans accumulate. While this at first might seem to contradict the idea that the shellmounds were situated at the lagoon margins, in the Acapetahua estuary the margins of lagoons are *not* contained by banks but are formed by the edge of the wetland mangrove forest formation. Accordingly, we think that the shellmounds have always been islands, but they were initially situated at lagoon margins.

The second line of reasoning is based on the assumption that the major features of the coast have been shifting seaward in a gradual way beginning about five thousand years ago, since the stabilization of sea level at its modern elevation (Lankford 1976:184-185, 197; see also Gagliano 1984:Figure 1.70). A series of inactive barrier beach formations mark the progress of this seaward movement but these features have not been studied and remain undated.

The Physiographic Setting

We describe both the terrestrial and the estuarine components of the Chantuto peoples' environment. We think that they probably participated in the ecosystems of both of these zones on an alternating basis but the known archaeological evidence pertains only to the estuarine system.

The Estuary

The Chantuto shellmounds are located within the Acapetahua estuary so we will begin our discussion with a description of that ecosystem.

Estuaries are coastal water bodies that are partly enclosed and within which there is a mixing of fresh and salt water. Freshwater is discharged into estuaries from rivers that drain adjacent land, whereas salt water is pumped into them by means of tidal flushes. These dynamic aquatic systems are characterized by constant and repeated pulsations of water from both rivers and the sea. Conceptually it is useful to view these aquatic systems as transitional between freshwater and marine ecosystems; many of the species that are found within them have a tolerance for a relatively wide range in salinity.

In the Acapetahua estuary there are three main zones: (1) the mangrove forest, (2) the herbaceous swamp, and (3) the open water lagoons and canals. These are discussed briefly here and in somewhat more detail in Voorhies (1976).

The mangrove forest formation consists of a high stand of two tree species, the red mangrove (*Rhizophora mangle*) and the white mangrove (*Laguncularia racemosa*), both of which tolerate inundated and saline soils. Since this forest stands in water it is technically a swamp. Animals that live in the forest include birds, semi-arboreal animals such as opossums, raccoons and porcupines, as well as termites and crabs. The zone occupies a band parallel to the coastline and is widest (approximately 8 km) near the middle of the Acapetahua estuary.

Herbaceous swamps occur at the eastern and western margins of the estuary. In the west, the swamp occurs in several relatively small patches and is dominated by a single species of cattail (*Typha*). At the eastern margin of the estuary there is a huge swamp, El Hueyate, that is formed by the discharge of the rivers Huixtla and Despoblado (Helbig 1976:219). Its extent is between 30 and 60 sq km, depending on the season, and water level fluctuates from 0.5 to 2.0 m (Helbig 1976:219). According to Helbig (1976), who gives a brief description, *papiros* (a tall member of the Ciperacae) and *palma real* are the dominant plants.

The fauna of the herbaceous swamp includes turtles and the migratory birds that are abundant from October through March. Other birds are continuous residents of this zone.

The open water within the estuary consists of canals and lagoons. This aquatic system is the home of many fish, turtles, crocodiles, shrimp, and mollusks. The lagoons are the habitat for the species of clam (*Polymesoda radiata*) whose shells make up the bulk of the archaeological sites we are discussing (Figure 4). They are the habitat also for shrimp, an animal that we believe was of major importance in the economy of the Chantuto people, despite the lack of direct evidence in support of this idea (Voorhies et al. 1991).

The Coastal Plain.

The coastal plain adjacent to the Acapetahua estuary has a very low gradient. This means that drainage is poor on the lowest slope with consequent flooding during the rainy season. The vegetation of the seasonally flooded zone is a palm savanna that is used today only for cattle pasture rather than for cultivation. Between the savanna and the mangrove forest there is another transitional community dominated by *Avicennia nitida*, a tree species that will tolerate seasonal but not continuous flooding.

The vegetation of the coastal plain probably once was tropical deciduous forest but it has been completely removed and replaced by fields and pastures. A gallery forest would have paralleled the major water courses. Due to the destruction of the climax vegetation we have great difficulty in determining what species may have been of economic importance. We speculate that there would have been deer, rabbit, jaguar, kinkajou, monkeys, *tepescuintle*, iguana and other animals. Tree fruits, fibers, roots and other plant products were almost certainly collected. Lowe et al. (1982:68-69) have published a species list of some of the more common animals in the vicinity of Izapa, an important archeological site located approximately 75 km east of our study area in a more inland and somewhat wetter zone.

Archaeological Evidence for the Ecology of the Chantuto People

Our discussion is divided into several sections that

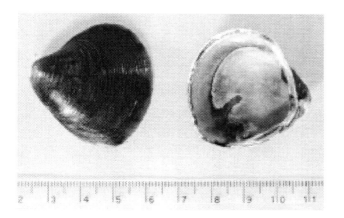

Figure 4. Two Examples of Marsh Clam Shells.

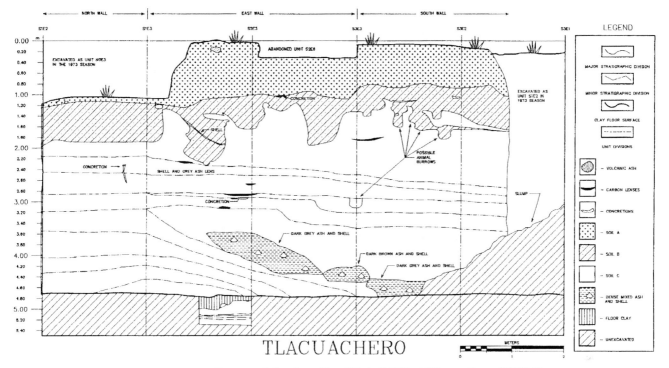

Figure 5. Profile of the North, East, and South walls of Unit S1E3 at Tlacuachero (CAP-7).

describe and interpret site stratigraphy, ecofacts and artifacts. We also include a section in which we generate a model of seasonality of site use based upon comparative data.

Stratigraphy, dating, and site occupation

This section focuses on stratigraphy at the Tlacuachero site (CAP-7), for which we have the most extensive data, but the findings are remarkably uniform at the other sites as well.

All of the studied Chantuto sites consist of two distinct cultural deposits. The upper deposit is characterized as a deep (1-3 m) mantle of dark, unbedded soil containing ceramics (Figure 5, Soil A). At Tlacuachero, Soil A contained a variety of cultural materials including chipped and ground stone artifacts, fragments of ceramic vessels and figurines, as well as a variety of faunal remains.

The next lower deposit, Soil B, was an unbedded, humus-rich soil similar to Soil A except that it contained noticeably more of the marsh clam shells that were the main constituent of the lowest component, Soil C. We consider Soil B to be mixed and to contain artifacts that derive from each of the two components represented at the site. This mixing probably occurred as a result of human disturbance of Soil C during the deposition of Soil A.

Underlying Soil B (or Soil A where B was not present) was Soil C. Soil C consisted of a thin-bedded formation composed overwhelmingly of marsh clam shells in either a whole or fragmented condition (Figure 6a and 6b). These

shells all came from the marsh clam (Figure 4). Soil C contained very few cultural materials. Ceramics were not found (with the exception of a handful of intrusive sherds). Chipped and ground stone tools were recovered, but occurred in very low frequencies and were limited in diversity. Examples of faunal remains other than marsh clam were recovered, but were also in very low frequencies. Charcoal was abundant in Soil C, but was generally thinly scattered through the layers of burned, fragmented shell, or was confined to small, thin, single-episode lenses (analogous to individual campfires).

The contact between the shell gravels and the upper, dark soils is distinct. This was made especially clear in the long profiles in the lateral excavations at Tlacuachero. The people responsible for the deposition of the A/B soils had dug pits into the underlying Soil C in all three sites studied by Voorhies (1976) and had entirely removed the uppermost portion of the C formation. There is no indication that these pits had been used for storage; they may represent the mining of shell from the shell gravel deposits by the later inhabitants of the sites. The mined shell may have been collected for burning to produce lime, a practice that is carried out today in the study area using modern shells. This lime would in turn have been used for processing corn. Such a practice is reported by Erasmus (1955:323) for Mayo men who use shell heaps for this purpose.

Whatever behavior was responsible for these pits, the end result is that the upper strata of the shell-bearing deposits have been truncated everywhere that we have excavated. Hence we have no surviving evidence from the youngest

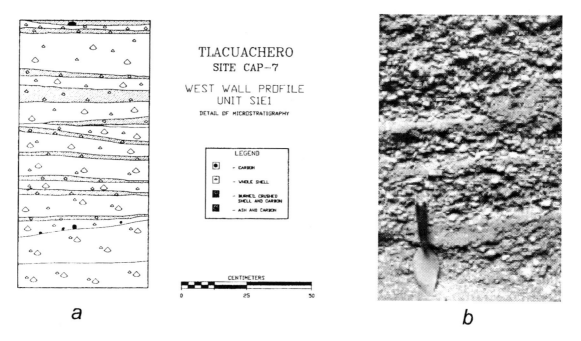

TLACUACHERO
SITE CAP-7

WEST WALL PROFILE
UNIT S1E1

DETAIL OF MICROSTRATIGRAPHY

LEGEND

⊙ - CARBON

◇ - WHOLE SHELL

▧ - BURNED, CRUSHED SHELL AND CARBON

▨ - ASH AND CARBON

CENTIMETERS
0   25   50

a

b

Figure 6. Details of Microstratigraphy at Tlacuachero: (*a*) Shows Detail of West Wall, Unit S1E1, (*b*) is a Photograph of Thin-bedded Layers of Soil C.

part of the Soil C occupation and are unable to date precisely the cessation of shell deposition at these sites.

It remains to establish the ages of the two components of the Chantuto sites. Previously, Voorhies (1976) dated the ceramic bearing deposits of the Chantuto sites to the Late Preclassic-Early Classic periods. This was done primarily on the basis of ceramic cross-dating to other known sites. One radiocarbon date was obtained from the ceramic deposits at Tlacuachero. Its age is 1900 ± 95 B.P. (HL=5,568 years).[2] This date is acceptable, as it falls within the Late Preclassic period, the earlier part of the time period indicated by the ceramics.

The preceramic component was previously dated, on the basis of radiocarbon assays, to between 3000 B.C. and 2000 B.C. (Voorhies 1976:42-43).[3] We obtained two new radiocarbon samples from just above the prepared clay floor feature during our 1988 investigations at Tlacuachero. The two new dates are 3900 ± 70 (Beta 25626) and 4060 ± 70 (Beta 25627) years B.P.[4]

Whereas the ceramic-bearing component of the sites has no internal stratigraphy, the Archaic deposits are complex. The three most striking features of the Archaic deposits are their thickness, the nature of their bedding, and the generally undisturbed condition of the beds. These characteristics have led us to develop a model of the formation processes responsible for them.

The thickness of the Archaic deposits at these sites, as well as their areal extent, indicates a very long and/or massive exploitation of the estuary, particularly of the marsh clam. At Zapotillo (CAP-8) the maximum known depth (as determined from a single test pit located near the site summit) is 10.30 meters (Voorhies 1976). At Tlacua-

chero (CAP-7) the maximum known thickness at the site summit is 6.4 meters, whereas at Campón (CAP-6) the deepest deposits exposed (in Test Pit N8W1) were measured at 5.6 meters. It should be noted that these are minimal thicknesses, as the bottoms of these formations were not reached due to current water table levels.

The second characteristic of note about these Archaic shell middens is the thinness and horizontal extent of the microstratigraphic beds. Figures 6a and 6b illustrate the microstratigraphy at Tlacuachero. The microstratigraphy can be characterized as spatially extensive layers of un-burned, whole shell alternating with layers of burned, fragmented shell. Many of these layers could be traced confidently across the full ten meter stratigraphic cut at Tlacuachero and they continued beyond the excavations. Individual dumps were rarely discernible but exceptions to this may be seen in Figure 5 where dark grey ash and shell lenses are located just above the floor. Overall, however, the deposits more closely conform to what Waselkov (1987:114) has referred to as blanket middens, which in his opinion are associated with industrial processing of shellfish for commercial exchange. Of great significance are the beds of burned, fragmented shell. The horizontal extent of these layers, and the regularity of their occurrence, indicate to us the possibility of periodic burning of the island's vegetation.[5]

We conducted experiments in the field with various heating regimes on marsh clams. These regimes sought to recreate the different conditions under which the archaeo-logical shell could have been burned. The regimes included several food preparation techniques such as steaming over coals, as well as direct burning, and indirect heating through a layer of soil. Direct burning and indirect heating produced results most like those observed at the sites. Direct burning resulted in significant heat fracturing and scorching of the shell, consistent with the characteristics of the shell in the beds of burned shell fragments. Indirect heating through an overlying layer of sand produced an orange discoloration of the shell that was very similar to the orange hue of the whole shell layers immediately underlying the burned, compacted layers.

These experimental results, coupled with the horizontal extent and regularity of the burned, fragmented shell layers led us to believe that they document the periodic burning of the islands. Today these islands are covered during the wet season either with grass or weeds. If, in the past, these sites were occupied only seasonally, it is probable that they would become vegetated between human visits. The vegetation, in turn, would have provided food and cover for a wide variety of animal species including snakes, iguana, crocodiles, turtles, and possibly jaguar (which was endemic to this area until the 1950's). Burning off the underbrush before reoccupying the islands would have cleared the area for general use and may have helped in catching animals scared off the island by the burning.

The final characteristic of the shell stratigraphy is its undisturbed nature. Long term occupation would surely have left traces in the strata such as worn paths or at least heavily trodden areas, pits, the accumulation of fairly substantial hearth deposits, sleeping depressions, post molds, and other traces of intense activity. None of these features has been noted in the Archaic strata (other than on the unique clay floor), although some of them are present in the later deposits at the same sites. Even the observed hearth deposits appear to be remains of single campfires. These factors suggest to us that during the Archaic period, occupations of the sites were short term and were not residential.

To summarize, the characteristics of the thermally altered shell and the extent of the layers across the islands are evidence for extensive burning. The stratigraphic repetitiveness of the burned layers argue for periodic, possibly seasonal, rather than long term occupation of the islands during the late Archaic period. The absence of features associated with generalized residential activities suggests to us that these sites were not residential base camps.

Faunal Evidence

The most striking aspect of the deposits pertaining to the Chantuto phase (Soil C) is that they consist almost exclusively of marsh clam shells (Table 2). There no actual soil in the matrix and the remains of other fauna are scarce. This fact has led us to the inevitable conclusion that the sites resulted from highly specialized procurement activities. Nevertheless, occasional remains of other mollusks, as well as vertebrates were found in all of the Chantuto phase

Table 2. Weights in grams of Marsh Clam, Barnacle and Miscellaneous Shell from S1E3, Tlacuachero.

Item	Size fraction		
	>0.500"	>0.250"	>0.125"
Marsh clam			
Whole valves	540.0	11.5	0.2
Fragments			
Unburned	190.1	550.0	
Burned	2.3	116.1	
All	-	-	2000.0
Barnacle	0.0	0.1	8.0
Other shell	0.0	0.0	1.2

deposits, but they were extremely scarce. In this section we discuss these remains and our interpretation of the food-getting strategy of the Chantuto people.

Invertebrates.

The marsh clams that dominate the faunal remains in the Chantuto sites live on the bottom of the lagoons. Procurement of these clams is simple and requires no special tools because they can be collected by simply ducking under water and picking them up. Some kind of container, such as a net bag, boat or basket, greatly facilitates the collection procedure, however. Our experience is that a few people are able to collect large quantities of these small clams in a relatively short period of time using this harvesting method.

The Chantuto people probably used a mass harvesting procedure rather than one in which each clam was collected individually, as we have done. We suspect this because very small, immature clams and small snails (*Neritina*) that also live in the lagoon mud are found when the deposits are analyzed carefully. We think their presence supports the idea that some tool, such as a scoop, was employed to harvest the marsh clams.

We also recover barnacle fragments during midden analysis, but they are small-sized and scarce (Table 2) so they could not possibly be the remains of food. Moreover, since these animals attach themselves to marsh clam shells, it appears that they reached the site along with the marsh clams. The only other invertebrates encountered are several individuals each of oyster (*Ostrea columbiensis*) and a land snail (*Orthalicus princeps*), both of which are large enough to be considered potential food sources; but their rarity (Voorhies 1976:46-48) means they were of little consequence in the ancient diet.

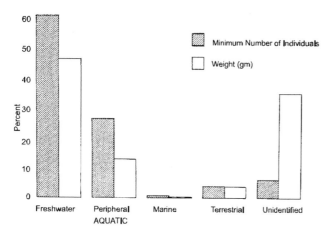

Figure 7. Animal Portion of Human Diet During the Archaic Period from Aquatic, Terrestrial, and Unidentified Organisms. Results Are Averaged Bone, by MNI and Weight, Recovered from Five Test Pits at Sites CAP-6 and CAP-7.

Thus, the invertebrate remains document an overwhelming emphasis on marsh clam compared to other species. We found no remains in the Chantuto phase deposits of the several mollusks that are eaten today and collected from either the sandy beach or the edges of canals by inhabitants of these wetlands. This suggests to us that the Chantuto people narrowly focused their procurement activities on the lagoon habitat while they were occupying the midden sites. This interpretation, which indicates that the sites may have been "locations," in Binford's site terminology, is strengthened by the remains of the vertebrate fauna as will be discussed below.

We have been assuming that the marsh clams were eaten by the human occupants of the Chantuto sites, but it is also possible that they were collected in order to be used for some other purpose. One possibility is that the clams were used for bait for the procurement of some other animal. It seems to us logically possible that clams might be used to attract either carnivorous fish or some kinds of shrimp[6] but we find it difficult to think that the clams were so used since it would have required the laborious extraction of clam meat from the shells at the site. A much more practical (i.e., quicker and less costly in labor) way to use these little clams as bait would be to smash them and to use the resultant mass of shell and meat as is. Such a practice, however, does not explain the shell buildup at the sites.

The second possibility is that clam shells were used in the processing of some other animal, such as fish or shrimp. We consider shrimp a likely candidate since it is a major component of the lagoon ecosystem, especially during the dry season when juveniles spend part of their developmental cycle there (Voorhies 1976:25).

The economy of modern inhabitants of the estuary is based heavily on shrimp (Voorhies 1976:26-28). During the time of the year when shrimp are abundant in the lagoons most men are full-time shrimpers and prior to the introduction of ice, most women processed them. The traditional method of processing entailed boiling the shrimp in brine and then sun drying them prior to their exportation to inland consumers. Today, with the introduction of electricity to the villages in the estuary, shrimp are refrigerated and exported fresh, rather than dried.

Using our understanding of shrimp exploitation today we reason that if shrimp were a major resource for the ancient Chantuto people, it would be very difficult to find evidence of this in the archaeological remains. First, shrimp preserve very poorly, especially in the midden environments where even pollen has not survived. Second, the juvenile shrimp may be and often are eaten whole, in which case the possibility of preservation is greatly lessened. Third, if shrimp were dried and exported to inland locations for their consumption we would expect few remains to have survived in the midden deposits.[7]

Despite these difficulties we plan to carefully analyze the deposits in search of the remains of shrimp, along with other small ecofacts. Other investigators (e.g., Reitz 1988; Reitz and Quitmyer 1988) have recovered shrimp remains from middens in the Southeastern U. S., so this technique may be productive.

In summary, the analysis of invertebrate remains shows that only one animal, the marsh clam, had a significant economic value for the people who created the shellmound sites, but we speculate that a second invertebrate, shrimp, may also have been important.

Vertebrates.

The vertebrate fauna from Chantuto phase deposits at two of the three sites excavated by Voorhies were identified to the lowest possible taxon by Elizabeth S. Wing (Voorhies 1976:54-62). Still to be studied are the bones excavated from Zapotillo (CAP-8), as well as those from our recent work at Tlacuachero. These analyses are planned for the near future.

Wing's study demonstrated that the Chantuto people concentrated their food procurement activities on estuarine aquatic resources (Figure 7). This conclusion was apparent when the data were compared either in terms of MNI's or by weight (Voorhies 1976:24). Marine animals (i.e., ones that are not known to enter the estuary) were present in very low frequencies and terrestrial animals represented only about 4% of MNI and weight. Most of the identified vertebrates were classed by Wing as either freshwater or peripheral (i.e., brackish water) and are present in the estuary (cf. Voorhies 1976:54).

Accordingly, the analysis of vertebrate fauna indicates that the Chantuto people were strongly focused on the estuary. This is completely consistent with the finding from the invertebrate study. People using the same two sites during the later occupation emphasized terrestrial fauna to a much greater extent than did the Chantuto people (Voorhies 1976:61).

Looking at the vertebrate data from the Chantuto phase deposits in more detail (Figure 8) we find that the most important class of vertebrates during the Chantuto phase was fish (75%), followed by mammal and turtle (each 11%), then other reptile (3%) and bird (1%). We assume that our findings give an accurate indication of that portion of the ancient diet for which remains survive but it does not assess the possible contribution of plants or of shrimp.

Recently Hudson, Walker and Voorhies (1989:143-144) have evaluated the relative contribution of clams compared with vertebrates using the assumption that both were components of the diet of the Chantuto people. They found that the amount of meat represented by all vertebrates was only 0.6% of the total meat (Figure 8). This overwhelming emphasis on clam procurement provides a very strong argument for interpreting the deposits as specialized activity locations rather than some other type of settlement. However, the predominance of clams over the remains of other organisms does not mean necessarily that they were eaten at the site, although that may have been the case.

We propose the hypothesis that clams were procured and processed at sites in the estuary prior to moving them inland to consumers. This scenario is akin to Waselkov's (1987) view of the industrial processing of shellfish for commercial purposes. If correct, then clam meat was one of the target resources processed in bulk quantities by the Chantuto people.

Another possibility is that shrimp, in addition to clams, were being processed in bulk quantities for movement to inland consumer locations. In this scenario, after the meat was extracted from the clam shells they were then used as construction material for shrimp drying platforms, an idea that was first suggested to us by George M. Riser (personal communication, 1988). This view is supported by ethnographic data for the area.

Floral Evidence

On the basis of the faunal evidence discussed above, we expect the paleobotanic evidence to show that (1) the plant environment was the same in the past as it is today, and (2) plants of economic value, if any, would be limited to very few species. We have discussed the major plant communities in a previous section so the first mentioned expectation requires no further explication. The second expectation is based on our interpretation that the Chantuto people were using the sites for a very restricted range of activities during short intervals of occupation. We reason that if any plants were economically important to those people while they were at the sites, they would have been restricted to a few species only, analogous to the finding that marsh clams were the main known target of animal procurement activities.

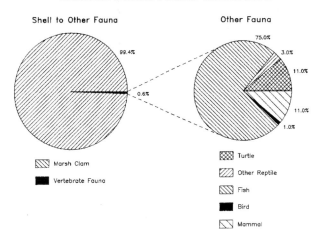

Figure 8. Percentage comparison of Chantuto site faunal constituents based on meat weight.

The two most likely candidates that we can think of are maize and cattails. Maize was being used by contemporary highland people (Mangelsdorf et al. 1967:180-183) of the Abejas phase in the Tehuacán Valley and MacNeish's reconstruction for that time period suggests that the establishment of a settlement pattern involving base camps was tied to an increasing reliance on maize horticulture. We feel that the lack of stratigraphic disturbance, however, argues against a residential population and therefore against this possibility. It is possible, however, that maize was grown on other estuarine islands or on the nearby mainland, although no known evidence exists.

Another plant with great economic potential for the Chantuto people is the cattail (*Typha* sp.). Cattails are the major floristic component of the herbaceous swamp, at least those patches that occur in the vicinity of the sites (Voorhies 1976:20-21). Logically, this plant may have been used by the Chantuto people. This is because cattails have general characteristics similar to other plants that have been targeted by humans for food. First, most parts of the cattail are edible (Niethammer 1974:88). For example, in the Southwestern U.S. native Americans used the greens as a vegetable, the pollen as an additive to soups and an ingredient for bread, and the roots as either a vegetable or processed flour. Second, cattails are found in single species stands and are easily procured. Third, recent experiments (Simms 1987) show that productivity of cattail collecting is very high. This is especially true for cattail pollen as compared to the roots. Simms (1987) found that the energetic return rate for cattail pollen was higher than any other plant studied. Fourth, cattails were eaten by native people in many different areas such as California (Jan Timbrook, personal communication, 1989), the American Southwest (Niethammer 1974), the American Plains (Fowler 1982; Simms 1987), and Australia (Lewis 1982).[8] For all these reasons the cattail could have been important for the Chantuto people and this possibility requires further examination.

It has not been a simple matter to obtain paleobotanical data from the Chantuto sites that would permit the investigation of these issues. Samples for pollen studies have been analyzed first by Matsuo Tsukada (Voorhies 1976:63-67) and more recently by John G. Jones, both of whom could find no identifiable fossil pollen. Phytoliths have been observed both by Jones and by Deborah Pearsall in samples from the shellmounds but a preliminary study by Pearsall failed to reveal data pertinent to the economic utilization of plants. Despite these discouraging results, we plan to pursue the possibility of phytolith studies before giving up entirely on this approach.

In summary, we have yet to obtain information on the paleobotany of the Chantuto people that would allow evaluation of the ideas presented above.

Seasonality and Scheduling

We have argued above that the stratigraphy indicates that the Chantuto shellmounds were occupied episodically and that each episode was relatively short in duration, or rather the features we expect to find in a general purpose residential site are absent. Accordingly, we interpret the mounds as special purpose locations. The issue then arises as to the scheduling of these periods of occupation. If this could be determined we would be better able to reconstruct the entire settlement system of the Chantuto people.

Archaeologists frequently rely on one of two methods to determine whether a site was occupied seasonally. In situations where a single activity site is related to one seasonally available resource, demonstrating the association between the site and the resource is usually adequate to establish the season of site occupation. In situations where the site occupants used either (1) a broad spectrum of resources, (2) a single resource whose seasonality is unknown, or (3) a single resource (like shellfish) that is available throughout the year, it is necessary to determine the seasonality of site occupation from constituents of the site itself. Frequently this is done by considering the season of capture of various animal species represented by archaeological ecofacts.

In sites where ecofacts document the ancient use of many different species, it may be possible to determine season of capture independently for several of them (e.g., Barber 1982), thus enhancing the reliability of conclusions regarding seasonality of occupation. However, such an approach is not possible for the Chantuto shellmounds, the contents of which are so heavily biased by a single species of clam. Although remains of other animals occur, the frequency of any particular species is so low that it would be very difficult to obtain large enough samples to be useful for determining season of death.

It is apparent that we must determine the season of capture of the marsh clams in order to establish the season of occupation of the sites. Like most shellfish (Waselkov 1987:111), marsh clams are available throughout the year in the Acapetahua estuary, so there is no easy association between time of capture and a particular season. We are in the process of subjecting these clams to growth ring studies in the hope that patterns of seasonal growth, or their absence, may be determined (cf. Claassen 1986; Quitmyer et al. 1985). A feasibility study, using marsh clams from the Acapetahua estuary, was performed by Cheryl Claassen. Claassen sectioned and examined some modern and archaeological specimens and found that growth rings could be observed on both groups of shell, although they were not present on all of the specimens that she examined. Her findings have encouraged us to begin an analysis of growth rings on modern clams so that seasonal patterns, if any, may be determined. This study is currently in progress.

In the meantime we have been evaluating the estuarine ecosystem in order to determine the nature of any resource pulsations. This approach was used by Voorhies (1976:23-28; Kennett 1989) and we will simply briefly review and update her earlier discussion.

As we mentioned above, the Acapetahua estuary is a highly dynamic aquatic system. From the perspective of the ecology of estuarine organisms, perhaps the most challenging change involves the regular alterations in salinity. Although these occur on a daily basis due to tidal action, salinity also changes seasonally due to increased riverine freshwater discharge during the rainy season compared to the dry season (Voorhies 1976:23). The climate of the Soconusco region, where the Acapetahua estuary is located, is strongly seasonal with a distinct wet and dry season;[9] rain is concentrated from mid-March to mid-October. In fact, the sharp seasonality of rainfall is the most dramatic aspect of the seasonal cycle, although temperature peaks toward the end of the dry season. Figure 9 is a diagram of the yearly cycle with the wet and dry

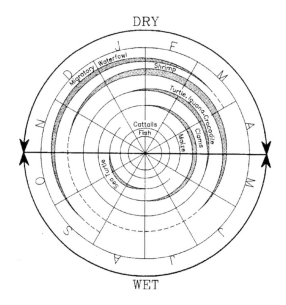

Figure 9. Graph of Resource Periodicities in the Littoral Zone of the Soconusco.

seasons, as well as the months, shown on the chart. Also included are some key resources with their relative availability indicated by the width of the line.

Most of the plants and animals in the estuary are available year round but four species that we emphasized show sharp seasonality in their local availability. These are sea turtle, migratory waterfowl, shrimp, and maize.

Migratory waterfowl and the sea turtle have peaks in the late wet/early dry season. The relative absence of remains of these animals in the Chantuto shellmounds might be due to a number of factors.[10] However, one possible explanation is that people were not using the midden sites when these animals were most abundant in the habitat.

Shrimp occupy the coastal lagoons in vast numbers as part of their seasonal cycle. They enter the lagoons as larvae and remain there throughout the juvenile stage of development, returning to the sea in order to reproduce (e.g., Bliss 1982; Edwards, 1977, 1978; Neal and Maris 1985). The dry season peak in shrimp availability is a major annual event in the estuary that triggers population increases in a number of species higher up the food chain.

Maize is sometimes grown today on some of the islands within the wetlands but this does not appear to be a highly viable enterprise. The nearest location in which maize thrives is farther inland on the coastal plain approximately midway between the edge of the wetlands and the foothills. The best milpas are located close to the foothills where three crops a year are possible using only rainfall irrigation. Only one crop may be grown in the lower gradient of the coastal plain where rainfall is less.

We have no botanical evidence that bears upon the question of maize use by the Chantuto people. Maize became a crucially important crop for later Mesoamericans and was undergoing morphological changes during the Late Archaic period. Results of a stable carbon isotope analysis of two human burials from Tlacuachero suggests that they both consumed C_4 plants–probably including maize–or, possibly, CAM plants, since their isotope ratios were as high as among later sedentary inhabitants of the region through to the Late Postclassic period (Blake et al. 1992). Our point here is to illustrate a potential scheduling conflict between maize and shrimp since both are available at the same season. At the end of the Archaic period, the wetland sites fell into disuse perhaps because people reorganized their subsistence to focus more upon certain plants, including maize, that can best be grown away from the estuary system.

Some circumstantial evidence exists to support the idea that the Chantuto people exploited the estuary during the dry season, the time of greatest resource availability. This evidence comes from the suite of other fauna whose remains were incorporated into the deposits. All species of turtles, crocodile and iguana that were procured by the Chantuto people are collected today during the dry season when the females are gravid. These species are generally ignored at other times of the year. These facts suggest to us the pos-

sibility that the Chantuto people were occupying the sites in the dry season. We wish to make clear, however, that the evidence for a dry season occupation is not strong, since it is based largely on the presence of the remains of reptiles, which are present throughout the year, although today they are procured with zeal only during the dry season.[11]

Another approach to understanding the ancient subsistence pattern of the Chantuto people would be to determine the season when terrestrial resources were waning. It is possible that the scheduling of estuarine resource use was determined primarily by this factor. We would be most interested to know about possible seasonal fluctuations in the availability of terrestrial protein sources, primarily animals. Unfortunately, we lack adequate knowledge of the terrestrial ecosystem on the coastal plain to enable a detailed discussion of resource availability. Almost all of the native forest has been removed and game animals are nonexistent. Although we believe that a concerted effort to learn more about the natural ecosystem of the coastal plain would produce significant insights, at the time of writing we have not attempted such a resource characterization. We speculate that the late dry season was the leanest time of the year for food resources for both hunter-gatherers and horticulturalists (at least until the maize harvest), since this is when biomass in the system is most reduced.

In summary, consideration of some plants and animals in the Acapetahua estuary shows that most species are constantly present but a few are seasonal visitors to the zone. The major pulse in resources takes place in the late dry season when shrimp juveniles occupy the coastal lagoons. This was the best time for humans to use estuarine resources and we have some weak evidence that the Chantuto sites were occupied at this time. At present, however, we cannot say with confidence that people were not using the sites at different times of the year, which must be done in order to support an argument for seasonal scheduling.

Artifacts

The artifact assemblage from the Chantuto phase deposits has a strikingly low diversity. We found only hammerstones, milling stones, and obsidian flakes, as well as the debitage resulting from the on-site production of the obsidian tools.

Hammerstones are hand-sized, waterworn rocks that are battered on either or both ends. The cobbles are unmodified except for the scars that have resulted from pounding. Thus, they are casual tools rather than manufactured ones. The rocks are usually one of the igneous or metamorphic rock types that outcrop in the coastal mountain range and foothills. Cobbles were selected by the Chantuto people at upriver locations where they abound.

Milling stones were also made of naturally occurring cobbles gathered from river beds. They consist of hand-sized manos that resemble the hammerstones except that they are polished and have striations across one or both of their broad faces, and usually are not end-battered. The metates are flat, oblong, water-worn rocks that have a concave ventral surface into which the manos fit comfortably. Both the manos and metates are of locally available stone.

The obsidian assemblage from the Chantuto component consists of small flake tools, as well as the nodules and debitage that resulted from their on-site production. This process, described by Clark (1989:220-221) and referred to as expedient flake technology, involved the direct percussion of imported obsidian nodules using a hard hammerstone. Sometimes a stone anvil was used in manufacturing flakes. Expedient flake technology requires relatively little skill and produces a great deal of waste, the most frequently found obsidian item in the Chantuto phase deposits. The obsidian that was used by the Chantuto people came from two Guatemalan sources, Tajumulco (72%) and El Chayal (28%) (Nelson and Voorhies 1980). The Tajumulco source is the closest known obsidian source to the Acapetahua estuary. We do not know whether obsidian was directly procured or was obtained through trade.

In summary, the diversity of tool types is very low and is limited to hammerstones, manos, metates, and obsidian flakes. This finding is consistent with our interpretation of the Chantuto sites as being special activity sites; general purpose sites are expected to produce a wider range of tools than we have observed.

The technology of tool production was very simple. This finding is in accord with Satterthwait's (1980:175) expectation that the technology of tool production should be simple at coastal sites used to exploit shellfish and other readily harvested resources. In fact, only one of the four types of tools that we found was actually produced on-site; the others were brought in. The obsidian production process was extremely simple and suggests that obsidian flakes were produced by the tool users when they were needed. That is, no specialization in production was present.

Another general observation is that the catchment area from which raw materials for artifacts was obtained is relatively limited. Hammerstones, and manos probably came from upstream locations along the same rivers that drain into the Acapetahua estuary. Obsidian and stones for metates were procured from farther away but we do not know how. Tajumulco obsidian may have been procured directly, but the El Chayal obsidian seems more likely to have been a trade item simply because of the considerable distance (250 km) from the source to the Chantuto sites. The overall picture that emerges is one of relative simplicity in economic organization as it related to manufactured goods.

Our final observation is that the artifact assemblage suggests to us that the shellmound sites may have been special activity loci for women and children rather than men. Ethnographically, in Mesoamerica, milling stones are generally part of women's tool kits and shellfish gathering seems to be female's work (e.g., Meehan 1982), but whether this pattern can be extended back to the Late Archaic period is unknown. We recognize, however, that shrimping is more likely to be a male activity, as it is today in the Acapetahua estuary and among the Anbarra (Rhys Jones, personal communication, 1989). We also note that no probable men's tools such as projectile points or fish hooks have been found at these sites.[12] Although we do not wish to overemphasize this interpretation before our studies have been completed, at present we see evidence to support the idea that the Chantuto sites were special activity "locations" frequented primarily by women and children.

Conclusions

The restudy of the Chantuto shellmounds is still in progress and the interpretations offered here vary in the degree to which they are demonstrably valid. Our basic view, which we consider strongly supported, is that the shell-bearing deposits are best interpreted as special activity locations. The large volume of shell in the deposits suggests that the sites were formed by logistically organized groups who were seeking goods for groups far larger than themselves. Our inference is that the Chantuto people were collectors rather than foragers. We predict that there are other settlement types in the settlement system of these people but the wetland island sites are the only sites in the system that have been found to date.[13] This interpretation is based on a consideration of the stratigraphy of the deposits, the overwhelming concentration on marsh clams, the limited range of unspecialized stone tools, along with our understanding of hunter-gatherer ways of life. Furthermore, we think that the sites were occupied periodically and probably seasonally, although the latter has not yet been established.

The faunal remains in the sites indicate a heavy emphasis on the collection of marsh clams, most likely as a food resource. It is possible that the clam shells might have also been used to facilitate the processing of shrimp, but the analyses to test this idea have not been completed. Last, we have offered the suggestion that the procurement of shellfish might have been carried out primarily by women and children, as widely documented ethnographically.

This model of the Late Archaic period coastal adaptation in the Acapetahua estuary has been generated from an admittedly small database. We have noted that no Late Archaic period sites have been found in the region that represent other components of the hypothetical settlement system (but see Note 13). Given the limited amount of archaeological research and the problems with detecting early sites from surface deposits in this region, this lack is not surprising to us. Future research may discover both base camps and other kinds of special activity sites at locations inland from the Chantuto sites.

The information currently available concerning the lifeways of contemporary peoples living along the Mesoamerican coasts is consistent with the proposed model.

However, there is insufficient evidence to permit a rigorous test. As we discussed above, there have been a small number of archaeological studies of coastal sites. Furthermore, the only ones relevant to our present objective are located on the Atlantic seaboard: Mountjoy's (1989) coastal Nayarit sites are younger than the time period considered here, Brush's (1965, 1969) coastal Guerrero data are severely limited since they derive from only 1.5 cubic meters of excavated material from the bottom of a single test pit, and Clark's et al. (1987, 1990) Cerro de las Conchas site seems to be best considered as another manifestation of the same local situation that we have been discussing (i.e., the site was deposited by the Chantuto people).

MacNeish's (1986; MacNeish and Nelken-Terner 1983) study along the coast of northern Belize has identified a series of sites that he dates to the Late Archaic period even though absolute dating has not been achieved. Although the reports that we have consulted are not detailed, and therefore we are unable to detect overall settlement patterns, MacNeish (1986:121) refers to a site that he speculates was either "a base camp or village." Inhabitants of the site relied on marine resources for food and firm evidence for agriculture was absent (but analysis was not complete at the time of writing). The artifact assemblage included projectile points, suggesting the practice of hunting, and milling stones, which suggest the use of plants. Given the reported data, this site could well be an example of a residential base for a group of collectors, although other interpretations are possible as well.

Another possible residential base is the Santa Luisa site along the banks of the Río Tecolutla in Veracruz (Wilkerson 1975). Wilkerson (1975) has interpreted the Palo Hueco phase (3100/3000 B.C. to 2700/2000 B.C.) occupation as evidence for a village but we think that it is equally possible that this was a residential base camp for a group of collectors. Wilkerson's preliminary report does not quantify food remains but our understanding is that there is both a greater diversity of species and evenness of these food items than in the case of the Chantuto shellmounds. Recovered food remains include shellfish (especially oyster but also estuarine and mudflat species), large land crabs, small mammals, howler monkey, and fish. Stone tools are also much more diverse than at the coeval Chantuto sites. They include crude blades, laterally worked unifaces, flake gravers, possible end scrapers, bifaces, block-core choppers, flake choppers, hammerstones and a possible net sinker. No projectile points were discovered. Likewise there were no indications of structures or cultivation, but since the site was deeply buried, and only a small area was excavated, these negative findings should not be given undue weight.

A contemporary Palo Hueco phase site in the nearby Tuxpan hills is interpreted by Wilkerson as an open air hunting camp. This site also is deeply buried with no surface indication. It consists of a possible hearth and artifacts that resemble those of the Palo Hueco phase material from Santa Luisa. Some limestone and sandstone tools were manufactured at the site but obsidian apparently was not worked there. Thus, Wilkerson's description suggests to us that this site could be considered as a field camp, one of the site types in Binford's model of collector settlement patterns.

In conclusion, we propose a model of Late Archaic period settlement and subsistence in the coastal lowlands of Mesoamerica, intended for heuristic purposes only. Our model proposes that the Late Archaic period coastal peoples of Mesoamerica manifested a subsistence/settlement pattern that, in its basic form, was much like that of their highland neighbors. That is, they were primarily hunter-gatherers, possibly with some horticulture, who were organizationally collectors rather than foragers. That is, their annual settlement pattern may have consisted of one or more base camp locations with a greater number of specialized activity stations, clustered as satellite settlements associated with each base camp.

Acknowledgments

Voorhies's earlier fieldwork was supported by a grant from the National Science Foundation, whereas our more recent fieldwork was funded by the National Geographic Society (No. 3689-87). We thank John G. Jones and Deborah Pearsall for their examination of samples in order to determine the feasibility of pollen and phytolith studies, and Cheryl Claassen for her trial study of marsh clam growth rings. Claassen also took the time and effort to give us a "crash course" on growth ring identification, for which we are very appreciative. Helpful suggestions for improving an earlier draft were made by Michael Blake, Andrea Gerstle, George Riser, and Greg Waselkov.

Notes

1. A second reason was to investigate, by means of a lateral exposure, a large deeply buried feature that Voorhies had discovered in 1973 but was unable to expose because of limitations in time and money. She suspected that the feature was a prepared clay floor, which we have verified during the recent field research (Voorhies and Michaels 1989; Voorhies et al. 1991).

2. Using recently proposed calibrations (Pearson and Stuiver 1986; Pearson et al. 1986) the date falls in the range 224 B.C. to A.D. 3 with 68% confidence (1 sigma on the calibration curve).

3. The previously obtained dates with revised calibrations are presented in Voorhies (1976), Voorhies and Michaels (1989), and Blake et al. (1995). See Voorhies (1989) for a discussion of the settlements and their dating in the Acapetahua region.

4. Beta 25626 and Beta 25627 have calibrated ranges (1 sigma on the calibration curve) of 2484-2298 B.C. and 2863-2495 B.C., respectively.

5. Another more probable interpretation is that these beds are due to the cooking of large batches of clams. This alternative view has been described in Voorhies (1996).

6. Although present day shrimpers in the Acapetahua estuary do not employ bait, it is known to be a viable procurement strategy (Alan P. Covich; Armand Kuris, personal communication, 1989). Our own observations suggest that some species in the Acapetahua estuary may respond to clam bait whereas the most preferred species do not.

7. This argument is developed more fully in Voorhies et al. (1991).

8. We have not found any references for cattails as a food resource among any Mesoamerican peoples whose ethnobotanies we have consulted. However, none of the groups (Huastec Maya [Alcorn 1984]; Yucatec Maya [Roys 1931; Lundell 1938]; or Seri [Felger and Moser 1985]) has significant cattail stands in its environment.

9. The climate is classified as Aw in the Köeppen system of climate classification (Vivo Escoto 1964; Helbig 1976).

10. Bones of a single sea turtle were recovered (Voorhies 1976:56) from one test pit at CAP-6.

11. Kennett and Voorhies (1996) have recently found at Tlacuachero that early in the Late Archaic period, clams were collected at various times of the year with an apparent preference for dry season site use. During the later part of the Late Archaic, site use had shifted strikingly to the wet season.

12. John E. Clark has cautioned us that projectile points seem to be entirely absent in all known sites of the Chiapas coast that predate the Late Preclassic period. Thus, it is possible that stone projectile points were not used by men of the Chantuto society. Instead, they might have been strictly net and club hunters or used blowguns or traps, none of which would survive.

13. While this chapter has been in press, two inland sites with possible Late Archaic period components have been identified.

References Cited

Alcorn, J. B.
1984 *Huastec Mayan Ethnobotany*. University of Texas Press, Austin.

Barber, R. J.
1982 *The Wheeler's Site: A Specialized Shellfish Processing Station of the Merrimack River*. Peabody Museum Monographs, No. 7. Harvard University, Cambridge.

Binford, L. R.
1980 Willow Smoke and Dogs' Tails: Hunter-gatherer Settlement Systems and Archaeological Site Formation. *American Antiquity* 45(1):5-20.

Blake, M., B. S. Chisholm, J. E. Clark, B. Voorhies, and M. Love
1992 Prehistoric Subsistence in the Soconusco Region. *Current Anthropology* 33(1):83-94.

Blake, M., J. E. Clark, B. Voorhies, M. Love, M. Pye, A. A. Demarest, and B. Arroyo
1995 A Revised Chronology for the Late Archaic and Formative Periods along the Pacific Coast of Southeastern Mesoamerica. *Ancient Mesoamerica* 6:161-183.

Bliss, D. E.
1982 *Shrimps, Lobsters and Crabs*. New Century Publishers, Inc., Piscataway, N.J.

Brush, C. F.
1965 Pox Pottery: Earliest Identified Mexican Ceramic. *Science* 149:194-195.
1969 *A Contribution to the Archaeology of Coastal Guerrero, Mexico*. Unpublished Ph.D. dissertation, Department of Anthropology, Columbia University, New York.

Claassen, C.
1986 Shellfish Seasons in the Prehistoric Southeastern United States. *American Antiquity* 51:21-37.

Clark, J. E.
1989 Obsidian Tool Manufacture. In *Ancient Trade and Tribute: Economies of the Soconusco Region, Mesoamerica*, edited by B. Voorhies, pp. 217-230. University of Utah Press, Salt Lake City.

Clark, J. E., M. Blake, P. Guzzy, P. Cuevas, and T. Salcedo
1987 *Proyecto: El Preclásico Temprano en la Costa del Pacífico*. Final Report to the Instituto Nacional de Antropología e Historia, México. Ms. on file, Department of Anthropology, Brigham Young University, Provo.

Clark, J. E., M. Blake, B. Arroyo, M. E. Pye, R. G. Lesure, V. Feddema, and M. Ryan
1990 *Reporte Final Del Proyecto Investigaciones del Formativo Temprano en el Litoral Chiapaneco*. Final Report to the Instituto Nacional de Antropología e Historia, México. Ms. on file, Department of Anthropology, Brigham Young University, Provo.

Drucker, P.
1948 Preliminary Notes on an Archaeological Survey of the Chiapas Coast. *Middle American Research Records* 1:151-169.

Edwards, R. R. C.
1977 Field Experiments on Growth and Mortality of *Penaeus vannamei* in a Mexican Coastal Lagoon Complex. *Estuarine Coastal Marine Science* 5:107-121.
1978 The Fishery and the Fisheries Biology of Penaeid Shrimp on the Pacific Coast of Mexico. *Oceanographic Marine Biology Annual Review* 16:145-180.

Erasmus, C. E.
1955   Work Patterns in a Mayo Village. *American Anthropologist* 57:322-333.

Felger, R. S. and, M. B. Moser
1985   *People of the Desert and Sea: Ethnobotany of the Seri Indians.* The University of Arizona Press, Tucson.

Flannery, K. V.
1983   Settlement, Subsistence and Social Organization of the Protomangueans. In *The Cloud People*, edited by K. V. Flannery and J. Marcus, pp. 32-36. Academic Press, New York.
1986   Guilá Naquitz in Spatial, Temporal and Cultural Context. In *Guilá Naquitz: Archaic Foraging and Early Agriculture in Oaxaca, Mexico*, edited by K. V. Flannery, pp. 31-42. Academic Press, Orlando.

Fowler, C. S.
1982   Food-named Groups Among the Northern Paiute in North America's Great Basin: An Ecological Interpretation. In *Resource Managers: North American and Australian Hunter-Gatherers*, edited by N. M. Williams and E. S. Hunn, pp. 113-129. Australian Institute of Aboriginal Studies, Canberra.

Gagliano, S. M.
1984   Geoarchaeology of the Northern Gulf Shore. In *Perspectives on Gulf Coast Prehistory*, edited by D. D. Davis, pp. 1-40. University of Florida Press-Florida State Museum, Gainesville.

Helbig, C. M. A.
1976   *Chiapas: Geografía de un Estado Méxicano*, Vol. 1. Gobierno del Estado de Chiapas, Tuxtla Gutíerrez, México.

Hudson, J. L., P. L. Walker, and B. Voorhies
1989   Changing Patterns of Faunal Exploitation. In *Ancient Trade and Tribute: Economies of the Soconusco Region of Mesoamerica*, edited by B. Voorhies, pp. 135-155. University of Utah Press, Salt Lake City.

Kennett, D. J.
1989   Analysis of Midden Sites Found on the Coast of Chiapas, Mexico. Ms. on file, Department of Anthropology, University of California, Santa Barbara.

Kennett, D. J., and B. Voorhies
1996   Oxygen Isotopic Analysis of Archaeological Shells to Detect Seasonal use of Wetlands on the Southern Pacific Coast of Mexico. *Journal of Archaeological Science* 23:689-704.

Lankford, R. R.
1976   Coastal Lagoons of Mexico: their Origin and Classification. In *Estuarine Processes, Vol. 2: Circulation, Sediments, and Transfer of Material in the Estuary*, edited by M. Wiley, pp. 182-215. Academic Press, New York.

Lewis, H. T.
1982   Fire Technology and Resource Management in Aboriginal North America and Australia. In *Resource Managers: North America and Australian Hunter-Gatherers*, edited by N. M. Williams and E. S. Hunn, pp. 45-67. Australian Institute of Aboriginal Studies, Canberra.

Lorenzo, J. L.
1955   Los Concheros de la Costa de Chiapas. *Anales del Instituto Nacional de Antropología y Historia* 7:41-50.

Lowe, G. W.
1978   Eastern Mesoamerica. In *Chronologies in New World Archaeology*, edited by R. E. Taylor and C. W. Meighan, pp. 331-393. Academic Press, N.Y.

Lowe, G. W., T. A. Lee Jr., and E. Martínez Espinosa
1982   *Izapa: An Introduction to the Ruins and Monuments.* Papers of the New World Archaeological Foundation No. 31. Brigham Young University, Provo.

Lundell, C. L.
1938   Plants Probably Utilized by the Old Empire Maya of Petén and Adjacent Lowlands. *Papers of the Mich. Acad. of Science Pt. 1*, pp. 37-56.

MacNeish, R. S.
1986   The Preceramic of Middle America. In *Advances in World Archaeology*, vol. 5, edited by F. Wendorf and A. E. Close, pp. 93-129. Academic Press, Orlando.

MacNeish, R. S. and, A. Nelken-Turner
1983   The Preceramic in Mesoamerica. *Journal of Field Archaeology* 10:71-84.

MacNeish, R. S., F. A. Peterson, and J. A. Neely
1972   The Archaeological Reconnaissance. In *The Prehistory of the Tehuacán Valley, Vol. 5, Excavations and Reconnaissance*, edited by R. S. MacNeish, M. L. Fowler, A. García Cook, F. A. Peterson, A. Nelken-Terner, and J. A. Neely, pp. 341-395. University of Texas Press, Austin.

Mangelsdorf, P. C., R. S. MacNeish, and W. C. Galinat
1967   Prehistoric Wild and Cultivated Maize. In *The Prehistory of the Tehuacán Valley, Vol. 1, Environment and Subsistence*, edited by D. S. Byers, pp. 178-200. University of Texas Press, Austin.

Meehan, B.
1982   *Shell Bed to Shell Midden.* Australian Institute of Aboriginal Studies, Canberra.

Mountjoy, J. B.
1971   *Prehispanic Culture History and Cultural Contact on the Southern Coast of Nayarit, Mexico.* Ph. D. dissertation, Southern Illinois University, Carbondale. University Microfilms, Ann Arbor.
1974   San Blas Complex Ecology. In *The Archaeology of West Mexico*, edited by B. Bell, pp. 106-119. Sociedad de Estudios Avanzados del Occidente de México, Ajijic, Jalisco.

1989 The Sampling of a Middle Formative Shell Midden at San Blas, Nayarit, Mexico. Paper presented at the 54th Annual Meeting of the Society for American Archaeology, Atlanta.

Navarrete, C.
1969 Resumen de las Exploraciones del Reconocimiento Arquelógico de la Costa de Chiapas (Región del Soconusco), en la Temporada de 1969. Ms. on file, New World Archaeological Foundation, San Cristóbal de las Casas, Mexico.

Neal, R. A., and R. C. Maris
1985 Fisheries Biology of Shrimps and Shrimplike Animals. In *The Biology of Crustacea. Economic Aspects: Fisheries and Culture, Vol. 10*, edited by A. J. Provenzano, pp. 101-110. Academic Press, Orlando.

Nelson, F. W., and B. Voorhies
1980 Trace Element Analysis of Obsidian Artifacts from Three Shell Midden Sites in the Littoral Zone, Chiapas, Mexico. *American Antiquity* 45:540-550.

Niethammer, C.
1974 *American Indian Food and Lore*. Collier, N.Y.

Pearson, G. W., and M. Stuiver
1986 High-precision Calibration of the Radiocarbon Time Scale 500-2500 B.C. *Radiocarbon* 28:839-862.

Pearson, G. W., J. R. Pilcher, M. G. Baille, D. M. Corbett, and F. Qua
1986 High Precision ^{14}C Measurement of Irish Oaks to Show the Natural ^{14}C Variations from A.D. 1840-5210 B.C. *Radiocarbon* 28:911-934.

Quitmyer, I., S. Hale, and D. Jones
1985 Paleoseasonality Determination Based on Incremental Shell Growth in the Hard Clam *Mercenaria mercenaria*, and its Implications for the Analysis of Three Southeast Georgia Coastal Shell Middens. *Southeastern Archaeology* 4:27-40.

Reitz, E. J.
1988 Evidence for Coastal Adaptations in Georgia and South Carolina. *Archaeology of Eastern North America* 16:137-158.

Reitz, E. J., and I. Quitmyer
1988 Faunal Remains from Two Coastal Georgia Swift Creek Sites. *Southeastern Archaeology* 7:95-108.

Roys, R. L.
1931 *The Ethno-Botany of the Maya*. Middle American Research Series, No. 2. Department of Middle American Research, Tulane University of Louisiana, New Orleans.

Satterthwait, L. D.
1980 *A Comparative Study of Australian Aborigine Food-Procurement Technologies*. Ph.D. dissertation. University Microfilms, Ann Arbor.

Scott, S. D.
1985 Core Versus Marginal Mesoamerica: a Coastal West Mexican Perspective. In *The Archaeology of West and Northwest Mesoamerica*, edited by M. Foster and P. Weigand, pp. 181-191. Westview Press, Boulder.

Simms, S. R.
1987 *Behavioral Ecology and Hunter-gatherer Foraging: An Example from the Great Basin*. BAR International Series 381. British Archaeological Reports, Oxford.

Vivo Escoto, J. A.
1964 Weather and Climate of Mexico and Central America. In *Natural Environment and Early Cultures*, edited by Robert West, pp. 187-215. Handbook of Middle American Indians Vol. 1, R. Wauchope, general editor. University of Texas Press, Austin.

Voorhies, B.
1976 *The Chantuto People: An Archaic Period Society of the Chiapas Littoral, Mexico*. Papers of the New World Archaeological Foundation No 41. Brigham Young University, Provo.

1978 Previous Research on Nearshore Coastal Adaptations in Middle America. In *Prehistoric Coastal Adaptations: The Economy and Ecology of Maritime Middle America*, edited by B. L. Stark and B. Voorhies, pp. 5-21. New York, Academic Press.

1989 Settlement Patterns in the Western Soconusco: Methods of Site Recovery and Dating Results. In *New Frontiers in the Archaeology of the Pacific Coast of Southern Mesoamerica*, edited by F. Bové and L. Heller, pp. 103-124. Anthropological Research Papers No. 39. Arizona State University, Tempe.

1996 The Transformation from Foraging to Farming in the Lowlands of Mesoamerica. In *The Managed Mosaic: Ancient Maya Agriculture and Resource Use*, edited by S. L. Fedick, pp. 17-29. University of Utah Press, Salt Lake City.

Voorhies, B., and G. H. Michaels
1989 *Final Report to National Geographic Society: Grant No. 3689-87*. Ms. on file, National Geographic Society, Washington, D.C.

Voorhies, B., G. H. Michaels, and G. M. Riser
1991 Ancient Shrimp Fishery. *National Geographic Research & Exploration* 7(1):20-35.

Waselkov, G. A.
1987 Shellfish Gathering and Shell Midden Archaeology. In *Advances in Archaeological Method and Theory*, vol. 10, edited by M. B. Schiffer, pp. 93-210. Academic Press, Orlando.

Wilkerson, S. J. K.
1973 An Archaeological Sequence from Santa Luisa, Veracruz, Mexico. *Contributions of the University of California Research Facility* 18:37-50.

1975 Pre-agricultural Village Life: The Late Preceramic Period in Veracruz. *Contrib. of the Univ. of Calif. Research Facility* 27:111-122.

5

The Emergence of Hereditary Inequality: the Case of Pacific Coastal Chiapas, Mexico

Michael Blake and John E. Clark

Introduction

How did societies, at different time periods and in different parts of the world, develop hereditary inequality? This is becoming one of the most widely asked research questions in archaeology today and one for which tentative answers are beginning to come forward (e.g., Arnold 1996, Price and Feinman 1995). The answer to this question is important because, for many archaeological cases, understanding the transition to hereditary social and political inequality means understanding one of the first significant cultural changes in a region's prehistory. Often too, it presages the development of increasingly complex societies leading to the emergence of regional polities such as chiefdoms or states, a process amply demonstrated in many recent studies (e.g., Earle 1991).

Most recent studies of chiefdom evolution, however, have focussed more on the changes in chiefdoms once they have come about rather than the processes that led to their initial emergence (e.g., Earle 1987, 1989, 1991; Drennan and Uribe 1987). Even so, a number of archaeologists have begun to focus on the processes of chiefly emergence and examine a range of causes and processes implicated in the transformation of egalitarian society. Archaeological case studies are now accumulating and provide diachronic documentation of the transition from egalitarian to non-egalitarian societies, both for hunting-fishing-gathering and early agricultural societies (see Price and Brown 1985; Arnold 1991, 1992; Gilman 1991; Upham 1990). Although some general statements or models describing how chiefdoms arose in the first place are available, they rarely apply to more than a few of the well-documented cases. It is becoming clear that there may be several distinctively different trajectories for the emergence of hereditary political inequality (Hayden 1995). These differences in the transformational processes need to be outlined in greater detail before theories of the emergence of inequality are likely to have much universality.

This paper explores several processes that may have been responsible for the transformation of egalitarian society in a specific environment and period: the Early Formative peoples (ca. 1600-900 B.C. uncal.) in the Mazatán region of the Pacific coastal lowlands of Chiapas, Mexico (Figure 1).[1] We do not claim that the processes we describe are universally applicable, instead, we simply evaluate the extent to which they can be monitored in one particular case. However, we expect to be able test the relevance of these processes in other well-documented archaeological examples of emerging inequality, as they become available.

Background

The Mazatán region is located in the highly-productive section of the southern Chiapas coast known as the Soconusco—an area famed for its productivity in both modern and pre-Columbian times (Voorhies 1989). The region is a patchwork of closely-packed environmental zones, with a narrow coastal plain sandwiched between the beach/estuary complex and the piedmont and Sierra Madre Mountains some 20 to 30 km inland (Figure 1). To the northwest, the plain borders an extensive swampy area that was especially important for obtaining subsistence resources from the Archaic through Early Formative periods. To the southeast it extends just past Río Suchiate, which now marks the boundary between Mexico and Guatemala.

Voorhies (1976) describes Late Archaic (Chantuto phase) shell middens that probably represent seasonal accumulations from occupations by residentially mobile hunter/-fisher/gatherers in the estuary zone. To date, few inland Chantuto sites have been located, so our knowledge of the total settlement and subsistence system remains hypothetical (Michaels and Voorhies, Chapter 4). We do know, however, that the Chantuto people engaged in long-distance exchange for highland Guatemalan obsidian (Nelson and Voorhies 1980).

We call the Early Formative peoples of this region the

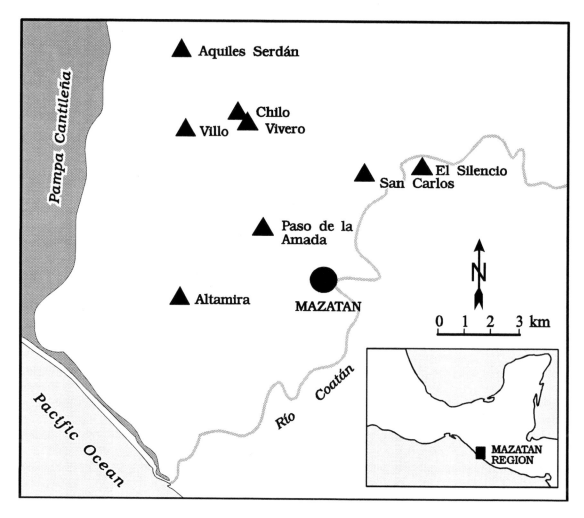

Figure 1. Map of the Mazatán Study Area.

Mokaya people: a term that comes from the Mixe language, meaning first people of the corn, and we use it to designate the people represented by four archaeological phases from 1550-1000 B.C. The earliest evidence of the Mokaya villagers dates to ca. 1550 B.C., or about 200 years after the last reliable data on the Archaic period. The first Mokaya tradition phase was the Barra phase (1550-1400 B.C.), a period that witnessed the founding of sedentary villages, with mixed agricultural and fishing and hunting economies, and the introduction of ceramics. We think it significant that the estuary shell middens saw only minimal use during this phase (Voorhies 1976), possibly signaling a shift in subsistence practices linked to a decrease in residential mobility.

Ambiguous hints of rank distinctions, perhaps denoting hereditary inequality, first appeared towards the end of the Barra phase, and became more convincing during the following Locona phase (1400-1250 B.C.) Briefly, the best indicators of emerging distinctions of social and/or political ranking during the Locona phase are: (1) a two-tiered hierarchy settlement pattern comprised of small villages and hamlets centered around large villages, (2) elite domestic architecture, (3) differential mortuary practices, (4) unequal access to sumptuary goods, (5) presence of patronized craft specialization centered around elite house mounds, (6) clues of increased public feasting, and (7) evidence of redistribution within each large village community (Clark 1991, 1994; Clark and Blake 1989; Blake 1991).

These patterns continued during the subsequent Ocós phase (1250-1100 B.C.). By the end of the Ocós phase, there was a significant increase in the evidence for external connections. During the following Cherla phase (1100-1000 B.C.), ceramic and figurine styles began to be introduced which show strong similarities to those in the Gulf Coast region of Mexico, and many other regions where there was a shift to increasing use of early Olmec styles. By the end of the Cherla phase the Mokaya tradition had become Olmecized: five and one-half centuries of local styles were being replaced by new ones that reflected the social and political changes sweeping through Mesoamerica.

The Mokaya present an ideal case for examining the question of how hereditary socio-political inequality emerged because there is a rich and well-preserved archaeo-

56

logical record spanning the entire period of the transition. This transformation was complete by the beginning of Middle Formative period (ca. 850 B.C.), when the material remains of cultures in the Soconusco region expressed strong similarities with their contemporaries in other parts of Mesoamerica: in a general sense they can be seen as "Olmecoid" (Clark 1990; Love 1991; Lee 1989; Demarest 1989; Pye and Demarest 1991:91). The evidence for the socio-political complexity of these Middle Formative societies includes remains at such sites as Izapa, in Chiapas, where there is a continuous occupation from the Early Formative period (Lowe et al. 1982; Ekholm 1969), and La Blanca in Guatemala where the same is true (Love 1991, Chapter 7). By this period along the Pacific Coast there were already in existence large-scale chiefdoms with four-tiered settlement hierarchies, sites with political centers displaying massive mound constructions, smaller minor centers, and out-lying villages and even smaller hamlets, single residences, as well a number of even smaller specialized sites (Love 1991:58; Pye and Demarest 1991:91-94; and Pye et al., Chapter 6).

During the Archaic period, ending sometime around 1800-1600 B.C., there was no evidence of such social inequality. Archaic sites along the coast of Chiapas and Guatemala are exceedingly rare (Voorhies 1976; Voorhies and Kennett 1995; Clark et al. 1987). But at the sites which have been studied, there is only evidence for small-scale, probably nomadic, hunter-fisher-gatherers (see Voorhies and Michaels 1989; Michaels and Voorhies, Chapter 4; Clark et al. 1990). Therefore, the transition from egalitarian societies to those with hereditary inequality and complex forms of social and political organization must have taken place sometime between the end of the Late Archaic period and the beginning of the Middle Formative: i.e., during the Early Formative period (ca. 1550-850 B.C.).

We have presented preliminary evidence for this transition in other papers and have argued that, during the Locona phase, Early Formative villagers in the Soconusco Region of Chiapas and the adjacent coast of Guatemala began to rapidly develop structures of social and political organization that permitted hereditary inequality (Clark and Blake 1994). Our central research question is: what were the causes of this transformation?

The following discussion of the Mazatán Early Formative will be more intelligible if we first review our thesis for the origins of rank, a central component of which is hereditary social inequality. We are convinced that the emergence of rank was an unintentional and unanticipated consequence of would-be-bigmen vying for prestige in a social milieu of complex hunter-fisher-gatherers (*sensu* Price and Brown 1985)—the primary engine of social change being private or local-level politics. Hayden and Gargett (1990) aptly label these would-be-leaders as "accumulators." We prefer the parallel term "aggrandizers" for these highly motivated prestige seekers.[2] In our view, the emergence of rank, or institutionalized inequality, is a long-term, unexpected

consequence of many individuals pursuing their own short-term interests (Clark and Blake 1994).

It should be clear that "prestige" is a euphemism for "adoring public" or "loyal following" and that competition for prestige is really competition for followers; the more the better. One's ability to compete rests, in turn, on his deployable resources, both material and ideal. These could include such things as esoteric knowledge, social commitments, subsistence resources, craft goods, and foreign products obtained through long-distance exchange. The complementary principles of (1) *quid pro quo* and (2) unreciprocated exchange are involved here. Followers follow because they believe they will benefit by doing so or because they feel obligated to do so. The aggrandizer becomes a focal point of beneficence; he bestows favors for factional loyalty.[3] Unreciprocated favors create obligations of social indebtedness which become deployable social resources themselves (Blau 1964; Sahlins 1972; Mauss 1967). For the Mazatán area, we suggest that the emergence of rank and its attendant phenomena may be viewed within such a competitive social setting.

Transegalitarian Societies

In this paper we reverse the traditional approach to the question of how hereditary social inequality emerged: instead, we ask how did egalitarianism disappear? The reason for this approach rests on our understanding of the processes and mechanisms of change. The change with which we are concerned is essentially long-term. Socio-political inequalities may emerge during a single generation but *hereditary* inequality must, by definition, extend over more than two generations, in effect, lasting past an individual's personal memory. We may be able to monitor the mechanisms that produce this long-term change over the short-run, but the overall process must be observed over the course of a century or two. Therefore, by the time hereditary inequality has emerged, the mechanisms that produced it may have long since passed. New mechanisms, those of the maintenance of inequality rather than the destruction of equality, would have taken over and become the most important social and political mechanisms.

In order to understand this transition it is necessary to look at the antecedents of change rather than their outcomes. It is necessary, therefore, to examine some aspects of egalitarian society before proceeding to chiefdoms. We argue that current terminologies and classifications obscure the sometimes subtle changes that take place during the transition to hereditary inequality. Although it is generally not very useful to introduce new terms for old concepts, we take the liberty of suggesting the term "transegalitarian" to describe societies that were in the process of transition from egalitarian to non-egalitarian organization and structure. Societies in this transformative stage may have shared characteristics with both egalitarian societies and chiefdoms, but, in sum, they may have looked like neither. The utility of the term transegalitarian lies in its ambiguity. It implies that the material characteristics that we might look for in any given archaeological case of transegalitarianism could be highly variable during the course of the transition. In other words, depending upon the political, social, historical, and economic conditions of each society, the length of time (i.e., number of generations) to complete the transformation to hereditary inequality could have varied greatly. The transegalitarian process may have lasted many generations in some cases, creating an archaeological record with no clear-cut evidence of ranking. We hope to show that by closely examining some of the mechanisms by which egalitarian societies were transformed to ones with increasing degrees of hereditary inequality, it may be possible to monitor these transformations in the archaeological record.

One of the main assumptions underlying this study is that egalitarian societies are particularly adept at suppressing most forms of inequality, especially hereditary inequality. Inequality and the forces that lead to it exist in all egalitarian societies as they do in all social groups, as the mechanisms and methods that people have developed to keep them in check attest. In fact, the egalitarian ethic is really only an ideal that groups and individuals may try to maintain, sometimes successfully and over the long-run, and sometimes unsuccessfully. In some complex egalitarian societies, such as tribes, confederations, big-man societies, and so forth, the egalitarian ethic is not as strictly enforced as it was in some hunting and gathering bands, and they could perhaps better be described as societies of "single generation" or temporary inequality. In all these societies status is derived from action, alliances, and on-going social relationships. It is essentially achieved during the lifetime of an individual and is not passed on to the individual's descendants.

This distinction is well discussed in Fried's (1967) and Service's (1971) dichotomy between societies that have "achieved" status differentiation and those that have "ascribed" status differentiation. When we examine egalitarian societies side-by-side with chiefdoms or states the dynamic power of achieved status appears diluted in comparison with the striking degrees of inherited social inequality common in the latter. However, when we look at a range of egalitarian societies and status differentiation within them, then it becomes clear that egalitarianism is a social strategy that can prevent hereditary inequality from emerging. In these societies hereditary inequality, or the threat of it, is potentially disruptive of social stability and threatens the well-being of both individuals within society and society as a whole.

The assumption underlying the foregoing is that there exist inherent social processes that lead to transgenerational social inequality lurking beneath the surface of even the most tranquil of egalitarian societies. Hayden and Gargett (1990; Hayden 1995) have recently argued that these processes may be an essential part of the primate social order. Wilson (1988) makes the reasonable observation that

social hierarchies in many primate societies are in direct contrast to the sorts of social orders in human societies. Human hunting and gathering societies have, possibly since *Homo erectus*, developed the social means of keeping these hierarchies under control. But the hierarchies that do develop in human egalitarian societies are not dominance hierarchies. Instead, they are social-categorical hierarchies based on achievement, skill, persuasiveness, and other abilities. When hereditary inequality emerges, it is not the re-emergence of primate dominance hierarchies, for these hierarchies are not hereditary and have little or nothing to do with the kinds of social and political systems that develop in the first rank societies or in simple chiefdoms. But, there may be some individual motivations for status acquisition and display that are deeply rooted in the human psyche. We are not prepared to argue this point in detail, but, for the present argument, simply accept that individual actions and motivations are highly variable. In all societies there will be individuals that will try to attain status and prestige, for social, developmental, and perhaps psychological reasons (Hayden 1995:20-23). For most of human history, cultures have developed means of channeling and, often, preventing the overt expression of these individual actions and differences. In some tribal societies where they clearly exist and are overtly expressed, mechanisms still are present to prevent advantages that have accrued to individuals during their lifetimes from being passed on to the next generation. In chiefdoms, these limiting mechanisms are overcome and the potential for transgenerational status, power, and wealth acquisition is fully realized.

We will examine two sets of mechanisms that operate in egalitarian and transegalitarian society: (1) those that serve to maintain an egalitarian social order and ideology and (2) those that can be used to over-ride it. One of the advantages, we hope, of taking this approach is that it provides some insights into the sorts of patterning that one might expect to find in the archaeological record as chiefdoms emerge. It might also help us to assess the relative importance of different mechanisms in the process of chiefdom formation.

Egalitarian-maintaining mechanisms

Of course, there is no single form of egalitarian society. There are many quite different societies with no hereditary status distinctions as the basis of political and social organization. These range from permanently mobile hunters and gatherers living in small groups of 25-30 people to sedentary farmers living in villages of 200 people or more. It is at this end of the spectrum that we begin to get overlap with rank societies or simple chiefdoms. But most societies that would fall into the category of egalitarian, regardless of whether they are large or small, mobile or sedentary, bring into action a number of mechanisms to forestall individuals from acquiring much social status, power, and wealth. And, in the cases where individuals may acquire higher standing than other members of the society, there are further mechanisms to prevent the transmission of such attributes to their offspring (Trigger 1990).

We are not so much concerned here with the transition from simple to complex egalitarian societies as we are with the transition from complex egalitarian societies to rank societies. The distinction between the first two is the presence or absence of marked differences in individual status. The distinction between the latter two is the presence or absence of hereditary differences in status. What are the natural conditions and social mechanisms that prevent individuals who, during their lifetimes, are able to acquire considerable status, power, and perhaps even wealth, from transmitting that social currency to their offspring?

The first two factors that we will look at result from natural conditions or human-environmental interactions:

1. Social mobility in response to unpredictability in the availability of food resources,
2. Under-exploitation of naturally occurring food resources,

while the following three are social mechanisms:

3. Social ostracism and witchcraft accusations,
4. Cross-cutting organizations,
5. Intra-group fissioning.

These factors, singly or in concert, conspire to prevent potential aggrandizing individuals from attaining and maintaining status, power, and wealth; but more importantly, all make it difficult for aggrandizers to pass on status to particular offspring in any predictable manner. They also make it difficult for an aggrandizer to claim the high status of a deceased parent or relative.

1. Social mobility in response to unpredictability in the Availability of Food Resources

One of the main concerns of people in many hunting and gathering economies is how to respond to unpredictability in the availability of food resources. Compared with agriculturalists, hunters and gatherers must be organized in smaller, much more fluid social groupings in order to adapt quickly to the constant changes in the availability of resources, both seasonally and yearly (Yellen 1977; Cashdan 1980; Woodburn 1982). Many aspects of this social fluidity lead to and perpetuate an egalitarian social ethos (Lee 1979). Social relations must be structured in a way to permit individual and group mobility as circumstances arise. Egalitarianism is actively encouraged because it is one effective means of allowing impermanence in social relations, thereby ensuring mobility.

Unpredictability in the availability of food resources therefore requires mobility and periodic group restructuring.

Permanent status and wealth differences would be extremely difficult to maintain in the face of these logistical requirements for two reasons. The first is that no individual could count on having access to resources in the same location or in the same quantities for long spans of time. The second is that the status hierarchy would have to be redefined every time the group restructured. Combined, these two factors would tend to level status and wealth differences within a community and enforce a strong sense of egalitarianism.

2. Over-Exploitation of Naturally Occurring Food Resources

In hunting and gathering economies the long-term harvesting of wild resources can lead to over-exploitation and, ultimately, reduced yields. Of course, a balance between group size, population growth rates, and resource abundance and stability tend to reduce over-exploitation. If hunter-gatherers were to attempt to increase individual or group status by increasing the harvesting of wild resources, the long-term effects of over-exploitation could lead to a collapse of the very resources that the group depended on. The collapse need not be long-lasting in order to undermine the social and political aspirations of the group.

The implications of this are that, even in the absence of social mechanisms to ensure that an egalitarian ethic remained in place, any aggrandizing individuals or groups that tried to increase their wealth and status by increasing the production of natural resources would find themseves, in the long-run and perhaps even in the short-run, reduced to ruin because of the limits of natural productivity. Even in the short-run, say within the span of one generation, if someone were able to increase his number of followers and invest greater and greater amounts of labor in production, the limits to natural productivity could soon be reached. Therefore, labor, and the control of it, is not as valuable in hunting and gathering economies as it is in agricultural societies. The more labor one invests in production, the more likely one is to undermine the very resources that supported any budding status and wealth differences. We will return to this point.

3. Social Ostracism and Witchcraft Accusations

The two egalitarian-maintaining processes discussed above could have very divisive, destructive effects on many hunting and gathering societies if social mechanisms were not developed to minimize their impact. One effective way of keeping individuals from accumulating status or wealth in egalitarian societies is to socialize against such behavior with scorn, criticism, ostracism, and even physical violence (Woodburn 1982:436; Cashdan 1980:116). For the Hadza and !Kung, such methods were used regularly to prevent individuals from boasting of their skills, aggrandizing themselves in any way, or accumulating wealth.

In more complex egalitarian societies where some degree

of resource accumulation and some status differentiation is allowed, sorcery and witchcraft are used as a means of focusing group disapproval of individual behavior. Individuals may attain status by sharing wealth, or giving resources away in very specifically prescribed circumstances. However, if they accumulate too much wealth or attempt to use it to enhance and maintain long-term status differences, then they may become the object of envy within the community. Group misfortune can be blamed on these individuals who go over the line of propriety and attempt to make their status and wealth differences greater than or more permanent than allowed.

In both types of society, the possibility of ostracism is sufficient enough a threat to prevent most people from transgressing the bounds of proper behavior. The sorts of individuals who would want to increase their status or prestige would be particularly prone to this sort of treatment. Wealth and status, after all, are relative: without a community they are meaningless.

Ostracism can work in two ways. In highly mobile communities people can readily remove themselves from the vicinity of the offending individual. In more sedentary communities the offending individual can be removed from the community. Either way, the threat of such sanctions, if not the reality, can be a powerful egalitarian-maintaining mechanism.

Witchcraft and sorcery accusations can focus attention on areas of social conflict resulting from unequal economic and political positions. In egalitarian societies witchcraft accusations can be mobilized to bring public scrutiny to someone who is perceived to be getting ahead at the community's expense. In stratified societies, the practice of witchcraft and sorcery is restricted almost entirely to the commoner classes where it tends to operate much as it did in smaller egalitarian society. However, this does not prevent nobles and rulers from using the services of sorcerers and witches, especially ones who can counteract the effects of witchcraft and sorcery directed against them. Evans-Pritchard (1937:251-252) provides a clear example of this for the Azande:

> nobles abstain from witch-doctors' activities which are entirely a commoner practice and mainly a commoner interest... [however]... Princes, like everyone else, have their interests to protect from witchcraft. They have, indeed, a wider range of interests, since political interests are added to those of householder, husband, and producer. It is one of the special cares of a witch-doctor summoned to court to inform his master of any unrest in his kingdom or principality.

Just as witchcraft may work to keep egalitarian societies egalitarian, it might also work to keep commoners common. It can be invoked as a leveling mechanism and serve to prevent individuals from reaching their aspirations that would allow them to be permanently higher in status than their fellows.

4. Cross-cutting Associations

Cross-cutting associations, such as moieties, phrateries, sodalities, age-sets, section systems, and secret men's societies provide a social mechanism that organizes people in ways both different from and complementary to kinship systems. Large-scale corporate and organizational groups that cut across a community's kinship or descent lines and that are responsible for most public activity tend to reduce the potential for individual wealth and status accumulation. They also tend to weaken the political power of kin groups because they distribute resources away from lineages or clans that could benefit from their control.

Membership in such organizations, if not compulsory, is usually encouraged because it provides access to the most important social networks in the community. Payment of goods and labor is usually required for membership in the group and elaborate initiation ceremonies are used to mark the incorporation of new members. Advancement in these groups, when not based solely on seniority, requires distribution of wealth and displays of skill. Because of this, the very mechanisms for achieving status in the organization also prevent individuals from passing either wealth or status to their offspring. Prestige might be passed on from one generation to the next, but unless one exhibits the organizational skills of one's father, it would be impossible to translate that prestige into permanent status.

Secret societies in Melanesia are good examples of voluntary organizations that have the effect of preventing long-term hereditary status differences from arising. Keesing (1981:278) in discussing the example of the Dukduk secret society of the Bismarck Archipelago says: "Entrance and passage through these grades [of membership] become progressively more difficult and expensive, especially in terms of ceremonial wealth distribution. The innermost circle comprises the most important leaders in the area." He also describes the *tamate* secret societies in the Banks and Torres Islands and mentions how initiates must pay to join and perform group labor such as preparing food for more senior members.

There are a large number of other such organizations in tribal societies around the world, and it would be misleading to claim that all had the same or even similar functions. Widely different groupings such as moieties, phrateries, sodalities, age-sets, sections, secret societies all have particular histories and functions in their own social contexts. However, they are generally more common in tribal, egalitarian societies than in hereditary chiefdoms. The hierarchical organization of chiefdoms and simpler stratified societies tends to replace these sorts of cross-cutting organizations. It is not until the appearance of the state that they start to appear once again, by which time they are often co-opted by the state. One of the reasons they become useful once again in state-level societies, is that they provide an effective way of dividing up kin groups that might become potential threats to centralized state-control.

For example, the 19th century Zulus' use of age-sets as a means of organizing warriors was a revolutionary means of using traditional methods of organizing tribal society to dilute the threat of rivals and strengthen the military powers of the state (Service 1975).

5. Intra-Group Fission

Finally, one of the most effective means of preventing permanent socio-political hierarchies from developing is group fission. Many anthropologists have discussed this mechanism in egalitarian societies as a means of resolving disputes. When an individual or group within a community decides that its interests are not being met or perceives that they are being abused, they simply pack up and leave. People can move to new territory as long as new land is available, or, more likely, stay put on territory that they think already belongs to them. The effect of this strategy on preventing long-term hereditary leadership from evolving is a profound one. An aspiring leader or aggrandizer would be unable to count on a population base for labor and resources if a large portion of the community abandoned him every time he did something not to their liking. Packing up and moving to a new community would have been one of the most effective and probably most often used means of maintaining an egalitarian ethic within the community. More importantly, however, it would have regularly undermined any tendency for cross-generational transmission of status, wealth, and power.

Egalitarian-Overriding Processes

Many of the above mechanisms, and no doubt more that we have not considered, could work effectively in egalitarian societies to prevent the occurrence of long-term inequality while at the same time encouraging or even validating short-term inequality. In order for long-term inequality to come about, the mechanisms that maintain egalitarianism must be over-come. Individuals competing for prestige within the domain of short-term inequality (that is achieved status) may occasionally be able to override the checks described in the last section. The more of these natural and cultural egalitarian-maintaining mechanisms they are able to over-come, the more likely they will be able to pass on their wealth and status to the next generation. This approach suggests that transegalitarian societies and emergent chiefdoms do not require the development of new ways of organizing society so much as new ways of disorganizing old society. The transegalitarian process, and ultimately, chiefdoms might then be considered to be the inevitable outcome of the breaking down of egalitarianism. In Cashdan's (1980:119-120) words: "Inequality ... can therefore be explained best not as the development of any formal organization of 'ranking' or 'stratification,' but, rather, as the inevitable result of the *lifting* of the constraints that produce strict egalitarianism." Cashdan reached this conclusion

after conducting an analysis of the //Gana, a group in Botswana, so of course, what she said does not refer directly to chiefdom development. However, she goes on to say (1980:120) that "there is nothing 'natural' (statistically or socially) about the extreme leveling typical of most Bushman groups and suggests that the type of inequality found among the //Gana can be seen as the inevitable result of economic buffers that make such leveling mechanisms unnecessary." Going one step beyond Cashdan's analysis, we suggest that the transformation to hereditary chiefdoms, from complex egalitarian societies, such as "Big-man societies," is the result of the successful actions of individuals and groups using a range of political and economic strategies to overcome these egalitarian leveling mechanisms.

The following strategies might have been among the most important ones for aggrandizers and their kin groups who were attempting to establish and maintain long-term social inequality:

1. Alliances with rivals within the community.
2. Alliances with other leaders in neighboring communities.
3. Investment of labor in producing resources that are highly predictable.
4. Support of descent-based rather than associational organizations and their symbols.

None of these would work individually to overcome egalitarian-maintaining mechanisms. In fact, many of these strategies are common in egalitarian societies and would always have been present. However, armed with all four, individuals within a traditionally egalitarian society could subvert the system and, in effect, disorganize the egalitarian ethos. It would be impossible to legitimize a status that is not acceptable in the community and is being continually undermined by the range of egalitarian-maintaining mechanisms that we described. The key to success would be disarming the egalitarian-maintaining mechanisms. Once disarmed, then a host of new tools could be brought to bear on the problem of legitimation, not the least of which is the manipulation of material symbols and information. The transegalitarian mechanisms we describe below are part of the disarming process, not the legitimation process. We see legitimation as part of the maintenance of hereditary inequality, and probably its expansion, not its initial formation.

1. Alliances with Rivals within the Community

The formation of within-community alliances can be used to over-come the effects of conflict that might undermine a leader's status and power. These alliances can become descent-based when they center on marriages and can therefore be used to transfer wealth, status, and power across generations (Bender 1985, 1990).

One way that leaders deflect sorcery and witchcraft accusations that could undermine their status is by bringing their envious rivals into their own sphere of activity. This would mean the distribution of resources to other powerful individuals within the community who might otherwise marshal support against the leader. These sorts of alliances would have the effect of channeling resources among a set of emerging elites rather than dispersing resources through cross-cutting organizations to the community as a whole. The prolongation of this pattern of intra-community exchange would be difficult in egalitarian society, not because the social constraints could not be over-come, but because the natural ones would eventually intervene. What we have, in effect, is an aggrandizer or big-man trying to use plentiful resources and superior organizational skills to buy-off or ally with potential rivals. While he may easily be able to convince them to support him in the short-run, only his prolonged access to resources would permit the alliances to continue. When the resources were no longer plentiful, the alliances would soon disappear. Big-men who attempted to prolong leadership, status, and power, would need to find ways to make resources both plentiful and predictable. Otherwise, they would not be able to maintain their supporters in the style to which they had become accustomed. In this respect, a disgruntled supporter is probably worse than an avowed enemy.

2. Alliances with other Leaders in Neighboring Communities

External alliances are one of the most obvious means of attaining supporters, both within one's own community and outside the community. But, as with internal alliances, external alliances need to be financed. Therefore, a leader who wants to maintain a network of allies in other communities must divert resources to people in similar positions in those communities. Inter-community exchanges of wives or husbands and material resources by individuals representing particular kin groups rather than the community as a whole, or cross-cutting organizations, would lead to a rapid restructuring of inter-community alliances. They would transform from community-based to individual-based. An individual with leadership aspirations could thereby begin to monopolize the benefits of such alliances and use the advantage to compete against rivals from within.

When the alliances are based on marriages as well as exchanges of goods, then there will be a descent-based dimension to the alliance, and one that could allow it to continue for more than one generation. If these alliances among individuals from different communities support the aspiring leader and buffer him from the effects of egalitarian-maintaining mechanisms, then they do the same for his descendants who also claim leadership roles. Combined with the same descent-based orientation of intra-community alliances, a relatively small group of related individuals should start to emerge that has the ability to

circumvent the traditional egalitarian ethic. These inter-marrying individuals and their offspring would have access to more resources both within the community and outside the community. In the long-run this might not generate hereditary inequality unless these individuals were able to make their resource base productive and predictable. Sooner or later, their alliances would break down and they would be unable to support their claims and deflect competitors if their resource base was unpredictable and unreliable.

3. Investment of Labor in Producing Predictable Resources

The foregoing argument suggests that the resource base is a key element of the transition to hereditary inequality. It certainly goes without saying that most societies around the world with any large degree of hereditary inequality, i.e., societies ranging from chiefdoms to states, have reliable systems of food production, either based on agriculture or intensive fishing. The increased predictability of food production may have been a key reason for its development in the first place as Flannery (1986:16) has argued. The initial domestication of plants and animals would have taken place in the context of egalitarian hunters and gatherers. For them the predictability of food production was not part of a status acquisition process, rather, it was simply a buffer to provide desired foods in during lean years. Continued domestication lasted for thousands of years in most parts of the world with no appreciable change in the social and political structure and no development of more complex societies. Hayden (1990) has recently suggested that the development of complex societies contributed to the process of domestication. We think it more likely that emerging complex societies adopted agricultural systems once they were productive enough to provide a buffer against both natural and social egalitarian-maintaining mechanisms (Blake, Clark, et al. 1992).

Agricultural production is so useful in the context of complex societies because it can provide an almost unfill-able hole in which to pour labor. This contrasts sharply with hunting and gathering economies where there are strict limits to the amount of labor that can be invested in most areas of food production. Over-harvesting of many wild resources would soon lead to the collapse of the resource base and be detrimental to the community in the long-run. Agriculture provides, in many environments, a way around this problem by yielding increased pay-offs in produce for additional amounts of labor invested. This implies that the reasons for the spread of agriculture may be quite different from the reasons for its initial development. If it developed for the reasons described by Flannery (1973, 1986) and others (e.g., Rindos 1984) then it probably spread as a result of social and political competition in the context of emerging complex society. Hayden's (1990) argument would apply to the wide-spread adoption of developed agricultural systems, not necessarily to initial domestication.

Based on our recent work along the Pacific Coast of Mexico and the work of others in this volume (e.g., Benz Chapter 3; Piperno, Chapter 9; and Pearsall, Chapter 12) it seems clear that agricultural products were present and used at least hundreds if not thousands of years before the first signs of complex society. But the role of agriculture in leading to increased cultural complexity does not become important until the products have undergone enough genetic change to make them more productive and more reliable. Kirkby (1973) has made a similar argument for the spread of corn cultivation in the valley of Oaxaca. The growth in the size of the average corn cob and the yields per hectare increase through the Formative period and there is a continuous increase in productive potential. The appearance of the first complex societies takes place long after agriculture is introduced but presumably coincides with the development of more productive strains of corn and other cultivated plants.

4. Support of Descent-Based Rather Than Associational Organizations

Any shift to hereditary inequality must, almost by definition, put an increased emphasis on "vertical" or descent-based claims to status rather than "horizontal" or achievement-based claims. Both dimensions are always present in all human societies, but as we have already discussed, both the internal and external alliances that high status individuals seek to maintain become increasingly kin-based as they are centered on spouse exchanges. We would expect that as individuals try to claim wealth and status positions based on their ancestry, they must also seek to legitimate the claim using methods that validated the concept of lineal descent.

This process might lead to conflicts between two sets of powerful people within the community: those who try to maintain the traditional egalitarian ethic and those who try to over-ride it by claiming ties to high-status ancestors. One logical avenue for establishing a descent-based claim is to divert resources into the retroactive elevation of an ancestor's status. An aspiring hereditary leader could compete with the traditionalists by sponsoring feasts or building monuments in the name of the venerated ancestor. This process of legitimation puts the burden directly on the descendants rather than the ancestors. We often tend to think of the process of chiefdom emergence as a question of how to transfer wealth status to the next generation. Instead, the above argument suggests that we should look at it from the opposite perspective: the appropriation of status and wealth from the previous generation.

The elaboration of new sets of material symbols that stress the primacy of descent-based social structures at the expense of cross-cutting associations and achievement-based groups is essential for the emergence of hereditary inequality. Blake (1991) has argued that residential architecture provides an ideal domain for the display of descent-based

status differentiation. Combined with mortuary symbols, exotic exchange goods, and a range of other material items, archaeologists have many avenues available for observing this transformation.

A Case from the Pacific Coast of Mexico

The model we have outlined for the transegalitarian process is particularly appropriate for cases where it is, on first inspection, unclear whether we are dealing with egalitarian or complex societies. One of the implications of the above model is that the lack of archaeological clarity is the result of the process itself, not a case of unfortunate lack of preservation or a strange quirk of the society under investigation. Once one is certain that evidence for hereditary inequality exists in the archaeological record, it is quite likely that the process of transformation had already passed. Evidence for the causes of the transformation must lie at an earlier stage when the egalitarian-maintaining mechanisms are under siege and being subverted and when egalitarian-overriding mechanisms are being promoted.

Following the points outlined above, we will discuss four lines of evidence for the presence of transegalitarian processes during the Early Formative period in the Mazatán region of coastal Chiapas: (1) population; (2) ceramics; (3) food production; and (4) symbols of prestige. It is not always easy to pinpoint the exact egalitarian-overriding mechanisms that might have been in play but the archaeological record does show some evidence for several that we have mentioned.

Population Growth and Concentration

The world-wide correlation of population increase and the beginnings of social complexity, discussed by Keeley (1988), relates to the fundamental requirement of self-aggrandizing individuals to build a following of loyal supporters. Therefore, an explosive population increase in the Mazatán region, as revealed by changes in the settlement patterns, may provide one of the key lines of evidence for the transegalitarian stage (Figure 2). Population increases could have helped aggrandizers build more internal alliances and, perhaps most important, invest more labor in the production of food and other goods.

The transegalitarian process in the Mazatán region precipitated the population increase, rather than vice versa. The absence of population pressure becomes clear when one follows Stark's (1990) recent suggestion and considers the demographics of Mesoamerica as a whole. During the Late Archaic and Early Formative, population was widely dispersed, with low population densities in most areas and many prime areas apparently unoccupied—including areas adjacent to Mazatán. There were a few exceptional areas, such as Mazatán. We are persuaded that demographic hot spots such as this were socially created or induced by aggrandizers competing for followers. The success of this

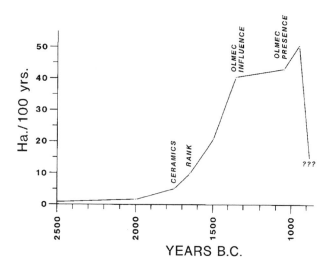

Figure 2. **Relative Curve for Hectares of Occupied Land in the Mazatán Area during the Late Archaic and Early Formative.**

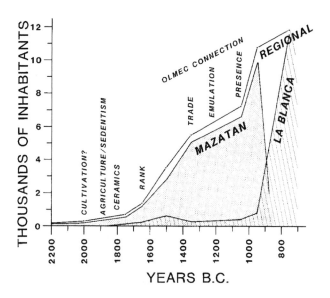

Figure 3. **Demographic Curves for the Mazatán and La Blanca Areas. The Relative Curve for the La Blanca Area is based upon data from Love (1989).**

strategy is apparent at sites like Paso de la Amada, San Carlos, and Aquiles Serdán, where population grew continually from the Barra phase through to the Cherla phase. As the size and number of communities grew in the region, the evidence for increased internal and external alliance-building also increased: more goods such as obsidian were exchanged, styles of material goods such as ceramics and figurines were relatively homogeneous over the whole region, and there was a long-term stability of the pattern, lasting from about 1550 to 1100 B.C.

The socially—and politically—contingent character of Mazatán population history becomes apparent if we broaden our spatial and temporal focus (Figure 3). The Mazatán region appears to have suffered massive depopulation about 900 B.C.—roughly the same time the region immediately to the south (the locus of the up-and-coming La Blanca paramount chiefdom documented by Love [Chapter 7]) experienced phenomenal population growth.[4] The population curves for each area are complementary—spatially and diachronically—suggesting a movement of most of the Mazatán population to the La Blanca area once sociopolitical conditions warranted it. Although we suspect warfare among paramount chiefdoms, the proximate causes of this demographic shift are not readily apparent at this time.

Ceramics and Social Competition

The prerequisites of what can be considered "competitive advantage" are implicated in the adoption of ceramics and highland cultigens. Competitive advantage in this context relates to the aggrandizer's deployable resources and ability

to provide material and spiritual benefits for his faction of followers vis-à-vis those offered by competitors. One can expect outside goods and ideas to be brought into an area under such heightened, competitive social conditions.[5] Ceramic technology and highland cultigens both fall into this category of long-distance or extra-local imports.

Ceramic technology of the Barra and Locona phases is problematical precisely because of its fully-developed technical and aesthetic sophistication. This observation led previous investigators to speculate that these first ceramic-using peoples came into the area from points south, perhaps Ecuador, Columbia, or Panama—all areas with earlier ceramic traditions (Coe 1960; Brush 1965; Lowe 1975). The colonization hypothesis gained force from juxtaposition to the technological arguments for ceramic origins in the Mesoamerican highland valleys of Tehuacán and Oaxaca (cf. MacNeish et al. 1970; Marcus 1983; Flannery and Marcus 1994). In the latter view, the first ceramics are seen as unsophisticated attempts to master a new, experimental technology, with major improvements coming with time and practice. Neither hypothesis can explain the timing of the adoption, the content of the Barra ceramic assemblage, or its technical sophistication.

In contrast, we think we are dealing with local adoption of ceramic technology, and technological transfer, rather than colonization or independent invention. Knowledge of ceramic techniques clearly came up the Pacific Coast, through a process of inter-group interaction, from points south. But the stylistic dissimilarities among the earliest ceramic assemblages known for northern South America, Central America, and Mesoamerica (cf. Hoopes 1987; Clark and Gosser 1995) is convincing evidence against the colonization hypothesis.

If we view the adoption of ceramic techniques within a social setting of competitive aggrandizers, the timing and content of the adoption of ceramics ceases to be problematical. We suggest that ceramic technology was brought into the Mazatán area by aggrandizers as part of their search for foreign goods that could be parlayed into personal gain. From this perspective, ceramic technology becomes a tool for overriding egalitarian-maintaining mechanisms. It is used in alliance-building both within and between communities and provides a new domain for the display of status. Most of the Barra and Locona phase ceramics were decorated serving vessels and may have featured prominently in the public display of food consumption.

If ceramic technology was brought in fully developed, or if aggrandizers sponsored a potter or two and persuaded them to come to the Mazatán area, how do we explain the differences in pottery styles in the borrowing area (Mazatán) and the donor area (Central America)? These are explicable, if not dictated, by technological transfer within the social milieu we have described. Undoubtedly, the complex hunter-fisher-gatherers in the Soconusco prior to the advent of ceramic technology had developed viable and suitable containers of perishable materials, such as gourds, baskets, skins, and cordage. We further assume that some of these containers and vessels were already functioning in a competitive sphere of ritual feasting, gift-giving, and public ritual display. Moreover, these perishable containers could have been elaborately decorated, expensive vessels.[6] If so, the containers most likely replaced and imitated by ceramic forms would have been stylistically bounded already. That is, vessel style was already socially meaningful in special social contexts. Copying these vessels in a new and more expensive medium (fired clay) would enhance their value but not tamper with fundamental social conventions of meaning. Introduction of different vessel forms and style, however, would not have been immediately meaningful, in terms of traditional conventions, and consequently would have been of less value to those seeking prestige through conspicuous consumption.

The idea of technological transfer in a milieu of competing aggrandizers can account for those aspects of ceramic technology that previous investigators found most puzzling. It can explain (1) the timing of the adoption, (2) vessel style or exterior decoration, (3) vessel forms, (4) the quality of the ceramics, (5) the odd nature of the ceramic assemblage as viewed archaeologically, and (6) the subsequent development of ceramics. Without going into detail, the timing was dictated by the heightened level of social competition in the Mazatán area. Vessel style and forms were predicated upon the style and forms of the ritual-feasting vessels already functioning in competitive social displays, for reasons noted above; all that changed was the base material and *some* of the fabrication processes (almost all the early vessel forms are phytomorphic, with carved, incised, or painted designs—likely forms of surface decorations for gourd and wooden vessels) (Figure 4). This hypothesis also accounts for the quality of the first vessels (they came in as sumptuary goods) and the puzzling absence of plain utilitarian vessels. Functions later performed by plain pottery continued to be performed, at this early date, by gourds or jicaras, net bags, and baskets.[7] Unslipped pottery became more common during the Locona phase, a time when techniques of ceramic manufacture were more widely known, and probably when the use of ceramic vessels in competitive displays had lost its novelty.

Beginning during the Barra phase there is evidence of internal alliance-building through feasting activities in domestic structures. Ceramics first came into wide-spread use during this phase, but they were almost completely restricted to serving vessels which were not designed for, nor do they show evidence of, use in cooking. Instead, they all appear appropriate for preparation of, or serving of, liquids (Figure 4), a point we will return to later. And, if we can assume that fire-cracked rock is a good indication of stone boiling, the major change in boiling technology occurred late in the Locona phase, when the frequency of fire-cracked rock declined dramatically (Clark and Gosser 1995). That is to say, we suspect that the adoption of ceramics did not alter the pre-existing food processing and preparation techniques. Rather, ceramics were adopted more for their power to impress others in competitive social displays than for their culinary (technological and functional) potential in food preparation. In other words, they were important in the transegalitarian process precisely because they could be used for status displays during occasions of alliance-building (rituals and feasting) that undermined the egalitarian-maintaining mechanisms of the past.

By the subsequent Locona phase there is much more evidence for the egalitarian-overriding mechanisms we described. Locona phase sites such as San Carlos and Paso de la Amada have large amounts of pottery that is highly

Figure 4. Reconstruction Drawing of Barra Vessels.

decorated and probably only used for serving vessels. Very few cooking vessels are represented, so traditional, pre-ceramic, methods of cooking were probably still in use. We think that these vessels represent higher levels of feasting than in the preceding Barra phase, and that this activity was related to the need to build up networks of supporters within the communities who would not then undermine the aspiring leader's claim to status.

Food Production

As with the introduction of ceramics, the beginnings of agriculture on the coast require an explanation: in terms of both timing and content. The primary questions in explaining coastal agriculture are: why were highland domesticates introduced and how important were they in the overall diet? Again, we suggest that the initial importation and cultivation of highland cultigens was, at least in part, the result of aggrandizers appropriating non-local materials in their never-ending quest for prestige.

The production of reliable and plentiful food resources became an important economic consideration during the Barra phase. Faunal remains from excavated sites show that fishing in the plentiful freshwater swamps and rivers of the Mazatán region was one of the main subsistence activities during this period. Continuing through all of the subsequent phases of the Mokaya tradition, large quantities of fish bones of several species indicate that fish of all sizes were being captured, probably by nets (Blake, Clark, et al. 1992.) In the few Barra phase deposits we have excavated so far, we have found good preservation of carbonized plant remains. The most common plants were all cultigens: maize, beans, and avocados; in fact few remains of any other plants have yet been recovered (Feddema 1993).

The evidence for food production during the Locona phase is similar to that described for the Barra phase. There is more direct evidence of net fishing with large numbers of notched sherd net-weights, and even greater amounts of freshwater estuary and riverine fish remains. Plant remains are more plentiful than before but include the same narrow range: charred maize kernels and cob fragments, beans, and avocado pits. Corn cobs recovered in Locona deposits are all quite small (4-5 cm long) and would not have been very productive. Moreover, grinding equipment such as manos and metates occur infrequently, suggesting that grinding of maize and other foods was limited.

The Ocós and Cherla phases have more evidence for agricultural food production. Corn and beans are present at a number of Ocós phase sites. Aquiles Serdán had the most evidence for agriculture with dozens of charred corn kernels, many cob fragments, many fragments of beans, avocado pits, and several other minor plant remains (Feddema 1993). Agricultural production was present during the previous two phases, but it does not seem to have been as important as during Ocós and Cherla times.

Even so, there is some contradictory evidence suggesting that maize, in spite of being the most common of the charred plant remains in all of the phases, was not yet a dietary staple for most people. This hypothesis is based on stable carbon and nitrogen isotope analyses of human bones from most of the sites excavated in the Mazatán region. We have found that the stable carbon isotope values measured in the skeletal population are more similar to non-maize eating peoples (Blake, Chisholm, et al. 1992; Blake, Clark, et al. 1992). Even during the Ocós and Cherla phases, the use of maize may have been a significantly less important part of the diet than during the Middle Formative period.

For the Mokaya people, maize may have been only one part of a system of food production that both required and could have absorbed greater labor input than previous hunting and gathering systems. It may also have been used occasionally during rituals and feasts and not as a staple of daily food consumption. However, in terms of our model, the important point to note is that, during the trans-egalitarian stage, there was increasing use of agriculture in the subsistence system. The incorporation of agricultural production into the subsistence system would have been an important first step in developing a reliable and predictable food base. Harnessing this new food production system for social and perhaps political purposes would have helped aggrandizers to afford strategies for circumventing egalitarian-maintaining mechanisms and for promoting notions of hereditary inequality.

How and why did this first step take place? We propose that the adoption of highland cultigens parallels and is linked to the adoption of ceramic technology, and for similar reasons. The highland seeds were imported into a self-sufficient system in terms of basic foodstuffs. Corn was not brought in as some sort of far-sighted, prehistoric agricultural improvement project. It should be recalled that the highland peoples who domesticated these plants were still not fully sedentary agriculturalists 4000 years ago (MacNeish 1964; Flannery 1986, Flannery and Marcus 1983; Marcus and Flannery 1996). In terms of our hypothesis, we would expect these cultigens to be adopted as sumptuary goods or status foods—a paradoxical proposition given the usual characterization of these early domesticates. But we need to avoid a pair of functional fallacies that posit the reasons the plants were imported had something to do with their function today or even their function 3000 or 6000 years ago.

The Barra phase ceramic assemblage provides a possible clue as to why corn may have been imported and cultivated. Barra ceramics (and if our argument is correct the perishable ritual vessels they mimicked) were designed almost exclusively for liquids, presumably liquids with ritual significance and prestige value for the giver. We suggest that corn was part of this complex and was introduced into the coastal area (prior to the adoption of ceramics) primarily as a source for making corn beer, or *chicha*. Alternatively, it may also have been brought in to be used with chocolate. Hayden (1990) has recently argued along similar lines that domestication of plants and animals resulted from their deployment and development as status foods. Use of corn as a ritual beverage ingredient, or as an alcoholic beverage in its own right, could explain (1) the initial importation and special cultivation of this relatively unproductive plant into the coastal zone, (2) the rarity and small size of seed-processing implements, and (3) the minor contribution of corn in the overall diet. Having said this, we should note that reconstructed proto-Mixe-Zoque terms support chocolate as the more important ritual beverage (Campbell and Kaufman 1976).[8]

Symbols of Prestige: Production, Exchange, and Display

External alliances are represented by the non-local exchanges in raw materials, and perhaps, finished items. Obsidian was imported in large quantities from at least three sources in the highlands of Guatemala (Clark et al. 1987). Scattered Barra phase ceramics also show up in a number of sites throughout Mesoamerica (Lowe 1975), indicating some movement of goods and people outside of local territories.

One of the areas where we do have good evidence of individuals attempting to circumvent traditional egalitarian-maintaining mechanisms is in descent-based, and possibly kin-related symbols of status. At the site of Vivero we excavated a burial of a child, perhaps 10 or 11 years old, with a forehead mirror disc that may have, as in later Olmec times, represented a symbol of high status (Clark 1991). Locona ceramic figurines show individuals that we think represent high status males also wearing forehead discs. The use of this symbol of high status in mortuary ritual for a young boy indicates that a good deal of his status must have been hereditary, since he could not have achieved it at his young age.

We have also excavated a series of Locona and Ocós phase structures at Paso de la Amada that may indicate the emergence of descent-based social distinctions. Mound 6 contained a stratigraphic sequence of at least six floors, several of which are among some of the largest structures yet known in Mesoamerica for this time period (Figure 5)(Blake 1991; Blake et al. 1993; Clark 1994). We interpret the structures in Mound 6 to represent a sequence of elite residences, perhaps those of successive chiefs, spanning several generations. The artifacts associated with the structures reflect the normal range of domestic activities that we have seen in smaller, non-elite houses at sites throughout the region (Lesure 1995). However, the large size of the structures in Mound 6 suggest that they may also have been used for community gatherings, perhaps ones sponsored by an emerging chiefly lineage resident in the structures.[9]

Some manufactures during the Locona phase would have required huge amounts of labor investment. For example, stone bowls became common and seem to concentrate in only a few locations. These and other stone items, such as

finely-carved stone pendants may have been exchanged within the community to build up elite alliances. There are also many more examples of non-local exchange goods in the Locona phase, representing the expansion of inter-community alliances. These goods are exemplified by obsidian once again, but other goods may also have been imported. For example we begin to see larger numbers of jade beads and carvings that probably came from afar.

Conclusions

One of the central points of this chapter is that the identification of chiefdoms is not as important to under-standing how they evolve as is tracing the strategies that individuals and groups may have used to initiate the transegalitarian process. By looking at the archaeological cases of chiefdom emergence in a number of different areas of the world it should be possible to trace recurrent patterns as well as differences in the way this transformation was achieved. We think that part of the key to doing this is to focus on the implications of the dynamic political processes that result from the quest for and competition for status in egalitarian societies. It becomes clear that while competition and rivalry may be inevitable in human societies, there is nothing inevitable about the maintenance of egalitarian-ism (Cashdan 1980) nor the overriding of it by accumula-tors or aggrandizers. We have attempted to outline some of the mechanisms whereby societies attempt to maintain their egalitarian political and social structures, as well as the conditions and mechanisms under which certain types of individuals and descent-based groups can overcome the egalitarian constraints imposed upon them.

In the case of the Mokaya of coastal Chiapas, Mexico, it appears that by the Early Formative period, the trend towards rank society was beginning. We noted some evidence for activities that may have initiated the transegal-itarian process during the Barra phase: i.e., internal and external alliance building. By the Locona phase, there is stronger evidence for both of these as well as added evi-dence for increased production of reliable resources and for descent-based social organization. During the Ocós phase, agricultural production continued, and the continuity of descent-based social units was maintained.

Throughout the Mokaya sequence, we can observe an elaboration of all types of material goods, especially goods that could have been used as symbols of status and prestige. There is some evidence for the aggrandizement of individu-als and groups through feasting and conspicuous consump-tion of crafts and imports, and the sequential elaboration of residential structures. However, there is little evidence for the elaboration of, or differentiation in, mortuary display. In sum, although there is no evidence for fully developed chiefdoms, the changes that took place from ca. 1550 B.C. to 1000 B.C. demonstrate that egalitarianism was breaking down and hereditary inequality was beginning to develop.

We have tried to answer the question of how rank

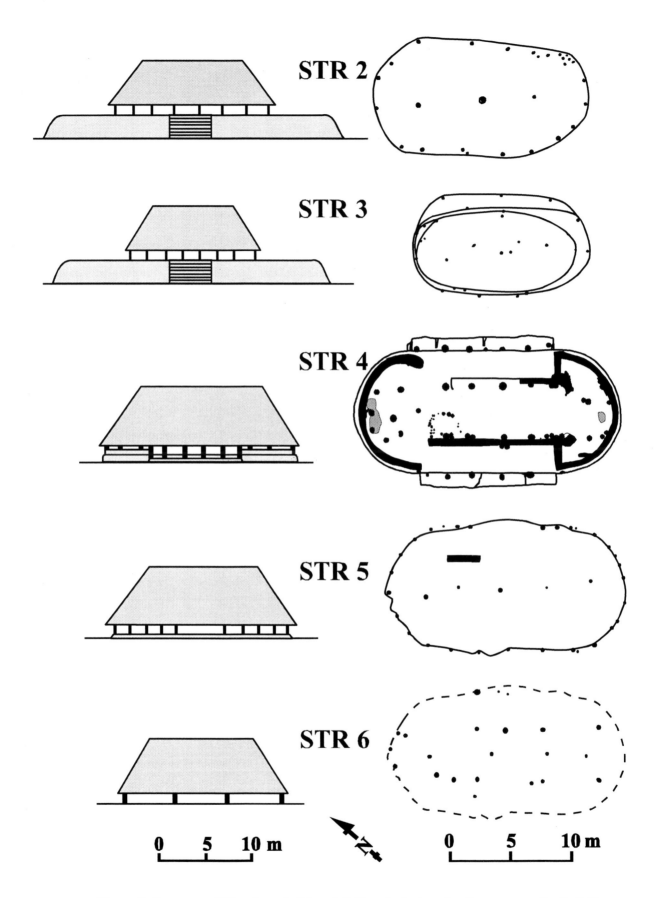

STR 2

STR 3

STR 4

STR 5

STR 6

0   5   10 m

N

0   5   10 m

Figure 5. Sequence of Structures in Mound 6, Paso de la Amada. Sequence on the Left Shows Reconstruction Drawings Based on Excavated Floor Plans Shown at Right.

societies emerged in the Mazatán region of Mexico. The available evidence indicates that these societies developed locally rather than being colonies from Central or South America. We should re-emphasize, however, that we still lack firm archaeological data for the crucial transitional period from the very end of the Late Archaic to the very beginning of the Early Formative (1800-1600 B.C.). For the present time, our reconstruction of this period should be taken as hypothetical. Similarly, our explanation of the transegalitarian process during the Early Formative period in the Mazatán region is preliminary and requires a great deal more documentation.

To summarize, we hypothesize that rank society, including hereditary social inequality and political complexity, arose as an unanticipated consequence of aggrandizers striving to increase their own prestige vis-à-vis their rivals. The necessary technological and environmental preconditions for this process are assumed to have been present by the Late Archaic period. At this time, the Chantuto people (Voorhies 1976) pursued a broad exploitative strategy of hunting, fishing, gathering, and probably cultivation of tropical plants—including root crops and fruits. This subsistence strategy continued into the Early Formative. Our reconstruction of the development of rank society presumes that the peoples of the Mazatán area were able to harvest swamp and tropical resources at a rate which allowed them to shift from residential mobility to sedentism. As Hayden (1981, 1990) points out, resilient resources such as fish resist over-exploitation. The productivity of these r-selected species also allowed for surplus accumulation and its competitive deployment by would-be-bigmen. Thus began a dynamic period of competitive borrowing, innovation, and development. Foreign goods and products were brought into the Mazatán area at this time. These included highland cultigens such as maize and beans and technology such as ceramics.

This initial social network of competing aggrandizers in an increasingly productive environment acted as a demographic magnet as each aggrandizer sought to expand his own support base through gift-giving and by sponsoring feasts and other productive activities such as craft production and long distance exchange. This competitive spiral eventually lead to the formation of rank societies on a regional scale.

Acknowledgments

Our research was generously funded by the New World Archaeological Foundation of Brigham Young University and the Social Sciences and Humanities Research Council of Canada grants. We thank Gareth W. Lowe, director of the N.W.A.F. when this project began in 1985, for the opportunity he provided us in initiating the Mazatán Project. All of our fieldwork has been carried out under permissions granted by the Consejo de Arqueología of the Instituto Nacional de Antropología e Historia in Mexico City. Our paper has benefited greatly from our ongoing discussions with Brian Hayden, Barbara Voorhies, Richard Lesure, Mary Pye, Michael Love, Barbara Arroyo, Joyce Marcus, Kent Flannery, Brian Chisholm, R. G. Matson, Richard Pearson, Vicki Feddema, Warren Hill, and Dennis Gosser. Barbara Stark, Barbara Voorhies, and Brian Hayden offered many constructive suggestions on previous drafts of this paper, for which we extend our appreciation.

Notes

1. All dates and age estimates for the phases and periods presented in this paper are in radiocarbon years (uncalibrated). We have decided not to present calibrated dates because we are more concerned with the relative age of archaeological sites and assemblages in evaluating the changing archaeological record than we are with absolute age estimates. See Blake et al. (1995) for a detailed presentation of the chronology and characteristics of each phase discussed in the text.

2. We opted for a term other than "accumulator" when we tried to translate this term into Spanish—its cognate refers to a car battery. We chose "aggrandizer" because it better captures that spectrum of behavior of interest. All aggrandizers must accumulate to finance their self-promoting activities, but not all accumulators need be self-aggrandizers (e.g., misers). Either term is preferable to "bigman" which is more restricted in meaning and bound to Melanesian societies.

3. Use of masculine pronouns is strictly intentional. We think an aggrandizer's competitive ability derives from his immediate access to the productive labor of his wife (or wives) and children, or what could be considered a form of familial exploitation (see Clark and Blake [1994] for more extensive discussion).

4. The population figures shown in Figure 3 are extrapolations of settlement data described by Love (1989). These population curves are just ballpark estimates. Each curve was calculated by the same procedures. We estimated the number of sites of each size class (or level in the settlement hierarchy) and multiplied each type by a population constant depending on the estimated average size of each type of settlement.

5. Albert (1988:169) in his discussion of Lak bigmen gives an example of this:

> Similarly, the Lak claim that innovations of any sort (e.g., use of a metal roof on a house) should come from a big-man, but they also mean that he should first run the risk of the leveling envy, sorcery, and illness that may follow.

6. Elaborate decoration of gourds persists today in Chiapas as an important native craft. Decoration consists of painting and carving. Some 100 years ago, gourds were also trained while on the tree or vine, using techniques similar to those used in cranial deformation. Tying the

gourd while it was growing resulted in lobed vessels similar to some of the Barra pots. An important point for early ritual vessels of perishable materials is that they be labor-intensive goods to distinguish them from common utilitarian vessels (see Clark and Parry 1990). We realize that for the moment, our argument for the relationship between early ceramics and perishable vessels remains circular—pending further data.

7. During the Barra phase, the container system would have consisted of ceramics and many types of perishable containers. Essentially, the ceramics were a type of elite goods. This creates a problem in our interpretation of the Barra phase. Households lacking ceramics would not have left any detectable trace. The degree to which this proves to be true, our demographic interpretations for the Barra phase will turn out to be conservative.

8. The ritual usage of chocolate conforms to later Meso-american practices. The evidence for the early importance of chocolate is the historical linguistic data for loan words into other Mesoamerican dialects. Cacao is one of the earliest and most extensively loaned terms from proto-Mixe-Zoque (Lyle Campbell, personal communication, 1989). This may relate to trade in cacao and/or an early ritual complex. Of course, if the Barra vessels were designed for chocolate drink, our argument for corn is fallacious and irrelevant. We should note here, also, that we have not discounted entirely the possibility of a more direct southern origin of Barra ceramics. Based upon current data at our disposal, however, we do not find the evidence of stylistic similarities convincing.

9. Excavations at Paso de la Amada in 1995 discovered a ballcourt dating to the Locona and Ocós phases (Hill 1996). The presence of a ballcourt in the largest village in the Mazatán region suggests that the ballgame was an important part of the transegalitarian process from the beginning of the Early Formative period.

References Cited

Albert, S. M.
1988   How Big are Melanesian Big-Men?: A Case Study from Southern New Ireland. *Research in Economic Anthropology* 10:159-200.
Arnold, J. E.
1991   Transformation of a Regional Economy: Sociopolitical Evolution and the Production of Valuables in Southern California. *Antiquity* 65: 953-962.
1992   Complex Hunter-gatherer-fishers of Prehistoric California: Chiefs, Specialists, and Maritime Adaptations of the Channel Islands. *American Antiquity* 57:60-84.
Arnold, J. E. (editor)
1996   *Emergent Complexity: The Evolution of Intermediate Societies*. International Monographs in Prehistory, Archaeological Series 9. Ann Arbor.

Bender, B.
1985   Prehistoric Developments in the American Midcontinent and in Brittany, Northwest France. In *Prehistoric Hunter-Gatherers: The Emergence of Cultural Complexity*, edited by T. D. Price and J. A. Brown, pp. 21-57. Academic Press, New York.
1990   The Dynamics of Non-hierarchical Societies. *The Evolution of Political Systems: Sociopolitics in Small-Scale Sedentary Societies*, edited by S. Upham, pp. 247-265. School of American Research Advanced Seminar Series, D. W. Schwartz, general editor. Cambridge University Press, Cambridge.
Blake, M.
1991   Paso de la Amada: An Early Formative Chiefdom in Chiapas, Mexico. In *The Formation of Complex Society in Southeastern Mesoamerica*, edited by W. R. Fowler, Jr., pp.27-46. CRC Press, Boca Raton.
Blake, M., B. S. Chisholm, J. E. Clark, B. Voorhies, and M. W. Love
1992   Prehistoric Subsistence in the Soconusco Region. *Current Anthropology* 33(1):83-94.
Blake, M., J. E. Clark, B. S. Chisholm, and K. Mudar
1992   Non-agricultural Staples and Agricultural Supplements: Early Formative Subsistence in the Soconusco Region, Mexico. In *Transitions to Agriculture in Prehistory*, edited by A. B. Gebauer and T. D. Price, pp. 133-152. Monographs in World Archaeology No. 4. Prehistory Press, Madison.
Blake, M., J. E. Clark, V. Feddema, M. Ryan, and R. G. Lesure
1993   Early Formative Architecture at Paso de la Amada, Chiapas, Mexico. Ms. on file, Department of Anthropology and Sociology, University of B.C., Vancouver.
Blake, M., J. E. Clark, V. Voorhies, G. Michaels, M. W. Love, M. E. Pye, A. A. Demarest, and B. Arroyo
1995   Radiocarbon Chronology for the Late Archaic and Formative Periods on the Pacific Coast of Southeastern Mesoamerica. *Ancient Mesoamerica* 6: 161-183.
Blau, P.
1964   *Exchange and Power in Social Life*. John Wiley and Sons, Inc. Reprinted, 1986 by Transaction Books, New Brunswick, New Jersey.
Brush, C. E.
1965   Pox Pottery: Earliest Identified Mexican Ceramic. *Science* 149(3680):194-195.
Campbell, L., and T. Kaufman
1976   A Linguistic Look at the Olmecs. *American Antiquity* 41(1):80-89.
Cashdan, E. A.
1980   Egalitarianism Among Hunters and Gatherers. *American Anthropologist* 82(1):116-120.

Clark, J. E.

1990 Olmecas, Olmequismo, y Olmequización en Meso-america. *Arqueología* 3:49-50.

1991 The beginnings of Mesoamerica: Apologia for the Soconusco Early Formative. In *The Formation of Complex Society in Southeastern Mesoamerica*, edited by W. R. Fowler, Jr., pp. 13-26. CRC Press, Boca Raton.

1994 *The Development of Early Formative Rank Societies in the Soconusco, Chiapas, Mexico.* Ph.D. Dissertation, Department of Anthropology, University of Michigan, Ann Arbor. University Microfilms, Ann Arbor.

Clark, J. E., and M. Blake

1989 El Origen de la Civilización en Mesoamerica: Los Olmecas y Mokaya del Soconusco de Chiapas, México. In *El Preclásico or Formativo: Avances y Perspectivas*, edited by Martha Carmona Macías, pp. 385-403. Museo Nacional de Antropología and Instituto Nacional de Antropología e Historia, México.

1994 The Power of Prestige: Competitive Generosity and the Emergence of Rank Societies in Lowland Mesoamerica. In *Factional Competition and Political Development in the New World*, edited by E. Brumfiel and J. Fox, pp. 17-30. Cambridge University Press, Cambridge.

Clark, J. E., M. Blake, P. Guzzy, M. Cuevas, and T. Salcedo

1987 *Proyecto: El Preclásico Temprano en la Costa del Pacífico.* Final Report to the Instituto Nacional de Antropología e Historia, México. Ms. on file, Department of Anthropology, Brigham Young University, Provo.

Clark, J. E., M. Blake, B. Arroyo, M. E. Pye, R. G. Lesure, V. Feddema, and M. Ryan

1990 *Reporte Final Del Proyecto Investigaciones del Formativo Temprano en el Litoral Chiapaneco.* Final Report to the Instituto Nacional de Antropología e Historia, México. Ms. on file, Department of Anthropology, Brigham Young University, Provo.

Clark, J. E., and D. Gosser

1995 Reinventing Mesoamerica's First Pottery. In *The Emergence of Pottery: Technology and Innovation in Ancient Societies*, edited by W. K. Barnett and J. W. Hoopes, pp. 209-221. Smithsonian Institution Press, Washington.

Clark, J. E., and W. J. Parry

1990 Craft Specialization and Cultural Complexity. In *Research in Economic Anthropology* 12:289-346.

Coe, M. D.

1960 Archaeological Linkages with North and South America at La Victoria, Guatemala. *American Anthropologist* 62:363-654.

Demarest, A. A.

1989 The Olmec and the Rise of Civilization in Eastern Mesoamerica. In *Regional Perspectives on the Olmec*, edited by R. J. Sharer and D. C. Grove, pp. 303-344. School of American Research Advanced Seminar Series. Cambridge University Press, Cambridge.

Drennan, R. D., and C. A. Uribe (editors)

1987 *Chiefdoms in the Americas.* University Press of America, Lanham.

Earle, T.

1987 Chiefdoms in Archaeological and Ethnohistorical Perspective. *Annual Review of Anthropology* 16: 279-308.

1989 The Evolution of Chiefdoms. *Current Anthropology* 30:84-88.

Earle, T. (editor)

1991 *Chiefdoms: Power, Economy, and Ideology.* School of American Research Advanced Seminar Series, D. W. Schwartz, general editor. Cambridge University Press, Cambridge.

Ekholm, S. M.

1969 *Mound 30a and the Early Preclassic Ceramic Sequence of Izapa, Chiapas, Mexico.* Papers of the New World Archaeological Foundation No. 25. Brigham Young University, Provo.

Evans-Pritchard, E. E.

1937 *Witchcraft, Oracles and Magic Among the Azande.* Oxford University Press, Oxford.

Feddema, V.

1993 *Early Formative Subsistence and Agriculture in Southeastern Mesoamerica.* Unpublished Master's. Thesis, Department of Anthropology and Sociology, University of British Columbia, Vancouver.

Flannery, K. V.

1973 The Origins of Agriculture. *Annual Review of Anthropology* 2:271-310.

Flannery, K. V. (editor)

1986 *Guilá Naquitz: Archaic Foraging and Early Agriculture in Oaxaca, Mexico.* Academic Press, Orlando.

Flannery, K. V., and J. Marcus (editors)

1983 *The Cloud People: Divergent Evolution of the Zapotec and Mixtec Civilizations.* Academic Press, New York.

Flannery, K. V., and J. Marcus

1994 *Early Formative Pottery of the Valley of Oaxaca.* Memoirs of the Museum of Anthropology, University of Michigan No. 27. Ann Arbor.

Fried, M. H.

1967 *The Evolution of Political Society: An Essay in Political Anthropology.* Random House, New York.

Gilman, A

1991 Trajectories Towards Social Complexity in the Later Prehistory of the Mediterranean. In *Chiefdoms: Power, Economy, and Ideology*, edited by T.

Earle, pp.146-168. School of American Research Advanced Seminar Series, D. W. Schwartz, general editor. Cambridge University Press, Cambridge.

Hayden, B.

1981 Subsistence and Ecological Adaptations of Modern Hunter/Gatherers. In *Omnivorous Primates: Gathering and Hunting in Human Evolution*, G. Teleki and R. Harding, eds., pp. 344-422. Columbia University Press, New York.

1990 Nimrods, Piscators, Pluckers and Planters: The Emergence of Food Production. *Journal of Anthropological Archaeology* 9:31-69.

1995 Pathways to Power: Principles for Creating Socioeconomic Inequalities. In *Foundations of Social Inequality*, edited by T. D. Price and G. M. Feinman, pp. 15-86. Plenum Press, New York.

Hayden, B., and R. Gargett

1990 Big Man, Big Heart?: A Mesoamerican View of the Emergence of Complex Society. *Ancient Mesoamerica* 1:3-20.

Hill, W. D.

1996 Mesoamerica's Earliest Ballcourt and the Origins of Inequality. Paper Presented at the 61st Annual Meeting of the Society for American Archaeology. New Orleans.

Hoopes, J. W.

1987 *Early Ceramics and the Origins of Village Life in Lower Central America*. Ph. D. Dissertation, Department of Anthropology, Harvard University, Cambridge. University Microfilms, Ann Arbor.

Keeley, L. H.

1988 Hunter-Gatherer Economic Complexity and "Population Pressure": A Cross-Cultural Analysis. *Journal of Anthropological Archaeology* 7(4): 373-411.

Keesing, R. M.

1981 *Cultural Anthropology: A Contemporary Perspective*. Holt, Rinehart, and Winston, New York.

Kirkby, A. V. T.

1973 *The Use of Land and Water Resources in the Past and Present Valley of Oaxaca, Mexico*. Memoirs No. 5. Museum of Anthropology, University of Michigan, Ann Arbor.

Lee, R. B.

1979 *The !Kung San: Men, Women, and Work in a Foraging Society*. Cambridge University Press, Cambridge.

Lee, T. A., Jr.

1989 Chiapas and the Olmec. In *Regional Perspectives on the Olmec*, edited by R. J. Sharer and D. C. Grove, pp. 198-226. School of American Research Advanced Seminar Series, J. Haas, general editor. Cambridge University Press, Cambridge.

Lesure, R. G.

1995 *Paso de la Amada: Sociopolitical Dynamics in an Early Formative Community*. Ph.D. Dissertation, Department of Anthropology, University of Michigan, Ann Arbor. University Microfilms, Ann Arbor.

Love, M. W.

1989 *Early Settlements and Chronology of the Río Naranjo, Guatemala*. Unpublished Ph. D. dissertation, Department of Anthropology, University of California, Berkeley.

1991 Style and Social Complexity in Formative Mesoamerica. In *The Formation of Complex Society in Southeastern Mesoamerica*, edited by W. R. Fowler, Jr., pp. 47-76. CRC Press, Boca Raton.

Lowe, G. W.

1975 *The Early Preclassic Barra Phase of Altamira, Chiapas; A Review with New Data*. Papers of the New World Archaeological Foundation No. 38. Brigham Young University, Provo.

Lowe, G. W., T. A. Lee, Jr., and E. Martínez E.

1982 *Izapa: An Introduction to the Ruins and Monuments*. Papers of the New World Archaeological Foundation No. 31. Brigham Young University, Provo.

MacNeish, R. S.

1964 Ancient Mesoamerican Civilization. *Science* 143: 531-537.

MacNeish, R. S., F. A. Peterson, and K. V. Flannery

1970 *Ceramics. The Prehistory of the Tehuacán Valley Vol. 3*. University of Texas Press, Austin.

Marcus, J.

1983 The Espiridión Complex and the Origins of the Oaxacan Formative. In *The Cloud People: Divergent Evolution of the Zapotec and Mixtec Civilizations*, edited by K. V. Flannery and J. Marcus, pp. 42-43. Academic Press, New York.

Marcus, J., and K. V. Flannery

1996 *Zapotec Civilization*. Thames and Hudson, London.

Mauss, M.

1967 *The Gift: Forms and Functions of Exchange in Archaic Societies*. Norton, New York.

Nelson, F. W., and B. Voorhies

1980 Trace Element Analysis of Obsidian Artifacts from Three Shell Midden Sites in the Littoral Zone, Chiapas, Mexico. *American Antiquity* 45(3):540-550.

Price, T. D., and J. A. Brown (editors)

1985 *Prehistoric Hunter-Gatherers: The Emergence of Cultural Complexity*. Academic Press, New York.

Price, T. D., and G. M. Feinman (editors)

1995 *Foundations of Social Inequality*. Plenum Press, New York.

Pye, M. E., and A. A. Demarest

1991 The Evolution of Complex Societies in Southeastern Mesoamerica: New Evidence from El Mesak, Guatemala. In *The Formation of Complex Society in Southeastern Mesoamerica*, edited by W. R. Fowler, Jr., pp.77-100. CRC Press, Boca Raton.

Rindos, D.
1984 *The Origins of Agriculture: An Evolutionary Perspective*. Academic Press, New York.

Sahlins, M.
1972 *Stone Age Economics*. Aldine, Chicago.

Service, E. R.
1971 *Primitive Social Organization: An Evolutionary Perspective* (Second Edition). Random House, New York.
1975 *Origins of the State and Civilization: The Process of Cultural Evolution*. W. W. Norton & Co., New York.

Stark, B.
1990 Gulf Coast and the Central Highlands of Mexico: Alternative Models for Interaction. *Research in Economic Anthropology* 12:243-285.

Trigger, B. G.
1990 Maintaining Economic Equality in Opposition to Complexity: an Iroquoian Case Study. In *The Evolution of Political Systems: Sociopolitics in Small-Scale Sedentary Societies*, edited by S. Upham, pp. 119-145. School of American Research Advanced Seminar Series, Cambridge University Press, Cambridge.

Upham, S. (editor)
1990 *The Evolution of Political Systems: Sociopolitics in Small-Scale Sedentary Societies*. School of American Research Advanced Seminar Series, Cambridge University Press, Cambridge.

Voorhies, B.
1976 *The Chantuto People: An Archaic Period Society of the Chiapas Littoral, Mexico*. Papers of the New World Archaeological Foundation No. 41. Brigham Young University, Provo.

Voorhies, B. (editor)
1989 *Ancient Economies of the Soconusco: The Prehistory and History of the Economic Development in the Coastal Lowlands of Chiapas, Mexico*. University of Utah Press, Salt Lake City.

Voorhies, B., and D. Kennett
1995 Buried Sites on the Soconusco Coastal Plain, Chiapas, Mexico. *Journal of Field Archaeology* 22:65-79.

Voorhies, B., and G. H. Michaels
1989 *Final Report to National Geographic Society: Grant No. 3689-87*. Ms. on file, National Geographic Society, Washington, D.C., and Department of Anthropology, University of California, Santa Barbara.

Wilson, P. J.
1988 *The Domestication of the Human Species*. Yale University Press, New Haven.

Woodburn, J.
1982 Egalitarian Societies. *Man* (N.S.) 17:431-51.

Yellen, J. E.
1977 *Archaeological Approaches to the Present*. Academic Press, New York.

6

Early Formative Societies
in Guatemala and El Salvador

Mary E. Pye, Arthur A. Demarest, and Barbara Arroyo

The Pacific Coastal plain of El Salvador and Guatemala is a strip of land ranging from only 10 to 20 km wide in El Salvador, and some 20 to 170 km in Guatemala. Numerous rivers run off the volcanic slopes to create one of the most fertile areas in southeastern Mesoamerica, while rich marine, estuarine, and riverine resources make the coastal plain an ideal area for fishing, gathering, and hunting. This corridor has also always been a natural trade route between the Isthmus of Tehuantepec and Central America (Figure 1). Given its ecology, it is no surprise that this corridor has

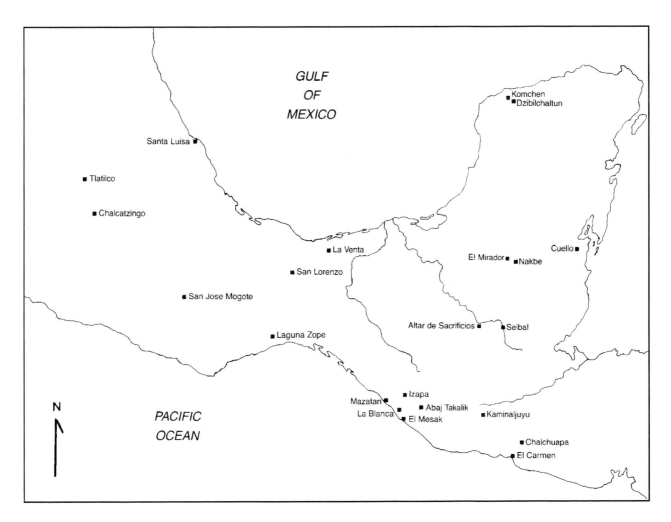

Figure 1. Some Early and Middle Formative Sites in Mesoamerica.

proven to be one of the richest areas of evidence for the origins of complex society in eastern Mesoamerica.

Early Research

Edwin Shook carried out one of the earliest surveys of the Guatemalan coastal plain (Shook 1948, 1965). Extensive Early and Middle Formative occupations were found in the Suchiate and Naranjo River valleys. Within these two river drainages, there are numerous sites from the shoreline to about 40 km inland, especially concentrated along the tributaries of these rivers (Shook 1965:185). Many of these Early and Middle Formative occupations are found beneath dense Late Preclassic and Late Classic remains.

Michael Coe (1961) selected and excavated at one of the Early Formative mounds in the far western Naranjo Valley. This site, La Victoria, is located approximately 2.5 km from the ocean, adjacent to an extinct lagoon system. It consists of 10 mounds all under 2 m in height. From his test excavations, Coe recovered both ceramic and ecological remains which indicated a subsistence pattern heavily reliant on marine and riverine resources. The ceramics of his Early Formative Ocós phase included iridescent, red-rimmed tecomates, some with banana tripod feet, the hallmark ceramic form of this culture (Figure 2). Stratigraphically above and slightly mixed with this Early Formative Ocós occupation, Coe encountered the later Middle Formative Conchas phase (ca. 800-400 B.C.). The stratigraphic position of Conchas material over Ocós, as well as similarities in the ceramics, led Coe to believe that the Early Formative Ocós phase developed directly into the Middle Formative Conchas phase (1961).

Coe and Flannery (1967) returned to the Naranjo area in an attempt to find occupations earlier than Ocós. They chose the site of Salinas La Blanca which consisted of two adjacent mounds on a salt flat 2 km from the ocean and across the Naranjo River from La Victoria. Test pit excavations revealed the existence of two other Formative period phases: Cuadros and Jocotal. These complexes also used tecomates, although they are thicker, unslipped, and have distinctive decorative motifs (Figures 3 and 4). After refining Coe's (1961) ceramic typology, Coe and Flannery (1967) argued that the Cuadros and Jocotal phases represented the transition between the Early and Middle Preclassic periods and should therefore be inserted between the Ocós and Conchas phases. They presented a cultural sequence which had the Ocós phase tentatively dated from 1300 to 1100 B.C., Cuadros from 1000 to 850 B.C., Jocotal from 850 to 800 B.C., and finally the Middle Formative Conchas from 800 to 300 B.C. (Coe and Flannery 1967:70). This sequence was essentially supported by numerous New World Archaeological Foundation excavations in Chiapas during the 1960s and 1970s (Green and Lowe 1967; Lowe 1978; Lowe 1975; Ceja Tenorio 1985). Ongoing research by the N.W.A.F. and others has continued to amplify and refine the sequence (Clark et al. 1987, 1990; Blake 1991; Blake et al. 1995). Earlier precursors of the Ocós phase (now dated from 1250 to 1100 B.C.) have been discovered: the Barra phase (1550-1400 B.C.) and the Locona phase (1400-1250 B.C.) (Blake and Clark, Chapter 5).[1] Locona

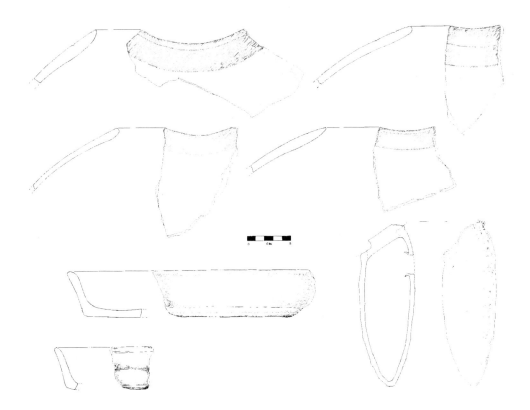

Figure 2. Typical Ocós Phase Ceramics from El Mesak, Guatemala.

phase ceramics have also been identified in Guatemala (Figure 5).

Shook and Hatch (1979) returned to Salinas La Blanca to test Coe and Flannery's (1967) chronology. A test pit was placed in the mound adjacent to their earlier excavation. Shook and Hatch found both Jocotal and Cuadros components, but below the Cuadros level, they also discovered new ceramic forms which they named the Navarijo complex. The new forms included tear-shaped tecomates distinct from the Cuadros phase Guamuchal Brushed types, and a distinctive cream-orange slipped ware. Guamuchal Brushed tecomates appeared in the upper level of the Navarijo mound suggesting that the Navarijo forms were antecedent to the Cuadros types. Notably, these Navarijo types were strikingly different from the Ocós phase materials, leading Shook and Hatch (1979:170-3) to argue that the Navarijo phase was probably coeval with Ocós and represented an unrelated ceramic tradition.

Farther east, at the site of El Bálsamo, Department of Escuintla, another Early Preclassic occupation was revealed when a mound was bulldozed during construction activity. This impressive site is located 40 km inland from the Pacific Ocean, and contains a number of pyramid mounds 1-5 m in height, constructed around two plazas. Also present are numerous jade artifacts and stone sculptures. The earliest ceramic material, named Coastal Undifferentiated Ware, was recovered from the surface and two test pits on the 2 m high Structure 1 which had originally stood about 6-8 m high (Shook and Hatch 1978). Forms and

decorative modes, especially of tecomates, correspond to Guamuchal Brushed of the Cuadros phase although "...one (Cuadros type) blends into the next (Jocotal type) without having distinct limits," and so the excavators could not easily distinguish between them (Shook and Hatch 1978:8). From analysis of the materials, they postulated that the Middle Preclassic was the primary period of occupation at the site.

Even farther east, at the site of Chalchuapa, in the Department of Ahuachapan, El Salvador, Sharer found Early Preclassic artifacts which he assigned to the Tok phase, dated to 1200 B.C. (Sharer 1978). Upon further reassessment of Tok ceramics, Demarest (1989) suggests that the bulk of the material, in particular the Macanse type, may only date to about 900 B.C. Near Chalchuapa, but closer to the coast at the site of San Nicholás, ceramics generally related to the Cuadros and Jocotal phase materials have also been reported (Navarrete 1972).

Other scattered distributions of Early Preclassic materials have been reported for southeastern Mesoamerica. A deeply buried component found at Copán contains some sherds similar to coastal Locona and Ocós phase ceramics and other sherds somewhat like coastal Cuadros phase ceramics (Fash and Viel 1992). Sharer and Sedat (1987) have a similar pattern in the Salama Valley, Guatemala. Ocós-like material is found in the Xox ceramic complex, while modal similarities to Cuadros and Jocotal phase ceramics appear in the late Xox and Max phases.

Overall, the pattern could be understood, up until the

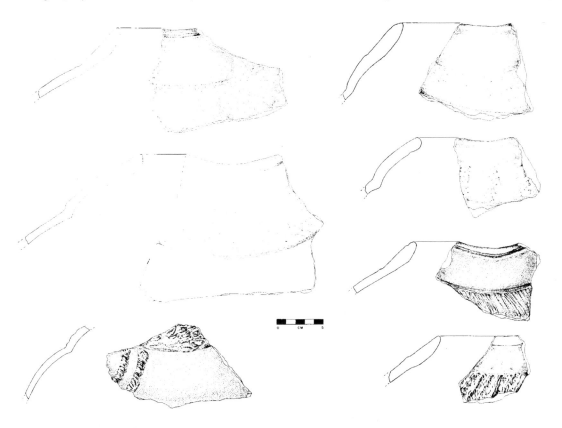

Figure 3. Typical Cuadros Phase Ceramics from El Mesak, Guatemala.

mid-1980s, as one of a continuous and complete, yet poorly understood, Early Preclassic culture (Ocós, Navarijo, Cuadros, Jocotal) with only scattered indications of its existence further to the east and south. At that time, it was not known whether the scarcity of materials east of the Department of San Marcos, and dated to before 1000 B.C., was the result of poor sampling or reflected the actual end of this early isthmian ceramic culture somewhere just beyond the Río Naranjo. As we will discuss below, researchers in the last four years have now demonstrated that the problem is one of sampling and that a rich initial Preclassic culture, very similar to that reported for Chiapas, probably extended along the Pacific coast, southeastward into western El Salvador. The degree of penetration of this culture inland and beyond western El Salvador remains unknown, but even so, new research has greatly extended the known distribution of what is generally referred to as "Greater Isthmian" culture (Lowe 1978).

Turning to culture-historical and processual considerations, it would be easy to criticize the flaws of the archaeological research carried out in the 1960s and 1970s. However, when viewed in historical perspective, one can see steady changes in the nature of the interpretations that were made. Coe's (1961) work at La Victoria initially produced a flawed chronology. Nevertheless, it also provided the first major evidence that Early Formative culture had a separate origin from the well-known early cultures of the Valley of Mexico. It helped to turn the attention of a small cadre of capable researchers to the lowlands and swampy coastal areas of Mesoamerica that we now know provided the

foundation for one of the earliest complex societies of Mesoamerica. Coe and Flannery's (1967) subsequent research at Salinas La Blanca consisted of two "telephone booth" excavations, later the source of self-deprecation by Flannery (1976). Still, viewed in its contemporary context their study was innovative in both approach and interpretation. It was heavily oriented to ecology, stressing analysis of the faunal and paleobotanical remains. More importantly, their characterization of the use of diverse microenvironments (Coe and Flannery 1964) by these early Preclassic cultures turned specialists' attention to the riverine and maritime aspects of these early societies and away from the assumption that cultural complexity and village life comes only with maize-dominated agriculture. Finally, the various studies of Shook and Hatch (1978, 1979) were perhaps overly concerned with ceramic chronology and taxonomy and shared the methodology of the "telephone booth," yet their challenges to the chronologies and discussion of the Navarijo phase turned our attention to regional differentiation within the Early Preclassic cultures and to variability in the rate of their spread—a theme which Hatch has explored and documented in her most recent research (Hatch 1989).

So each of these studies, and the subsequent discussion and debates represented an advance in our understanding of the southeast coast. Still, however ably researched and interpreted, the major problem with these studies was that they were all based on very small excavations. A total of five or six test pits and small trenches were the basis for all discussion and interpretation. The controversies surround-

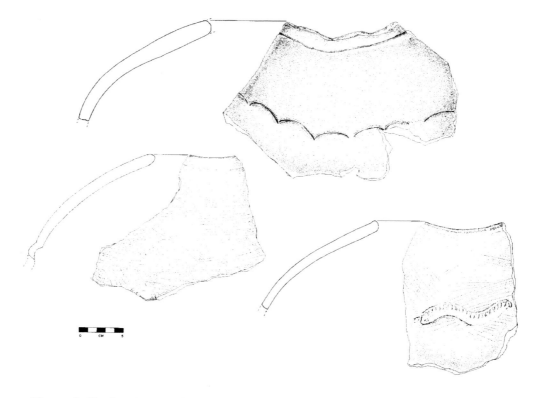

Figure 4. Typical Jocotal Phase Ceramics from El Mesak, Guatemala.

78

ing chronology, the regional extent of these cultures, their relationship to the sequences to the west in Chiapas, and even their basic nature can all be attributed to the attempt to extract a view of a vast area from a small excavated sample. The researchers who embarked on a series of projects in the late 1980s (Hatch, Bove, Love, and the present authors) were all determined to increase the physical sample of materials, regional coverage, and especially, the sheer volume of excavated Early Formative deposits. The new insights which are emerging in Guatemalan Formative cultures are primarily attributable to the increased bulk of relevant materials studied.

Recent Research

Knowledge of the Early and Middle Formative periods on the Pacific coast of Guatemala has been greatly expanded and refined by a number of projects in the past several years. Love's research (Love 1986, 1989, 1991) in western San Marcos Department has given us the first regional settlement pattern study of Early and Middle Formative sites in Guatemala. His excavations at La Blanca are also providing a detailed understanding of the Conchas phase (850-650 B.C.) chiefdoms on the coast (Love 1991, see Chapter 7).

Excavations at the site of El Bálsamo have revealed networks of local and interregional exchange suggesting considerable cultural complexity (Stark et al. 1985; Heller and Stark 1989). At present, there is some debate as to whether primary mound construction, residential occupation at the site, and trade networks occurred during the Middle Formative as posited by Shook and Hatch (1978), or in the Late Formative as recently proposed by Stark and colleagues (1985). Their re-interpretation is based on the dating of specific ceramic types. This issue is at present unresolved, and must be addressed "before any definitive models of South Coast evolution can be tested adequately" (Bove 1989a:7).

Other important Early and Middle Formative discoveries include the site of Vista Hermosa located 3 km from the coast in the Department of Escuintla (Bove 1981, 1989b). Middle Formative ceramic types were found in the materials of his surface survey making this perhaps the earliest site in the area with public architecture (Bove 1981:105). A preliminary reconnaissance of the coast of Jutiapa and Santa Rosa was undertaken in 1985 (Demarest et al. 1992). Figurine heads in the Middle Formative Conchas phase style (Demarest 1987) were found, but no definite Early Formative occupations were discovered, perhaps due to the heavy alluviation in the area. Finally, excavations are presently underway at the site of Abaj Takalik, Department of Retalhuleu, under the direction of Orrego Corzo (1988), which should contribute to a better understanding of the nature and chronology at that important Middle to Late Formative center.

The largest corpus of new evidence on the Early Formative in Guatemala comes from extensive excavations at the site of El Mesak (Demarest et al. 1988; Pye and Demarest 1991; Pye 1990, 1995). El Mesak, located to the east of Champerico in the Department of Retalhuleu, is in an area of rich estuaries and swamps. Bove discovered the site in 1986, and the Vanderbilt University investigations were carried out in 1987 and 1988. We explored an extensive site system consisting of over 50 mounds spread along the edge of a lagoon and dense mangrove (Figure 6).

Excavations at El Mesak uncovered living floors and associated features, ceramics, and other artifacts, and subsistence remains that have now been radiocarbon dated to the Locona (1400-1250 B.C.) and Ocós phases (1250-1100 B.C.). More than 60 carbon samples were recovered, but only seven have been analyzed so far (Table 1). Sherds and associated Ocós phase remains are scattered throughout the site, including middens, storage pits, hearths, and living floors. Three Ocós phase components (Mounds 1, 3, and 11) also contained Locona phase ceramics.

Preservation of fauna at El Mesak was excellent in all deposits and has provided an interesting picture of the Early Formative diet and subsistence strategy. Preliminary studies by Wake and Hyland (1989) reveal a mixed subsistence system with a reliance on a wide variety of aquatic resources, including more than 28 varieties of mollusks, and other animals such as crab, catfish, grunts, ciclids, and gar. Other animals so far identified include crocodile, deer, monkey, and various reptiles birds. Farming may have been

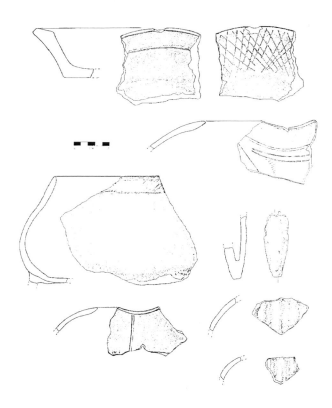

Figure 5. Typical Locona Phase Ceramics from El Mesak.

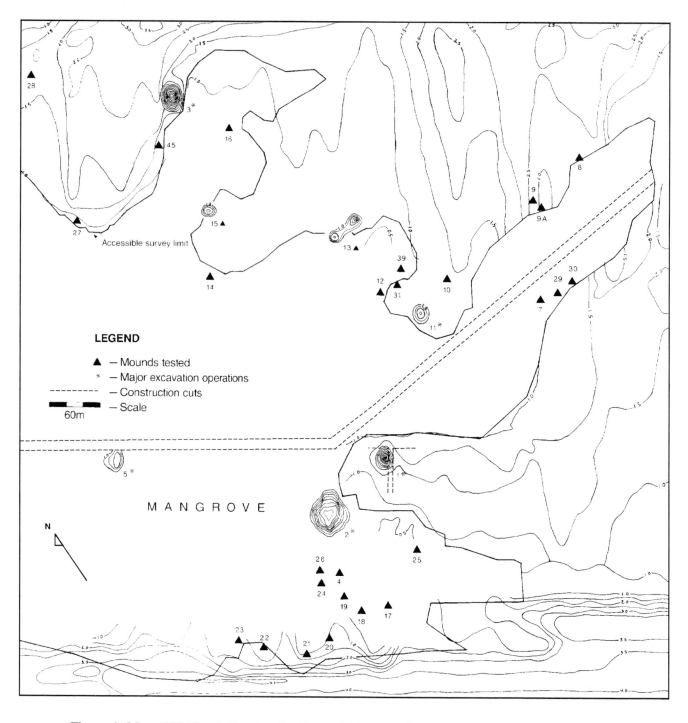

Figure 6. Map of El Mesak Showing the Site and Mangrove Lagoon System with Mounds Tested—(▲), and Mounds with Major Excavations—(✳).

only a minor supplement to the regional diet at El Mesak. Work is continuing on these materials to uncover potential chronological trends in subsistence patterns, as well as the seasonality of resource exploitation.

In one area of El Mesak, overlying a Locona occupation, was a 6.5 meter high mound, the tallest at the site. Deep excavations into this mound by Marion Hatch, indicate that it was a ceremonial construction of carefully selected sand

fills. All of the ceramic remains are of Ocós style and it dates to 1090±60 B.C., indicating that it was constructed, using Ocós fill, at the end of, or immediately following the Ocós phase. The existence of this mound in the late Ocós phase indicates a much greater degree of social complexity than earlier research had revealed (Coe 1961; Coe and Flannery 1967).

To the east, in western El Salvador, the important new

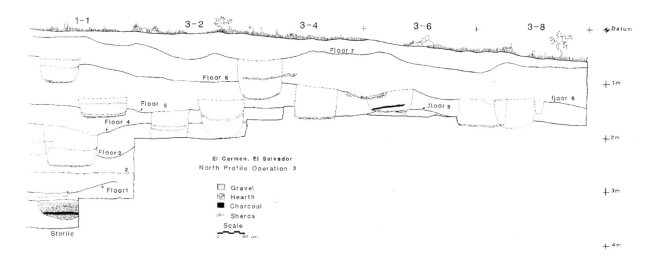

Figure 7. North Profile of Operation 3 at El Carmen, Showing Floors and Hearths.

site of El Carmen consists of a single large mound also adjacent to a mangrove system. Excavations there in 1988, by Arroyo and colleagues (1989a, 1989b), uncovered a finely stratified series of occupation floors, storage pits, hearths, and middens (Figure 7). Also uncovered was an unusual deposit consisting of an occupation area with seven sequential floors, probably the household remains of an extended family. Two hearths at the edges of the mound

and one at the center, as well as fourteen well-defined storage pits, provided both carbon and evidence of early corn agriculture. From the stratigraphy and placement of the features, there seem to have been two different occupations at El Carmen. The first one was associated with the three hearths found inside sterile soil. These hearths suggest a specialized and/or seasonal occupation; no metates or seed remains were associated with the hearths, so the first occupation may not have involved agriculture. The later seven occupation floors and associated storage pits were possibly more permanent. These posterior floors and storage pits did uncover metates, manos, and seed remains.

The associated ceramic assemblage is a variant of the Locona complex (Figure 8), with red-rimmed tecomates,

Figure 8. Metalio Type Sherds Resembling the Locona Complex.

Table 1. Radiocarbon Dates from El Mesak, Guatemala, and El Carmen, El Salvador.

Site	Sample Number	Uncalibrated Radiocarbon date	
		Age B.P.	Date B.C.
El Mesak		Beta-30297	3460±60
			1510 ± 120
	Beta-27088	3140±100	1190±200
	Beta-30295	3060±80	1110±160
	Beta-27090	3040±70	1090±140
	Beta-30703	2890±65	940±130
	Beta-27089	2860±70	910±140
	Beta-30298	2840±60	890±120
El Carmen	Beta 29794	3130±80	1180±160
	Beta 29795	3430±90	1480±180
	Beta 29796	3150±90	1200±180
	Beta 29797	3220±90	1270±180

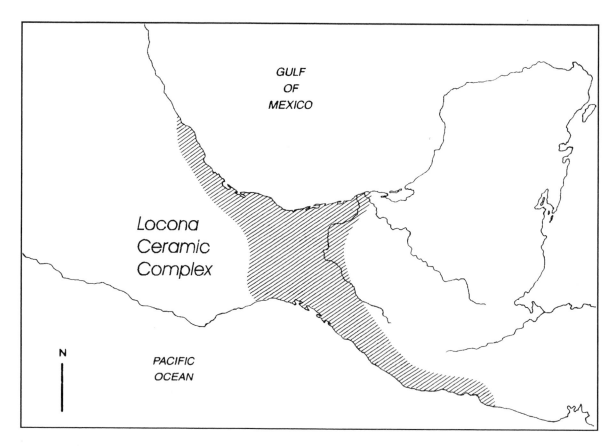

Figure 9. Locona Ceramic Complex Distribution.

most often with diagnostic early Locona modes including grooved lines, slight necks and cross-hatched burnished zones (Arroyo et al. 1989a, 1989b; Arroyo 1990, 1991). Carbon samples dating from 1480 to 1180 B.C. (Table 1) correspond to the dating of the Locona complex in Chiapas (Blake et al. 1995).

The identification and the location of El Carmen in El Salvador greatly increases the known area of distribution of the Locona and Ocós complexes, raising questions about the precise significance of this vast area of artifact similarity. The nature and mechanisms of the spread of the Locona complex are now becoming one of the central questions of the Early Formative era.

The Locona Phase Pattern Emerges

The research at El Mesak and El Carmen, combined with the studies in the Mazatán region of Chiapas, clearly indicates the existence of a unified and widespread ceramic complex in the Early Formative. In the Mazatán region, Clark and Blake (1989, 1994; Clark 1991, 1994) have termed it the Locona phase (1400-1250 B.C.), which appears to be similar to other complexes ranging all the way from Veracruz across the isthmus along the Pacific coast from Chiapas to El Salvador (Figure 9). These similarities include the red-rimmed tecomate forms, flaring-wall, flat-

bottomed bowls, and rocker-stamping and shell impression decorative motifs. This Early Formative tradition or "Greater Isthmian Region" forms the basis of a shared cultural substratum which eventually evolves by the Middle Formative into a series of regional chiefdoms (Demarest 1989).

An obvious interpretive problem will be elucidating in socio-processual terms the significance of this regional similarity in ceramics. A number of alternative hypotheses can be suggested. Previously, Lowe (1977) has attributed this early Ocós distribution to the unified ethnic character of the Mixe-Zoque speaking peoples of the isthmus and adjacent coastal plain. Needless to say, we should be cautious about moving from ceramic similarities to ethnic and linguistic interpretations. The new evidence from El Mesak and El Carmen could be seen to strengthen the Mixe-Zoque hypothesis, but, in fact, the extent of Locona ceramic distribution has now become so great as to require a vast early distribution of the Mixe-Zoque language group, an issue which we will leave to the linguists to examine. Alternative hypotheses could invoke intense economic exchange along this trade corridor or, as Clark and Blake (1989, 1994) have done, posit an interrelated or allied series of political units, what they have dubbed the "Mokaya" group (Clark 1991, 1994).

Again, we feel that such interpretations are intriguing, but at this point extremely speculative. A simpler, but not improbable, possibility is that the widespread distribution and uniformity of Ocós and Locona complexes may have represented the initial introduction of ceramic technology. Clark and Blake have presented evidence that the Ocós and Locona cultures have their antecedents in the Barra culture best known from the coast of Chiapas. Yet even there, Barra materials are relatively rare, restricted in distribution, and, according to Clark and Blake (1989, 1994, Chapter 5) are possibly the result of artistic elaboration of a pre-existing gourd decorative tradition, rather than being widespread functional materials. It seems likely to us that, wherever its origin, the Locona ceramic complex might have been rapidly spread as a technological innovation with great functional utility. Archaeological, historic, and ethnographic studies have shown that technology can spread rapidly across cultural political boundaries. Decorative styles, on the other hand, tend to be more closely linked to regional ethnic cultures.

Thus, the initial introduction of ceramic technology to societies throughout the isthmus and down the coast of Central America could represent such a unique situation of the introduction of new technology. The Locona ceramic complex may have been the first such technology introduced into a given region, therefore, most of the repertoire of stylistic elements remained since the complex was moving into a vacuum—cultures which previously had little or no ceramics, and therefore, no local regional style that would provide a conservative tradition against new stylistic influences (cf. Wright 1989; Wobst 1977; Barth 1969). Such an interpretation, while no more strongly supported by the current evidence, is easily testable since it posits that Locona would be the first ceramic complex in a particular region.[2] Furthermore, Occam's Razor dictates that we should give this processually simpler hypothesis serious consideration before we turn to interpretations of the Locona distribution as a product of migration, ethnic expansion, or related political units.

Transition to the Middle Formative: The Cuadros and Jocotal Phases

While the chronological development of the Locona and Ocós ceramic complexes are becoming clearer and better documented, the relationship of these to succeeding phases remains obscure in Guatemala. Some mounds at El Mesak do contain well-preserved deposits of Cuadros phase remains, now dated in Chiapas to between 1000 to 900 B.C. Mound 5 at El Mesak has several levels of Cuadros phase materials which contain the diagnostic Guamuchal Brushed tecomates. However, the Navarijo Type 1B tecomates as well as the cream-orange slipped ware (Shook and Hatch 1979) were also found with the Guamuchal material.

While the presence of these ceramics at El Mesak confirms the existence of Navarijo types and indicates a relationship between Navarijo and Cuadros, it also suggests that the Navarijo material could represent an early type or

an early facet of the Cuadros phase. The El Mesak Navarijo tecomates are tear-shaped with slightly out-curved or everted, smoothed rim bands and raked body surfaces; all examples measure 17-18 cm in orifice diameter. Given their more "jar-like" and "standardized" aspect, these Navarijo forms, in contrast to the globular tecomates of Guamuchal Brushed, may represent a functional ceramic type of earlier Cuadros assemblages. In addition, Clark and Blake (Clark et al. 1987; Blake et al. 1995) have defined a new phase between Ocós and Cuadros—the Cherla phase (1100-1000 B.C.). Navarijo forms show some similarities with the Cherla forms. However, the samples of Navarijo material from both El Mesak and the Navarijo Mound at Salinas La Blanca samples are at present fairly small. The transition from Ocós to Cuadros remains unclear in Guatemala. Future excavation is planned at El Mesak in other mounds with Cuadros material which, we hope, will clarify the relation of Ocós to the later Navarijo and Cuadros phases, as well as to the Cherla phase in Chiapas.

Coe and Flannery (1967) viewed the Jocotal ceramic complex as clearly a short period of transition between the Cuadros and Conchas phases. The excavators stressed the continuity seen in both subsistence and settlement patterns. However, it should be noted that the Jocotal material comprised a significantly smaller percentage of the total material of the excavations and was located only in the very upper, generally disturbed, levels of the Salinas La Blanca mound.. This suggests that, rather than being a generally

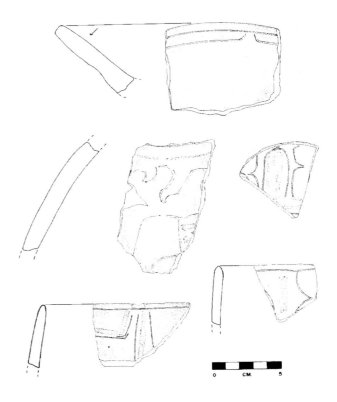

Figure 10. Jocotal Phase Ceramics with So-called "Olmec" Motifs.

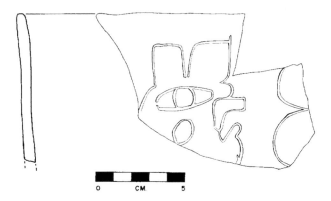

Figure 11. "Olmec Were-jaguar" Motif on White, Fine-paste Cylinder.

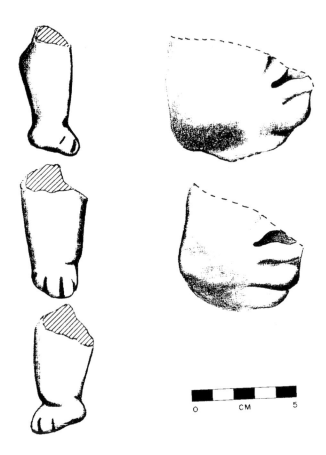

Figure 12. Fragment of "Olmec" Baby Figure and Limb Fragments from Late Jocotal Figurines.

ephemeral and short-lived complex, the Jocotal phase was simply not as well-represented as the Cuadros phase at Salinas La Blanca.

Recent systematic survey of the Naranjo River basin by Love (1989, 1991) suggests a settlement pattern shift occurred between the Ocós and Cuadros/Jocotal phases. The distribution of Ocós sites occurs along the coast and interior, while in the Cuadros/Jocotal phases, he notes a preference for site locations close to estuaries and mangroves. Discrete differences between the Cuadros and Jocotal phases could not be defined because the ceramic material was found mixed in the surface collections. Similar problems in the definition of the Jocotal phase also occur in the eastern coastal area of Chiapas adjacent to Guatemala; Jocotal phase components most commonly occur at the surface and are highly eroded (Clark et al. 1990). Farther west along the Chiapas coast, excavations at the sites of Tzutzuculli (McDonald 1983, Pampa el Pajón (Paillés 1980), and the inland site of Mirador (Agrinier 1984) have revealed Cuadros and Jocotal related occupations. At these sites, the Jocotal sample is larger and shows the clearer evolution of these sites into major centers of the subsequent Middle Formative era.

Given the relative paucity of Jocotal material in Guatemala, the most informative deposit of this phase is definitely Mound 2 at El Mesak. It is a large, wide mound measuring approximately 100 m in diameter and approximately 4.5 m in height, with an exposed road cut creating a stratigraphic profile of more than 26 m in length. Extensive excavation into the mound's stratigraphic profile revealed many finely-laminated layers of occupation floors and midden deposits spanning the Jocotal phase. Preliminary analysis of the El Mesak materials shows the transition from late Cuadros to Jocotal, subsequent development of Jocotal forms, and appearance of initial Conchas features. Comparison of the El Mesak Jocotal material to the Salinas La Blanca ceramics examined by both Coe and Flannery (1967) and Shook and Hatch (1979), suggests that the Salinas La Blanca tecomates characterized as "typical Jocotal phase" actually occur very

late in the Jocotal phase. More "typical" Jocotal tecomates have some trace of a rim band, albeit less exaggerated than Cuadros tecomates. In Chiapas, material from Mirador (Suchiate phase [Agrinier 1984:Figure 44b-g,i,m]), and Pampa El Pajón (Islas phase Variety 2 [Paillés 1980:Figure 29]) provide good examples of these forms which are most characteristic of the Jocotal phase. Statistical analysis of Mound 2 ceramics at El Mesak should give us a more refined chronological development of the tecomate tradition for the Early to Middle Formative transition. Continuing study of materials recovered from the 23 Jocotal stratigraphic levels will not only help define and seriate this poorly known phase, but also clarify the evolution of social and economic complexity at the end of the Early Formative period.

Operations on top of Mound 2 also recovered evidence of a village dating to the end of the Early Formative period at about 950-800 B.C. From the domestic refuse of this village, sherds were found of the Tacaná Incised variety seen in Chiapas, carrying iconographic motifs of the so-called "Olmec" style, including cleft heads, flame eyebrows, clover leafs, and star or lozenge shapes (Figure 10). Close resemblances can be seen in the El Mesak fine white wares, Temblor Incised from Salinas La Blanca, Tacaná Incised at

Altamira (Green and Lowe 1967:119), Socorro Fine Gray in Oaxaca (Drennan 1976:34), and Amatzinac White at the distant site of Chalcatzingo (Guillén 1987:211-22). These sherds include examples of stylized Olmec were-jaguar images (Figure 11).

In this region, such vessels have generally been considered an elite ceramic tied to the Middle Formative Olmec phenomenon. Nonetheless, here they seem to gradually evolve from slightly thicker local white wares found in the lower early Jocotal levels of the Mound 2 midden. Other artifacts, including a fragment of a baby-faced figurine (Figure 12) and several fragments of fine jade celts, suggest wider contacts or an elite presence. At this time, we are not certain what the presence of such "elite" markers might mean. One possibility is that, contrary to general interpretation, these elements are not truly elite markers, but were more widely distributed. Another possibility is that the El Mesak estuary could have functioned as a portage on a southeast Mesoamerican trade route during the Early and Middle Formative periods. Sharer and others have posited a major trade route along the Pacific Coast and up the Río Paz near Chalchuapa to the Motagua River valley jade source and nearby Ixtepeque obsidian source (Sharer 1989; Demarest 1989).

In general, the extent, depth, and gradual evolution of cultures represented by the Jocotal deposits at El Mesak tends to imply a phase that is both longer and includes within it a considerably greater degree of cultural development than was previously thought. Love has observed that the subsequent Middle Formative Conchas phase saw a burst of cultural development as manifested in settlement hierarchy, elite goods, and ceremonial construction at ceremonial centers like La Blanca (Love 1991). However, the complexity and development of the Jocotal sequence at El Mesak could be seen as indicative of a local evolutionary process. There are no grounds to argue that the El Mesak Jocotal component is in anyway atypical, as it is the only extensive Jocotal deposit yet excavated in Guatemala. Future research will seek to link the El Mesak Jocotal and earlier materials to settlement studies of the region and to the transition from Early to Middle Formative cultures at other sites on the western coast of Guatemala (Pye 1989).

Conclusions

The recent research briefly characterized here has built upon two decades of work in the area. Nevertheless, it is still based upon a fairly small corpus of excavated material. Recent studies have altered our conceptions in several ways regarding the various phases of the Early Formative period.

The most intriguing pattern to emerge concerns the extensive distribution of the Locona and complexes. The origin, spread, and social correlates of this wide distribution of stylistically related material is, as yet, poorly understood. Previously, shared stylistic elements and even linguistic commonalities have been attributed to a hypothesized late Early Formative "Olmec" expansion and dominance of the area from their centers in Veracruz and Tabasco (Campbell and Kaufman 1976). It is now apparent that the period of greatest stylistic uniformity occurred centuries earlier during the Locona and Ocós phases, and that the shared features of later cultures throughout this zone results from the processes that generated the Locona distribution at the beginning of the Formative era. The new evidence has shown that the later developments of the Cuadros and Jocotal complexes as well as the subsequent chiefdoms of the Middle Formative can best be viewed in terms of the gradual evolution and subsequent regionalization of this Locona substratum, rather than in terms of intrusive complexes or foreign influences.

This interpretation sets the stage for what should logically be the next phase of Early Formative research along the Guatemalan and El Salvadoran littorals: regional ecological studies, studies of site differentiation, and settlement pattern studies. Moving beyond the comparison of isolated, excavated sites and their assemblages, we can then characterize the economic nature, and cultural evolution of societies in each of these regions. Only then will it be possible to define the interplay between local adaptation and outside influences in the development of the first complex societies along the Pacific coast of Central America.

Notes

1. Dates for these Early and Middle Formative phases are presented in uncalibrated form. For the complete sample of recent radiocarbon dates from the Soconusco region, on which the absolute dating of the phase sequence is based, see Blake et al. (1995).

2. However, this is obviously not the case for the Mazatán region where we have known for more than 20 years of the presence of an earlier Barra phase ceramic complex (Lowe 1975; Ceja Tenorio 1985).

References Cited

Agrinier, P.
1984 *The Early Olmec Horizon of Mirador, Chiapas, Mexico.* Papers of the New World Archaeological Foundation No. 48. Brigham Young University, Provo.

Arroyo, B.
1990 Early Formative Ceramics from El Salvador: Sitio El Carmen. Paper presented at the 55th Annual Meetings of the Society for American Archaeology., Las Vegas.
1991 El Formativo Temprano en Chiapas, Guatemala y El Salvador. *Utz'ib* 1(1):7-13.

Arroyo, B., A. A. Demarest, and P. Amaroli
1989a Informe Preliminar: Proyecto El Carmen, El

Salvador. Final Report Submitted to the Dirección General del Patrimonio Cultural, El Salvador. Ms. on file, Department of Anthropology, Vanderbilt University, Nashville.

Arroyo, B., A. A. Demarest, P. Amaroli, and T. Jackson
1989b The El Carmen Site, El Salvador: New Information on the Early Preclassic of Southeastern Mesoamerica. Paper presented at the 54th Annual Meeting of the S.A.A., Atlanta.

Barth, F.
1969 *Nomads of South Persia*. Little, Brown, and Co., Boston.

Blake, M.
1991 Paso de la Amada: An Early Formative Chiefdom in Chiapas,Mexico. In *The Formation of Complex Society in Southeastern Mesoamerica*, edited by W. R. Fowler, Jr., pp. 27-46. CRC Press, Boca Raton.

Blake, M., J. E. Clark, B. Voorhies, G. Michaels, M. W. Love, M. E. Pye, A. A. Demarest, and B. Arroyo
1995 Radiocarbon Chronology for the Late Archaic and Formative Periods on the Pacific Coast of Southeastern Mesoamerica. *Ancient Mesoamerica* 6:161-183.

Bove, F.
1981 *The Evolution of Chiefdoms and States on the Pacific Slope of Guatemala: A Spatial Analysis*. Unpublished Ph.D. dissertation, Dept. of Anthropology, University of California, Los Angeles.
1989a Dedicated to the Costeños: Introduction and New Insights. In *New Frontiers in the Archaeology of the Pacific Coast of Southern Mesoamerica*, edited by F. Bove and L. Heller, pp. 1-14. Anthropological Research Papers No. 39. Arizona State University, Tempe.
1989b *Formative Settlement Patterns on the Pacific Coast of Guatemala: A Spatial Analysis of Complex Societal Evolution*. BAR International Series 493. British Archaeological Reports, Oxford.

Campbell, L., and T. Kaufman
1976 A Linguistic Look at the Olmec. *American Antiquity* 41:81-89.

Ceja Tenorio, Jorge F.
1985 *Paso de la Amada, An Early Preclassic Site in the Soconusco, Chiapas, Mexico*. Papers of the New World Archaeological Foundation No. 49. Brigham Young University, Provo.

Clark, J. E.
1991 The Beginnings of Mesoamerica: Apologia for the Soconusco Early Formative. In *The Formation of Complex Society in Southeastern Mesoamerica*, edited by W. R. Fowler, Jr., pp. 13-26. CRC Press, Boca Raton.
1994 *The Development of Early Formative Rank Societies in the Soconusco, Chiapas, Mexico*. Unpublished Ph.D. dissertation, Department of Anthro-

pology, University of Michigan, Ann Arbor.

Clark, J. E., and M. Blake
1989 El Origen de la Civilización en Mesoamerica: Los Olmecas y Mokaya del Soconusco de Chiapas, México. In *El Preclásico or Formativo: Avances y Perspectivas*, edited by M. Carmona Macías, pp. 385-403. Museo Nacional de Antropología and I.N.A.H., México.
1994 The Power of Prestige: Competitive Generosity and the Emergence of Rank Societies in Lowland Mesoamerica. In *Factional Competition and Political Development in the New World*, edited by E. M. Brumfiel and J. W. Fox, pp. 17-30. Cambridge University Press, Cambridge.

Clark, J. E., M. Blake, P. Guzzy, M. Cuevas, and T. Salcedo
1987 *Proyecto: El Preclásico Temprano en la Costa del Pacífico*. Final Report to the Instituto Nacional de Antropología e Historia, México. Ms. on file, Department of Anthropology, Brigham Young University, Provo.

Clark, J. E., M. Blake, B. Arroyo, M. E. Pye, R. G. Lesure, V. Feddema, and M. Ryan
1990 *Reporte Final Del Proyecto Investigaciones del Formativo Temprano en el Litoral Chiapaneco*. Final Report to the Instituto Nacional de Antropología e Historia, México. Ms. on file, Department of Anthropology, Brigham Young University, Provo.

Coe M. D.
1961 *La Victoria, an Early Site on the Pacific Coast of Guatemala*. Papers of the Peabody Museum of American Archaeology and Ethnology Vol. 53. Harvard University, Cambridge.

Coe, M. D., and K. V. Flannery
1964 Microenvironments and Mesoamerican Prehistory. *Science* 143:650-654.
1967 *Early Cultures and Human Ecology in South Coastal Guatemala*. Smithsonian Contributions to Anthropology Vol. 3. Smithsonian Institution, Washington, D. C.

Demarest, A. A.
1987 Recent Research on the Preclassic Ceramics of the Southeastern Highlands and Pacific Coast of Guatemala. *British Archaeological Reports* 345(1):329-339.
1989 The Olmec and the Rise of Civilization in Eastern Mesoamerica. In *Regional Perspectives on the Olmec*, edited by R. J. Sharer and D. C. Grove, pp. 303-344. School of American Research Advanced Seminar Series, J. Haas, general editor. Cambridge University Press, Cambridge.

Demarest, A. A., B. Arroyo, and S. Medrano
1992 Survey of the Pacific Coast of Guatemala, Departments of Santa Rosa and Jutiapa. Ms. on file, Department of Anthropology, Vanderbilt University, Nashville.

Demarest, A. A., M. E. Pye, J. T. Myers, and R. Mendez
1988　El Proyecto Mar Azul/El Mesak. Preliminary report to Instituto de Antropología e Historia, Guatemala. Ms. on file, Department of Anthropology, Vanderbilt University, Nashville.

Drennan, R.
1976　*Fábrica San José and Middle Formative Society in the Valley of Oaxaca.* Memoirs No. 8. Museum of Anthropology, University of Michigan, Ann Arbor.

Fash, W. and R. Viel
1992　An Early Preclassic Level in Copán, Honduras. Ms. on file, Proyecto Arqueológico Copán, Ruinas de Copán, Honduras.

Flannery, K. V. (editor)
1976　*The Early Mesoamerican Village.* Academic Press, New York.

Green, D., and G. W. Lowe
1967　*Altamira and Padre Piedra, Early Preclassic Sites in Chiapas, Mexico.* Papers of the New World Archaeological Foundation No. 20. Brigham Young University, Provo.

Guillén, A. C.
1987　Ceramics. In *Ancient Chalcatzingo*, edited by D. C. Grove, pp. 200-251. University of Texas Press, Austin.

Hatch, M. P.
1989　Observaciones sobre el desarollo cultural prehistórico en la Costa Sur de Guatemala. In *Investigaciones Arqueológicas en la Costa Sur de Guatemala*, edited by D. Whitley and M. Beaudry, pp.4-36. Institute of Archaeology Monograph No. 31. University of California, Los Angeles.

Heller, L., and B. Stark
1989　Economic Organization and Social Context of a Preclassic Center on the Pacific Coast of Guatemala: El Bálsamo, Escuintla. In *New Frontiers in the Archaeology of the Pacific Coast of Southern Mesoamerica*, edited by F. Bove and L. Heller, pp. 43-64. Anthropological Research Papers No. 39. Arizona State University, Tempe.

Lowe, G. W.
1975　*The Early Preclassic Barra Phase of Altamira, Chiapas.* Papers of the New World Archaeological Foundation No.38. Brigham Young University, Provo.

1977　The Mixe-Zoque as Competing Neighbors of the Maya. In *The Origins of Maya Civilization*, edited by R. E. W. Adams, pp. 197-248. School of American Research Advanced Seminar Series, University of New Mexico Press, Albuquerque.

1978　Eastern Mesoamerica. In *Chronologies in New World Archaeology*, edited by R. E. Taylor and C. W. Meighan, pp. 331-393. Academic Press, New York.

Love, M. W.
1986　Preliminary Report on Archaeological Work in Ocós, San Marcos 1984-85. Report to Instituto de Antropología e Historia, Guatemala. Ms. on file, Department of Anthropology, University of California, Berkeley.

1989　Early Settlements and Chronology of the Río Naranjo. Unpublished Ph.D dissertation, Department of Anthropology, University of California, Berkeley.

1991　Style and Social Complexity in Formative Mesoamerica. In *The Formation of Complex Society in Southeastern Mesoamerica*, edited by W. R. Fowler, Jr., pp. 47-76. CRC Press, Boca Raton.

McDonald, A.
1983　*Tzutzuculli: A Middle Preclassic Site on the Pacific Coast of Chiapas, Mexico.* Papers of the New World Archaeological Foundation No. 47. Brigham Young University, Provo.

Navarrete, C.
1972　El Sitio Arqueológico de San Nicholás, Municipio de Ahuachapan, El Salvador. *Estudios de Cultura Maya* 7:57-66.

Orrego Corzo, M.
1988　Enfoque del Sitio Arqueológico de Abaj Takalik. Paper presented at the Second Symposium of Archaeological Investigations in Guatemala, Guatemala City.

Paillés H., M.
1980　*Pampa El Pajón: An Early Middle Preclassic Site on the Coast of Chiapas, Mexico.* Papers of the New World Archaeological Foundation No. 44. Brigham Young University, Provo.

Pye, M. E.
1989　The Río Jesus Regional Settlement Project: The Evolution of the Cultural System in Southeastern Mesoamerica. Grant Proposal Submitted to the Wenner-Gren Foundation, New York. Ms. on file, Department of Anthropology, Vanderbilt University, Nashville.

1995　*Settlement, Specialization, and Adaptation in the Rio Jesus Drainage, Retalhuleu, Guatemala.* Unpublished Ph.D. dissertation, Department of Anthropology, Vanderbilt University, Nashville.

Pye, M. E. (editor)
1990　Informe Preliminar de los Resultados del Análisis del Laboratório del Proyecto El Mesak. Report submitted to the Instituto de Antropología e Historia, Guatemala. Ms. on file, Department of Anthropology, Vanderbilt University, Nashville.

Pye, M. E., and A. A. Demarest
1991　The Evolution of Complex Societies in Southeastern Mesoamerica: New Evidence from El Mesak, Guatemala. In *The Formation of Complex Society in Southeastern Mesoamerica*, edited by W. R. Fowler, Jr., pp.77-100. CRC Press, Boca Raton.

Sharer, R. J.

1978 Pottery and Conclusions. In *The Prehistory of Chalchuapa, El Salvador* Vol. 3. University of Pennsylvania Press, Philadelphia.

1989 The Olmec and the Southeast Periphery of Meso-america. In *Regional Perspectives on the Olmec*, edited by R. J. Sharer and D. C. Grove, pp. 247-271. School of American Research Advanced Seminar Series, J. Haas, general editor. Cambridge University Press, Cambridge.

Sharer, R. J., and D. Sedat

1987 *Archaeological Investigations in the Northern Maya Highlands, Guatemala: Interaction and the Development of Maya Civilization.* University Museum Monographs No. 59. University of Pennsylvania, Philadelphia.

Shook, E. N.

1948 Guatemala Highlands. *Carnegie Institution of Washington Yearbook, 1946-1947*, pp.214-218. Washington, D. C.

1965 Archeological Survey of the Pacific Coast of Guatemala. In *Archaeology of Southern Mesoamerica Pt. 1*, edited by G. R. Willey, pp. 180-194. Handbook of Middle American Indians, Vol. 2, R. Wauchope, general editor. University of Texas Press, Austin.

Shook, E. N., and M. P. Hatch

1978 The Ruins of El Bálsamo. *Journal of New World Archaeology* 3(1):1-38.

1979 *The Early Preclassic Sequence in the Ocós-Salinas La Blanca Area, South Coast of Guatemala.* Contributions of the University of California Archaeological Research Facility No. 41. University of California, Berkeley.

Stark, B., L. Heller, F. Nelson, R. Bishop, D. Pearsall, D. Whitley, and H. Wells

1985 El Bálsamo Residential Investigations: A Pilot Project and Research Issues. *American Anthropologist* 87:100-111.

Wake, T., and J. Hyland

1989 A Preliminary Analysis of Faunal Remains from El Mesak, Guatemala. Paper presented at the 54th Annual Meeting of the Society for American Archaeology, Atlanta.

Wobst, H. M.

1977 Stylistic Behavior and Information Exchange. In *For the Director: Research Essays in Honor of James B. Griffin*, edited by C. E. Cleland, pp.317-342. Anthropological Papers No. 61, University of Michigan, Ann Arbor.

Wright, R.

1989 New Tracks on Ancient Frontiers: Ceramic Technology on the Indo-Iranian Borderlands. In *Archaeological Thought in America*, edited by C.C. Lamberg-Karlovsky, pp. 268-279. Cambridge University Press, Cambridge.

7

Economic Patterns in the Development of Complex Society in Pacific Guatemala

Michael W. Love

The shift from food-procurement to food-production is viewed by most archaeologists as a critical process in human history. In Mesoamerica, the development of civilization has long been seen as being linked inextricably to the development of agriculture, and especially to the domestication of maize and its propagation as a staple crop (MacNeish 1964). There is little question that maize agriculture provided the subsistence base upon which complex societies in Mesoamerica were built (Grove 1981), but we can question whether the factors linking agriculture and complexity are really well understood. It can be questioned especially whether we understand the historical courses followed by various regional societies between the initial adoption of agriculture and the subsequent appearance of complex societies.

The processes that led to the initial genetic modification and subsequent domestication of maize and other cultivars were undoubtedly crucial to the creation of a sedentary residence pattern (Flannery 1968; Stark 1981). According to evolutionary systems models, this led in turn to more rapid population growth, social disputes in search of regulatory institutions, and new systems of exchange to move geographically constrained products (Stark 1981). Such systems models place emphasis on the interaction of plant genetics, human demography, and the technology linking human societies with plant reproduction. Very little attention is given to the desires or strategies of social actors, other than to assume a desire for maximization and efficiency. Instead, emphasis is placed on the selection and amplification of certain behavioral traits through feedback throughout the system (Flannery 1973).

Although systems models seek to portray domestication and sedentism as processes, rather than events, an inordinate amount of attention is still fixed on origins. What transpires, subsequently, is often viewed as postscript, as though once our subjects were firmly fixed in one place with an array of domesticates the development of civilization was axiomatic. These models do not deny that important innovations followed domestication and sedentism, but posit that the basic cycle of population growth, technological change, and cultural elaboration was set.

Bender's (1978) critique of systems models calls for greater attention to the role of social relations in the intensification of production and the beginnings of both agriculture and sedentism. She notes that while some systems theorists (e.g., Flannery 1973) have attempted to integrate social factors into their models, they still fail to overcome the limits of functionalism and thus cannot view social relations as an active force in change. Bender (1978:214) argued that social relations can be a source of demand on the economy and that "demography and technology are products of social structure rather than independent variables."

Bender does not pursue the subject beyond the initial stages of sedentism and early agriculture. Her model, too, is concerned principally with the question of origins. But while Bender's discussion ostensibly concerns the social causes of sedentism and domestication, a more critical contribution lay in linking social demands and economic transformation; sedentism and domestication are the means of satisfying new demands generated by emergent leaders. Her premise is that the intensification of production associated with sedentism involved the change from a "Domestic Mode of Production" (Sahlins 1972), aimed at meeting household needs, to public economy, aimed at surplus production.

Viewing this shift to a public economy, rather than any particular technological innovation or genetic modifications in cultivars, as fundamental, enables the formulation of a more broadly applicable model. The change in social relations is central, and generates the need for new economic systems. The particular constellation of factors leading to a solution of those economic problems may vary widely.

In the case of Mesoamerica, I argue that the emphasis placed on agricultural "origins" is unwarranted if what we

89

seek to understand is the development of complex society. I maintain that the key process in the development of complex society was not the development of agriculture, but the transformation of agriculture, and other productive technologies, in order to meet social goals. The most important juncture was not any material change, but a change in social relations that organized production. I also propose that the changes seen in agriculture are part of a pattern of economic intensification echoed in other realms of subsistence as well as exchange and non-subsistence production, and that we should not assign a privileged position to agriculture in our models of change.

Here I explore the links between economic change and the development of social complexity in Pacific Guatemala during the Middle Formative period (900-600 B.C.)(Figure 1), when there developed large-scale regional structures of political organization and economic integration, resulting in one of the largest and most powerful societies of Mesoamerica at the time. Agriculture and sedentism had been in place for many centuries, so that the origin of these traits is not at issue. Furthermore, maize had been cultivated in the region for at least 500 years, so its diffusion is also not at issue. At issue is how already existing modes of production, including maize agriculture, were intensified in the process of change. The process I am concerned with in this paper is the economic intensification that transformed the domestic mode of production to one that generated large-scale surpluses for a public economy. I will try to shown that the key factor in these changes was not the creation of new products or technologies, but the adaptation of already existing technologies. What changed was not the material potential for intensification, but the social conditions in which that existing technology was applied.

This discussion will emphasize the fundamental impor tance of including social relations and the choices made by social actors in our models of the formation of complex social institutions. This highlights the need for the development of models that recognize both the role of social actors and the historically defined situations in which they act. Cybernetic models as presently utilized do not give sufficient recognition to the ability of human actors to reflect and act upon their circumstances. Nor do they recognize the unique aspects of historical situations in which social acts take place. A social transformation cannot be understood solely by reference to processes begun millennia earlier, but must also refer to conditions existing at the time of the transformation.

Early Complexity on the Pacific Coast of Mesoamerica

The documentation and understanding of the development of complex society on the Pacific coast of Chiapas, Mexico and Guatemala has important implications for understanding the emergence of civilization in Mesoamerica as a whole. As detailed by Blake and Clark (Chapter 5) and Pye, Demarest, and Arroyo (Chapter 6), the

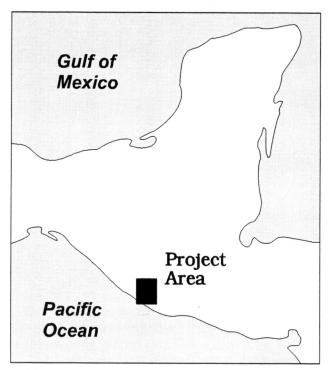

Figure 1. Map of Southern Mesoamerica Showing the Project Area.

societies of this region were among the first in Mesoamerica to exhibit features of complex social organization such as settlement hierarchies, intra-community social inequality, and possibly craft specialization. Clark and Blake (1989, 1994; Clark 1991; Blake 1991) have gathered evidence for this social differentiation as early as the Locona phase (1400-1250 B.C.), and its continuation into the later Ocós (1250-1100 B.C.), Cherla (1100-1000 B.C.), Cuadros (1000-900 B.C.), and Jocotal (900-850 B.C.) phases, ending at about 900 B.C.[1] These developments follow the first appearance of maize and other presumed cultigens during the Barra phase (1550-1400 B.C.) (Blake et al. 1992a, 1992b), and follow from the hunting, gathering, and collection subsistence modes of the Chantuto period (Michaels and Voorhies, Chapter 4).

With the transition to the Middle Formative, which is locally defined as the Conchas phase (ca. 900 to 600 B.C.), the stage shifts from the Mazatán region to the region centered on the Río Naranjo, some 40 km to the east. The complementary patterns of regional demography (with reduced population in Mazatán as population in the Río Naranjo zone increases), the continuity of socio-political change, as well as the similarity and continuity of material culture traits, makes it clear that we are dealing with a single integrated process of change, played out over great time and a relatively large expanse. It should also be clear that the early appearance of complexity and its continued development through time belies any diffusionist argument for the origins of social change in the region. Instead, we must look principally to local processes, although the integration of these processes with pan-Mesoamerican events cannot be denied.

The data presented here come from a settlement survey conducted from 1983 to 1985 and excavations undertaken in 1985. The settlement survey intensively covered an area of approximately 170 km² with less intensive coverage of an additional 30-40 km². Excavations were undertaken at the Middle Formative center of La Blanca. Excavations were limited to residential zones of the site, and all of the botanical, lithic, and faunal remains discussed come from domestic deposits at La Blanca.

The Setting and the Growth of Complexity

The coastal plain of Guatemala and Chiapas was formed by the erosion of sediment from the highlands and its capture in a tectonic trench (Kuenzi, Horst, and McGehee 1979). The recent origin of the soils, which are generally deep and replenished by alluvial and aeolian deposits, makes the area one of the most fertile zones of Central America. Rainfall becomes heavier as one moves inland from the coast, but is generally sufficient to produce at least two crops of maize a year throughout most of the plain (McBryde 1947; Coe 1961). A third crop may be harvested by using humid depressions that occur on the plain 5-12 km

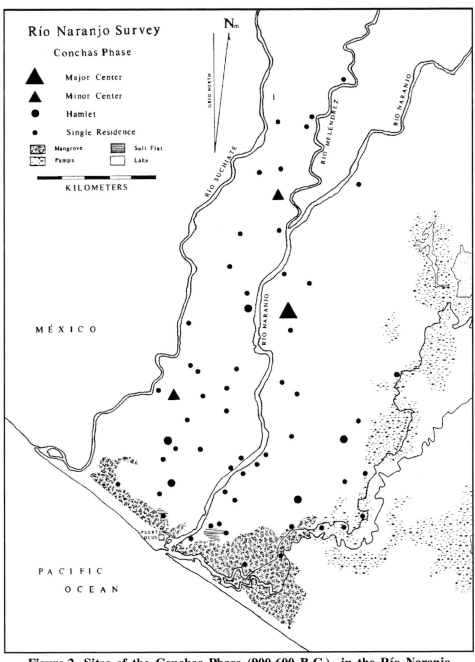

Figure 2. Sites of the Conchas Phase (900-600 B.C.) in the Río Naranjo Region.

Figure 3. La Blanca, Mound 1 as it is Being Destroyed in 1973 (Photo by E. M. Shook).

inland, where the water table is shallow. The extreme coastal areas are subject to flooding in the rainy season, and otherwise suffer from poor drainage and salinity, so that their productivity is limited.

Although there is a tendency for ecological and resource zones to be correlated with distance from the coast, the distribution is much more mosaic than stratified. Edaphic factors vary widely with minor differences in topography, creating patches of poorly drained, low quality soils adjacent to better drained, fertile ones. Two large rivers, the Naranjo and the Suchiate, drain water from the piedmont slopes directly into the ocean, while smaller channels originating on the plain drain through estuary/lagoon systems of immense primary productivity.

During the Early Formative period the occupations present in the Río Naranjo zone were small, with little differentiation, and with population not exceeding 30 households for the region during any single phase. Subsistence during this period does not appear to have been estuarine-oriented, since sites are found evenly distributed across the landscape from the coast to the inland limit of survey. A mixed economy is thus indicated. This supposition for the Río Naranjo zone is supported by research in the Mazatán region where carbonized cultivars have been found in almost all household contexts dating from the Barra

through to the Cuadros phase (Clark et al. 1987, 1990; Blake et al. 1992b)

The size and relative density of sites for the Early Formative suggests that the Río Naranjo region was peripheral to the more nucleated and regionally structured polities of the Mazatán region during this time period. The precise nature of this relationship, as well as the relations with the El Mesak zone to the east, are in need of investigation, but the similarity of the Río Naranjo region's material culture with that of its neighbors indicates a high degree of interaction.

The regional population and its organization changed dramatically at the beginning of the Middle Formative period. The Conchas phase, dated from 900 to 600 B.C., witnessed a massive surge in population, combined with the formation of a multi-tiered settlement hierarchy, dominated by the site of La Blanca (Figure 2) (Love 1989, 1993). The regional population for this phase is estimated at a minimum of 116 households at 56 sites. The complementary demographic patterns from the Mazatán zone and the Río Naranjo zone suggests that part of the population growth in the latter region may be due to the relocation of people from the Mazatán zone (Clark and Blake 1994). The difficulty in locating Middle Formative sites from coastal Retalhuleu (Mark Johnson, personal communication, 1981) may also indicate movement from the El Mesak zone to the Río

Naranjo zone. However, the apparent population explosion that took place in Mesoamerica at this time should make us wary of viewing these possible population movements as the principal cause of growth in the Río Naranjo system.

La Blanca, the paramount settlement of the Río Naranjo zone during the Conchas phase, was one of Mesoamerica's largest settlements at this time. It covered a minimum of 100 hectares and was the site of at least 43 households. Both of these figures are minima, and the destruction of the southern portion of the site may obscure areas of occupation that would double both of those estimates. La Blanca was also the site of immense monumental constructions that may be considered as public or ceremonial structures. The largest of these was Mound 1, a large truncated cone of clay and earth that measured 25 m in height and 140 m by 160 m at its base, according to a map made by the Instituto de Antropología e Historia de Guatemala (Love 1989). This structure was levelled to a height of 2 m in 1973, when it was used as a source of fill for a local highway project (Edwin Shook, personal communication 1981)(Figure 3).

Excavations at La Blanca found differences between thehouseholds in many classes of material culture. In comparison to samples available from regional surface collections and additional excavated households at La Blanca and La Victoria, two of the three residences excavated had more valuables and exotics, such as jade, mica jewelry, fine past ceramics, and decorated earspools. These two residences also had ceramics decorated with motifs and icons not found elsewhere in the region. These icons and symbols included many that might be called "Olmec," but also many without such connotation.[2]

Compared with the Early Formative period, the combination of Conchas phase settlement and excavation data suggest an increase in social and political inequality at both the regional and household levels. This transformation was associated with the development of new forms of material culture, new types of economic organization, and increased social competition.

The Nature of Social Complexity

Elsewhere, I have presented arguments for viewing the development of complex society as consisting in part of the aggregation of separate and possibly competitive groups into an articulated, but not completely integrated social network (Love 1991). There is evidence that during the Middle Formative period in the Río Naranjo region the competition and social negotiation between groups was played out in expressive material culture.

In this view, complex societies are by their nature comprised of many social groups with differing goals and viewpoints, so that models which treat societies as integrated wholes analogous to biological systems are misleading. Groups and individuals, because they have differing goals, will be in frequent conflict and competition, a process that may contribute to social and economic change. These

are by no means the only factors determining the course of social history, because these actions take place within the context of larger social, economic, and ecological settings, but within the local framework they are undeniably significant.

This perspective is quite similar to that presented by Clark and Blake (1994) in their model of the development of complex social forms in the Mazatán area. Both views place an emphasis on social conflict, competition, and negotiation as key forces in change. Before proceeding further, however, I wish to highlight two essential aspects of this model. First, I believe that in the early development of inequality, competition for prestige is generally structured by kinship, so that prestige is not freely floating and available to the highest bidder, but is structured within and between groups. In all societies, inequality is structured by age, sex, and kin relations, and there are no truly "egalitarian" societies. The crucial transition is not the development of inequality per se, but the ranking and evaluation of groups relative to one another (Berreman 1981). This is my reason for emphasizing group relations, rather than those between individuals, such as competitive political aspirants. Secondly, although competition is a social act and evaluations involve social constructions played out through economic means; it is in the economic realm that we find the best evidence of social relations and strategies that shaped group actions. We see reflected in the archaeological record a series of choices among economic resources, technologies, and labor forms that allow those social relations and strategies to be reconstructed.

The Costs of Complexity

The social acts of competition for status and power involve economic costs, as many authors have noted (e.g., Bender 1978; Clark and Blake 1994; Earle 1978; Gilman 1981; Renfrew 1986). The sponsorship of feasts, festivals, and public works, as well as the direct support of followers and other strategies used by political aspirants to increase their power and prestige, produce increasing demands on the economy of the entire society. These and other economic demands were undoubtedly present in the Río Naranjo area by the Conchas phase, as new pressures for labor, goods, and increased subsistence production are evident in the monumental constructions, use of status markers, and increased population.

The studies of social change in proto-historic Hawaiian polities by Goldman (1970) and Earle (1978) provide specific links between competition and economics. Both Goldman and Earle emphasize that competition or status rivalry was an essential aspect of Hawaiian society. Earle (1978:168) develops the observation further and proposes that this competition is financed through a strategy of economic intensification, which created a dual economy, with subsistence and political components:

A subsistence economy has a minimizing strategy for

which the goal is to meet the needs of the household unit. In contrast, a political economy has a maximizing strategy for which the goal is to produce the greatest possible income to finance political aspirations.

The subsistence economy represents a quasi "original state," which Sahlins (1972) labels as the "Domestic Mode of Production." For Sahlins (1972:86), life in the "original state" of the DMP is far worse than nasty, brutish, and short; it is under-productive:

> ...the DMP harbors an anti-surplus principle. Geared to the production of livelihood, it is endowed with the tendency to come to a halt at that point. Hence, if "surplus" is defined as output above the producer's requirements, the household system is not organized for it. Nothing within the structure of production for use pushes it to transcend itself.

Economic intensification requires that the autonomy of the household be undermined and that it be integrated into the larger social fabric. As it is "mobilized in a larger social cause" (Sahlins 1972:130), the productive capacity of the household is unleashed, and a surplus can be extracted from it. It can be said then, that politics is the mother's milk of money (or at least surplus), in that politics provides the motivation for surplus production.

Intensification and loss of household autonomy are twin aspects of the same phenomenon: the adoption of maximizing and surplus producing economic strategies. In the following sections I will present evidence for these two phenomena in the Middle Formative period of Pacific Guatemala. The topic of intensification will be addressed by looking at a series of economic choices made during the Conchas phase by members of that society. Loss of household autonomy will be examined by considering regionalization, or the process by which the household was integrated into a regional economy.

Intensification

"Intensification" is generally taken to mean the process by which the yield of existing resources is increased (Boserup 1965). Kaiser and Voytek (1983:329), in considering the effects of sedentism in Neolithic Europe, note that intensification may take many forms: "(1) intensification proper, an increase in the net labor and resources devoted to productive activity, (2) specialization, the channeling of labor and resources to achieve certain restricted ends, and (3) diversification of labor and resources to produce a greater yield."

Several different strategies of intensification are evident in the economic choices made by the residents of the Formative period Río Naranjo area. I wish briefly to consider three examples of those choices: labor, subsistence production, and lithic production. These three examples show not only that intensification took place in diverse areas of the economy, but that separate and distinct strategies were undertaken in each.

Labor

Labor is the most essential aspect of intensification. As Sahlins (1972:93) notes, in primitive economies the right to things is realized through a hold on persons. The ability to mobilize labor and convert effort into product is the means by which surplus is accumulated.

The first form of intensification named by Kaiser and Voytek, an increase in the net input of labor and resources dedicated to productive activities, could be accomplished by at least three strategies: (1) a rise in per capita labor by increasing the amount of labor performed per worker, (2) by increasing efficiency of labor through improved technology, and (3) an increase in the labor force.

The first alternative is certainly viable, and is the topic that is the principal concern of Sahlin's (1972) comparison of cultural differences, duration, and intensity of labor and the correlation of these with political organization. Moreover, the possible emergence of power relationships and an ideology justifying inequality during the Middle Formative period make such a strategy attractive as an explanation, but there is no direct archaeological correlate of such a process, and further inquiry does not appear possible at this time.

The evidence for more productive technology is certainly evident. Some of these aspects will be discussed in the following section. The third alternative, however, is also viable and is manifested archaeologically. Intensification begins at home, and aspiring individuals or groups must initiate the process of intensification by increasing their own household production. The most direct way to do this is to increase the size of the household. Sahlins (1972:136) notes that in Melanesia, leaders typically seek to enlarge their domestic working force by polygyny. This provides not only additional wives for labor, but also additional offspring for future labor.

While, according to Boserup's (1965) model, agricultural production is intensified at the impetus of population expansion, the strategy considered here views population expansion as itself being a form of intensification. Provided that population increases within a given area, it may be considered to be intensification rather than simple expansion. Given that in an economy directed towards surplus production any working person creates more than he/she uses, any population increase will perfunctorily increase surplus. Hence it represents the simplest and most direct form of economic intensification. This strategy would account for the widespread pattern of population increases following the emergence of inequality, noted by Clark and Blake (1994).

Subsistence Production

The intensification of subsistence production is evident in two phenomena: the increased production and consumption of maize, and the increased use of the domestic dog as a meat source. The increase in maize consumption shows a selection for increased labor investment in a highly productive crop in order to increase the absolute size of the surplus. The increased use of the dog manifests a maximizing strategy favoring easily harvested protein sources over hunting.

Corn

As already mentioned, the Pacific coast of Guatemala is a highly productive zone, with fertile soils and abundant terrestrial, riverine, and estuarine fauna. Evidence presently available suggests that all of these zones were exploited by early sedentary populations. The evidence from Salinas La Blanca led Coe and Flannery (1967) to state that people of the Cuadros and Jocotal phases were primarily agriculturalists who supplemented their diet with marine resources. However, other lines of evidence, discussed below, suggest that during the Early Formative period, maize agriculture, although practiced, did not make a significant contribution to the diet. In contrast, by the Conchas phase, maize had become a much more important part of the diet.

Coe and Flannery (1967) note that grinding stones are rare in Early Formative deposits at estuary sites. A total of three mano and metate fragments are recorded in the Salinas La Blanca excavations for Cuadros and Jocotal levels (Coe and Flannery 1967:126). A stark contrast is shown in the surface collections and excavated levels of Conchas period sites, which show an omnipresence of complete and fragmentary grinding stones.

Another, more direct line of evidence for the changing use of corn is the stable carbon and nitrogen isotope analyses of human bone. Blake et al. (1992b) argue that although macrobotanical corn remains were common in Early Formative contexts in the Mazatán region, it may have only been a dietary supplement. The low stable carbon ratios and abundant remains of estuary fauna suggest that fish, turtles, C_3 plants, and C_3 plant-eaters were the most common elements of peoples' diets. However, in our analysis of Conchas phase human bones from La Blanca, we found much higher stable carbon isotope ratios, indicating the increased importance of C_4 plants, presumably maize, in the diet (Blake et al. 1992a). Clark and Blake (1994) have suggested that, during the Early Formative period in the Mazatán region, the use of maize may have been primarily in the form of a fermented beverage, possibly for ritual purposes. This is clearly not the case in the Conchas phase, by which time maize had become an important dietary staple.

The reason for this shift from limited to broad scale use of maize lies in its unique potential for surplus production. Under normal conditions, maize yields a higher return of calories for labor invested than other staple crops. Logan and Sanders (1976) calculate that for sandy loam soils, broadly similar to those of the coastal plain, an input-output

ratio of 1:16 to 1:24 is obtained when neolithic tool kits are used. Even when differences between modern and ancient maize are taken into account, the surplus generated in ancient times would have been substantial and would have exceeded that of any other staple crops that may have been cultivated, such as manioc (Cowgill 1971). The short growing cycle of some maize varieties, in combination with the environment of the Pacific coastal plain, compounded the advantage by allowing multiple crops to be harvested during the year.

Some present-day farmers in the Río Naranjo region plant up to three crops of maize in a single year. The first and second crops are grown during the rainy season. The third is planted during the dry season in humid depressions and along the margins of seasonally inundated pampas. It surely is not coincidental that the largest expanse of these humid soils lies immediately east of La Blanca.

The advantage of maize is not simply that it is surplus producing, but that the size of the surplus is largely determined by labor input. Hence, the production of maize is capable of being increased either through expansion of the area brought under cultivation or by producing multiple crops from the same plot. In the expansive and fertile coastal plain either or both strategies can be followed, but undoubtedly the chief advantage of maize lies in the facility for multi-cropping; this not only increases surplus production, it maximizes it relative to other possible strategies.

For instance, it would have been possible to increase the

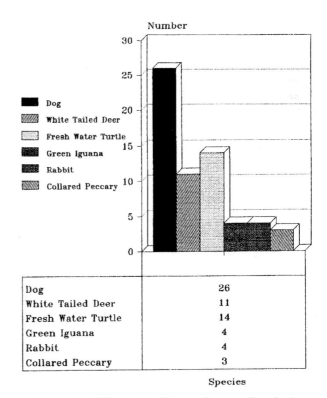

Dog	26
White Tailed Deer	11
Fresh Water Turtle	14
Green Iguana	4
Rabbit	4
Collared Peccary	3

Figure 4. MNI for La Blanca Fauna. Totals Are for All Conchas Subphases (after Harrington 1991).

labor devoted to the collection of shellfish and other estuarine resources. The estuary/mangrove system has the highest primary productivity of exploitable biomass (Odum 1971; Yesner 1980). Yet, in spite of this high productivity, the estuarine resources are finite, and the constraints on production are not set by labor input, but by the reproductive capacity of the exploited species. Hence, the intensification of collection is possible, and such a strategy would increase the available surplus, but it would not maximize it.

Dogs

A different aspect of intensification is found in the use of faunal resources. In this realm of subsistence, the strategy was not one of increasing labor input to increase production, but of minimizing labor used in the procurement of protein to allow its investment in other activities. The strategy is thus one of increased efficiency, rather than increased output per se.

Early Formative period assemblages in the coastal zones of Chiapas and Guatemala show a nearly exclusive use hunting, fishing, and collecting to procure animal protein. Faunal exploitation shows extremely high diversity in the number and type of species captured. Quantitative data for this time period are very limited, but studies in progress on the Mazatán data (Blake et al. 1992b) and El Mesak (Wake and Hyland 1989) will permit more detailed assessment of procurement strategies for that time period.

Studies of the faunal assemblage from La Blanca (Harrington 1991) show two important trends in animal resource use. First is a strategy focusing on a more limited number of species. Three species, domestic dog (*Canis familiaris*), deer (*Odocoileus virgianus*), and fresh water turtle (*Pseudomys ornata*) dominate the assemblage (Figure 4).

The use of these three species represents an emphasis on minimizing time spent in procurement. Turtles and deer are species that could both be captured at locations close to the site. Turtles would be taken in the pampas immediately east of the site or on the banks of the Río Naranjo, which at that time flowed immediately west of the site. Deer would probably have been taken in woods near the site or in cleared areas adjacent to agricultural plots (Linares 1976).

The increased use of a domestic protein source is perhaps the most telling point. Domestic dog is rare in Early Formative archaeological contexts in the area. None were found at Salinas la Blanca (Coe and Flannery 1967) nor at El Mesak (Wake and Hyland 1989). However, dogs are present in faunal samples from the Mazatán area, and Blake et al. (1992b) report that in a Cherla phase deposit they are the second most common larger mammal species (after deer) by MNI.

At La Blanca, as in many Middle Formative sites in Mesoamerica, the domestic dog represents the most common animal in the assemblage, when calculated by MNI (Figure 4). A large percentage of the bones are fractured and burned, so there is no doubt of their role as food. The estimated weight of these dogs ranges from 10.6 to 22.6 lbs,

with a mean of 14.7 (Harrington 1991). There are no estimates of the live weight represented by the deer specimens at La Blanca, but given that these animals can frequently reach 100 lbs in weight, it is clear that dogs are not the greatest overall contributor to the diet. However, what more is germane to present considerations is the increase in the use of dogs as a food source from the Early to the Middle Preclassic, reaching a level where they approach deer in overall importance. This increase in the use of dogs for food, relative to deer, suggests an increased emphasis on food production.

Dogs require virtually no effort to tend, nourish, and harvest. They can be kept in pens with only minimal supervision, fed by scraps, and collected with the least effort. Care and feeding could also be undertaken by small children otherwise unable to participate in productive activity. The role of dogs in the household labor regime and subsistence economy may well have been analogous to that of pigs in the modern Mesoamerican household. The result would be an abundant and reliable food source with a net labor and resource input that is minimal.

Lithics

Both the Early and Middle Formative period lithic assemblages from coastal Chiapas and Guatemala are dominated by obsidian, a material imported from highland locations. The Early Formative assemblages consist mainly of casually flaked material, produced either by direct hard hammer percussion or bi-polar percussion. Both techniques required minimal skill, and apparently were practiced by every household (Clark 1987).

The assemblages of the Conchas phase show evidence of a second industry, the production of pressure flaked prismatic blades (Jackson and Love 1991). The techniques for producing these blades have been discussed extensively by Clark (1987, 1988). Briefly, the production of prismatic blades requires the forming of a core and the removal of blades by pressure flaking with a specialized tool. Clark has argued convincingly that requirements of skill and constant practice make it nearly certain that this was a task performed by specialists. He proposed that, initially, specialists were sponsored by chiefs at substantial cost. Clark believes that the adoption of blade technology was based not on economic factors of production but on political factors, in which "blades were distributed by chiefs as a type of political payola—as gifts used to keep subordinates from getting restless" (Clark 1987:280-281).

Evidence from the Basin of Mexico and San Lorenzo, Veracruz indicates that the technology for prismatic blade manufacture existed by 1100 B.C. (Cobean et al. 1972; Tolstoy 1989). Hence, what we see in the Pacific coast area is not the invention of technology, but the adoption of a previously existing one.

I am in agreement with Clark on the key point that the adoption of blade technology was linked to the development of rank societies, but the evidence from the Naranjo region indicates that the reasons for adoption of blade technology were primarily functional and economically motivated. The evidence for this is twofold: (1) blades are found in all Conchas phase site surface collections containing obsidian, indicating minimal restriction on their distribution, and (2) almost all blades show evidence of extensive use. In many instances the blades have been retouched or an attempt has been made to regenerate then through bi-polar flaking (C. Roger Nance, personal communication 1988). This later point indicates both that blades were highly prized tools and that the technology of producing them was restricted. Obsidian in the form of unworked nodules or spalls was apparently abundant and if these households had the capacity for producing blades they would have done so, rather than attempting to regenerate exhausted ones.

Prismatic blades are superior to household-produced flake tools in almost all technical aspects. At La Blanca, the flakes were produced by smashing spalls or nodules that were originally under 10 cm in size. The flakes had irregular cutting edges that were generally under 3 cm in length. The flakes are awkward to hold and use by hand and would be very difficult to haft. In marked contrast, the prismatic blade tools have two straight and regular edges that often reach 10 cm in length. These tools are easily held in the hand and would be well suited for hafting.

Given this evidence, I believe that the adoption of blade technology stems from the demand for more efficient tools capable of increasing productivity. This argument for technical superiority would be bolstered if we could specify, through edge wear analysis, the precise uses of these blade and flake tools. These analyses have not yet been carried out, so that at present we cannot link the tools to specific economic activities.

The locus of blade production has not been determined. There were no prismatic blade cores recovered in the La Blanca excavations, and they were also absent from all surface collections from Conchas phase sites. It is possible that (1) the blades were manufactured at very limited loci in the Río Naranjo area by specialists, or (2) the blades were imported already made. Although Jackson and I have made a case for the second alternative (Jackson and Love 1991), the issue has not been empirically resolved.

As Clark (1987) notes, the production of prismatic blades entails substantially higher costs than the production of casual tools. These costs are present whether the blades are produced locally or at a great distance. In either case, the procurement of blades represents a "capital intensification" (Gilman 1981) that would allow increased production.

Regionalization

Regionalization of the economy serves the purposes of intensification by undermining the autonomy of the house-hold economy, which otherwise tends toward underproduction. At no time, however, were households so completely isolated from one another that complete autonomy existed, as the widespread exchange of obsidian and other goods in the Early Formative attests. The changes of the Middle Formative must therefore be viewed as the amplification of this pattern and not its creation.

There can be little doubt that the process regionalization was more fully developed by the Conchas phase. The ability to construct public works of such monumentality as are present at La Blanca is ample evidence of the ability to mobilize labor on a regional scale, although the basis by which this was done cannot be specified.

Beyond this, however, much of the evidence already mentioned indicates that regional patterns of production and exchange had become not only part of, but integral to, the economy of the Río Naranjo region. The presence of exchange in earlier times has already been discussed, but specialization was also apparently in place by the Locona phase. In the Early Formative period, exchange was limited to raw materials, such as obsidian spalls, and specialization, if present, was probably restricted to limited production of a few commodities, such as elite pottery (Clark and Blake 1994). In the Conchas phase specialization and exchange are extended into the realm of finished products essential to productive technology. I will provide two brief examples, both of which draw upon evidence already presented.

As already mentioned, in the Early Formative, the production of obsidian tools was done on a household basis; each of these units obtained the raw material and had the means needed to manufacture its own obsidian tools. In the Conchas phase, the expedient household production of simple obsidian tools continued, but was supplemented by acquisition of prismatic blades, which the household did not produce. If one accepts the argument that blades represent a more efficient technology and that a household seeking to increase its production would find them desirable, the dilemma is obvious: the household must obtain these tools from another individual or household that is capable of producing them. This represents a significant juncture, because it is the first time that one household has been dependent upon the specialized knowledge of another in order to increase its own productive capacity. This link is far stronger than the bonds formed by exchange of raw materials. Raw materials may be obtained from many sources, but specialized production demands that links be established and maintained with a specific household or individual. The person in control of this specialized production, whether the artisan or someone controlling his or her labor, obtains a position of tremendous power.

One final example is less powerful, but similarly focuses on productive means. As mentioned, the production of maize is indicated by both bone isotope data and by the presence of increased numbers of grinding tools. The raw materials used to produce these tools is not native to the coastal plain, which is alluvial. Rather, the stone is derived from piedmont sources, some 20-30 km inland. The absence of debitage at La Blanca indicates that these grinding tools were probably manufactured in the piedmont zone. This, then provides another instance where acquisition of technology essential to the process of intensification demands increased reliance on other households, in this case ones outside the immediate area.

Conclusions

This discussion has presented evidence for the growth of complex societies in Pacific Guatemala during the Middle Formative period and the economic processes linked to that development. These limited examples show that technological innovations in productive means, especially agriculture, were necessary, but not sufficient, to the growth of complex society. In the examples discussed, the means for intensification had been in place for several hundred years before they were used. The essential process in the growth of complexity was a change in social relationships that provided the rationale for economic transformation. The technology of production provided the means for economic intensification, but not the rationale.

A key to understanding the changes in Preclassic Pacific Guatemala lies in answering the question of why economic intensification and the growth of regional economic structures took place. I argue that economic intensification was driven by the demands of emerging social inequality and social competition for status, processes that began in the Early Formative period but which became more clearly manifest by the Middle Formative period. The demands of emergent elites for increased production and surplus were central to the intensification of the economy. Intensification was needed both to support a non-productive group of elites and specialists, and to finance increased demand for goods and labor needed for their competitive displays. A reason why the highly productive resources of the mangrove/estuary zone became increasingly marginal to the production of subsistence goods may be that they were finite, and their productivity could not be increased to meet the demands of a maximizing strategy. In contrast, the production of corn, in the proper ecological zone, can be increased in proportion to the amount of labor invested. The increased reliance on the domestic dog represents a different type of choice that focused on efficiency.

Regionalization was part of this process, because it represents a loss of household autonomy and linked each household inextricably to others in order to obtain productive means. This is the expression of changing social relations that in turn fed back upon the growth of a maximizing surplus-producing economy. It created a conundrum of embedded economic and social relations which continued to fuel the processes of change.

Acknowledgements

Fieldwork and analysis of materials were conducted under permission granted by the Instituto de Antropología e Historia de Guatemala. Licenciada Edna Núñez de Rodas was director of the Instituto during the inception of the project and authorized the export of lithic and faunal materials for analysis in the United States. Miguel Valencia A., chief of Monumentos Prehispánicos y Coloniales, supervised fieldwork and facilitated all of the above permits.

Many sources of funding made this work possible. Travel in 1982 and 1983 was supported by grants from the Tinker Foundation through the Center for Latin American Studies at the University of California at Berkeley. Field work in 1983 was financed by a Graduate Humanities Research Fund grant from the Graduate Division, University of California at Berkeley. Field work in 1984 and 1985 was funded by a Fulbright-Hayes Dissertation Research Abroad Fellowship from the United States Department of Education. Analysis of the materials was made possible by a Dissertation Improvement grant from the National Science Foundation, Grant BNS-8611064. Grants from the Robert H. Lowie Scholarship Fund and the Ronald O. Olson Fund by the University of California at Berkeley Department of Anthropology aided research from 1983 through 1987.

Many people have provided comments on various drafts of this paper. Comments by Mark Edmonds, Christine Hastorf, Matthew Johnson, Kent Lightfoot, Margaret Purser helped greatly to improve the paper.

Notes

1. The phase ages presented throughout are based on uncalibrated radiocarbon dates. See Love (1993) and Blake et al. (1995) for a detailed account of the chronology for the Pacific Coast region.

2. An extensive discussion of the nature and meaning of these symbols may be found in Love (1991). For the present purposes, I wish only to note that I do not view any of these icons and symbols, whether they may be called "Olmec" or not, to indicate influence, conquest, or migration from the Gulf Coast of Mexico.

References Cited

Bender, B.
  1978   Gatherer-Hunter to Farmer: A Social Perspective. *World Archaeology* 10:204-222.
Berreman, G. D.
  1981   Social Inequality: A Cross-Cultural Perspective. In *Social Inequality: Comparative and Developmental Approaches*, edited by G. D. Berreman., pp. 3-40. Academic Press, New York.
Blake, M.
  1991   Paso de la Amada: An Early Formative Chiefdom in Chiapas, Mexico. In *The Formation of Complex Society in Southeastern Mesoamerica*, edited by W. R. Fowler, Jr., pp.27-46. CRC Press, Boca Raton.

Blake, M., B. S. Chisholm, J. E. Clark, B. Voorhies, and M. W. Love
1992a Prehistoric Subsistence in the Soconusco Region. *Current Anthropology* 33(1):83-94.

Blake, M., B. S. Chisholm, J. E. Clark, K. Mudar
1992b Non-agricultural Staples and Agricultural Supplements: Early Formative Subsistence in the Soconusco Region, Mexico. In *Transitions to Agriculture in Prehistory*, edited by A. B. Gebauer and T. D. Price, pp. 133-151. Monographs in World Archaeology No. 4. Prehistory Press, Madison.

Blake, M., J. E. Clark, B. Voorhies, G. Michaels, M. W. Love, M. E. Pye, A. A. Demarest, and B. Arroyo
1995 Radiocarbon Chronology for the Late Archaic and Formative Periods on the Pacific Coast of Southeastern Mesoamerica. *Ancient Mesoamerica* 6:161-183.

Boserup, E.
1965 *The Conditions of Agricultural Growth*. Aldine, Chicago.

Clark, J. E.
1987 Politics, Prismatic Blades, and Mesoamerican Civilization. In *The Organization of Core Technology*, edited by J. K. Johnson and C. A. Morrow, pp. 259-284. Westview Press, Boulder and London.
1988 *The Lithic Artifacts of La Libertad, Chiapas, Mexico: An Economic Perspective*. Papers of the New World Archaeological Foundation No. 52. Brigham Young University, Provo.
1991 The beginnings of Mesoamerica: *Apología* for the Soconusco Early Formative. In *The Formation of Complex Society in Southeastern Mesoamerica*, edited by W. R. Fowler, Jr., pp. 13-26. CRC Press, Boca Raton.

Clark, J. E., and M. Blake
1989 El Origen de la Civilización en Mesoamerica: Los Olmecas y Mokaya del Soconusco de Chiapas, México. In *El Preclásico o Formativo: Avances y Perspectivas*, edited by M. Carmona Macías, pp. 385-403. Museo Nacional de Antropología and Instituto Nacional de Antropología e Historia, México.
1994 The Power of Prestige: Competitive Generosity and the Emergence of Rank Societies in Lowland Mesoamerica. In *Factional Competition and Political Development in the New World*, edited by E. M. Brumfiel and J. W. Fox, pp. 17-30. University of Cambridge Press, Cambridge.

Clark, J. E., M. Blake, P. Guzzy, M. Cuevas, and T. Salcedo
1987 *Proyecto: El Preclásico Temprano en la Costa del Pacífico*. Final Report to the Instituto Nacional de Antropología e Historia, México. Ms. on file, Department of Anthropology, Brigham Young University, Provo.

Clark, J. E., M. Blake, B. Arroyo, M. E. Pye, R. G. Lesure, V. Feddema, and M. Ryan
1990 *Reporte Final Del Proyecto Investigaciones del Formativo Temprano en el Litoral Chiapaneco*. Final Report to the Instituto Nacional de Antropología e Historia, México. Ms. on file, Department of Anthropology, Brigham Young University, Provo.

Cobean, R. H., M. D. Coe, E. A. Perry, K. D. Turekian, and D. P. Kharkar
1971 Obsidian Trade at San Lorenzo Tenochtitlan, Mexico. *Science* 174: 666-671.

Coe, M. D.
1961 *La Victoria: An Early Site on the Pacific Coast of Guatemala*. Papers of the Peabody Museum of American Archaeology and Ethnology Vol. 53. Harvard University, Cambridge.

Coe, M. D., and K. V. Flannery
1967 *Early Cultures and Human Ecology in South Coastal Guatemala*. Smithsonian Contributions to Anthropology Vol. 3. Smithsonian Institution, Washington, D.C.

Cowgill, U. M.
1971 Some Comments on Manihot Subsistence and the Ancient Maya. *Southwestern Journal of Anthropology* 27: 51-63.

Earle, T. K.
1978 *Economic and Social Organization of a Complex Chiefdom The Halele'a District, Kaua'i, Hawaii*. Anthropological Papers No. 63. Museum of Anthropology, University of Michigan, Ann Arbor.

Flannery, K. V.
1968 Archaeological Systems Theory and Early Mesoamerica. In, *Anthropological Archaeology in the Americas*, edited by B. J. Meggers, pp. 67-87. Anthropological Society of Washington, Washington, D.C.
1972 The Cultural Evolution of Civilizations. *Annual Review of Ecology and Systematics* 3:399-426.
1973 The Origins of Agriculture. *Annual Review of Anthropology* 2:271-310.

Gilman, A.
1981 The Development of Social Stratification in Bronze Age Europe. *Current Anthropology* 22:1-23.

Goldman, I.
1970 *Ancient Polynesian Society*. University of Chicago Press, Chicago.

Grove, D. C.
1981 The Formative Period and the Evolution of Complex Culture. In *The Handbook of Middle American Indians*, Supplement 1, edited by V. R. Bricker and J. A. Sabloff, pp.373-391. University of Texas Press, Austin.

Harrington, L. R.
1991 The Fauna Of La Blanca, Guatemala. Ms. on file,

Department of Anthropology, University of California, Los Angeles.

Jackson, T. L., and M. W. Love
1991   Bladerunning: Obsidian Production and the Introduction of Prismatic Blades at La Blanca, Guatemala. *Ancient Mesoamerica* 2:47-59..

Kaiser, T., and B. Voytek
1983   Economic Intensification and the European Neolithic. *Journal of Anthropological Archaeology* 2:329-351.

Kuenzi, W. D., O. H. Horst, and R. V. McGehee
1979   Effects of Volcanic Activity on Fluvial-deltaic Sedimentation in a Modern Arc-trench Gap, Southwestern Guatemala. *Geological Society of America Bulletin* 90:827-838.

Linares, O. F.
1976   Garden Hunting in the American Tropics. *Human Ecology* 4:331-350.

Logan, M. H., and W. T. Sanders
1976   The Model. In *The Valley of Mexico*, edited by E. R. Wolf, pp. 31-58. University of New Mexico Press, Albuquerque.

Love, M. W.
1989   *Early Settlements and Chronology of the Río Naranjo, Guatemala*. Unpublished Ph.D. dissertation. Department of Anthropology, University of California at Berkeley. University Microfilms, Ann Arbor.
1991   Style and Social Complexity in Formative Mesoamerica. In *The Formation of Complex Society in Southeastern Mesoamerica*, edited by W, R. Fowler, Jr. pp. 47-76. CRC Press, Boca Raton.
1993   Ceramic Chronology and Chronometric Dating: Stratigraphy and Seriation at La Blanca, Guatemala. *Ancient Mesoamerica* 4:17-29.

MacNeish, R. S.
1964   Ancient Mesoamerican Civilization. *Science* 143:531-537.

McBryde, F. W.
1947   *Cultural and Historical Geography of Southwest Guatemala*. Smithsonian Institution, Institute of Social Anthropology No. 4. Smithsonian Institution, Washington, D.C.

Odum, E. P.
1971   *Fundamentals of Ecology*. Saunders, Philadelphia.

Renfrew, C.
1986   Varna and the Emergence of Wealth in Prehistoric Europe. In *The Social Life of Things*, edited by A. Apparadurai, pp.141-168. Cambridge University Press, Cambridge.

Sahlins, M.
1972   *Stone Age Economics*. Aldine, Chicago.

Stark, B. L.
1981   The Rise of Sedentary Life. In *The Handbook of Middle American Indians*, Supplement 1, edited by V. R. Bricker and J. A. Sabloff, pp.345-372. University of Texas Press, Austin.

Wake, T., and J. Hyland
1989   Early Formative Flora, Fauna, and Estuarine Subsistence Systems in South Coastal Guatemala. Paper presented at the 54th Annual Meeting of the Society for American Archaeology, Atlanta.

Yesner, D. R.
1980   Maritime Hunter-Gatherer Ecology and Prehistory. *Current Anthropology* 21:727-750.

Part II
CENTRAL AMERICA

8

Precolumbian Fishing on the Pacific Coast of Panama

Richard G. Cooke and Anthony J. Ranere

Introduction: Estuarine Fishing in the Eastern Tropical Pacific

It is well known that the productivity, biotic diversity and geological heterogeneity of large estuary-lagoon systems along the Pacific coast of tropical America were causally related to the precocity and intensity of sedentism and civilization in Precolumbian times. Most archaeologists are aware that the abundance, variety and accessibility of estuarine animals offered pre-Spanish hunter-gatherers and farmers many alternatives for exploitation. Intrinsic resource diversity is conducive to intensification from within a biome. Each estuarine system, however, has its own biological, physical and historical peculiarities. Many eastern tropical Pacific (henceforth ETP) estuaries are quite extensive. They harbored contemporary human groups with different social and cultural histories. Therefore it is important to inventory resource distribution in space and time within specific estuarine systems in order to determine their relevance to local, regional and universal correlates of economic development.

In recent years, archaeologists have benefitted from improving standards of archaeofaunal and geoarchaeological field and laboratory techniques. Nevertheless, reports on animal exploitation in the ETP are still biased towards invertebrates and large terrestrial vertebrates. Molluscs and mammal and bird bones are easier to see and collect than tiny fish bones. Furthermore, they generally represent fewer utilized species, whose skeletons and shells are stored in accessible reference collections. Many archaeologists have learnt to handle identifications themselves with the help of practical guidebooks.

ETP fish faunas are a different matter. Many families and genera that live in or enter estuaries are "speciose," i.e., they contain several species. Although they often resemble each other morphologically, these species partition particular estuarine systems in subtle ways. This diversity means that archaeozoologists must collect large numbers of skeletons in ontogenetic series (i.e., representing different life stages) in order to identify their ichthyofaunas to the satisfaction of the archaeologists who recover them so painstakingly in the field. Objective interpretation of human exploitation requires baseline biological data on how individual species behave and are distributed in the many different sectors of an estuary. This is a tricky task because ETP estuarine fish have been surprisingly poorly studied (Cooke 1992). Fisheries research has concentrated on commercially important non-estuarine fish, such as tunnies, big jack, and groupers. Field biologists have emphasized fish that live on reefs or near rocks because they are easier to observe than species that swim in turbid waters subjected to strong tidal influences.

Research Rationale

Our chapter refers to the Santa María estuary on the central Pacific Coast of Panama (Figure 1). This is the region where the "Coclé" culture developed, now more prosaically known as the "Central Region" of Panama (Cooke and Ranere 1992b; Lothrop 1937, 1942). This culture is considered to be typical of complex and stratified chiefdoms in the lowlands of tropical America (Helms 1979; Linares 1977; Willey 1971). The regional chronology has been well-defined. However, Precolumbian settlement patterns in the region are imperfectly understood (Cooke 1984a; Cooke and Ranere 1992b).

Investigations into regional subsistence economies are still in an interim stage. We cannot collate all the relevant bodies of data to the satisfaction of a demanding cultural historian. For this reason, we have chosen a topic that the existing information can address reasonably objectively, if not completely: the degree to which the taxonomic composition and proportionality of dietary fish remains from two sites with different ^{14}C ages and topographies within the Santa María estuary can be used to infer cultural parameters (i.e., habitat use, capture techniques and foraging ranges) as

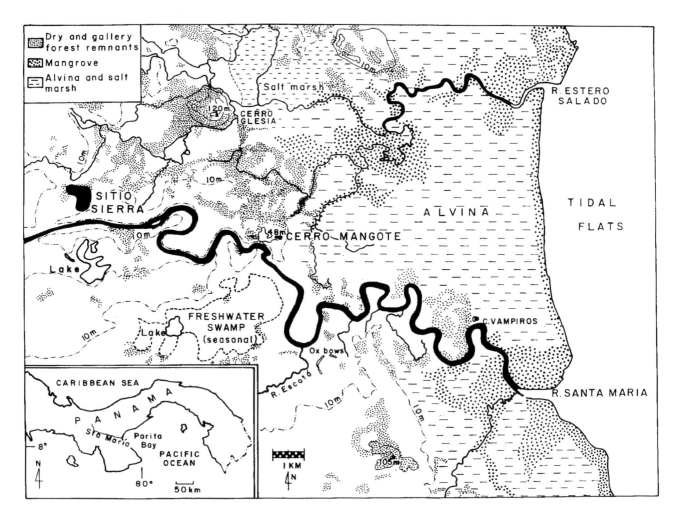

Figure 1.   The Middle Estuary of the Santa María River in Central Panama, Showing the Locations of Cerro Mangote and Sitio Sierra.

well as topographical ones (i.e., site location vis-à-vis the evolving coastline).

The two sites are: Cerro Mangote and Sitio Sierra. Cerro Mangote was a preceramic camp or hamlet occupied between ca. 5650 and 3600 cal B.C. and, during this period, located about 1.2-5.5 km from the coastline. Sitio Sierra was a nucleated farming village which would have been about 12 km inland between approximately cal A.D. 1 and 400.[1]

Summaries of the peculiarities of ETP estuarine fish diversity, ecology and distribution are presented elsewhere (Cooke 1992, 1993a, 1993b; Cooke and Tapia 1994a, 1994b). Even so, the following text contains detailed information about fish. In case some readers find this tedious, we employ the scientific binomial the first time we mention a taxon, and thereafter rely on English common names. Our marine fish reference is Allen and Robertson's *Fishes of the Eastern Tropical Pacific* (1994). Their nomenclature differs from that of other monographs (e.g., Bussing and López 1993; FAO 1995; Thomson et al. 1979), but since we applaud their attempt to standardize vernacular

names, we follow their lead. Where we cannot find an English name, we have invented one (for example, we translate *amblops* as "bluntnosed"). Table 1 lists all the fish taxa recorded in the archaeological bone samples so that readers can cross-check popular and biological nomenclature.

The Santa María River Estuary

Our multidisciplinary project in the Santa María basin began in the early 1980s (Cooke and Ranere 1984, 1992a, 1992b). The eponymous river enters the sea at Parita Bay. Geological sediment cores extracted with a "Vibracore" allow us to correlate some aspects of the evolution of its delta with sea-level change (Barber 1981; Clary et al. 1984) and, thence, with archaeological sites where fish bones are important components of middens (Cooke and Ranere 1984, 1989; Cooke 1992, 1993b).

To compensate for the scant information about ETP estuarine fish faunas, we sponsored three parallel investigations into modern fish distribution and fishing techniques within this system (localities are identified in Figure 1): (1)

the ethnology of fishing at two Parita Bay coastal villages (El Rompío, Aguadulce, and Boca de Parita, Monagrillo) (directed by John Bort), (2) a taxonomic and quantitative evaluation of the nektonic (i.e., free swimming) fauna captured in an intertidal net-and-pole trap in the Estero Palo Blanco, Aguadulce, a mangrove-fringed inlet just north of the Estero Salado channel (Cooke and Tapia 1994b), and (3) a survey of marine fish amphidromy (i.e., periodic upward and downward movements) in the middle (mixing) and upper (fluvial) estuary of the Santa María River, based on bi-monthly captures made with different fishing techniques at four stations located between .8 and 20 km from the mouth (Table 1; Cooke and Tapia 1994a).

Although this research promises to fine-tune our interpretations of Precolumbian fishing, there remain several unresolved problems. The first is insoluble: the native population in this part of Panama was exterminated, hybridized or radically hispanicized soon after initial contact (Romoli 1987). Hence we cannot assume continuity between pre- and post-contact fishing methods. All that our "middle range research" (Trigger 1989:362-7) has achieved so far is to point out which fishing techniques may have been used, and in which estuarine habitats the fish taxa identified in the archaeological bone samples may have been caught. It is possible that some modern techniques were actually used in Precolumbian times—e.g., intertidal traps like the one we are studying—but we may never be able to prove this.

Another defect is recovery bias. Using .25 inch mesh screen for recovering large mammal bones is in some situations methodologically defensible (Shaffer 1992). However, it is not viable for recovering fish remains (Wheeler and Jones 1989:38-43). The samples to which we refer herein represent the fraction recovered using .125 inch mesh screen. Bones recovered beneath this mesh size have not been analyzed to our satisfaction. These comprise mostly tiny individuals of the taxa identified with larger meshes. So their absence from our quantifications affects appreciations of fish size ranges to a greater degree than fish taxonomic richness and diversity.

Present-day Environment

This section is based on descriptions in Barber (1981) and Clary et al. (1984) and on personal observations. It is quite long; but the detail is necessary to emphasize two particularly relevant features of tropical estuaries: (1) the variety and patchiness of terrestrial and aquatic habitats, and (2) the jigsaw-like, temporally unpredictable juxtaposition of freshwater, brackish and saline habitats. Illustrations of some of the habitats and landforms can be found in Clary et al. (1984).

Day et al. (1989:3) define estuaries as "that portion of the earth's coastal zone where there is interaction of ocean water, fresh water, land, and atmosphere." Fairbridge (1980) divides estuaries into three sectors: (1) *marine* or

Table 1. List of Fish Taxa Identified at Cerro Mangote and Sitio Sierra.

Genus and species	English name	Synthesis of fishing records
Elasmobranchs		
CARCHARHINIDAE:		
Carcharhinus altimus[a]	bignose shark	
C. leucas	bull shark	
C. limbatus	blacktip shark	R
Rhizoprionodon longurio	Pacific sharpnose shark	
DASYATIDAE:		
Dasyatis longus	long-tailed stingray	O
MYLIOBATIDAE:		
Aeteobatus narinari	spotted eagle ray	1
PRISTIDAE:		
Pristis	sawfish	2, 4
SPHYRNIDAE:		
Sphyrna lewini	scalloped hammerhead	R
Sphyrna tiburo	bonnethead	
UROLOPHIDAE:		
Urotrygon asterias	stingray	O
Teleosts		
ALBULIDAE:		
Albula neoguinaica	Pacific bonefish	
ARIIDAE[b]:		
"*Arius*" *dasycephalus*	broadhead catfish	
"*A.*" species B[c]	widemouthed catfish	1, 2, 3, 4
"*A.*" *kessleri*	Kessler's catfish	A, 1, 2
"*A*". *lentiginosus*	Panamanian catfish	
"*A*". "*osculus*"[d]	thick-lipped catfish	O, 1
"*A*". *platypogon*	slender-spined catfish	R
"*A.*" *seemanni*	Seemann's catfish	A, 1, 2
Bagre panamensis	chihuil catfish	R
B. pinnimaculatus	long-barbled catfish	O, 1, 2
Cathorops hypophthalmus	gloomy catfish	A, 1, 2
C. multiradiatus	many-rayed catfish	O, 1
C. species A[e]	congo catfish?	O, 1, 2
C. species B	Taylor's catfish?	A, 1
C. tuyra	Tuyra catfish	A, 1, 2, 3
Sciadeops troscheli	chili catfish	
Sciadeichthys dowii	flap-nosed catfish	O, 1, 2
AUCHENIPTERIDAE:		
Parauchenipterus amblops	blunt-nosed driftcat	1, 2, 3, 4
BATRACHOIDIDAE:		
Batrachoides[f]	toadfish	O, 1
Daector	toadfish	A
BELONIDAE:		
Strongylura scapularis	yellowfin needlefish	O, 2
Tylosurus crocodilus	crocodile needlefish	R
BOTHIDAE:		
Citharichthys gilberti	Gilbert's flounder	O, 1, 2, 4
CARANGIDAE:		
Alectis ciliaris	African pompano	

Table 1. (Continued)

Genus and species	English name	Synthesis of fishing records
Carangoides otrynter	threadfin jack	
Caranx caballus	green jack	R
C. caninus	Pacific crevalle jack	O, 1
Chloroscombrus orqueta	Pacific bumper	A
Oligoplites altus	longjaw leatherjacket	A, 1
O. refulgens	shortjaw leatherjacket	O
O. saurus	yellowtail leatherjacket	O
Selar crumenophthalmus	purse-eyed scad	
Selene brevoortii	Pacific lookdown	O (juv)
S. oerstedii	hairfin lookdown	O (juv)
S. peruviana	Pacific moonfish	R (juv)
Trachinotus kennedyi	blackblotch pompano	O, 1
CENTROPOMIDAE:		
Centropomus armatus	longspine snook	A, 1, 2
C. medius	bigeye snook	O, 1
C. nigrescens	black snook	O, 1, 2, 3, 4
C. robalito	little snook	A, 1-4 (juv)
C. unionensis	humpback snook	A, 2
C. viridis	white snook	A, 1, 2, 3, 4
CICHLIDAE:		
Aequidens coeruleopunctatus	blue-spotted cichlid	3, 4
CLUPEIDAE:		
Opisthonema libertate[g]	Pacific thread-herring	R
CTENOLUCIIDAE:		
Ctenolucius hujeta	pike characin	3, 4
CURIMATIDAE:		
Curimata magdalenae	Magdalena curimata	2, 3, 4
ELOPIDAE:		
Elops affinis	machete	O, 1, 2, 3, 4
ENGRAULIDAE:		
Anchoa	anchovy	O, 1, 2
Cetengraulis mysticetus	Pacific anchoveta	A, 1
EPHIPPIDAE:		
Parapsettus panamensis	Panama spadefish	O
ERYTHRINIDAE:		
Hoplias sp.[h]	Santa Maria trahira	2, 3
GERREIDAE:		
Diapterus peruvianus	Peruvian mojarra	A
Eucinostomus currani	blackspot mojarra	O, 3, 4 (juv)
Eugerres brevimanus	short-finned mojarra	O, 2
E. lineatus	striped mojarra	O
Gerres cinereus	yellowfin mojarra	O
GOBIIDAE/ELEOTRIDIDAE:		
Bathygobius cf. *andrei*	estuary frillfin	O, 1
Dormitator latifrons	spotted sleeper	2
Eleotris picta	painted gudgeon	2, 3
Gobioides peruanus	Peruvian eelgoby	2
Gobiomorus maculatus	pike gudgeon	2, 3, 4
HAEMULIDAE:		
Anisotremus dovii	blackbarred grunt[i]	
A. pacifici	Pacific grunt	O, 1, 2
Haemulon flaviguttatum	Cortez grunt	
Orthopristis chalceus	brassy grunt	R
Pomadasys bayanus	freshwater grunt	O, 1, 2[j]

Genus and species	English name	Synthesis of fishing records
P. macracanthus	bigspine grunt	O, 1, 2
P. panamensis	Panamanian grunt	
Pomadasys (H.) elongatus	elongate grunt	A
P. (H.) leuciscus	white grunt	A
P. (H.) nitidus	silver grunt	R
LOBOTIDAE:		
Lobotes surinamensis	tripletail	O, 1, 2
LORICARIIDAE:		
Hypostomus panamensis	Panamanian armored cat	1, 2, 3, 4
LUTJANIDAE:		
Lutjanus argentiventris	yellow snapper	R[k]
L. colorado	colorado snapper	O, 1
L. guttatus	spotted rose snapper	
L. novemfasciatus	dog snapper	O, 1, 3, 4
MUGILIDAE:		
Mugil curema	white mullet	A, 1, 2, 3
PIMELODIDAE:		
Rhamdia guatemalensis[l]	Guatemalan rivercat	2
POLYNEMIDAE:		
Polydactylus approximans	blue bobo	O
P. opercularis	yellow bobo	A
PRISTIGASTERIDAE:		
Ilisha furthii	Pacific ilisha	A, 1, 2
Opisthopterus	longfin herring	A, 1 (*O. dovii*)
SCIAENIDAE:		
Bairdiella. armata	armed croaker	O, 1
B. ensifera	swordspine croaker	A, 1, 2
Cynoscion albus	white corvina	A, 1, 2
C. squamipinnis	scalefin weakfish	
C. stolzmanni	Stolzmann's weakfish	O
Menticirrhus panamensis	Panama kingcroaker	O
Micropogonias altipinnis	high-fin corvina	R (juv)
Ophioscion scierus	tuza croaker	O
O. typicus	point-nosed croaker	A, 1
O. vermicularis	worm-lined croaker	
Paralonchurus dumerilii	suco croaker	O
Stellifer chrysoleuca	shortnose stardrum	O
S. oscitans	yawning stardrum	A, 1
SCOMBRIDAE:		
Euthynnus lineatus	black skipjack tuna	
Scomberomorus sierra	sierra mackerel	R
SERRANIDAE:		
Epinephelus analogus	spotted cabrilla	R
SPHYRAENIDAE:		
Sphyraena ensis	Pacific barracuda	
STERNARCHIDAE:		
Sternopygus dariensis	Darien knifefish	2, 3, 4
STROMATEIDAE:		
Peprilus snyderi	Snyder's butterfly-fish	O
SYNBRANCHIDAE:		
Synbranchus marmoratus	freshwater eel	
TETRAODONTIDAE:		
Sphoeroides annulatus	bullseye puffer	A, 1
Guentheridia formosa	Guenther's puffer	A

Table 1. (Continued)

Note: Taxa are presented together with their English names and information on their presence in an intertidal fish trap in the Estero Palo Blanco, Aguadulce and at four collection stations up the Santa María River (Figure 1). Trap records: A—abundant, O—occasional, R—rare. River collection stations: 1—Mouth (0.8 km), 2—París (7 km), 3—El Rincón (12 km), 4—Santa María (20 km) (Cooke 1993b; Cooke and Tapia 1994a, 1994b).

[a]   Our collection contains two Parita Bay skeletons identified as this species. Confusion with *C. obscurus* (also with a dorsal ridge) is possible. This species is more likely to enter ETP inshore waters.

[b]   The sea catfish family (Ariidae) is under revision. The genus *"Arius"* comprises species of distinct phylogenetic origins (hence our use of inverted commas). Lapillus morphology suggests that *"Arius" seemanni* and *"A."* platypogon are divergent from the other *"Arius"* species (Cooke, 1996).

[c]   This appears to be the species that was erroneously assigned by Meek and Hildebrand (1923:120-22) to their *"Netuma oscula."* See Bussing and López (1993:62-63).

[d]   The type specimen of this species has been lost.

[e]   We believe that our *Cathorops* species A corresponds to *C. furthii* and *C.* species B, to *C. taylori* (Allen and Robertson 1994:69, Plate V-7), which Bussing and López (1993) consider to be synonymous with *C. steindachneri*. See also Cooke (1996).

[f]   Both *Batrachoides boulengeri* (estuary toadfish) and *B. pacifici* (Pacific toadfish) are captured frequently in the Santa María estuary. We have identified the former 22 km from the mouth in freshwater. They are difficult (but not impossible) to separate osteologically.

[g]   We do not possess skeletons of *Opisthonema bulleri* or *O. medirastre*. Both species occur in Panama, but not, as far as we know, in turbid shallow waters in Parita Bay.

[h]   Two species are known from Panama: *Hoplias malabaricus* and *H. microlepis*. A. Martin (personal communication), who is investigating mtDNA in Panamanian freshwater fish, believes that the Santa María population may be a distinct species.

[i]   This species is abundant at the mouth of the Estero Salado inlet near the fishing village of El Rompío (Cooke, personal observation).

[j]   We have recorded this species 60 km from the coast at 300 m elevation (Cooke and Tapia 1994a).

[k]   Although rare in the intertidal trap, young adults are abundant at the edge of mangrove-fringed inlets where they can be readily caught with hook and line (Cooke, personal observation).

[l]   This is the only *Rhamdia* species that has been reported in the Santa María lower drainage. It is also the only *Rhamdia* in our reference collection. Other species may occur, however.

lower estuary, in free connection with the open sea, (2) *middle estuary,* subject to strong salt and fresh water *mixing,* and (3) *upper* or *fluvial estuary,* characterized by fresh water but subject to daily tidal action (emphasis ours).

These definitions are germane to regional-historical studies because they stress the fact that an archaeological site can be a considerable distance from the sea yet still be technically estuarine (Day et al. 1989:6; Day and Yáñez A. 1982). Sitio Sierra's location and large size between cal A.D. 1 and 400 can be viewed as a topographical compromise between proximity to fertile colluvium for maize-dominated agriculture (Cooke 1984a), and access to the rich nektonic and littoral resources of the middle and upper estuary. Although the Santa María River now flows fresh about 12 km inland, it is still weakly tidal at this point. Hence, sensu Day et.al. (1989) and Fairbridge (1980), Sitio Sierra is an estuarine site. As we shall see, its fishing practices were markedly estuary-dependent.

By global standards, the Santa María River is small, about 145 km from source to mouth (Weiland 1984:34). Nevertheless, the basin it drains (3315 km²) is the second largest in Panama and the largest in the Central Region. Its delta is one of the driest zones in Central America with an average annual rainfall between 1000 and 1400 mm and an intense 4-5 month dry season. But the mountains and foothills through which it descends are humid: annual precipitation is 3800 mm at one well-known station (La Yeguada, 650 m elevation [Estadística Panameña 1975]) and even more above 1000 m, where orography causes more constant dry season precipitation.

The flood-plain drainage systems to the north and south of the main river channel are poorly integrated: during the heaviest floods, water flows northwards in front of Cerro Iglesia and crosses into the drainage of the Estero Salado, which is probably an ancient primary channel of the Santa María. Here the landscape is dotted with meander scars, elbows of capture, swamps and some freshwater ponds, which expand after floods and retract rapidly in the dry season. Evanescent bodies of freshwater are often dammed up close to the *alvina* (see below), covered with water lilies and crowded with herons, woodstorks and other aquatic birds.

Seasonal pools are important to modern fishing because when they evaporate during dry periods, they concentrate freshwater and euryhaline species (i.e., tolerant of a wide range of salinity), facilitating their capture in large quantities with simple fishing methods.

We shall see that freshwater species were fished frequently at Sitio Sierra, but not at Cerro Mangote.

The C-shaped coastline of Parita Bay is a recent marine invasion of the Pacific continental shelf. Its tidal range averages 4.5 m during most of the year and 6 m during spring tides (Fleming 1938). However, the low angle of the coastal slope, weak wave action, and the lack of a restricted channel for tides make it a low energy environment, heavily colonized by mangrove. Intertidal mudflats extend for 2-3 km into Parita Bay, criss-crossed by runnels and channels.

Where the Santa María River discharges into the marine environment, it breaches the strandline *Rhizophora* mangroves. These often extend inland along tidal and run-off channels for as much as 8 km enabling some marine organisms to penetrate almost to the foot of the hill upon which the site of Cerro Mangote is located. Further inland stretch the coastal *alvinas*. These comprise mid-tidal, high-tidal and supra-tidal zones. Near its seaward edge, the mid-tidal zone contains patches of *Avicennia* mangroves. At its widest point, the high-tidal *alvina* is a barren plain surface. It supports algal growth when moist, becomes a quagmire during heavy rains, and desiccates during the dry season when patches are covered with a dazzling film of salt. The supra-tidal *alvina* supports sparse grassy vegetation, xerophilous trees, and cacti. This grades into anthropogenically altered tropical dry forest. Woods present in 1955 are shown in Figure 1. Their vegetational composition is probably quite different from that of Precolumbian woods; but they may approximate the extent of continuous vegetative cover when the two sites were occupied. According to sediment core data from Lake La Yeguada, the premontane forest of the upper Santa María drainage had been extensively cleared by ca. 2000 B.C. (Piperno et al. 1991). By A.D. 1, the lower course of the river was well settled by farming peoples. The terrestrial vertebrates identified alongside the fish at Cerro Mangote and Sitio Sierra are, with very few exceptions, denizens of grassland, marsh-swamp, and secondary or dry woods (Cooke 1984a, 1984b; Cooke and Ranere 1989, 1992c; Cooke et al. 1996).

Site History and Paleogeography

Cerro Mangote's refuse covers 1750 m^2 of a prominent flat-topped hill of the same name. This is 1.2 km long and .2 km from the Santa María River's present north bank. Its eastern edge is now 8 km from the shoreline of Parita Bay. First recognized and excavated by McGimsey (1956), it was re-tested in 1979 by Ranere (Cooke 1984a). Seven acceptable dates range (at the 2 sigma level) from 5930 (5660-5640) 5450 cal B.C. to 3834 (3623) 3348 cal B.C.[1]

Five strata (McGimsey 1956) represent two distinguishable events. A basal "red zone" of laterized clay has fewer cultural materials per sediment unit than an overlying "brown zone". This is an organically rich refuse deposit that probably accumulated rapidly. The fish bone sample to which we refer comes from .45 m^3 of this "brown zone" (1.25-2.05 m below surface). The distribution of ^{14}C dates suggests that it was deposited sometime between 5000 and 3600 cal B.C.

Barber (1981) summarized Cerro Mangote's relation to continental and marine sediments on the basis of two 2.6 m "Vibracore" samples. By correlating sedimentology, ^{14}C dates and sea-level curves for Panama (Bartlett and Barghoorn 1973; Golik 1968), he proposed a facies change model, which related archaeological sites to coastline mechanics (Cooke and Ranere 1992a). He inferred that Cerro Mangote's initial occupation (ca. 5600 cal B.C.) coincided with the closest approach of a marine setting (1.2 km) and its abandonment (ca. 3600 cal B.C.) with the end of a period of rapid delta progradation. At this time, a marine setting would have been about 5 km distant.

We took salinometer readings during 1992-3 in the lower course of the Santa María River. Surface salinity at the mouth varies from 0‰ to 30‰ in a single tide cycle. This is the archetypal mesohaline "mixing" zone of a tropical estuary where riverine and marine influences are constantly and often violently juxtaposed.

Seven kilometers upstream, at París, surface salinity was generally 0-1‰ and occasionally 3-5‰. In this sector, the highest tides create a strong bore and turbid water. During rainy season floods, the downriver current is very strong: the water turns orange-brown with suspended sediments. This location represents the inward edge of the oligohaline section of the "middle estuary."

Twelve and 20 km upriver we recorded zero salinity although weak tidal influences cause the water level to fluctuate slightly (1.5 m at El Rincón and .5 m at Santa María). These locations correspond to Fairbridge's (1980) "upper or fluvial estuary" and Day et al.'s (1989:50) "tidal river zone."

If Cerro Mangote was between 1.2 and 5.5 km from the Santa María outlet during its Late Preceramic occupation, it would have been alongside the mesohaline mixing zone of the middle estuary. It is possible, however, that it was not actually along the primary river channel.

Sitio Sierra occupies a low knoll 10-15 m above sea level. It is .4-1.2 km north of the main channel of the Santa María River and 14 km from the mouth. A farming village with a maximum surveyed extent of 45 ha, it was occupied between ca. 200 cal B.C. and the Spanish Conquest. The fish bone sample presented herein comes from a 3.5 m^2 (1.4 m^3) cut, excavated into a 20 m^2 refuse midden that has not been dated by ^{14}C. Two domestic features lying directly beneath it were associated with two charcoal dates whose 2 sigma maximum range is 195 cal B.C. to cal A.D. 233 (with means of cal A.D. 2 to cal A.D. 29-56)(Cooke 1979, 1984a; Isaza-Aizuprúa 1993). The Aristide pottery (Cooke 1985) contained in the midden suggests that it was laid down before cal A.D. 400. Deposition seems to have been rapid.

If we apply an average sedimentation rate of 3 mm/1000 years (Clary et al. 1984:61) to Barber's facies change model, the central portion of the Santa María has prograded approximately 1 km/1000 years for the last four millennia. This is a "smoothed" estimate that does not take into account fluctuations in sedimentation rates due to deforestation, changes in precipitation patterns or local tectonic events. Nevertheless, Pb-210 dating of marine cores elsewhere in Panama Bay gives sedimentation rates which are similar to Barber's (Suman 1983:71). Hence, the active shoreline was probably 12-12.5 km away from Sitio Sierra at cal A.D. 1-400.

The Fish Bone Samples

We compare fish bones collected over a .125 inch standard metal mesh, laid flat. The Cerro Mangote sample

Table 2. Ratio of Fish Bone Elements (E) to Volume, and MNI, and the Estimated Average. Weight.

Site	Fish E per m³	Fish E/ MNI	Average estimated weight of teleosts (kg)
Cerro Mangote	7,100	12.6	.723
Sitio Sierra (all fish)	14,094	26.5	.325
Sitio Sierra (marine fish)			.407

comprises 3,195 skeletal elements: 3,107 (97.2 percent) are teleost (bony fish) and 88 (2.8 percent) elasmobranch (shark and ray). The Sitio Sierra sample totals 19,731 elements, of which 19,623 (99.5 percent) are teleost, and 108 (.5 percent) elasmobranch.

The two samples were buried in organic-rich soils with similar crumb structure. They were recovered over the same kinds of screen. This validates their comparison. Sitio Sierra's sample, however, was taken after the retained sediments were hosed down with water. This action surely influenced the differences exhibited by the two samples with regard to (1) the ratio of fish bone elements (E) to estimated numbers of individuals (MNI), and (2) the estimated average size of the identified fish (Table 2). We summarize identifications in Table 3 (Cerro Mangote) and Table 4 (Sitio Sierra). Table 1 includes simplified comments on the distribution of each identified taxon within the Santa María estuary based on our actualistic studies in Parita Bay.

Taxonomically secure identifications of bones are fundamental to the significance of this research. So some comments on our procedures are not out of place. These are not at the cutting edge of modern archaeozoology! Rather, they are subservient to the complexities generated by large, fragmented and diverse fish bone samples, which include many species of the same ETP genus or family—sometimes, *all* the currently recorded species (Cooke 1992, 1993b).

Our strategy consisted of three stages: (1) the assignment of body parts (fish E) identified with a binocular microscope to the most exact category on the taxonomic scale (i.e., Order, Family, Genus, Species), (2) the calculation of minimum numbers of individuals (MNI) based on size groups estimated by reference to specimens in the Smithsonian Tropical Research Institute's comparative skeletal collection, and (3) the calculation of the "estimated dietary biomass" (EDBM). This is the sum of the inferred body masses of all the individuals identified in each taxon.[2]

Readers with a modicum of experience in archaeozoology may be concerned about the imprecision of this procedure.

Table 3. Distribution of Fish Bones Recovered Using .125 Inch Metal Mesh Screen in a Refuse Deposit at Cerro Mangote, Panama. E—skeletal parts. MNI—minimum number of individuals. EDBM—estimated dietary biomass.

Genus and species	E	MNI	EDBM (kg)
Elasmobranchs			
Shark	10		
Shark, unid. species[a]	4	1	>2
CARCHARHINIDAE:			
Carcharhinus cf *altimus*	7	1	5
C. leucas	59	1	3.5
Ray	2		
Ray, unid. species	1	1	?
DASYATIDAE:			
Dasyatis	2	1	>10
PRISTIDAE:			
Pristis	1	1	?
UROLOPHIDAE:			
Urotrygon cf *asterias*	2	2	15
Teleosts			
ALBULIDAE:			
Albula neoguinaica	10	2	.7
ARIIDAE:	747		
"*Arius*"	28		
"*A.*" species B	20	4	3.15
"*A.*" *kessleri*	39	8	4.3
"*A.*" cf *kessleri*	3		
"*A.*" *kessleri* or "*A.*" sp. B	14		
"*A.*" *lentiginosus*	3	1	.45
"*A.*" cf *lentiginosus*	1		
"*A.*" "*osculus*"	1	1	.45
"*A.*" cf "*osculus*"	1		
"*A.*" *osculus* or "*A.*" species B	2		
"*A.*" *platypogon*	4	2	1.15
"*A.*" *seemanni*	112	15	3.73
Bagre panamensis	2	1	.45
B. pinnimaculatus	7	3	2.95
Cathorops	39		
Cathorops, not species A	2		
C. species A	31	6	1.3
C. cf species A	6		
C. hypophthalmus	2	1	.45
C. cf *hypophthalmus*	2		
C. multiradiatus	2	2	.55
C. tuyra	7	3	1.2
C. cf *tuyra*	1		
C. species A or *C. tuyra*	1		
Sciadeichthys dowii	339	24	46.6
cf *S. dowii*	6		
BATRACHOIDIDAE:			
Batrachoides	63	15	7.275
BELONIDAE:			
Strongylura cf *scapularis*	1	1	.15
CARANGIDAE:	4		

Table 3. (Continued)

Table 3. (Continued)

Genus and species	E	MNI	EDBM (kg)
Carangoides otrynter	1	1	.25
Caranx caninus	8	5	3.9
C. cf caninus	3	1	.25
Chloroscombrus orqueta	2	1	.075
Oligoplites altus	3	2	.9
O. altus or *O. saurus*	2	1	.15
Selene peruviana	3	2	.425
CENTROPOMIDAE:			
Centropomus	19		
Centropomus ("gualajo" group[b])	11	1	.075
Centropomus armatus	18	5	2.2
C. cf armatus	2		
C. armatus or *C. unionensis*	1		
C. robalito	4	3	1.1
C. cf robalito	1		
C. robalito or *C. unionensis*	1		
Centropomus ("elongate")	25	3	5.58
C. medius	16	5	4
C. nigrescens	1	1	1.5
C. viridis	5	4	4.475
C. nigrescens or *C. viridis*	21	1	.55
CLUPEIFORMES:	1		
CLUPEIDAE:			
Opisthonema cf *libertate*	16	2	.2
PRISTIGASTERIDAE:			
Ilisha furthii	6	3	.7
Opisthopterus	1	1	.03
ELOPIDAE:			
Elops affinis	1	1	.075
ENGRAULIDAE:			
cf *Cetengraulis mysticetus*	2	1	.01
GERREIDAE:	9		
Diapterus peruvianus	9	3	.8
cf *D. peruvianus*	4		
Eucinostomus currani	1	1	.15
Eugerres	8		
E. brevimanus	2	1	.15
E. lineatus	8	3	1.25
Gerres cinereus	3	1	.15
GOBIIDAE/ELEOTRIDIDAE:	1		
Bathygobius cf *andrei*	2	1	.03
Dormitator latifrons	388	20	2.775
Eleotris picta	3	2	.6
Gobioides peruanus	11	3	.325
Gobiomorus maculatus	3	2	.2
HAEMULIDAE:	5		
Anisotremus	1	1	.25
Anisotremus dovii	1	1	.15
Haemulon flaviguttatum	1	1	.15
Orthopristis chalceus	21	5	1.225
cf *O. chalceus*	1		
Pomadasys	2		
Pomadasys macracanthus	18	4	2.65
P. cf *macracanthus*	5		
Pomadasys (*Haemuliopsis*)	3		

Genus and species	E	MNI	EDBM (kg)
Pomadasys (*H.*) cf *elongatus*	1	1	.2
P. (*H.*) *leuciscus*	1	1	1
P. (*H.*) cf *leuciscus*	2		
P. (*H.*) *nitidus*	2	1	.25
LOBOTIDAE:			
Lobotes surinamensis	9	4	7.65
LUTJANIDAE:	7	3	1.15
Lutjanus argentiventris	2	2	3.5
L. cf *argentiventris*	1	1	.45
L. colorado	1	1	.5
L. guttatus	1	1	.45
L. novemfasciatus	2	2	3.5
MUGILIDAE:			
Mugil cf *curema*	15	5	1.325
POLYNEMIDAE:			
Polydactylus approximans	2	1	.35
P. opercularis	35	7	2.025
SCIAENIDAE:	8		
Bairdiella	1		
B. armata	4	2	.3
B. ensifera	2	1	.2
Cynoscion	3		
C. albus	17	4	11
C. albus or *C. stolzmanni*	7		
C. squamipinnis	1	1	3.5
C. stolzmanni	7	4	3.55
Menticirrhus panamensis	1	1	1
M. cf *panamensis*	1	1	.25
Micropogonias altipinnis	8	5	10.35
cf *M. altipinnis*	2		
Ophioscion scierus	2	1	.25
Ophioscion typicus	8	3	.275
O. cf *typicus*	1		
O. vermicularis	1	1	.15
Stellifer oscitans	3	2	.2
Paralonchurus dumerilii	2	2	.7
SERRANIDAE:			
Epinephelus analogus	1	1	1.75
E. cf *analogus*	6	2	8
TETRAODONTIDAE:			
Sphoeroides annulatus	7	3	1.95
Total, Elasmobranch:	88	8	>35.5
Total, Teleost:	3107	246	177.93
Total, Fish:	3195	254	213.43

[a] unid.—unidentified; a taxon that is not present in the Smithsonian Tropical Research Institute's comparative skeletal collection.

[b] The following three species are known as "gualajos" by Parita Bay fisherfolk. Osteologically, they are somewhat distinct from the three "elongated" species. Hence specifically undiagnostic bones can sometimes be assigned to either group.

Table 4. Distribution of Fish Bones Recovered Using a .125 Inch Metal Mesh Screen in a Refuse Deposit at Sitio Sierra, Panama. E—skeletal parts. MNI—minimum number of individuals. EDBM—estimated dietary biomass. *—primary freshwater taxon.

Genus and species	E	MNI	EDBM (kg)
Elasmobranchs			
Elasmobranch, unid. species	25	1	?
Elasmobranch, unid. species	10	1	?
CARCHARHINIDAE:			
Carcharhinus cf *altimus*	2	1	1
C. leucas	6	2	11
C. limbatus	1	1	?
Rhizoprionodon longurio	33	2	1
Ray	1		
DASYATIDAE:			
Dasyatis cf *longus*	1	1	?
MYLIOBATIDAE:			
Aeteobatus narinari	4	1	3
SPHYRNIDAE:			
Sphyrna	1	1	
cf *Sphyrna*	1	1	>10
Sphyrna cf *tiburo*	19	1	1
PRISTIDAE:			
Pristis	3	1	?
UROLOPHIDAE:	1	1	?
Teleosts	3320		
Teleost, unid. species	1	1	.1
SILURIFORMES:	52		
ARIIDAE:	1529		
"*Arius*"	85	1	.025
"*Arius*" *dasycephalus*	2	1	.15
"*A.*" cf *dasycephalus*	1		
"*A.*" species B	89	10	9.5
"*A.*" cf species B	5		
"*A.*" *kessleri*	111	13	9.3
"*A.*" cf *kessleri*	11		
"*A.*" "*osculus*"	14	3	1.5
"*A.*" cf "*osculus*"	1		
"*A.*" *platypogon*	1	1	.9
"*A.*" cf *platypogon*	1		
"*A.*" *seemanni*	80	8	2.05
cf "*A.*" *seemanni*	5		
Bagre	12		
B. panamensis	48	6	2.6
B. pinnimaculatus	35	5	6.825
Cathorops	114		
Cathorops (not species A or *hypophthalmus*)	1		
C. species A	13	3	.85
C. cf species A	1	1	.03
C. sp. A or *hypophthalmus*	1		
C. species B	8	4	.575
C. cf species B	3		

Table 4. (Continued)

Genus and species	E	MNI	EDBM (kg)
Cathorops species A or *C. tuyra*		1	
C. multiradiatus	5	2	.35
C. cf *multiradiatus*	1		
C. tuyra	20	4	1.15
C. cf *tuyra*	4		
Sciadeops troscheli	3	2	.8
Sciadeichthys dowii	333	18	35.45
cf *S. dowii*	8		
AUCHENIPTERIDAE:			
*Parauchenipterus amblops**	863	112	3.84
PIMELODIDAE:			
Rhamdia cf *guatemalensis**	509	23	5.15
LORICARIIDAE:			
*Hypostomus panamensis**	3	1	.3
cf ALBULIDAE unid. species	6	1	.5
ALBULIDAE:			
Albula neoguinaica	52	2	1.1
cf BATRACHOIDIDAE:	1		
BATRACHOIDIDAE:			
Batrachoides pacifici	1	1	.75
Daector	1	1	.275
cf BELONIDAE unid. species	1	1	.2
BELONIDAE:	2		
Strongylura	1	1	.25
Tylosurus	2	2	.65
BOTHIDAE:			
Citharichthys gilberti	1	1	.05
CARANGIDAE:	194		
Alectis ciliaris	1	1	.15
Carangoides otrynter	10	2	.85
Caranx	4		
C. caballus	39	4	.7
C. caninus	29	6	18.9
Chloroscombrus orqueta	251	13	1.075
cf *C. orqueta*	2		
Oligoplites	51		
O. altus	9	1	1
O. refulgens	25	5	1
O. cf *refulgens*	1		
O. saurus	1	1	.25
Selar crumenophthalmus	25	2	.35
Selene	354		
Selene brevoortii	54	4	2.075
S. oerstedii	2	1	.2
S. peruviana	1154	50	7.5
Trachinotus kennedyi	2	1	3
CENTROPOMIDAE:			
Centropomus	21		
C. medius	3	1	.075
Centropomus cf *medius*	2	1	.8
C. nigrescens/viridis[a]	47	9	14.55
C. robalito	1	1	.075
CHARACIFORMES:	2		
CTENOLUCIIDAE:			
*Ctenolucius hujeta**	17	3	.225
CURIMATIDAE:			
*Curimata magdalenae**	26	7	.355

Table 4. (Continued)

Genus and species	E	MNI	EDBM (kg)
ERYTHRINIDAE:			
Hoplias sp*	2090	50	15.55
CICHLIDAE:			
Aequidens coeruleopunctatus*	26	9	.4
CLUPEIFORMES:	105		
CLUPEIDAE:			
Opisthonema cf libertate	3263	119	11.9
ENGRAULIDAE:			
cf Anchoa	3	1	.1
PRISTIGASTERIDAE:			
Ilisha furthii	76	5	1.95
EPHIPPIDAE:			
Parapsettus panamensis	1	1	.15
GERREIDAE:		1	
cf Diapterus peruvianus	1	1	.15
GOBIIDAE/ELEOTRIDIDAE:			
Dormitator latifrons	223	15	3.575
Eleotris picta	18	4	1.225
Gobiomorus maculatus	2	1	.075
cf G. maculatus	2	1	.15
HAEMULIDAE:	467		
Anisotremus	3		
Anisotremus dovii	16	2	.9
A. pacifici	13	4	1.45
Orthopristis chalceus	2967	87	13.25
cf O. chalceus	3		
Pomadasys	6		
Pomadasys bayanus	7	2	1.8
P. cf bayanus	1	1	.2
P. macracanthus	32	6	4.15
P. panamensis	2	2	1.2
P. cf panamensis	1	1	.5
Pomadasys (Haemuliopsis)	19	2	.45
Pomadasys (H.) elongatus	3	2	.35
P. (H.) cf elongatus	1		
cf P. (H.) elongatus	3		
P. (H.) leuciscus	6	2	.75
P. (H.) cf leuciscus	2	1	.1
P. (H.) cf nitidus	1	1	.25
LOBOTIDAE:			
Lobotes surinamensis	8	3	7.25
LUTJANIDAE:			
Lutjanus cf colorado	1	1	.5
MUGILIDAE:			
Mugil cf curema	2	1	.45
POLYNEMIDAE:			
Polydactylus	1		
P. approximans	1	1	.4
P. opercularis	109	10	4.2
SCIAENIDAE:	20		
Bairdiella	1		
B. ensifera	3	2	.375
Cynoscion	18		
C. albus	17	3	5.35
C. albus or C. stolzmanni	1	1	2.75
C. stolzmanni	27	4	1.6
C. cf stolzmanni	2	2	.225

Table 4. (Continued)

Genus and species	E	MNI	EDBM (kg)
Menticirrhus panamensis	1	1	.55
Micropogonias altipinnis	22	4	4.15
Ophioscion	1		
Ophioscion scierus	7	3	.55
O. typicus	13	3	.4
O. cf typicus	5		
Paralonchurus dumerilii	1	1	.8
Stellifer chrysoleuca	1	1	.2
SCOMBRIDAE:			
Euthynnus lineatus	5	1	.8
Scomberomorus sierra	7	4	1.95
SPHYRAENIDAE:			
Sphyraena ensis	2	2	.95
STERNARCHIDAE:			
Sternopygus dariensis*	161	9	2.4
STROMATEIDAE:			
Peprilus snyderi	2	2	.35
SYNBRANCHIDAE:			
Synbranchus marmoratus*	117	4	.725
TETRAODONTIDAE:	6	1	.15
Sphoeroides	3		
Sphoeroides annulatus	1	1	.35
Guentheridia formosa	4	2	.5
Total, Elasmobranch:	108	15	>27
Total, Teleost:	19,623	729	236.8
Freshwater:	3,812	218	28.945
Marine (incl. gobiids):	12,436	510	207.805[b]
Total, Fish:	19,731	744	263.850

[a] 3—C. nigrescens, 1—C. cf nigrescens, 1—C. nigrescens or C. viridis, 4—C. viridis.

[b] One individual of an unidentified species could be either marine or freshwater.

Allometry (i.e., estimating the size of archaeological individuals by plotting accurate measurements of whole bones against biometric data acquired from fresh specimens) is a much more reliable way of calculating the size of individuals and, it follows, the relative importance of each taxon.

Statistically meaningful allometry, however, requires well preserved archaeological bones and ontogenically complete series of modern skeletons. Very few bones that survived in our samples are measurable. Very few identified species were represented by numerically meaningful groups of measurable bones. Individual sizes within a taxon were often estimated from different body parts. In two cases, we verified our EDBM with allometric calculations. The results were statistically identical. In this situation, the comparative method is far from perfect, but is practical. We will present allometric reconstructions of fish size when the comparative skeletal collection has been expanded.

Molecular biology is casting doubts on the significance of some current taxonomic treatments of ETP fish, especially freshwater taxa. Even so, we believe that archaeo-ichthyologists should strive to identify species as rationally as their ancient and modern fish samples permit (Cooke 1992). Of course, this is easier said than done. Osteological differentiation at the species level is variable and unpredictable. Externally, the two ETP bobos (*Polydactylus approximans* and *P. opercularis*) are distinguished only by different fin coloration and pelvic fin ray counts. Skeletally, however, they are strikingly dissimilar. The ETP sea catfish of the Ariidae family comprise about 20 poorly categorized species. Even freshly caught specimens are notoriously tricky to identify (Cooke 1993b). Their head bones, however, can be differentiated accurately (Cooke, 1996).[3]

Our final methodological point is that it is much easier to infer MNI and EDBM for teleosts than for elasmobranchs, which have fewer and morphologically more homogeneous ossified elements. At both sites, the dietary contribution of sharks and rays appears to be disproportionate to the abundance of their bones. Our current reconstructions, whose accuracy is affected by our not possessing skeletons of a few unidentified taxa, suggest that at Cerro Mangote eight elasmobranch individuals (3.2 percent fish MNI) supplied at least 16.6 percent EDBM. At Sitio Sierra, 15 sharks and rays (2.1 percent fish MNI) represent 10.2 percent EDBM. Sharks and rays, then, were important food items. However, from a cultural-ecological perspective, their archaeofaunal distribution is broadly consistent with the inferences we derive from the teleost samples. All positively identified taxa enter shallow meso/oligohaline waters; the bull shark (*Carcharhinus leucas*) and sawfish (*Pristis* spp.) are capable of spending long periods of time in freshwater (Table 1; Vásquez and Thorson 1982). For these reasons, we focus the following discussion on bony fish whose levels of "identifiability" are presented in Table 5.

Table 5. Bone Identified to Family, Genus, and Species.

Site	Family	Genus	Species[a]
	% = proportion of teleost E		
Cerro Mangote	2,357 (76%)	1,576 (51%)	1,226 (40%)
Sitio Sierra	16,135 (82%)	13,903 (71%)	6,988 (36%)[b]

[a] Only incontrovertible identifications according to our criteria.

[b] If we assume that *Hoplias* and *Opisthonema* bones represent single species—as they probably do—this figure would be 12,341 (63%).

Fish Taxa Found in Freshwater

Loftin (1965:193) collected only 21 primary freshwater fish in the Santa María River basin, a species poverty that is typical of the fish fauna of the Central American land-bridge (Miller 1966). Our own collections have added two species: the Darien knifefish (*Sternopygus dariensis*) and the bluntnosed driftcat (*Parauchenipterus* [=*Trachycorystes*] *amblops*). Both are common to abundant in the freshwater and oligohaline stretches of the river (Cooke and Tapia 1994a).

The Santa María River basin also harbors some secondary (or peripheral) sleepers and gobies. These evolved in the sea, but have adapted to spending all or part of their lives in freshwater. We have collected 25 genuinely marine species in the oligohaline (less than 1‰ to less than 5‰) riverine zone (París collection station), and ten in the freshwater fluvial estuary (Figure 1; Cooke and Tapia 1994a).

In spite of their low diversity in nature and in the archaeological bone samples (nine families, genera and species), primary freshwater fish are quite abundant in the lower stretches of the Santa María River. Not surprisingly, Sitio Sierra's inhabitants regularly caught and ate them (together they represent 19 percent E, 30 percent MNI and 12 percent EDBM). The Santa María trahira ranks third for E, fourth for MNI and third for EDBM. Four of the listed species—Santa María trahira, Darien knifefish, Panamanian armored cat, and Guatemalan rivercat—grow to more than .5 kg. The others, though very small, can occur in large shoals, so that biomass compensates for low body mass. For example, the bluntnosed driftcat, whose maximum recorded adult weight is 80 gm, is the second most abundant teleost at Sitio Sierra. These frenetic little cats are difficult to extricate from nets because they have serrated and poisonous pectoral spines that can inflict nasty wounds. They are also most active at night, which complicates handling. A large proportion of the pectoral spines found at Sitio Sierra were intact, suggesting that these fish were captured with baskets or poison, rather than with nets.

In contrast, no primary freshwater fish occurred at Cerro Mangote. Our present-day sampling program shows that curimatas, knifefish, tahiras and driftcats thrive in oligohaline waters 7 km upriver, seaward of Cerro Mangote's current location. But we caught only two primary freshwater fish in one year at the river mouth: one driftcat and one Panamanian armored catfish (*Hypostomus panamensis*). These were probably washed down by strong wet season currents. Therefore, the absence of these freshwater species in the "brown zone" refuse provides indirect support for geomorphological indications that Late Preceramic Cerro Mangote was close to the mesohaline (mixing) zone of the estuary.

But what if Cerro Mangote was not, in fact, adjacent to the main channel of the Santa María River? Perhaps the absence of primary freshwater fish indicates this. This question can only be answered satisfactorily with continued geomorphological research. Nevertheless, the archaeo-faunal distribution of two marine teleosts suggests that it may have been near a major channel. One is the wide-mouthed catfish (*"Arius"* species B, the eighth ranked teleost taxon [MNI]). Although this species is still undescribed, it is very common in the Santa María River, but only in the main channel, where it occurs from the mouth to at least 20 km inland. We have not recorded it in the Estero Palo Blanco fish trap where salinity ranges from 15‰ to 34‰. It probably spends its entire life cycle within the main channel where it attains a large size (640 mm standard length, 4.8 kg [Cooke 1993b; Cooke and Tapia 1994a, b]).

The other relevant species is the Peruvian eelgoby (*Gobioides peruanus*). This fossorial fish is most unlikely to be caught away from the main river channel since it lives in burrows in the muddy banks of the tidal river to at least 8 km upstream. Local fishermen cut eelgobies up with machetes and use the pieces to bait hooks. They think they are repugnant and inedible. But since Cerro Mangote lies on top of a hill, up quite a steep slope, it is likely that the bones deposited in the Late Preceramic middens are food remains.

The three local euryhaline sleepers—the spotted sleeper, painted gudgeon, and pike-gudgeon (*Gobiomorus maculatus*)— are also indicators of estuarine topography. Their absence in the Estero Palo Blanco fish trap suggests that they reject salinities greater than 15‰. The least salt-tolerant is the pike-gudgeon, which is found in quite fast-flowing streams. We have collected large adult painted gudgeons and spotted sleepers (.5-1.5 kg) in oxbows and in the freshwater and oligohaline zones of the main river channel. Smaller spotted sleepers are also abundant in shallow coastal pools where they can be caught in large numbers when water levels drop. This species is the second-ranked teleost at Cerro Mangote (8 percent MNI). Average individual weight is ca. 140 gm, in contrast to ca. 240 gm at Sitio Sierra. It is reasonable to suppose, then, that Cerro Mangote's spotted sleepers were collected, possibly by women and children, in mangrove channels or pockets of water in the *alvina*.

Marine Teleosts

At a macro-ecological level, the marine archaeo-ichthyofaunas from Cerro Mangote and Sitio Sierra are similar. Their estuarine nature is underscored by the fact that we have observed all of the recorded taxa in the middle and/or upper estuary at least once. Both samples lack many widespread and popular foodfish taxa that are associated by preference or obligation with coral reefs, the offshore epipelagic zone, and deeper, clearer water around rocks. The best known examples are: tunnies, wahoos and their allies (*Thunnus, Katsuwonus, Auxis, Acanthocybium*); dolphinfish (*Coryphaena*); tilefish (*Caulolatilus*); brotulas (*Brotula*) (a popular food fish in Ecuador); moray eels

(Muraenidae); parrotfish (*Scarus*); damselfishes (Pomacentridae); and wrasses (Labridae) (Allen and Robertson 1994; Cooke 1992; Phillips and Pérez-Cruet 1984; Thomson et al. 1979).

"Estuarineness" is also underlined by the presence or absence of individual species that belong to ethologically and ecologically heterogeneous families and genera. For example, the only grouper recorded at the two study sites—the spotted cabrilla (*Epinephelus analogus*)—is acknowledged to be the most estuarine ETP species. The most deep-water and most coralline snappers (*Lutjanus peru* and *L. viridis*) are absent. So are the least estuarine corvina (*Cynoscion reticulatus*), and carangids that prefer to swim offshore in clear water, such as amberjacks (*Seriola*), and rainbow runners (*Elagatis bipinnulata*).

Taxonomic Richness

Table 6 presents the numbers of positively identified marine families, genera and species (excluding gobies and sleepers). The two samples are similarly diverse; the slightly greater richness at Sitio Sierra reflects larger sample size.

Table 6. Numbers of Positively Identified Marine Fish Families, Genera and Species (Excluding Gobies and Sleepers).

Site	Families	Genera	Species
Cerro Mangote	19	40	59
Sitio Sierra	22	43	72

Table 7 shows that 10 genera and 19 species are recorded only at Cerro Mangote and 13 genera and 19 species exclusively at Sitio Sierra. At first sight, this "mutual taxonomic exclusivity," appears to be a significant difference between the samples. All these taxa, however, represent 1 percent E or less, except for the longspine snook (*Centropomus armatus*) (more than 2 percent MNI at Cerro Mangote). Hence, some of this variability can be explained by the randomness of fish behavior, fishing, taphonomy, and archaeological sampling procedures.

We have not captured 12 of the 38 mutually exclusive species in the stationary fish trap nor in the main channel of the tidal river. These are: broadhead catfish (*"Arius" dasycephalus*), Panamanian catfish (*"A." lentiginosus*), chili catfish (*Sciadeops troscheli*), African pompano (*Alectis ciliaris*), purse-eyed scad (*Selar crumenophthalmus*), spotted rose snapper (*Lutjanus guttatus*), Cortez grunt (*Haemulon flaviguttatum*), Panamanian grunt (*Pomadasys panamensis*), scalefin weakfish (*Cynoscion squamipinnis*), worm-lined croaker (*Ophioscion vermicularis*), Pacific

Table 7. **Genera and Species of Marine Teleosts Reported in only One of the Two Analyzed Archaeological Fish Bone Samples (Cerro Mangote and Sitio Sierra, Panama).** Mutually exclusive genera are <u>underlined</u>.

Cerro Mangote	%E	%MNI	Sitio Sierra	%E	%MNI
			"Arius"	.02	.20
"Arius" lentiginosus	.13	.41	<u>*Sciadeops troschelii*</u>	.02	.40
<u>*Centropomus armatus*</u>	.64	2.03	<u>*Daector*</u>	<.01	.20
<u>*Opisthopterus*</u>	.03	.41	<u>*Tylosurus*</u>	.01	.40
<u>*Elops affinis*</u>	.03	.41	<u>*Citharichthys gilberti*</u>	<.01	.20
<u>*Cetengraulis mysticetus*</u>	.06	.41	<u>*Alectis ciliaris*</u>	<.01	.20
<u>*Eucinostomus currani*</u>	.03	.41	*Caranx caballus*	.31	.78
<u>*Eugerres*</u>	.03	.41	*Oligoplites refulgens*	.21	.97
E. lineatus	.26	1.22	<u>*Selar crumenophthalmus*</u>	.20	.40
<u>*Gerres cinereus*</u>	.10	.41	*Selene brevoortii*	.43	.78
<u>*Bathygobius andrei*</u>	.06	.41	*S. oerstedii*	<.01	.20
<u>*Gobioides peruanus*</u>	.35	1.22	<u>*Trachinotus kennedyi*</u>	.01	.20
<u>*Haemulon flaviguttatum*</u>	.03	.41	<u>*Anchoa*</u>	<.01	.20
Lutjanus argentiventris	.10	1.22	<u>*Parapsettus panamensis*</u>	<.01	.20
L. guttatus	.03	.41	*Anisotremus pacifici*	.10	.78
L. novemfasciatus	.06	.82	*Pomadasys bayanus*	.32	.59
Bairdiella armata	.13	.41	*Stellifer chrysoleuca*	<.01	.20
Cynoscion squamipinnis	.03	.41	<u>*Euthynnus lineatus*</u>	.04	.20
Ophioscion vermicularis	.03	.41	<u>*Scomberomorus sierra*</u>	.06	.78
Stellifer oscitans	.10	.41	<u>*Sphyraena ensis*</u>	.01	.56
<u>*Epinephelus analogus*</u>	.23	1.22	<u>*Peprilus snyderi*</u>	.01	.40
			Guentheridia formosa	.03	.40

barracuda (*Sphyraena ensis*), and black skipjack tuna (*Euthynnus lineatus*).

Cooke (1992) argued that the African pompano, Pacific barracuda, and black skipjack tuna belong to a "transitional or outer (lower) estuarine" species cluster: "the component taxa probably move into estuaries opportunistically to feed or when salinity and/or visibility is unusually high, i.e., at the end of dry season." These, and three other species in this hypothetical grouping, including green jack (*Caranx caballus*), Panama spadefish (*Parapsettus panamensis*) and sierra mackerel (*Scomberomorus sierra*), were recorded only at Sitio Sierra where together they represent .5 percent marine teleost E and 3 percent MNI.[4]

The above distributions, both archaeofaunal and contemporary, suggest that Sitio Sierra had more regular, albeit sporadic, access to fish caught at the seaward edge of the marine (or lower) estuary than did Cerro Mangote. Even so, a few fish species (when adults) at Cerro Mangote appear to avoid shallow muddy bottoms close to shore, according to our actualistic research, e.g., slender-spined catfish ("*Arius*" *platypogon*), chihuil catfish (*Bagre*

panamensis), Pacific bonefish (*Albula neoguinaica*), high-fin corvina (*Micropogonias altipinnis*), Cortez grunt (*Haemulon flaviguttatum*), Pacific moonfish (*Selene peruviana*), spotted rose snapper, and scalefin weakfish. The Cortez grunt is usually associated with reefs and rocks, although juveniles sometimes occur in mangroves (Cooke 1992). Fisheries data suggest that the scalefin corvina is commonest in the deeper waters of the marine estuary (Bartels et al. 1983, 1984; Cooke 1992). In sum, this cluster of species could indicate that Cerro Mangote's inhabitants fished occasionally from watercraft in the marine estuary; but it is also possible that Parita Bay inshore waters were less sedimented (and less turbid) at the time of this site's occupation, than they are today, and favored the inshore encroachment of the above species.[5]

Dominance

Dominance (McNaughton 1968), construed culturally, can be assessed by looking at frequency of capture (percent MNI) and contribution to diet (percent EDBM).

Frequency of capture (percent MNI)

Table 8 summarizes dominance by MNI. Sea catfish were landed more frequently at Cerro Mangote (29 percent) than at Sitio Sierra (16 percent). The genera *"Arius"* and *Sciadeichthys* together represent more than 22 percent MNI, and the flap-nosed, Seemann's and Kessler's catfish more than 19 percent MNI. These three species, in addition to the widemouthed and thick-lipped catfish (*"Arius" "osculus"*), the five ETP *Cathorops* species, and the long-barbled catfish (*Bagre pinnimaculatus*) are permanent and ubiquitous residents in the middle estuaries of Parita Bay (Cooke 1993b; Cooke and Tapia 1994a, b). Seemann's catfish teem near river mouth human settlements where they feed voraciously on domestic refuse. Flap-nosed catfish—the largest ETP sea cats which often weigh more than 10 kg—are common in mangrove channels and in the oligohaline stretches of the Santa María River. We have taken widemouthed and Tuyra catfish (*Cathorops tuyra*) in the freshwater fluvial or upper estuary (Cooke 1992, 1993b; Cooke and Tapia 1994a).

At Sitio Sierra, MNI dominance exhibits a different pattern. Three species, none of which exceed 300 gm weight, comprise 50 percent marine fish MNI: Pacific threadfin herring (*Opisthonema* cf. *libertate*), Pacific moonfish, and brassy grunt (*Orthopristis chalceus*). Together they are more dominant than the first five ranked species at Cerro Mangote, where they are also present, but in noticeably smaller numbers.

Thesethree species appeared sporadically in Estero Palo Blanco fish trap, but in very small numbers. We did not capture them n the Santa María River (Cooke and Tapia 1994a, b). D'Croz et al. (1977), however, recorded large shoals of Pacific moonfish in stationary intertidal traps set close to Veracruz Beach, near Panama City. This locale lacks the extensive mudflats typical of central Parita Bay. We have observed large gillnet catches of thread-herrings about .5 km seaward of El Rompío in clearish water. El Rompío fisherfolk say that they net the brassy grunt and Pacific moonfish in currents of clear water on the incoming tide and also close to sandbanks within Parita Bay. Hence, it is likely that water-column clarity and substrate type are relevant paramerters to the intra-estuarine distribution of moonfish, thread-herrings, and brassy grunts. We not reject the inference that their dominance at Sitio Sierra is correlated with the use of gill-nets set some distance offshore

Table 8. Marine Families, Genera and Species Ranked 1-5 in the Archaeological Teleost Samples at Cerro Mangote and Sitio Sierra, Panama Expressed as Percent MNI (Includes Gobies and Sleepers).

Cerro Mangote		Percent MNI	Sitio Sierra		Percent MNI
Family					
1. Sea catfish	Ariidae	28.9	Herrings	Clupeidae	23.3
2. Sleepers etc.	Eleotrididae/Gobiidae	11.4	Grunts	Haemulidae	22.1
Corvinas etc.	Sciaenidae	11.4			
3.			Jacks etc.	Carangidae	17.7
4. Snook	Centropomidae	9.3	Sea catfish	Ariidae	16
5. Grunts	Haemulidae	6.1	Corvinas etc.	Sciaenidae	4.9
Toadfish	Batrachoididae	6.1			
Genus					
1. Sea catfish	*"Arius"*	12.6	Thread herring	*Opisthonema*	23
2. Sea catfish	*Sciadeichthys*	9.8	Grunt	*Orthopristis*	17
3. Snook	*Centropomus*	9.3	Moonfish etc.	*Selene*	10.8
4. Sleeper	*Dormitator*	8.1	Sea catfish	*"Arius"*	7.2
5. Toadfish	*Batrachoides*	6.1	Grunt	*Pomadasys*	3.9
Species					
1. Flap-nosed catfish	*Sciadeichthys dowii*	9.8	Thread herring	*Opisthonema libertate*	23
2. Spotted sleeper	*Dormitator latifrons*	8.1	Brassy grunt	*Orthopristis chalceus*	17
3. Seemann's catfish	*"Arius" seemanni*	6.1	Pac. moonfish	*Selene peruviana*	9.8
Toadfish	*Batrachoides* spp.	6.1	Flap-nosed catfish	*Sciadeichthys dowii*	3.5
5. Kessler's catfish	*"Arius" kessleri*	3.3	Spotted sleeper	*Dormitator latifrons*	3

(*contra* Cooke 1988, 1992). We must determine experimentally whether stationary traps set over sandbanks are appropriate for catching shoals of these taxa.

Contribution to diet (percent EDBM)

At Cerro Mangote, sea catfish account for 38 percent EDBM. One species alone—the flap-nosed catfish— represents 26 percent. Snook, the second-ranked teleost family, account for 11 percent EDBM. In spite of their small average size, the Pacific thread-herring, Pacific moonfish, and brassy grunt represent 16 percent marine fish EDBM at Sitio Sierra.

Fish with average adult body masses of more than 1 kg contribute a larger proportion of EDBM at Cerro Mangote. Thirty-seven individuals (15 percent) represent 61 percent EDBM, while at Sitio Sierra, 34 individuals (7 percent) provide 46 percent EDBM (Table 9).

Since we are dealing with samples which differ taphonomically and have some collection-induced biases, we should beware of exaggerating the significance of size-range discrepancies. Furthermore, bones smaller than .125 inches have yet to be considered in our calculations. However, it is possible that the larger number of sizeable fish captured at Cerro Mangote reflects a stronger emphasis on land-based capture techniques. For example, the high dominance levels of estuarine sea cats and snook would be consistent with damming up mangrove channel outlets with large-meshed nets or baskets and spearing from the channel and river edge. The two middle and upper estuary toadfish species, fifth-ranked by numbers at Cerro Mangote, but rare at Sitio Sierra, are ungainly, bulky and wholesome fish that hug muddy bottoms. They too would have been captured regularly if Preceramic fisherfolk had blocked off outlets with some kind of barrier that permitted the exit of smaller fish.

Concluding Remarks

Geomorphological Considerations

The fish bone samples collected using .125 inch mesh screens at Cerro Mangote and Sitio Sierra lend support to the principal events outlined in Barber's (1981) facies change model for the evolution of the Santa María delta. They also draw attention to details in local topography, which, though speculative, can be verified by geographical prospection at a later date.

No primary freshwater fish were identified in the Cerro Mangote sample. This suggests that this site's fisherfolk did not operate in the fluvial estuary and, probably, not in the oligohaline stretches of the river, either.

The hypothesis that Cerro Mangote was situated at some distance from the main river channel is challenged, albeit tenuously, by (1) the high rank of the widemouthed catfish which has not yet been recorded seaward of the main river mouth and (2) the use, apparently for food, of the Peruvian eelgoby. The abundance of small spotted sleepers (averaging less than 140 gm) alludes to fishing in shallow *alvina* pools or mangrove channels in the high and supra-tidal zones.

Other aspects of Cerro Mangote's fish bone proportionality infer fishing along intertidal mudflats and near the river mouth: the general dominance of sea catfish, particularly flap-nosed, Kessler's and Seemann's catfish, and the high rank of toadfish and snook.[6]

As befits its location in the upper, or fluvial, estuary, freshwater fish were captured regularly at Sitio Sierra. If this village had been near a smaller river than the Santa María, we believe that we would have recorded more bones of the ubiquitous blue-spotted cichlid. This species is most abundant in the stagnant shallows of streams and rivulets (Conkel 1993:181).

The archaeofaunal distribution of the marine mojarras (Gerreidae) may have implications for geomorphological reconstructions. These fish are abundant in Mexican coastal lagoons where they are present the year-round (Aguirre and Yáñez A. 1986; Warburton 1979). They are occasional within the Santa María River and along the mesohaline littoral, but generally as juveniles and young adults. Their bones dominate samples from the lagoonal Puerto Chacho site in northern Colombia (Legros

Table 9. Marine Teleosts in Archaeological Bone Samples from Cerro Mangote and Sitio Sierra, Panama, Whose Weight is Estimated to Exceed 1 kg.

	Cerro Mangote		Sitio Sierra	
	Inds. > 1kg	EDBM (kg)	Inds. > 1 kg	EDBM (kg)
"Arius" kessleri	1	1.30	3	4.00
"A." species B	1	1.20	5	7.25
Bagre pinnimaculatus	1	1.50	2	5.25
Sciadeichthys dowii	12	40.50	9	29.75
Caranx caninus	1	2.00	3	16.75
Trachinotus kennedyi			1	3.00
Centropomus nig/vir	5	13.25	3	10.25
Pomadasys macracanthus	1	1.25	1	1.25
Lobotes surinamensis	2	6.80	3	7.25
Cynoscion albus	3	10.75	2	4.75
C. albus or *stolzmanni*			1	2.75
C. squamipinnis	1	3.50		
Micropogonias altipinnis	3	9.75	1	2.50
Lutjanus argentiventris	2	3.50		
Lutjanus novemfasciatus	2	3.50		
Epinephelus analogus	2	8.75		
Totals:	37	107.55	34	94.75

1992:191). Their fairly low archaeofaunal visibility in Parita Bay is not consistent with a fishing strategy that concentrates on shallow bar-formed lagoons (*sensu* Barnes 1980). Perhaps these ecologically special landforms did not exist near our two sites when their archaeo-ichthyofaunas were deposited.

Fishing Practices and Cultural History

It is hardly surprising that the purveyors of marine foods for Cerro Mangote (5000-3600 cal B.C.) and at Sitio Sierra (cal A.D. 1-400) did not make forays into deep clear water to search out shoals of epipelagic piscivores and their prey, and that they did not fish around coral reefs or rocky substrates, given the intrinsic taxonomic richness and productivity of this and other ETP estuaries. Even so, Cerro Mangote's age and Sitio Sierra's inland position vis-à-vis the delta, confirm the longevity and geographical amplitude of Precolumbian fishing in turbid littoral waters (Cooke 1988).

With regard to Cerro Mangote's "brown zone" sample, the lack of primary freshwater fish, the dominance of sea catfish, snook, toadfish, and spotted sleepers, and the distribution of sea catfish and croaker species, point strongly towards fishing in intertidal mudflats, *Rhizophora* mangroves, *alvinas*, and the lowest (mesohaline and mixing) sections of the Santa María River. The presence of a few species that normally stay away from shallow soft-bottom waters, particularly the chihuil catfish and high-fin corvina, may be suggestive of fishing in deeper water. However, since these species occasionally wander towards the littoral, their generally low numbers cannot be considered proof of nets and hooks and lines. All told, even if Cerro Mangote was approximately 5 km from the active shore, its fisherfolk probably never had to travel more than 7 km to keep their families and kin well supplied with fish.

The considerably greater abundance of thread herrings, brassy grunts, and Pacific moonfish at Sitio Sierra may indicate the growing importance of watercraft and gillnets. The thread herring is a filter-feeder and will not take a hook. We have taken care, however, not to overstate relationships between fishing methods and fish distribution within the estuary, in the expectation that continuing study of present-day fish distributions will provide better analogies than those we have at hand.

At "inland" Sitio Sierra freshwater fish were important dietary items notwithstanding the small adult size of some species such as the bluntnose cat. In spite of their having lived about 12 km from the coast, as the crow flies, and much further taking into consideration the river's meanders, villagers could have obtained some marine species nearby. For example, in the upper fluvial estuary and at the inward edge of the oligohaline zone, they could have caught white corvina; widemouthed, flap-nosed and Tuyra catfish; dog snapper; freshwater grunt; and white and black snook. Many of the marine species they used, however, have not been recorded in the main channel of the Santa María River. This suggests either that villagers had to undertake the quite arduous and probably dangerous canoe trip down the river and into the delta or that they obtained some fish from other communities. Bearing in mind that occupational and settlement specialization is apparent at this stage in the development of central Panamanian society (Cooke and Ranere 1992b; Hansell 1988; Linares 1977) exchange in foodstuffs should have existed among related sectors of the regional population. The Spanish lieutenant Gaspar de Espinosa (1913:166) saw coastal peoples at Natá, whose geographical location is similar to that of Sitio Sierra, exchanging crabs for maize. The occasional consumption of a few "outer estuarine" species, such as green jack and sierra mackerel, is, perhaps, the best indication that Sitio Sierra was in contact with distant or technologically sophisticated fisherfolk. Since these oily fish spoil quickly, salting and drying would have been the most practical way to preserve them.

Acknowledgments

Conrado Tapia, Máximo Jiménez and Aureliano Valencia provided assistance with the identification and quantification of the archaeological fish bone samples at the Smithsonian Tropical Research Institute's Archaeology Laboratory in Panama. Thanks are due to William Bussing and Patricia Kailola for providing access to and sharing collections, and for discussions about taxonomy. The first author, however, takes full responsibility for any inconsistencies and inaccuracies in the taxonomic treatment presented in this paper. The financial support of the James Smithson Society of the Smithsonian Institution is gratefully acknowledged. Last but not least, we applaud Michael Blake for his patience in coping with the various versions of this paper he had the misfortune to read.

Notes

1. All estimates for site occupation spans are presented in calibrated years using Stuiver and Reimer (1993). For marine calibrations, ∂R was estimated as 5.0 ± 50.0.

2. "Dietary" means that we assume the fish were eaten rather than used for something else. "Biomass" is the aggregate of estimated "body masses," i.e., "live" weights.

3. Our species-level identifications were made by reference only to species known unequivocally to occur in Panamanian waters. They were accepted as valid only if all species for a particular genus were present in the comparative collection. Since this text was written, however, we have become aware of *Orthopristis cantharinus*, which according to the 1995 FAO guide is sympatric with *O. chalceus*. Hence it behooves us to test whether these species can be distinguished osteologically. We have also become skeptical whether *Centropomus viridis* and *C. nigrescens*

can be differentiated safely on the basis of their osteology, and believe they may belong to a single polymorphic species.

4. Contra Cooke (1992), we have eliminated the black-blotch pompano from this group because it frequently enters the Estero Palo Blanco fish trap.

5. We know nothing about the habits and distribution of the Panamanian catfish and worm-lined croaker, recorded only at Cerro Mangote. They seem to be rare in nature.

6. We identified all six ETP snook species in the "brown zone" sample, but we have not captured longspine and humpback snook (*Centropomus unionensis*) more than 7 km up the Santa María River. We believe that these two species are the least anadromous ETP snook.

References Cited

Aguirre L. A., and A. Yáñez A.
1986 The "Mojarras" from Términos Lagoon: Taxonomy, Biology, Ecology and Trophic Dynamics (Pisces: Gerreidae). *Anales del Instituto de Ciencias del Mar y Limnología* 13:369-444. Universidad Nacional Autónoma de México.

Allen, G., and D. R. Robertson
1994 *The Fishes of the Tropical Eastern Pacific.* Bathurst Press, Bathurst, Australia.

Barnes, R. S. K.
1980 *Coastal Lagoons: the Natural History of a Neglected Habitat.* Cambridge University Press, Cambridge.

Barber, J.
1981 *Geomorphology, Stratigraphy and Sedimentology of the Santa María Drainage Basin.* Unpublished M.A. Thesis, Temple University.

Bartels, C. E., K. S. Price, M. I. López, and W. A. Bussing
1983 Occurrence, Distribution, Abundance and Diversity of Fishes in the Gulf of Nicoya, Costa Rica. *Revista de Biología Tropical* 31:75-101.

Bartels, C. E., K. S. Price, M. L. Bussing, and W. A. Bussing
1984 Ecological Assessment of Finfish as Indicators of Habitats in the Gulf of Nicoya, Costa Rica. *Hydrobiologia* 112:197-207.

Bartlett, A. S., and E. S. Barghoorn
1973 Phytogeographic History of the Isthmus of Panama During the Past 12,000 Years. In *Vegetation and Vegetational History of Northern South America,* edited by A. Graham, pp. 203-299. Elsevier Scientific Publishing Company, New York.

Bussing, W. A., and M. I. Lopéz
1993 *Demersal and Pelagic Inshore Fishes of the Pacific Coast of Lower Central America: an Illustrated Guide.* Special Publication of the *Revista de Biología Tropical.*

Clary, J., P. Hansell, A. J. Ranere, and T. Buggey
1984 The Holocene Geology of the Western Parita Bay Coastline of Central Panama. In *Recent Developments in Isthmian Archaeology,* edited by F. Lange, pp. 55-83. BAR International Series 212. British Archaeological Reports, Oxford.

Conkel, D.
1993 *Cichlids of North and Central America.* TFH, Neptune City, New Jersey.

Cooke, R. G.
1979 Los Impactos de las Comunidades Agrícolas Precolombinas Sobre los Ambientes del Trópico Estacional: Datos del Panamá Prehistórico. *Actas del IV Simposio Internacional de Ecología Tropical, Tomo III.* pp. 917-973. Instituto de Cultura, Panama.

1984a Archaeological Research in Central and Eastern Panama: a Review of Some Problems. In *The Archaeology of Lower Central America,* edited by F. W. Lange and D. Z. Stone, pp. 263-302. University of New Mexico Press, Albuquerque.

1984b Birds and Men in Prehistoric Central Panama. In *Recent Developments in Isthmian Archaeology,* edited by F. Lange, pp. 243-281. BAR International Series 212. British Archaeological Reports, Oxford.

1985 Ancient Painted Pottery from Central Panama. *Archaeology* July/August 34-39.

1988 Some Social and Technological Correlates of Inshore Fishing in Formative Central Panama. In, *Diet and Subsistence: Current Archaeological Perspectives,* edited by B. V. Kennedy and G. M. Le Moine, pp. 140. Proceedings of the Chacmool Conference, Archaeological Association of the University of Calgary, Calgary.

1992 Prehistoric Nearshore and Littoral Fishing in the Eastern Tropical Pacific: an Ichthyological Evaluation. *World Archaeology* 6:1-49.

1993a Relación Entre Recursos Pesqueros, Geografía y Estrategias de Subsistencia en Dos Sitios Arqueológicos de Diferentes Edades en un Estuario del Pacífico Central de Panamá. *Actas del Primer Congreso Sobre la Defensa del Patrimonio Nacional,* Panamá.

1993b The Past and Present Distribution of Sea Catfishes (Ariidae) in a Small Estuarine Embayment in Panama: Relevance to Precolumbian Fishing Practices. In, *Explotación de Recursos Faunísticos en Sistemas Adaptativos Americanos,* compiled by J. L. Lanata. Arqueología Contemporánea, Vol. 4, Edición Especial, pp. 57-74.

1996 Aportes Preliminares de la Arqueozoología y Etnología a Investigaciones Sobre la Taxonomía, Ecología y Zoogeografía de las Especies de la Familia Ariidae en el Pacífico Oriental Tropical. *Cespedesia,* in press.

Cooke, R. G., L. Norr, and D. R. Piperno
1996   Native Americans and the Panamanian Landscape. In *Case Studies in Environmental Archaeology*, edited by E. J. Reitz, L. A. Newsom, and S. J. Scudder, pp. 103-126. Plenum Press, New York.

Cooke, R. G., and A. J. Ranere
1984   The "Proyecto Santa María": A Multidisciplinary Analysis of Human Adaptations to a Tropical Watershed in Panama. In *Recent Developments in Isthmian Archaeology,* edited by F. W. Lange, pp. 3-30. BAR International Series 212. British Archaeological Reports, Oxford.

1989   Hunting in Precolumbian Panama: a Diachronic Perspective. In, *The Walking Larder*, edited by J. Clutton-Brock, pp. 295-315. One World Archaeology, Unwin Hyman, London.

1992a   Prehistoric Human Adaptations to the Seasonally Dry Forests of Panama. *World Archaeology* 24:114-133.

1992b   The Origin of Wealth and Hierarchy in the Central Region of Panama (12,000-2,000 B.P.). In, *Wealth and Hierarchy in the Intermediate Area*, edited by F. W. Lange, pp. 243-316. Dumbarton Oaks, Washington, D.C.

1992c   Human Influences on the Zoogeography of Panama: an Update Based on Archaeological and Ethnohistorical Evidence. In, *Biogeography of Mesoamerica*, edited by S. P. Darwin and A. L. Welden. Special Publication of the Mesoamerican Ecology Institute, pp. 21-58. Mérida, Yucatán, México.

Cooke, R. G., and G. Tapia R.
1994a   Marine and Freshwater Fish Amphidromy in a Small Tropical River on the Pacific Coast of Panama: Implications for the Study of Precolumbian Fishing Practices. Proceedings of 7th. Meeting of Fish Working Group of the International Council for Zooarchaeology. *Annales du Musée Royale de l'Afrique Centrale* 274:99-106.

1994b   Stationary Intertidal Fish Traps in Estuarine Inlets on the Pacific Coast of Panama: Descriptions, Evaluations of Early Dry Season Catches and Relevance to the Interpretation of Dietary Archaeofaunas. Proceedings of 6th. Meeting of Fish Working Group of the International Council for Zooarchaeology. *Offa* 51:287-298.

Day, J. W., Jr., and A. Yáñez A.
1982   Coastal Lagoons and Estuaries, Ecosystem Approach. *Ciencia Interamericana* 22:11-26.

Day, J. W., Jr., C. A. S. Hall, W.M. Kemp, and A. Yáñez A.
1989   *Estuarine Ecology*. Wiley, New York.

D'Croz, L., R. Rivera, and E. Pineda
1977   Observaciones Sobre un Arte de Pesca Fija en las Costas de la Bahía de Panamá. *Conciencia* 3:14-17.

Espinosa, Gaspar de
1913   Relación del Proceso quel Licenciado Gaspar de Espinosa, Alcalde Mayor, Hizo en el Viaje Mandado por el muy Mágnifico Señor Pedrarias Dávila...desde esta Ciudad a las Provincias de Natá e París e a las Otras Provincias Comarcanas (1517). In, *El Descubrimiento del Océano Pacífico: Vasco Núñez de Balboa, Fernando de Magallanes y sus Compañeros*, edited by J. T. Medina, pp. 154-183. Editorial Universitaria, Santiago de Chile.

Estadística Panameña
1975   *Situación Física, Meteorología: Año 1975.* Contraloría General de la República, Dirección de Estadística y Censo. Panama.

Fairbridge, R.
1980   The Estuary: its Definition and Geodynamic Cycle. In, *Chemistry and Biochemistry of Estuaries,* edited by E. Olausson and I. Cato, pp. 1-35. Wiley, New York.

FAO
1995   *Guía FAO Para la Identificacíon de Especies Para los Fines de la Pesca.* Pacífico Centro-Oriental. Vol. 2. Rome.

Fleming, R. H.
1938   Tides and Tidal Currents in the Gulf of Panama. *Journal of Marine Research* 1:192-206.

Golik, A.
1968   History of Holocene Transgression in the Gulf of Panama. *Journal of Geology* 76:497-507.

Hansell, P.
1988   *The Rise and Fall of an Early Formative Community: La Mula-Sarigua, Central Pacific Panama.* Unpublished Ph.D. dissertation, Department of Anthropology, Temple University.

Helms, M. W.
1979   *Ancient Panama: Chiefs in Search of Power.* University of Texas Press, Austin.

Isaza-Aizuprúa, I.
1993   *Desarrollo Estilístico de la Cerámica Pintada del Panamá Central con Énfasis en el Período 500 a.C.-500 d.C.* Tesis Profesional, Escuela de Antropología, Universidad Autónoma de Guadalajara, México.

Legros, T.
1992   *Puerto Chacho et les Premiers Céramistes Américains.* Vol. 1. Thèse de Doctorat, Université de Paris, France.

Linares, O. F.
1977   *Ecology and the Arts in Ancient Panama: on the Development of Rank and Symbolism in the Central Provinces.* Studies in Precolumbian Art and Archaeology, No. 17. Dumbarton Oaks, Washington D.C.

Loftin, H. G.
1965   *The Geographical Distribution of Freshwater*

120

Fishes in Panama. Unpublished Ph.D. dissertation, Florida State University.

Lothrop, S. K.
1937 *Coclé: An Archaeological Study of Central Panama, Part 1*. Memoirs of the Peabody Museum of American Archaeology and Ethnology Vol. 7. Harvard University, Cambridge.
1942 *Coclé: An Archaeological Study of Central Panama, Part 2*. Memoirs of the Peabody Museum of American Archaeology and Ethnology Vol. 8. Harvard University, Cambridge.

McGimsey, C. R. III
1956 Cerro Mangote, a Preceramic Site in Panama. *American Antiquity* 22:151-161.

McNaughton, S. J.
1968 Structure and Function in California Grasslands. *Ecology* 49:962-972.

Meek, S. E., and S. F. Hildebrand
1923 The Marine Fishes of Panama. *Field Museum of Natural History Zoological Series* 15:1-1045.

Miller, R. R.
1966 Geographical Distribution of Central American Freshwater Fishes. *Copeia* 1966(4):773-802.

Phillips, P. C., and Pérez-Cruet, M. J.
1984 A Comparative Survey of Reef Fishes in Caribbean and Pacific Costa Rica. *Revista de Biología Tropical* 32:95-102.

Piperno, D. R., Bush, M. B., and Colinvaux, P. A.
1991 Paleoecological Perspectives on Human Adaptation in Panama. II. The Holocene. *Geoarchaeology* 6:227-250.

Romoli, K.
1987 *Los de la Lengua Cueva: los Grupos Indígenas del Istmo Oriental en la Epoca de la Conquista Española*. Instituto Colombiano de Antropología and Instituto Colombiano de Cultura, Bogotá.

Shaffer, B. S.
1992 Quarter-inch Screening: Understanding Biases in Recovery of Vertebrate Faunal Remains. *American Antiquity* 57:129-136.

Stuiver, M., and P. J. Reimer
1993 Radiocarbon Calibration Program Rev. 3.0.2. *Radiocarbon* 35:215-230.

Suman, D. O.
1983 *Agricultural Burning in Panama and Central America: Burning Parameters and the Coastal Sedimentary Record*. Unpublished Ph.D. thesis, Department of Oceanography, University of California, San Diego.

Thomson, D. A., Findley, L. T., and Kerstitch, A. N.
1979 *Reef Fishes of the Sea of Cortez*. Wiley, New York.

Trigger, B. G.
1989 *A History of Archaeological Thought*. Cambridge University Press, Cambridge.

Vásquez, R., and T. B. Thorson
1982 The Bull Shark (*Carcharhinus leucas*) and Largetooth Sawfish (*Pristis perotteti*) in Lake Bayano, a Tropical Man-made Impoundment in Panama. *Environmental Biology of Fish* 7:341-347.

Warburton, K.
1979 Growth and Production of Some Important Species of Fish in a Mexican Coastal Lagoon System. *Journal of Fish Biology* 14:449-464.

Weiland, D.
1984 Prehistoric Settlement Patterns in the Santa María Drainage of Panama: a Preliminary Analysis. In, *Recent Developments in Isthmian Archaeology*, edited by F. W. Lange, pp. 31-53. BAR International Series 212. British Archaeological Reports, Oxford.

Wheeler, A., and A. K. G. Jones
1989 *Fishes*. Cambridge University Press, Cambridge.

Willey, G. R.
1971 *An Introduction to American Archaeology, Vol. 2, South America*. Prentice-Hall, Englewood Cliffs New Jersey.

9

The Origins and Development of Food Production in Pacific Panama

Dolores R. Piperno

Introduction

Paleobotanical research in recent years has given Pacific Panama a key role in expanding our knowledge about the origins and development of food production in the New World. In this paper, I will examine five main themes concerning early food production, each buttressed by plant microfossil evidence from archaeological and geological sites:

1. Food production was an indigenous development in Panama. It evolved out of late glacial-early Holocene foraging in tropical forests partly as a response to severe resource unpredictability.

2. The cultivation of native plants like arrowroot (*Maranta arundinacea*) was underway by the ninth millennium B.P. A Mesoamerican domesticate, maize, was accepted into socioeconomic systems of the Pacific watershed by the end of the eighth millennium B.P., an event that, in any case, would be difficult to explain in the absence of articulated systems of cultivation.

3. In looking at the origins of food production in the tropics, it is essential to distinguish between the terms cultivation, domestication, and agriculture. It is also important to distinguish between tropical and temperate zone cultivation systems.

4. When hunters and gatherers in tropical forests turned to cultivation they may not have had to work harder than their foraging ancestors. In fact, they may have been rewarded with certain advantages derived from more favorable cost-benefit ratios of energy procurement and decreased mobility.

5. Diffusionist concepts of plant domestication are not being supported by recent evidence from archaeology and genetics. Rather, New World tropical forests may have seen repeated independent evolution of systems of plant husbandry.

The central Pacific watershed of Panama is a region where intensive archaeological survey and excavation have revealed a continuous 11,000 year record spanning Paleoindian though Contact-period occupations (Cooke and Ranere 1984, 1989, 1992a; Ranere and Cooke 1991, 1994; Weiland 1984) (Figure 1). Excavated soils spanning the entire Holocene period have been analyzed for plant macro- and micro-fossils (Piperno and Husum-Clary 1984; Piperno 1988). A program of coring and analyzing lake sediments has also been initiated, providing paleoecological information on prehistoric environments, settlement patterns, agriculture, and land use (Piperno et al. 1990, 1991a, 1991b). The temporal focus will comprise the Paleoindian to the beginning of the Formative period (ca. 11,500-3000 B.P.). Formative period developments have already been well-studied in western and central Panama (Cooke 1984; Hansell 1987; Linares et al. 1975; Linares 1977; Linares and Ranere 1980).

Late Pleistocene and Early Holocene Environments and Subsistence

The temporal frame encompassing the earliest occupation of Panama and hunter-gatherer adaptations associated with, and immediately subsequent to, initial human entry are important elements of this chapter. The archaeological record of human habitation begins with Paleoindian lithic assemblages that have been found at two lowland sites. One, La Mula, is on the Pacific coastal plain, and the other, at Lake Madden, is situated 240 km eastward in the less seasonal Caribbean watershed (Bird and Cooke 1978; Ranere and Cooke 1991; Ranere 1980). At a third lowland site, Lake La Yeguada, located at an elevation of 650 m (Figure 1), a disturbance and fire horizon in Pleistocene sediments has been identified that is most probably human in origin and starts at 11,000 B.P. (Piperno et al. 1990, 1991a). These data provide evidence for Paleoindian penetration of environments reconstructed as mixed

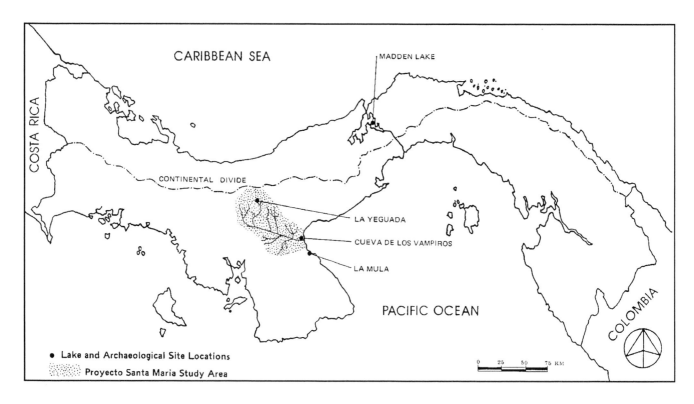

Figure 1. Location of the Archaeological Sites and Lake Yeguada.

montane-lowland evergreen forests, and are *contra* hypotheses that tropical forests never supported hunting and gathering adaptations (e.g., Bailey et al. 1989).

The timing of the disturbance horizon is in remarkable agreement with presumed dates for the Paleoindian penetration of Lower Central America (Lynch 1983; Ranere and Cooke 1991) and we view it as evidence not only for early anthropogenic alteration of vegetation, but also for "late entry" of humans into tropical America. Thus, developments leading from the earliest foraging to the first indigenous cultivation to the acceptance of introduced crops are probably telescoped within a 4000 year period. Consideration of one development cannot proceed without reference to the other two.

Pollen, phytolith, and diatom records from Lake La Yeguada show that Late Pleistocene environments (14,000-11,000 B.P.) were significantly cooler and drier than at present (Piperno et al. 1990, 1991a, 1991b). Oak and Magnolia were important constituents of the montane forest that replaced lowland forests of non-glacial periods at elevations between 500 m and 1000 m. A downward movement of vegetation zones on the order of 800 m indicates an annual temperature depression of about 4°-5° C. The presence of a shallow lake, as evidenced from diatom and sedimentological studies, documents significant reduction in annual precipitation. The Lake La Yeguada watershed today receives an average of 3800 mm of rainfall per annum, thus even a 40 percent reduction in precipitation during the Late Glacial would probably have provided enough moisture to support the forest reconstructed from

pollen and phytolith data. This data set makes it very likely that the environment of the Late Glacial Pacific coastal plain was dry and that vegetation responded to such conditions through the expansion of open, thorn-scrub and savanna environments, with the former type being more widespread (Piperno et al. 1991a, 1992).

The subsistence strategies of Paleoindians cannot as yet be addressed using archaeological food remains themselves, as no excavated soils have been analyzed. Judging from paleoecological reconstructions and distribution of archaeological sites (Ranere and Cooke, 1991, 1994; Piperno et al. 1992), we can assume that they probably exploited a range of environments, from thorn-scrub savannas to semi-evergreen and montane forests. This information, along with use of models derived from evolutionary ecology, allows reasonable projections of Paleoindian subsistence that will be tested in the future with direct archaeological evidence.

Application of the diet breadth and patch choice models of optimal foraging theory (Winterhalder and Smith 1981) to diets of modern hunters and gatherers have revealed several aspects of resource choice and change that may be fundamental to all human foragers (O'Connell and Hawkes 1981; Hill 1982; Hames and Vickers 1982; Hawkes et al. 1982). The assumptions, workings, and results of optimal foraging models have been elaborated in detail by these workers and will not be reviewed here. Briefly, the main predictions of the model appear to have been met with cultural data, in that humans are rational actors in their environment. The resource set is often chosen so as to

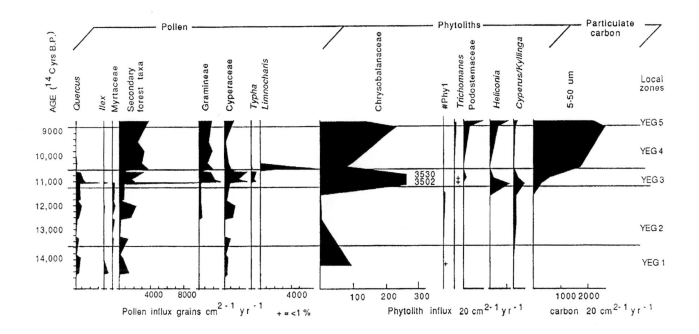

Figure 2. Pleistocene-Early Holocene Pollen and Phytolith Records from Lake Yeguada (after Piperno et al. 1990).

maximize net energy intake. It has been shown with sound quantitative data that a trend of increasing return of energy generally occurs along a resource gradient leading from plants to small animals to larger game. Lower ranked resources (usually, plants) assume greater importance in the diet not as a function of their own abundance, but as the abundance of higher ranked items (usually, animals) fluctuates.

It is worthwhile to view Paleoindian subsistence in terms of optimal foraging strategies and diet sets rather than in simple comparisons of generalized and specialized systems. Use of this robust model allows testable predictions about the range and proportions of resources in the diet, while recognizing the fact that as humans forage they encounter and have intimate knowledge of many species in the environment. The final dietary mix is little reflection on their ability to exploit other resources more intensively.

Following the tenets of optimal foraging, one reasonably concludes that megafauna provided the bulk of calories in environments where such animals roamed in some abundance. On the coastal plain the optimal diet set probably included mastodons and horses, but it is quite possible that some plants (e.g., cactuses) made the optimal set as well, and it is virtually certain that others (tubers, palms, and fruits) were eaten from time to time. The important point is that hunting horses and mastodons does not indicate a parochial Paleoindian cognition of their environment oriented toward the animal kingdom, but rather a correct set of subsistence choices, given available options.

Economic strategies would have been oriented differently in the forests, for it is difficult to envision a focus on the taking of big game in such environments, where its density is notoriously low (Meltzer and Smith 1987). Here, small mammals, birds, and plants would have been more valued resources and supplied proportionately more energy in the diet. That Paleoindian exploitation of forests included vegetation clearance and modification using fire has been evidenced in the Lake La Yeguada phytolith and pollen record. A disturbance horizon appears suddenly at 11,000 B.P., after having been absent for the previous 3000 years of the lake's history. It is characterized by massive increases in particulate carbon and the appearance of herbaceous plants of forest gaps, like *Heliconia* and sedges (Piperno et al. 1990) (Figure 2). Over 90 percent of the phytoliths from these early successional plants have the characteristic carbon residue indicating that they were burnt, suggesting that clearings were being created and also *maintained*. Evidence for the disturbance and forest occupation continues unabated and intensifies across the Pleistocene-Holocene boundary, further discouraging the suggestion that use of forested habitats may have involved simply the casual search for sources of stone, with little exploitation of their subsistence resources.

Determining whether such activity was directed toward encouraging the growth of useful plants, increasing the biomass of game animals, or maintaining habitats for base camps, (probably all three goals were operative) is less important than the fact that clearings were created and probably sustained in tropical forests by the earliest human occupants. Intimate associations between plants and people that lead to increasingly dependent relationships and co-evolutionary developments (Rindos 1984) have a long

125

history in Panama. Patterns of plant use and manipulation that saw their inflorescence during the post-Pleistocene were components of Paleoindian adaptations.

The Pleistocene-Holocene transition in Pacific Panama (11,100-10,000 B.P.) was a period of profound and continuous change of the flora and fauna (Piperno et al. 1991b). The climatic snap to significantly warmer and wetter conditions beginning at ca. 11,100 B.P. appears to have been very rapid, perhaps taking place in no more than 60-70 years. However, a complete change to conditions more or less approximating the modern non-glacial period may not have occurred until several thousand years later, as the decline of all montane taxa to background levels and the establishment of lowland evergreen forest did not take place until ca. 8600 B.P.

Present evidence suggests considerable vegetation assembly and reassembly during the early Holocene, probably due to conditions cooler and wetter than at present, and also to differential rates of lowland taxa from their Pleistocene locations. The result is likely to have been continuously changing forest composition and species densities. The vegetational formations engendered by these changes had not been seen before and probably will not be seen again.

Pleistocene-Holocene perturbations had three main implications for human subsistence strategies. The megafauna was lost, tropical forests were now the dominant biome as the open settings of the coastal plain were replaced by deciduous forest, and people were forced to adjust to persistent change and *unpredictable* environments.

Optimal foraging theory predicts that a decline in resource availability will result in the expansion of diet breadth, if previously used resources were in the optimal set (Winterhalder 1987). Decline in resource availability may come about through actual drops in the abundance of resources or increased population density. There is no evidence suggesting that the early Holocene in Panama saw significant population growth (Cooke and Ranere 1984; Weiland 1984). Economic logic, therefore, tells us that the decline in big game availability led to a diversification of the resource base to include species of plants and small mammals that had not been intensively exploited because of previously unfavorable procurement costs.

It is important to emphasize that a broadening of the food base is an expected cultural response in situations of resource fluctuation, where it acts as a hedge against sudden crashes of particular foods in an ever-changing environment. Risk avoidance and resource reliability are viewed as integral components of economic strategies in Hayden's (1981) and Hassan's (1977, 1978) models of pre-Neolithic economic development, and they are being incorporated into new models of optimal foraging theories as well (Winterhalder 1987). Thus, under certain conditions, humans may combine a balance of risk reduction and energetic efficiency in foraging decisions, leading to more generalized strategies.

10,000-7000 B.P.: The Horizon of Indigenous Food Production

I have argued elsewhere (Piperno 1989a) that tropical forests are energy poor, unpredictable, and generally unfavorable environments for hunters and gatherers, leading to adaptations that favor small and highly mobile social groups. Calories available from plant stuffs, which may be the critical element influencing population size and stability, are in short supply, and fluctuations in the resource base occur over seasonal and multi-annual time frames. These characteristics of tropical biomes seem to be true both of Old World and New World systems (e.g. Milton 1984; Hart and Hart 1986; Headland 1987). I contended that in such environments strategies that sought higher caloric returns in tandem with a more reliable and predictable food base had particular adaptive value, and into such contexts a starch-rich, easily storable, and reliable cultigen, maize, was accepted by socioeconomic groups of mid-Holocene Panama.

A possible pre-maize indigenous pattern of cultivation was not addressed because such evidence did not exist at that time and it would not alter the basic developmental processes or their ecological milieu. It simply pushes the picture back by a few thousand years and takes into account the affect both of short-term and long-term environmental perturbations on human subsistence choices.

Phytolith spectra from pre-maize (pre-7000 B.P.) archaeological strata at the site of Cueva de los Vampiros (Cooke and Ranere 1984) are revealing the presence of arrowroot (*Maranta arundinacea*) in deposits ^{14}C dated to 8600 B.P. Species level identification is possible with arrowroot phytoliths because their origin in the epidermis of seeds results in silicified versions of individual cells of the seed coat, and, hence, highly distinctive shapes (Piperno 1989b). Vampiros is presently situated on the *alvinas* only a mile from the coast. High numbers of sponge spicules, presence of marine diatoms, and paucity of tree phytoliths in arrowroot-bearing samples suggest that at the time of occupation the site was in a habitat comparable to today's, close to the sea in a dry, non-forested setting (Piperno 1988). Arrowroot is not found today near the site and accounts of its natural distribution place it as a plant of deciduous and semi-evergreen forest, where it grows in the understorey near well-watered situations (Andersson 1986). Its presence at Vampiros may then reflect a situation where the plant has been moved outside of its natural range and planted.

Arrowroot is today a minor cultigen that is grown in indigenous economies of northern South America, Central America, and the Antilles (Helen Kennedy, pers. comm. 1994). Nowhere is it a staple crop and Panamanian *campesinos* include it as a casual element of their gardens. The antiquity and nature of its uses in the past are extremely poorly understood. The Panamanian record is the first documentation of its occurrence in prehistoric economies.

Early documentary records from the Antilles point to indigenous use of the root not as a food plant, but as an antidote to arrow poison (Sturtevant 1969). Processing the tuber to release the starch is thought to be a development of modern technology, as European recorders apparently never noted that this plant was even eaten, much less processed prior to ingestion (Sauer 1950). However, its use in many contemporary, native food producing systems (e.g., Alcorn 1984; Dufour 1988) may point to a much earlier and more important exploitation in ancient times.

The following lines of evidence lead me to hypothesize that arrowroot and other native plants such as *Calathea latifolia* and *Dioscorea* spp. were cultivated in Panama before the introduction of maize: (1) the record of the use of arrowroot itself, (2) its present-day natural distribution, (3) the appearance of a grinding stone technology in the study region between 9000 and 7000 B.P. that may have been used to process arrowroot, (4) evidence for extensive ground-clearing and vegetation firing by 8600 B.P., and (5) the acceptance of fully domesticated, exogenous crops by 7000 B.P. Some of these points need further elaboration.

Evidence for the presence of maize in Central Pacific Panama by 7000 B.P. has been presented in detail elsewhere (Piperno et al. 1985; Piperno 1988). The record of material culture does not suggest a population replacement near the end of the eighth millennium B.P., nor the influx of significant numbers of people who brought with them the ideas and techniques of cultivation (Cooke and Ranere 1992b). Rather, it bears witness to the acceptance of a fully developed domesticate in various local economies of the region. As Lathrap (1987) has argued for some regions of South America, this pattern is difficult to explain in the absence of pre-existing pattern of cultivation already articulated with necessary changes in mobility and scheduling of resource acquisition. Once again, the geologic record has provided appropriate evidence.

At Lake La Yeguada, the anthropogenic habitat modification that had first appeared at 11,000 B.P. intensified over time, so that shortly after 8600 B.P. frequencies of weedy plants, burnt secondary taxa, and particulate carbon from woody species reached very high levels (Figure 2) (Piperno et al. 1991b). High proportions of 5-50 micron-sized carbon indicate that, as in Pleistocene periods, modification was not confined to the immediate lake edge, but occurred throughout the watershed. Spiralling frequencies of carbon and burnt, disturbed growth indicate both substantial expansion of cleared ground and continual maintenance of areas already cleared. Such patterns are the expected manifestation of a well-developed system of plant exploitation so, in light of the arrowroot data from Vampiros, I suggest that local plants of the La Yeguada watershed were being cultivated as well.

The archaeological evidence cannot yet provide relevant data, but the ninth millennium B.P. vegetational alterations probably also reflect some significant changes in seasonal rounds and scheduling patterns necessary for the mainte-nance of a cultivated food supply. Sites may have been occupied over longer time periods, and the same areas may have seen long-term annual reoccupation and reuse. The ninth millennium B.P. also saw the appearance of a plant-grinding stone technology (Valerio L. 1987), whose functions may well have included processing arrowroot.

Questions of Causation

If an ancient pattern of food production was developed independently in Panama, we need to address some questions concerning causation and the nature of the pre-maize food productive system that has been proposed. What I view as the basic developmental processes and entwined ecological circumstances have already been alluded to in the discussion of early Holocene environments above. The decline of the megafauna and spread of ever-changing forested biomes from 11,000 to 8600 B.P. created an environment that was both seriously deficient in available calories and unpredictable over seasonal and multi-annual temporal frames. Such conditions favored subsistence options that diversified the food base and intensified exploitation of plants that previously were underemphasized because of unfavorable energy costs. They also put a premium on the search for good, reliable energy sources. Starch-rich products like arrowroot, *Calathea* spp., *Zamia* spp., the Araceae, and palms would now be valued items and would be increasingly taken where they were encountered despite their abundance, which is not particularly impressive in undisturbed forests.

The anthropogenic modification in evidence from the Pleistocene onward would have increased the densities of many of these taxa (Piperno 1989a). This modification by Late Glacial foragers was significant in their successful colonization of tropical forests, because it created environments more favorable to growth of useful plants (Piperno et al. 1992). For example, *Calathea latifolia*, another prime candidate for early cultivation, is found in greatest densities beside forest trails.[1] Many native palm taxa like *Scheelia* and *Astrocaryum* are more common in gaps and in secondary forests than in mature forests and observation of stands of arrowroot in open waste places indicates that it can be considered a plant with weedy tendencies as well.[2] Many of our postulated contributors to indigenous food production would have thrived in the disturbed habitats of campsites, providing a basic vehicle by which human control of plant propagation proceeded.

In the scheme of human plant management, and especially after having already interacted closely with such plants for several generations, it would have been a very small step to further increase their density by planting them around existing campsites, or, as in the likely case of Vampiros, to move them outside of their natural range and plant them elsewhere. It would not have required any sudden burst of knowledge or insight on the part of the human actor, and, as I will discuss below, it probably did not involve unfavorable cost-benefit ratios. It was a predictable step in the continuum of human-plant interactions that began with simple harvesting and ended in domestication. However, the continuum involved many different kinds of interactions and often did not wind irreversibly towards genetic and phenotypic change (domestication) of the plants in question (Harlan 1975; Ford 1981; King 1987).

There are various definitions of cultivation and domestication in the literature. The ones I find most useful in thinking about tropical plants have been provided by Harlan (1975:64):

> To cultivate means to conduct those activities involved in caring for a plant, such as tilling the soil, preparing a seedbed, weeding, pruning, protecting, watering, and manuring. Cultivation is concerned with human activities, while domestication deals with the genetic response of the plants or animals being tended or cultivated. It is therefore quite possible to cultivate wild plants, and cultivated plants are not necessarily domesticated.

Harlan (1975:67) goes on to stress that in the tropics the differences between wild, tolerated, and cultivated are very fuzzy when compared to temperate zones and that "...the movement of useful plants from the wild condition to the cultivated and back again is a relatively simple and common occurrence."

Simple temperate zone typologies of plants as weed, wild, cultivated, or domesticated and of cultures as hunter-gatherers, cultivators, or agriculturalists become difficult to use when hunters and gatherers maintain gardens in their hunting ranges (Holmberg 1950), and shifting cultivators dramatically increase the density of useful wild trees and change their genetic composition "...without anyone deliberately planting a seed" (Harlan 1975:66). Presuming that such activities had prehistoric antecedents, I suggest that something near to them characterized the plant management systems of 10,000 B.P. to 8000 B.P. in central Pacific Panama. Arrowroot may well be the Panamanian equivalent of *Setaria* (foxtail), a plant that was cultivated in early Archaic Mexico and was probably well down the road to domestication (Callen 1967), when maize and other crops were introduced and supplanted it in subsistence economies.

Recently, there has been a lot made of the relative costs of hunting and gathering as compared to food producing subsistence strategies. Cohen (1977, 1987) and Harris (1979) have suggested that early farmers probably experienced diminishing returns to labor as they were forced to rely increasingly on lower quality, less preferred foodstuffs. The Post-Pleistocene "broad-spectrum revolution" was a time of increasing reliance on foodstuffs like seeds, molluscs, starchy tubers, and small game; items that seem to be less-preferred and costlier when compared to larger mammals. For example, O'Connell and Hawkes (1981), Hawkes (et al. 1982), Hames and Vickers (1982) and Hill (1982) have shown that exploiting terrestrial fauna is more energetically efficient than gathering plants. Two of these studies

dealt directly with tropical groups and it will be noted that the optimal diet set included some plants, especially palm products. As predicted, resources entered the optimal diet set by virtue of their procurement (search and handling) costs and the abundance of higher-ranked resources.

If studies of modern preferences and how foodstuffs enter and leave diets can be used to evaluate prehistoric strategies, and the general worldwide Pleistocene subsistence trends (Cohen 1987) indicate to me that they can, then one should not view the development of food production and associated technologies as progress in human evolution (Hayden 1981, has been a prominent spokesman of this viewpoint), but as a necessary, stress-induced adjustment to a deteriorating food base, brought on by territory reduction, population pressure, or some combination of both (Cohen 1977, 1987; Harris 1979, 1987; Binford 1983).

Stress models appeal to me for a number of reasons, not least of which are their compatibility with economic models and the roles of natural-cultural selection in influencing patterns of human behavior over time. Moreover, as we gather more data on Late Pleistocene climate change in the tropics it is becoming increasingly apparent that the dramatic environmental oscillations seen elsewhere in the world and associated with Neolithic developments (Wright 1977) also occurred at low latitudes. However, I am not convinced that the kind of subsistence pattern we are postulating for the indigenous cultivation horizon in Panama entailed an increase of work effort.

First of all, there are very few data on the relative costs of hunting and gathering when compared to small-scale cultivation. If, as Johnson's (1982) and Johnson and Baksh's (1987) data suggest, tropical horticulture is a less expensive strategy than wild plant exploitation, then casual cultivation combined with hunting and collecting of high-ranked plant resources may have been less expensive than wild resource specialization (Piperno 1989a). Also, re-evaluations of hunter-gatherer work effort in groups previously considered "affluent" (Hawkes and O'Connell 1981; O'Connell and Hawkes 1981) have shown that their costs have been seriously underestimated because resource processing was not considered.

It seems to me that while the symbolic lore of early Holocene peoples may have recalled to them the enviable taste of mastodon meat, other pursuits, such as planting arrowroot, collecting palm hearts, and hunting garden-raiding agoutis (Linares 1976) involved no more work effort than foraging in tropical forests. Farming may well have entailed less effort, and in the process, options for reduced mobility that became available (or necessary) further improved certain aspects of life. Moran (1983) has reminded us that mobility is associated with negative factors in the tropics and studies of the foraging Ache (Hawkes 1987) make clear the difficult work demands that woman face in moving camps every day and caring for children.

If increased work effort is not correlated with the development of tropical forest food production, what about other stress factors? Population pressure can be ruled out because there is no suggestion that early Holocene environments were anywhere near saturation level, and territory reduction can be dismissed for the same reason. On the contrary, population growth and pressure on land became significant factors *after* the introduction of maize. This brings us to other kinds of environmental factors that were associated with the decline of prey and development of modern habitats.

When applied to Late Pleistocene and Holocene tropical habitats, I find appealing a combination of general evolutionary- ecological models and more specific models such as Hayden's (1981) and Hassan's (1978). The latter view risk avoidance and resource reliability as primary objectives of human subsistence strategies, and the former assume that efficient foraging strategies were favored by natural-cultural selection. The transition to food production can then be viewed as the natural outcome of opportunistic, economically rational adjustments to the kinds of resources that became available, and to the limitations of such resources in providing a secure food base. There is no monolithic causal factor involved and no external prime movers forcing developments. Human actors, behaving in ways that ensured short term success and stability (the *proximate* motivator), chose strategies that in the long-run were successful.

It will also be noticed that the argument has not been dichotomized into a highland *vs.* lowland or seed cropping *vs.* root cropping one. Rather, cultures interacted with biota that were available to them, developed close relationships with plants that were most useful to them, and in the process took some of them under cultivation.

7000-3000 B.P.: The Florescence of Shifting Horticulture

By 7000 years ago, central Panamanian cultivators had augmented their economies with maize and, possibly, squash (*Cucurbita* spp.). These new strategies of cultivation must have been successful because during the succeeding 4000 years increasingly large populations cut down and disturbed huge expanses of the primary forest (Piperno 1988; Piperno et al. 1991b). Settlements were numerous, often less than one hectare in size, and situated on promontories overlooking streams or on interfluvial spurs (Weiland 1984). These patterns are similar to some modern shifting horticulturalists who live in dispersed single or multi-family settlements.

Results of the systematic survey carried out by the Proyecto Santa María provide provocative data on the contrast between pre- and post-7000 B.P. population trends (Cooke and Ranere 1984, 1992a; Weiland 1984). A four percent coverage survey of the Río Santa María watershed (Figure 1) located about 15 sites dating from 10,000 B.P. to 7000 B.P. In contrast, late preceramic and early ceramic occupations (7000-3000 B.P.) numbered around 250.

Phytolith and pollen records from nearby Lake Ya

Yeguada reveal that by 4000 B.P., these shifting cultivators had deforested much of the watershed (Piperno et al. 1991b). Significant denudation of interior forests and probable declining agricultural yields may have played significant roles in the settlement of the alluvium of major rivers of the coastal plain. In these contexts, the first nucleated and sedentary villages with economies dependent on staple crops like maize are first found during the third millennium B.P., when deforestation around Lake La Yeguada was severe, and become common shortly after 2000 B.P. (Hansell 1987; Cooke 1984).

Relationship to other Regions in Tropical America

Data accumulated since 1980, from both archaeological and geological sites, and studies of protein and cytological relationships in extant domesticates and putative wild ancestors, are altering views of New World plant domestication. The diffusionist concepts of Sauer (1952) and his students (Carter 1977) are being replaced by an awareness that independent systems of cultivation arose in many widely separated areas.

For example, an independent center of domestication in the Eastern Woodlands of North America now seems likely (Smith 1987; Decker and Wilson 1986; Decker 1988; Heiser 1989). The common bean (*Phaseolus vulgaris*) was domesticated in at least three areas: Mexico, lowland Colombia, and highland Peru and Argentina (Gepts and Bliss 1986; Gepts et al. 1986), the latter event occurring by 7,700 B.P. Prehistoric cultivators in a least two disparate regions of South America and one region of Mexico domesticated four different species of *Capsicum* (chile peppers) (Pickersgill 1977). Some now think that maize was not brought under domestication in the familiar highland valleys of Mexico, but in lower, wetter, and warmer environments near the Río Balsas watershed of Guerrero province (Iltis and Doebley 1984; see Benz, Chapter 3). This domestication must have been well underway by 8500 years ago, because maize had spread through Panama and into northern South America by 7000 B.P. (Pearsall and Piperno 1990), and was present in Amazonia by 5300 B.P. (Bush et al. 1989). If we ever obtain relevant evidence from the eastern slopes of the Andes, a bewildering array of zones of cultivation and associated plants will probably be revealed (Pickersgill and Heiser 1977). To this list of regions and plants we have added central Panama and arrowroot.

Harlan (1975) and Pickersgill (1977) have noted that species of the same genera were repeatedly domesticated in widely separated areas of the world, and America, in particular, had a remarkable number of these "vicariant domestications" (e.g., *Cucurbita, Capsicum, Phaseolus, Dioscorea*). Such patterns imply that similar processes operated in divergent areas and this led to parallel evolutions of domestication. These processes had much to do with evolutionary ecology and the nature of Late Pleistocene and Holocene environments in tropical America.

Many of the plants that were taken under cultivation during the early Holocene must have been subsequently abandoned or nearly so, as others were fully domesticated and became favorites in subsistence economies because of desirable traits. It is these latter plants that dominate the later prehistoric and ethnohistoric records.

My thesis is that plant cultivation evolved repeatedly and independently in tropical America following the major climatic perturbations that marked the end of the Pleistocene. Combined with this process was the early, long-distance transmission of primitive domesticates such as maize. The spread of crop plants may have occurred through population migration and colonization or through exchange networks. Pickersgill and Heiser (1977) and Harlan (1986) commented that known patterns of transmission seem to indicate plant-by-plant transfer, rather than movement of whole complexes. This contrasts sharply with the situation in the Near East and Europe (Ammerman and Cavalli-Sforza 1984; Harlan 1986), and argues against large-scale movement of populations acting as the main mechanism of early plant transfer (or as an impetus for interregional domestication).

Simple forms of down-the-line exchange have often been invoked to account for the spread of early cultivars (Pearsall 1977-78; Piperno 1983), but I now believe that transmission may have been even simpler than that, perhaps having much to do with the nature of early Archaic settlement characteristics and reproductive networks. Early Holocene mobile forager-cultivators were spread over the landscape at very low densities and were likely to have interacted with other groups and to have chosen mates who lived in far-flung and distant regions (Wobst 1978). Such behavior would have had positive political and economic implications (Turnbull 1986), and it also served to maintain viable reproductive networks (Wobst 1974). The Pygmy, for example, who have a prescription to "marry far" (Turnbull 1986) choose mates who live, on average, 53 km away (Hewlett et al. 1986). The mean mating distance for the !Kung is 66 km (Harpending 1976).

Such interactions, when considered over centuries, would serve to move new ideas and plants long distances. The transfer of crops and requisite agro-economic knowledge could occur very causally and quickly (a central Panamanian says to a visitor, "Have you seen the new plant we are growing?"), or merely entail semi-bounded populations and changes in residence of a husband or a wife at marriage. As populations grew and systems of land tenure became somewhat more formal, one would expect that mating distances and "exploration ranges" (Ammerman and Cavalli-Sforza 1984) of individuals over their lifetimes became smaller. Increased population densities no longer made social closure reproductively disadvantageous. The "regionalization" of the archaeological record from Panama by 7000 B.P., (Cooke and Ranere 1992b) may reflect such a situation.

Conclusions

Fleshing out these concepts of the development and dispersals of tropical forest plant domestication will not be easy. That Late Pleistocene and early Holocene populations existed at low densities, shifted locations frequently, and left few material items by which to locate and date their settlements adds to the difficulty of tropical archaeology. In formulating research designs, however, we need to be aware that geological phytolith and pollen records in tandem with genetic data from modern species are currently providing more information on the problem than are archaeological data. The intensification and refinement of such research foci should, therefore, become of highest priority.

Notes

1. Personal observation by author, 1989.
2. Personal observation by author, 1989.

References Cited

Alcorn, J. B.
  1984   *Huastec Mayan Ethnobotany*. University of Texas Press, Austin.
Ammerman, A., and L. L. Cavalli-Sforza
  1984   *The Neolithic Transition and the Genetics of Populations in Europe*. Princeton University Press, Princeton.
Andersson, L.
  1986   Revision of Maranta subgen. Maranta (Marantaceae). *Nordic Journal of Botany* 6:729-756.
Bailey, R. C., G. Head, M. Jenike, B. Owen, R. Rechtman, and E. Zechenter
  1989   Hunting and Gathering in Tropical Rain Forests: Is It Possible? *American Anthropologist* 91:59-82.
Bird, J., and R. Cooke
  1978   The Occurrence in Panama of Two Types of Paleoindian Projectile Points. In *Early Man in America from a Circum-Pacific Perspective*, edited by A. Bryan, pp. 263-272. Occasional Papers No. 1. Department of Anthropology, University of Alberta, Edmonton.
Binford, L. R.
  1983   *In Pursuit of the Past*. Thames and Hudson, New York.
Bush, M. B., D. R. Piperno, and P. Colinvaux
  1989   A 6000 Year History of Amazonian Maize Cultivation. *Nature* 340:303-305.
Callen, E. O.
  1967   The First New World Cereal. *American Antiquity* 32:535-538.
Carter, G. F.
  1977   A Hypothesis Suggesting a Single Origin of Agriculture. In *Origins of Agriculture*, edited by

C. A. Reed, pp. 89-133. Mouton, The Hague.

Cohen, M.
1977   *The Food Crisis in Prehistory.* Yale University Press, New Haven.
1987   The Significance of Long-Term Changes in Human Diet and Food Economy. In *Food and Evolution: Toward a Theory of Human Food Habits*, edited by M. Harris and E. B. Ross, pp. 261-283. Temple University Press, Philadelphia.

Cooke, R.
1984   Archaeological Research in Central and Eastern Panama: A Review of Some Problems. In *The Archaeology of Lower Central America*, edited by F. Lange and D. Z. Stone, pp. 263-302. University of New Mexico Press, Albuquerque.

Cooke, R., and A. J. Ranere
1984   The "Proyecto Santa María." A Multidisciplinary Analysis of Prehistoric Adaptations to a Tropical Watershed in Panama. In *Recent Developments in Isthmian Archaeology*, edited by F. Lange, pp. 3-30. BAR 212, Oxford.
1989   Hunting in Prehistoric Panama: A Diachronic Perspective. In *The Walking Larder*, edited by J. Clutton-Brock, pp. 295-315. George Allen and Unwin, London.
1992a   Prehistoric Human Adaptations to the Seasonally Dry Forests of Panama. *World Archaeology* 24:114-133.
1992b   The Origins of Wealth and Hierarchy in the Central Region of Panama with Observations on its Relevance to the Phylogeny of Chibchan-speaking Polities of Panama and Elsewhere. In *Wealth and Hierarchy in the Intermediate Area*, edited by F. W. Lange, pp. 243-316. Dumbarton Oaks, Washington, D.C.

Decker, D.
1988   Origin(s), Evolution, and Systematics of *Cucurbita pepo* (Cucurbitaceae). *Economic Botany* 42:4-15.

Decker, D., and H. D. Wilson
1986   Numerical Analysis of Seed Morphology in *Cucurbita pepo*. *Systematic Botany* 11:595-607.

Dufour, D.
1988   Cyanide Content of Cassava (*Manihot esculenta*, Euphorbiaceae) Cultivars Used by Tukanoan Indians in Northwest Amazonia. *Economic Botany* 42:255-266.

Ford, R. I.
1981   Gardening and Farming Before A.D. 1000: Patterns of Prehistoric Cultivation North of Mexico. *Journal of Ethnobiology* 1:6-27.

Gepts, P., and F. A. Bliss
1986   Phaseolin Variability among Wild and Cultivated Common Beans (*Phaseolus vulgaris*) from Colombia. *Economic Botany* 40:469-478.

Gepts, P., T. C. Osborn, K. Rashka, and F. A. Bliss
1986   Phaseolin-protein Variability in Wild Forms and Landraces of the Common Bean (*Phaseolus vulgaris*): Evidence for Multiple Centers of Domestication. *Economic Botany* 40:451-468.

Hames, R. B., and W. T. Vickers
1982   Optimal Diet Breadth as a Model to Explain Variability in Amazonian Hunting. *American Ethnologist* 9:358-378.

Hansell, P.
1987   The Formative in Central Pacific Panama: La Mula-Sarigua. In *Chiefdoms in the Americas*, edited by R. D. Drennan and C. A. Uribe, pp. 119-139. University Press of America.

Harlan, J.
1975   *Crops and Man.* American Society of Agronomy, Crop Science Society of America, Madison.
1986   Plant Domestication: Diffuse Origins and Diffusions. In *The Origin and Domestication of Cultivated Plants*, edited by C. Barigozzi, pp. 21-34. Elsevier Science Amsterdam.

Harpending, H.
1976   Regional Variation in Kung Populations. In *Kalahari Hunter-Gatherers*, edited by R. B. Lee and I. DeVore. Harvard University Press, Cambridge.

Harris, M.
1979   *Cultural Materialism.* Random House, New York.

Hart, T., and J. Hart
1986   The Ecological Basis of Hunter-Gatherer Subsistence in African Rain Forests: The Mbuti of Eastern Zaire. *Human Ecology* 14:29-55.

Hassan, F.
1977   The Dynamics of Agricultural Origins in Palestine: A Theoretical Model. In *Origins of Agriculture*, edited by C. A. Reed, pp. 589-609. Mouton, The Hague.
1978   Demographic Archaeology. In *Advances in Archaeological Method and Theory, Vol. 1*, edited by M. Schiffer, pp. 49-103. Academic Press, New York.

Hawkes, K.
1987   How Much Food do Foragers Need? In *Food and Evolution: Toward a Theory of Human Food Habits*, edited by M. Harris and E. B. Ross, pp. 341-355. Temple University Press, Philadelphia.

Hawkes, K. and J. F. O'Connell
1981   Affluent Hunters? Some Comments in Light of the Alyawara Case. *American Anthropologist* 83:622-626.

Hawkes, K., K. Hill, and J. F. O'Connell
1982   Why Hunters Gather: Optimal Foraging and the Ache of Eastern Paraguay. *American Ethnologist* 9:379-398.

Hayden, B.

1981 Research and Development in the Stone Age: Technological Transitions Among Hunter-Gatherers. *Current Anthropology* 22:519-548.

Headland, T. N.

1987 The Wild Yam Question: How Well Could Independent Hunter-Gatherers Live in a Tropical Rain Forest Ecosystem? *Human Ecology* 15:463-491.

Heiser, C. B., Jr.

1989 Domestication of Cucurbitaceae: Cucurbita and Lagenaria. In *Foraging and Farming: The Evolution of Plant Exploitation*, edited by D. R. Harris and G. C. Hillman, pp. 471-480. Unwin-Hyman, London.

Hewlett, B. S., J. M. H. van de Koppel, and L. L. Cavalli-Sforza

1986 Exploration and Mating Range of Aka Pygmies of the Central African Republic. In *African Pygmies*, edited by L. L. Cavalli-Sforza, pp. 65-79. Academic Press, Orlando.

Hill, K.

1982 Hunting and Human Evolution. *Journal of Human Evolution* 11:521-544.

Holmberg, A. R.

1950 *Nomads of the Longbow*. Smithsonian Institution Press, Washington, D.C.

Iltis, H. H., and J. F. Doebley

1984 Zea—A Biosystematical Odyssey. In *Plant Biosystematics*, edited by W. F. Grant, pp. 587-616. Academic Press, Toronto.

Johnson, A.

1982 Reductionism in Cultural Ecology: The Amazon Case. *Current Anthropology* 23:413-428.

Johnson, A., and A. Baksh

1987 Ecological and Structural Influences on the Proportions of Wild Foods in the Diets of Two Machiguenga Communities. In *Food and Evolution: Toward a Theory of Human Food Habits*, edited by M. Harris and E. B. Ross, pp. 387-405. Temple University Press, Philadelphia.

King, F.

1987 The Evolutionary Effects of Plant Cultivation. In *Emergent Horticultural Economies of the Eastern Woodlands*, edited by W. F. Keegan, pp. 51-65. Occasional Paper No. 7. Center for Archaeological Investigations, Southern Illinois University, Carbondale.

Lathrap, D.

1987 The Introduction of Maize in Prehistoric Eastern North America: The View from Amazonia and the Santa Elena Peninsula. In *Emergent Horticultural Economies of the Eastern Woodlands*, edited by W. F. Keegan, pp. 345-371. Occasional Paper No. 7. Center for Archaeological Investigations, Southern Illinois University, Carbondale.

Linares, O. F.

1976 "Garden Hunting" in the American Tropics. *Human Ecology* 4:331-349.

1977 *Ecology and the Arts in Central Panama*. Studies in Precolumbian Art and Archaeology No. 17. Dumbarton Oaks Washington, D.C.

Linares, O. F., and A. J. Ranere

1980 *Adaptive Radiations in Prehistoric Panama*. Peabody Museum Monograph No. 5. Harvard University Press, Cambridge.

Linares, O. F., P. D. Sheets, and E. J. Rosenthal

1975 Prehistoric Agriculture in Tropical Highlands. *Science* 187:137-145.

Lynch, T.

1983 The Paleoindians. In *Ancient South Americans*, edited by J. D. Jennings, pp. 87-137. W. H. Freeman and Co., San Francisco.

Meltzer, D. J., and B. Smith

1987 Paleoindian and Early Archaic Subsistence Strategies in Eastern North America. In *Foraging, Collecting, and Harvesting: Archaic Period Subsistence and Settlement in the Eastern Woodlands*, edited by S. W. Neusius, pp. 3-31. Occasional Paper No. 6. Center for Archaeological Investigations, Southern Illinois University, Carbondale.

Milton, K.

1984 Protein and Carbohydrate Resources of the Maku Indians of Northwestern Amazonia. *American Anthropologist* 86:7-27.

Moran, E.

1983 Mobility as a Negative Factor in Human Adaptability: The Case of South American Tropical Forest Populations. In *Rethinking Human Adaptation: Biological and Cultural Models*, edited by R. Dyson-Hudson and M. A. Little, pp. 117-135. Westview Press, Boulder.

O'Connell, J. and K. Hawkes

1981 Alyawara Plant Use and Optimal Foraging Theory. In *Hunter-Gatherer Foraging Strategies: Ethnographic and Archaeological Analyses*, edited by B. Winterhalder and E. Smith, pp. 788-793. University of Chicago Press, Chicago.

Pearsall, D. M.

1977-78 Early Movements of Maize Between Mesoamerica and South America. *Journal of the Steward Anthropological Society* 9:41-75.

Pearsall, D. M., and D. R. Piperno

1990 The Antiquity of Maize in Ecuador: Summary and Re-evaluation of the Evidence. *American Antiquity* 55:324-337.

Pickersgill, B.

1977 Taxonomy and the Origin and Evolution of Cultivated Plants in the New World. *Nature* 268:591-595.

132

Pickersgill, B., and C. B. Heiser, Jr.

1977   Origins and Distributions of Plants Domesticated in the New World Tropics. In *The Origins of Agriculture*, edited by C. A. Reed, pp. 803-835. Mouton, The Hague.

Piperno, D. R.

1983   *The Application of Phytolith Analysis to the Reconstruction of Plant Subsistence and Environments in Prehistoric Panama.* Unpublished Ph.D. Dissertation, Department of Anthropology, Temple University. University Microfilms, Ann Arbor.

1988   *Phytolith Analysis: An Archaeological and Geological Perspective.* Academic Press, San Diego.

1989a   Non-affluent Foragers: Resource Availability, Seasonal Shortages, and the Emergence of Agriculture in Panamanian Tropical Forests. In *Foraging and Farming: The Evolution of Plant Exploitation*, edited by D. R. Harris and G. C. Hillman, pp. 538-554. Unwin-Hyman, London.

1989b   The Occurrence and Significance of Phytoliths in the Reproductive Structures of Tropical Angiosperms. *Review of Paleobotany and Palynology* 61:147-173.

Piperno, D. R., and K. Husum-Clary

1984   Early Plant Use and Cultivation in the Santa María Basin, Panama: Data from Phytoliths and Pollen. In *Recent Developments in Isthmian Archaeology*, edited by F. Lange, pp. 85-121. BAR 212, Oxford.

Piperno, D. R., K. Husum-Clary, R. Cooke, A. J. Ranere, and D. Weiland

1985   Preceramic Maize in Central Panama: Evidence from Phytoliths and Pollen. *American Anthropologist* 87:871-878.

Piperno, D. R., M. B. Bush, and P. C. Colinvaux

1990   Paleoenvironments and Human Occupation in Late Glacial Panama. *Quaternary Research* 33:108-116.

1991a   Paleoecological Perspectives on Human Adaptation in Central Panama. I. The Pleistocene. *Geoarchaeology* 6:210-226.

1991b   Paleoecological Perspectives on Human Adaptation in Central Panama. II. The Holocene. *Geoarchaeology* 6:227-250.

1992   Patterns of Articulation of Culture and the Plant World in Prehistoric Panama: 11,500 B.P. - 3000 B.P. In *Archaeology and Environment in Latin America*, edited by O. R. Ortiz-Troncoso and T. Van der Hammen, pp. 109-127. Instituut Voot Pre-El Protohistorische Archeologie Albert Egget Val Giffen, (IPP) Amsterdam.

Ranere, A. J.

1980   Human Movement into Tropical America at the End of the Pleistocene. In *Anthropological Papers in Memory of Earl H. Swanson*, edited by

L. B. Harten, C. N. Warren, and D. R. Tuohy, pp. 41-47. Idaho Museum of Natural History, Pocatello.

Ranere, A. J., and R. G. Cooke

1991   Paleo-Indian Occupation in the Central American Tropics. In *Clovis: Origins and Adaptations*, edited by R. Bonnichsen and K. L. Turnmire, pp. 237-253. Center for the Study of Early Man, Korvallis, Oregon.

1994   Early Human Migration Through the Isthmus of Panama. In *Human Occupation of the Pacific Continents and Islands*, edited by R. E. Ackerman. Washington State University Press, Pullman, in press. Ms. 1994.

Rindos, D.

1984   *The Origins of Agriculture: An Evolutionary Perspective.* Academic Press, San Francisco.

Sauer, C. O.

1950   Cultivated Plants of South and Central America. *Handbook of South American Indians*, Bull. 143, pp. 487-543. Bureau of American Ethnology, Smithsonian Institution, Washington, D.C.

1952   *Agricultural Origins and Dispersals.* M.I.T. Press, Cambridge.

Smith, B.

1987   The Independent Domestication of Indigenous Seed-Bearing Plants in Eastern North America. In *Emergent Horticultural Economies of the Eastern Woodlands*, edited by W. F. Keegan, pp.3-47. Occasional Paper No. 7. Center for Archaeological Investigations, Southern Illinois University, Carbondale.

Sturtevant

1969   History and Ethnography of Some West Indian Starches. In *The Domestication and Exploitation of Plants and Animals*, edited by P. J. Ucko and G. W. Dimbleby, pp. 177-199. Duckworth, London.

Turnbull, C. M.

1986   Survival Factors Among Mbuti and Other Hunters of the Equatorial Rain Forest. In *African Pygmies*, edited by L. Cavalli-Sforza, pp. 103-123. Academic Press, Orlando.

Valerio L., W.

1987   Análisis Funcional y Estratigráfico de Sf-9 (Carabali), un Abrico Rocoso en la Región Central de Panama. Unpublished Thesis. University of Costa Rica, San Jose.

Weiland, D.

1984   Prehistoric Settlement Patterns in the Santa María Drainage of Panama: A Preliminary Analysis. In *Recent Developments in Isthmian Archaeology*, edited by F. Lange, pp. 31-53. BAR 212, Oxford.

Winterhalder, B.

1987   The Analysis of Hunter-Gatherer Diets: Stalking an Optimal Foraging Model. In *Food and Evolution: Toward a Theory of Human Food Habits,*

edited by M. Harris and E. B. Ross. Temple
University Press, Philadelphia.

Winterhalder, B. and Smith, E.
1981   *Hunter-Gatherer Foraging Strategies.* University
of Chicago Press, Chicago.

Wobst, H. M.
1974   Boundary Conditions for Paleolithic Social Systems: A Simulation Approach. *American Antiquity* 39:147-178.

1978   The Archaeo-Ethnology of Hunter-Gatherers or
the Tyranny of the Ethnographic Record in Archaeology. *American Antiquity* 43:303-308.

Wright, H. E.
1977   Environmental Change and the Origin of Agriculture in the Old and New Worlds. In *Origins of
Agriculture*, edited by C. A. Reed, pp. 281-318.
Mouton, The Hague.

Part III
SOUTH AMERICA

10

Wetlands as Resource Concentrations in Southwestern Ecuador

Alfred H. Siemens

Introduction

The development of subsistence systems has long interested geographers, particularly those who would dare to call themselves human or cultural geographers. This has always required collaboration with those working in the physical environmental wing of the discipline and indeed an array of specialists from other disciplines, particularly those able to manipulate the various recently developed testing procedures. Various techniques and even methodologies must be brought into alignment. When this goes well one may achieve synthesis and arrive at insights that would not have occurred otherwise. There is an extensive literature on such an approach to prehistory, often called "the new archaeology" or "geoarchaeology" and it does not need to be reviewed here. With these sorts of predispositions and aspirations, I became involved in an investigation of the significance of wetlands for the interpretation of early subsistence in the lowlands of southwestern Ecuador.

Substantively, this foray had its beginnings in a series of wetland studies in the state of Veracruz, Mexico. In one of them, various colleagues and I had been monitoring current use of one particular wetland margin, relating it to what was being done around wetlands elsewhere in the lowland part of the state and to the relics of Prehispanic use of wetlands, that is "raised fields," in the same region (Siemens 1981). It had become apparent that the nature and circumstances of recent incursions by *campesinos* (peasant farmers), commercial farmers, and *ganaderos* (cattle ranchers) into wetland, could yield some very useful propositions for the interpretation of the relics. The relationship of cropping and grazing in the wetlands to other economic activities in neighboring communities, particularly the seasonal rhythm of these activities, their expansion and retraction over longer periods of time, and various other aspects, was perceived to be instructive generally. In fact, it was deduced that land use on the wetland margin, or the *orilla*, had much to suggest regarding the processes of intensification and disintensification.

Before going further, it will be useful to clarify the typical elements of landscapes enclosing wetlands by means of a series of diagrams (Figure 1). They condense numerous actual landscapes encountered in lowland Mesoamerica, as well as examples from elsewhere discussed in the literature, and attempt to make some links with what has been examined in southwestern Ecuador. They begin with a simple schematic profile: stream channel, levee, back-slope, back-swamp and *terra firma*, which can occur in countless variations and combinations. The top of the levee is a typical, preferred settlement site, in the past as in the present; it was probably also an important site for the early development of cultivation (Figure 1b). Its significance will be examined along the Arenillas River. The back-slope of the levee, in particular the zone subject to yearly inundation, the *orilla* already referred to (Figure 1c), is often the context for complex, seasonally pulsing agriculture. A strong example of this is the endlessly complex traditional agriculture on the back-slopes of the labyrinthine lowlands of the Mexican state of Tabasco. The echos of something similar may still be detected along the back-slopes of the Arenillas floodplain, on the margins of water-bodies called *pozas*.

A careful consideration of the use of terrain subject to regular inundation seems critical. On such terrain one often finds the remains of "raised fields", or one might say the proto-*chinampa*, as seen in Figure 1d. Such agriculture often stopped short of the core of swampland with open water all year round, but it may also have extended entirely across a wetland, depending on the details of topography and hydrology. Full scale *chinampa* agriculture, as we know it in the Valley of Mexico, developed once the water level could be controlled, fluctuations reduced, and platform levels maintained above high water level all year. There is no evidence yet of "raised field" agriculture around the wetlands of southwestern Ecuador, but there are abundant remains of it northward in the Guayas River delta.

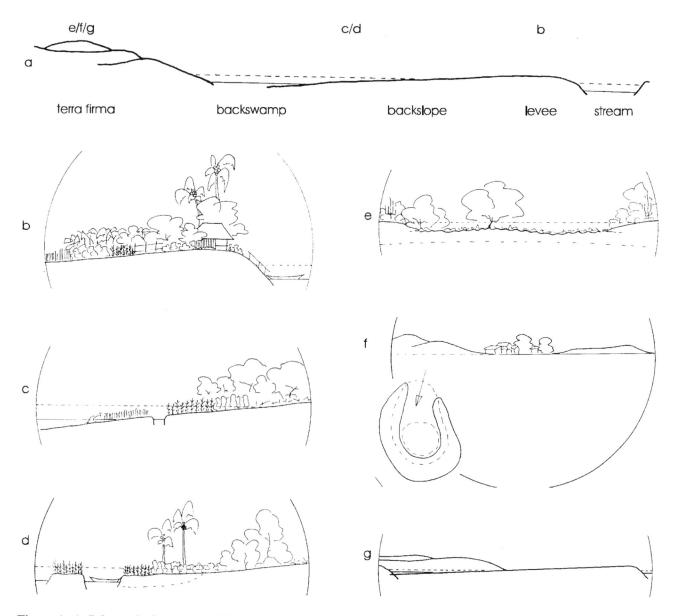

Figure 1. A Schematic Summary of Landscape Elements Recurring in the Study of Wetlands as Sustaining Areas, Including: (*a*) a general profile of the five basic landscape elements; (*b*) the levee—favored settlement and horticulture site; (*c*) the margin of the wetland, subject to inundation, often used for dry season cultivation; (*d*) the same margin as it will have appeared under cultivation by means of a raise field system; (*e*) perched wetlands, as dealt within greater detail in figure 4; (*f*) an *albarrada*, as found on *terra firma* on the Santa Elena Peninsula; (*g*) a *poza*—ponded water forming lakes between fingers of higher ground, with seasonally variable levels.

One must not lose sight of neighboring *terra firma*. What was done there was likely to have been complementary to the cultivation around the wetlands. This has become strongly apparent in our investigations of the remains of field systems on *terra firma* just west of the wetlands of Central Veracruz. In the lowlands of south western Ecuador we have found wetlands perched on *terra firma* (Figure 1e). These too, seem to be complementary to subsistence activities in neighboring microenvironments, and we will return to them later. They bear a good deal of

comparison with *aguadas* or even *bajos* (seasonally flooded low-lying areas) in the Maya realm.

Early in the planning for an investigation south of the Guayas Estuary, the possibility was raised of finding examples of the *albarrada*, or artificial catchment basin, as described for the Santa Elena Peninsula north of the estuary by many observers, but discussed particularly well by Stothert (1989). Figure 1f represents such a feature, in profile and in plan view. It captures the run-off at some advantageous focal point in the hydrography during a *buen*

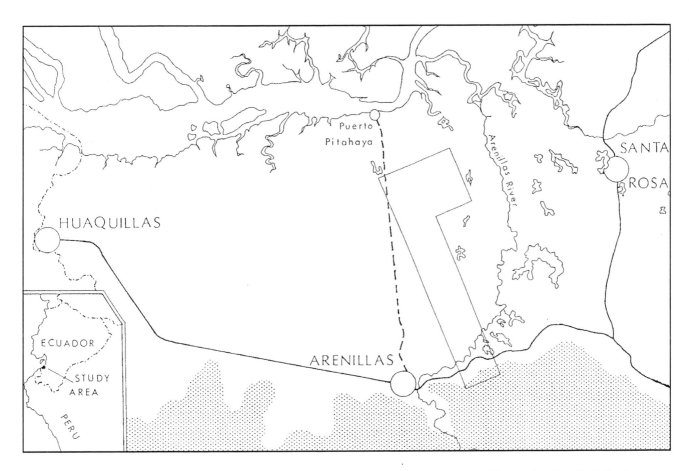

Figure 2. Map of the Arenillas Lowlands Showing the Outlines of the Transect Chosen for Detailed Study.

invierno, that is during the rains associated with an El Niño. Related settlement and tree growth of the genus *Prosopis* is shown, as well as the drop in the water level in the months after the end of the rains. The falling water is often followed on the exposed *albarrada* floor by plantings of various crops—another instance of the use of a wetland margin.

As it has turned out, there is little evidence yet for full-scale *albarradas* south of the estuary, but these may perhaps be seen as artificial versions of *pozas*, natural, water-filled depressions that are frequent on both sides of the Arenillas River (Figure 1g). The origin of some of the other types of wetlands in the El Oro region is still debatable.

In the background of the Ecuadorean investigations there was also fascinating work on the margins of lakes in the Basin of Mexico. Niederberger (1979) outlined the nature of this advantageous biotope and showed how it had been used by settled people practicing a pre-agriculture subsistence system some six millennia B.C. Robertson (1980) has provided thoughtful interpretation of the evolution of intensive agriculture in these same circumstances. Tichy (1979) expanded on the concept of lake margin and wetlands in Central Mexico as favored places before Conquest, which was echoed by research on Prehispanic wetland agriculture in the lowlands of Mesoamerica (e.g., Siemens

1983).

A further, rather fundamental and well known line of research on early subsistence in the Americas influenced the new Ecuadorean work as well: the wide range of early subsistence possibilities found to exist in the rather arid hill land near Tehuacán, Mexico, and the impulse given to the development of agriculture under these circumstances (Byers 1967).

The arid coastal regions of southwestern Ecuador had already been found to be interesting with respect to early occupance and the development of subsistence strategies on the South American continent (e.g., Meggers et al. 1965; Lathrap et al. 1975; Zevallos et al. 1977). The Arenillas Lowlands in the southwestern extremity, pockmarked with wetlands, promised to be an interesting region in which to pursue this further.

A good deal of thought had already been given, of course, and evidence adduced, on the antiquity of settlement and agriculture in western Ecuador generally and in the low-lands to the south of the Guayas Estuary in particular (Netherly 1984). Various settlement sites have been excavated (e.g., Marcos 1982; Staller 1994). This is, therefore, not the place to attempt to summarize what has been found, except to note that Valdivia period occupation had been found along the litoral (Phases VII and VIII,

139

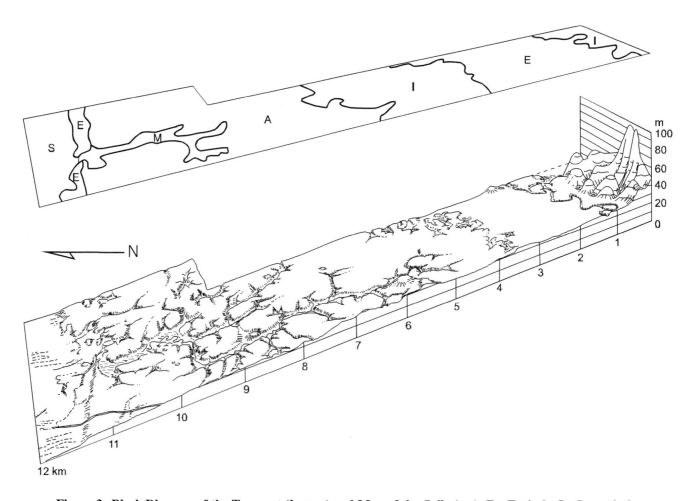

Figure 3. Block Diagram of the Transect (*bottom*) and Map of the Soils (*top*): E—Entisols, I—Inceptisols, A—Aridisols, M—Intermittently Flooded Marsh, S—Saline Beach Deposits.

1700-1500 B.C.) and along the lower river (Phases III and IV, 2300-2200 B.C., as well as Early Formative, 3500-1500 B.C.). Numerous sites of other,subsequent periods have also been found (Netherly et al. 1980; Lathrap et al. 1977). The settlement survey continues at the present time and will be reported elsewhere (see Raymond, Chapter 11). In any case, there was chronological latitude for the interpretation of the wetlands, and there were cultural points of reference.

There was also excellent vertical air photo and topographic map coverage, as well as a good deal of environmental information available from published sources and various governmental agencies. There remained lacunae on such matters as the behavior of ground water in the lowlands, for example, and on Holocene sea level changes, but the potential existed to contribute to the interpretation of the environmental context of the wetlands.

In 1982, I was invited to study the wetlands in the lowland region to the south of the Guayas River estuary (Figure 2). This study was part of the Tahuín Project, a long-term investigation of ancient settlement above and below a new dam on the Arenillas River. The specific objectives of the study were: to generate a taxonomy of the wetlands of the Arenillas Lowlands, to determine the

climatic context of the wetlands, in particular, the variation of precipitation at several time scales, to trace the resulting surface and subsurface hydrology, to collect botanical data on the wetlands, and to interview local inhabitants about environmental constraints traditional practices of gathering, hunting, fishing, and agriculture in areas subject to inundation.

All of the above was to assist in the interpretation of such evidence regarding subsistence and settlement as might emerge from the archaeological investigations already underway, to facilitate the modeling of Prehispanic subsistence systems, and to provide data toward an overview of change in both environment and subsistence within the region. It was also to integrate scattered environmental data in aid of an ongoing investigation of a cultural phenomenon, somewhat like a study of karst in the Yucatan Peninsula undertaken some years ago in order to clarify the limits of the "raised field" phenomenon in that region (Siemens 1978).

Physical Environmental Characteristics

Little published information was available regarding the

140

Arenillas Lowlands to the south of the Guayas River estuary; this region it has often been viewed as a stepsister of the Santa Elena Peninsula to the north. The arid Arenillas Lowlands are often only briefly mentioned in discussions of the vast Peruvian coastal desert region. They are similar in physical characteristics but less well known, possibly because they are isolated by an international boundary.

The coastal plain to the north of Arenillas is composed of Pliocene and Pleistocene (i.e., late Tertiary and early Quaternary) sediments of various textures, which have been uplifted by tectonic processes, and dissected by both indigenous and exotic streams (Fairbridge 1968). These sediments are overlain on the coast by Holocene fluvio-marine deposits; on the floodplains of the larger exotic streams by Holocene clay, silt, and sand deposits; and on the boundary between the coastal plains and the foothills of the Andes by Holocene piedmont formations, which have been dissected to some extent (Orstrom-Francia 1983).

The soils of the Arenillas Lowlands (Consortio Internacional Puyango-Tumbes n.d.) are shown together with a block diagram of a transect through the Lowlands in Figure 3. The main soil groups, from the beach ridge to the mountains include, first of all, *Aridisols* on the coastal plain. These develop in areas that are not normally moist more than 90 consecutive days and they have well-developed horizons, including a deep and distinctive clay horizon. They are subject to churning that results from repeated wetting and drying. These soils are of considerable interest in the interpretation of certain kinds of wetlands, as will be seen.

To the south are *Inceptisols*, recent soils that developed on sediments of an earlier floodplain and have weakly developed horizons. *Entisols* fringe our region to the north and the south. They are very recent, with no horizons, and underlie both the current floodplain of the Arenillas and the beach ridge.

The climate is highly seasonal, with rains normally occurring only in February and March. It is semi-arid, with precipitation exceeding potential evaporation only in these two months. With regard to the availability of water for agriculture, the climate is formally described as *deficiente* in January, *algo excesivo* in February, *algo deficiente* in March and April, and as *muy deficiente* for the remaining eight months of the year (IGM n.d.). The degree of annual rainfall variability remains to be formulated. In addition, there is vast and irregular variation, at intervals of several years, attributable to El Niño (Sheppard 1933). El Niño has become the subject of increasing attention in the clarification of synoptic weather patterns.

Climatically, this is an environment of great risk, but also, of great opportunity. The role of the various kinds of wetlands is almost certainly going to prove of key importance in the interpretation of past and present exploitation of the region because wetlands provide greater stability in water supply and therefore, reduce risk.

The vegetation of the lowlands grades from *manglares* on the coast, to desert associations described as *Xerofilla Humboltiana* slightly inland, *deciduous coastal woodlands* yet further inland, and then pluvial *selva* on the rising piedmont (IGM n.d.). The second and third of these are most relevant for the interpretation of the wetlands, as will be shown.

Phreatophytic species are particularly interesting in the xerophytic context. The genus *Prosopis* of the Leguminosae or Mimosaceae families is commonly referred to as *mesquite* in North America, *algarrobo* in South America, and *kiawe* in Hawaii. *Prosopis pallida* is the species most strongly represented near some types of wetlands in the Arenillas Lowlands. *Prosopis pallida* grows to about 20 m, bears fruit and is valuable for lumber, fuel-wood, and fodder. It is native to the driest areas of Peru, Colombia, and Ecuador, especially along the coast (Habit 1981).

The Quechua Indians of Precolumbian Peru called the *algarrobo* plant *thacco* or *taco* meaning, "the tree" or "great one," probably because the tree bore fruit even in years of drought when all other crops died (D'Antoni and Solbrig 1977). *Hualtaco* is an important place name in the northwest part of our region, where there a great deal of wetland and many *algarrobo* stumps. Nowadays, trucks bearing *algarrobo* wood may be seen along the highways of the region on any given day. Their tracks, visible on the vertical air photos from the early 1970's, lead from wetland to wetland, as their operators searched for fuel-wood. Fresh stumps around many wetlands bear witness to the continuing usefulness of the wood and to the stresses being put on this landscape by population increase and urbanization.

Types of Wetlands

Methodological Interjection

Excellent quality air photos, at a scale of 1:5000, were available for the Arenillas Lowlands. They were scanned in their entirety and interpreted in a preliminary fashion, after which, a transect was chosen for detailed analysis (Figure 2).

Throughout this analysis there were frequent reminders of the extent of recent change in this landscape. The air photos we used were taken late in the dry season of 1974. In the interim there had been several El Niño events, one of which was strong enough to obliterate many roads and trails. In addition, immigration from the highlands, population increase within the region, rapid urbanization, especially around Huaquillas, the expansion of ranching and of commercial agriculture, involving bananas, cacao, and rice, the related small irrigation schemes, as well as the dramatic leveling and flooding of large sections of the litoral in aid of shrimp farming, have all had a visible impact on the landscape.

There is also good quality air photo coverage at a scale of 1:60,000, taken in 1983. These photos show the landscape under the full effect of El Niño and will be very helpful in defining the extremes of environmental change in the region.

A program of oblique air reconnaissance was undertaken. It yielded large-scale imagery that helps update the previous vertical coverage and, in addition, allows visual probing from various perspectives (Figure 5). One feels saddened during such reconnaissance because many of the features of interest to this study are being rapidly obliterated. Once the subtle remains of ancient landscapes are covered by plantations and ponds, they are gone.

1. Esteros

Valleys so named occur in various of the maps at our disposal. They have steep sides and apparently level floors; they extend into the lowlands from the litoral. The transect includes a prominent example. They are apparently saline, subject to intermittent inundation, and support a growth of marsh and swamp plant communities. There is little evidence for exploitation within or immediately around them on the 1974 air photos. Ethnographic inquiry near the coast has not yielded any clues regarding their usefulness either, but they might nevertheless support animals and plants that at sometime were important to a hunting and gathering or incipient agricultural economy.

2. Arenillas River Valley Bottom-land

Bars and low, sloping banks are exposed in the bottoms of the entrenched valley during each dry season. There are instances of scattered small plots under various crops, apparent on the 1974 air photos, which are examples of small scale fugitive subsistence agriculture with perhaps some cash cropping. This is a variant on a kind of rudimentary seasonal land use to be found in the bottom-lands of many other regions—a matter of catch-as-catch-can, in supplement to agriculture and other subsistence activities in neighboring microenvironments. This type of wetland fades quickly with the advance of modernization.

3. Arenillas River Floodplain

The present main channel north of Arenillas is a sequence of meanders incised several meters into the floodplain; there are vestiges to the north and west of an earlier meandering channel. The soils (*Entisols*) are recent and deep, and, as might be expected, they are now being used almost entirely for agriculture and ranching. The first predominates near the river and the second on the peripheries. Variable access to irrigation water would not seem to be a problem, considering the location of the main canals running roughly parallel to the river. There must be other reasons for this differentiation, including the possibility of variability in the depth and frequency of flooding. Even the highest riverside locations are reported to have been flooded in the strong El Niño of 1982-3.

This is a complex landscape, offering various seasonally inter-phased cropping possibilities. It is quite likely that it was exploited in Prehispanic times. There are also opportunities for hydrological manipulation, particularly vis-à-vis the *pozas*, which are discussed below, by means of dams that could keep out rising stream waters, or more likely, keep them in.

4. Pozas

Against the abrupt breaks in slopes on both sides of the Arenillas floodplain, one finds many lakes or ponds that are commonly referred to as *pozas*. They are irregular, often dendritic in shape, with steep banks away from the Arenillas River and low, gentle banks toward it. They were formed as a result of the aggradation of the floodplain, which blocked small tributaries.

The margins of the *pozas* have been of particular interest to this study from the beginning. Water levels rise and fall; good agricultural land is exposed and flooded, especially on the lower river-ward margins. It seemed that there would be a situation here that would yield instances of the agricultural incursions referred to at the outset of this paper. On the 1974 air photos can be seen several instances of what must be dry season use of exposed wetland margin. This is a residue of an activity that seems to have been highly important in the long-term development of tropical lowland agriculture. However, by 1985 when we undertook our first field-checking excursions, much of this had fallen prey to modernization.

It has been possible to inquire into several farmers' use of such land near the community of San Vicente. In one case down-slope canalization had been resorted to in order to speed the drainage of the low river-ward margin—exactly the sort of canalization that is hypothesized to have taken place at an early stage in the development of complexes of platforms and canals ("raised fields") on wetland margins. Water is pumped or manually lifted out of *pozas* for irrigation at many locations, at least until evaporation raises the salinity unacceptably in the longer dry periods.

It has long been recognized that there was a clustering of Prehispanic sites along the Arenillas River and around the *pozas* (Netherly et al. 1980).

5. Rounded Depressions on the Coastal Plain (Pans)

The terrain from the left margin of the Arenillas River floodplain, northwestward to the beginning of mangrove is dotted with rounded depressions (Figure 2). Their investigation was hampered for some time by curious configurations on the 1974 1:5000 vertical air photo coverage of the regions underlain by *Aridisols* just inland from the beach ridge (Figure 3). These were dotted by numerous, 10 m diameter, dark features, connected into a network by double lines. It seemed from the beginning that they were a type of wetland to which woodcutters had come with their heavy vehicles in order to take out the various phreatophytes, especially *algarrobo*. However such small round wetlands could not be found in the contemporary landscape.

It eventually became apparent, from information provided by informants who had finally been asked the right questions, and some evidence on the ground, that these features were the round blots of charcoal litter that remain from the large conical mounds erected and removed by charcoal burners. These were particularly active in the 1970's as immigration from the Sierra was accelerating and the need for household fuel was increasing. The forest on the *Aridisols* was the principal remaining source in the lowlands. The supply of hard wood suitable for the production of good charcoal was soon depleted. Several El Niño events helped to stimulate the growth of succession species in what remained of the forested area, and obscure the

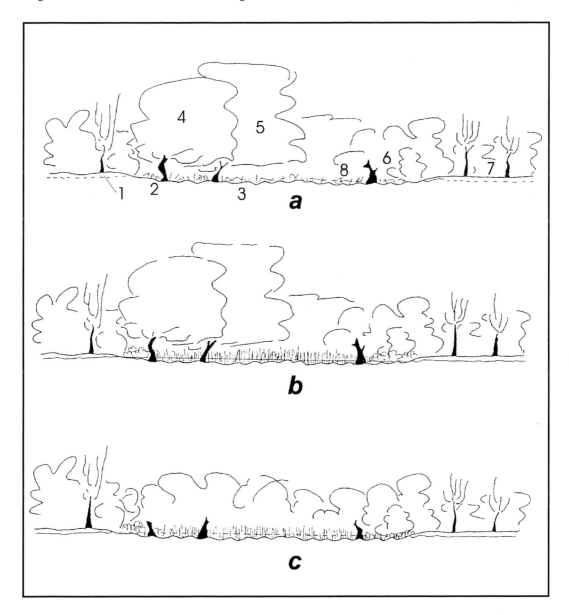

Figure 4. A Series of Three Schematic Diagrams Showing One Particular Example of the Larger of the Round Depressions (*pans*) at Various Stages: (*a*) the depression as seen late in the dry season. The numbers indicate the following: 1) sandy topsoil, 2) clay subsoil, 3) hummocks with intervening cracks, characteristic of a clay horizon subject to wetting and drying, 4) and 5) various species of the genus *Prosopis*, 6) a stump of an *Algarrobo*, 7) xerophytic surrounding vegetation, 8) dry hydrophytes. (*b*) The same depression as one would expect to see it after rains, with a lush new growth of hydrophytes, swarms of insects and the sound of birds. Open water is visible among plants, it has just covered the highest of the hummocks around the edge. (c) The depression as it was actually seen after the rains. The above conditions obtained, but the remaining *Prosopis* had been cut down and we were assured that in the next dry season the surface of the entire area would be leveled for agriculture.

143

rounded features with the connecting tracks that were so prominent on the 1974 air photographs. More and more of the forest is being cleared now for irrigated cropping, especially rice, which obliterates the marks of previous occupance and use—phantom wetlands, tracks, ancient settlements, and all.

Larger rounded features are also apparent on the same air photos, but these have persisted and are indeed wetlands. Two types can be tentatively differentiated on pragmatic grounds, but further work may very well show that they are only variations in degree. The first measures 100-200 m in diameter. Such wetlands seem to be distentions in the courses of intermittent streams. They can be manipulated by damming to enhance storage of water. This provides an opportunity for dry season cropping on soil with residual moisture. During the wetter months, such depressions are flooded.

Other rounded depressions, also on the order 100-200 m in diameter, are enclosed all around, or almost all around. They have an open, flat and light-toned appearance,

particularly during the latter parts of the long dry season, from which we have derived the designation: *pan*. They flood during the rains, hold open water for some months after that, then dry out.

We have been able to observe the behavior of water and plant response in several such depressions at different times of year, sampled the soil stratigraphy within and on the margins of two of them, and obtained ethnographic evidence on some current uses. Some of the results of the work on these features to date are presented on the diagrams that make up Figure 4, and are illustrated in Figure 5.

One of the intriguing aspects of the *pans* apparent from the air during the dry season is the network of paths and rough roads connecting them. People searched them out, moving repeatedly around their peripheries, perhaps to utilize the pods of the *algarrobo*, but more likely to cut down specimens of this or other species. The paths were undoubtedly also used by the deer in their search for edibles in those same *pan* peripheries, and indeed by domesticated animals.

Figure 5. An Oblique Air Photograph of a *pan* Similar in its Seasonal Hydrology and Botany to the Depression Described in Figure 4.

Even more intriguing is the rounded periphery of the *pans*. Before commercial agriculture and urbanization rolled over the pans of northern El Oro, and the reference here is to *pans* in the drier, less continuously vegetated western parts of our region, as well as the more densely forested areas such as those shown in Figure 5, many were fringed by tree growth that is somewhat denser than in the surroundings. These are the phreatophytes, notably *algarrobo*, that were of interest to the charcoal-burners and the wood-cutters that sought building materials during the region's urbanization. They may have been used by the early inhabitants who would also have found concentrations of resources around the pans.

The shape of the *pans* of this type, as surveyed in the various kinds of air photo coverage available for the northern part of the lowlands, particularly the region underlain by the *Aridisols*, is predominantly circular, but some are distended along a part of their circumference into a pear shape. These distentions seem to coincide with vague intermittent stream channels. There is the suggestion, therefore, that the remainder of the rounded margins represent an artificial catchment basin. However, careful ground examination, measurement of profiles and excavations around several *pans* have not shown them to be surrounded by traces of the spoil that would have had to result from human excavation.

None of the situations described in the literature on clay-soil landforms seems to fit with the features observed in El Oro. Any interpretation of these wetlands and their context will need to take into account that there has been sequential uplift along this coast and some of the characteristics of the landforms are probably attributable to marine conditions.

In the earlier Mesoamerican wetland studies (Siemens 1983), it became apparent that natural processes stimulated imitative human adaptations. The rounded islands that appear in a wetland as it fills itself in are a virtual prototype for the "raised field." As Stothert (1989:4) has suggested, it may be that the various rounded depressions in lowland El Oro, or indeed the *pozas*, such as those mentioned in this chapter, constitute prototypes for or early stages in the development of the *albarrada*. This is a rounded basin traditionally constructed on gentle slopes to catch periodic run-off in areas where wetlands do not occur naturally. Those discussed in the literature are substantial, stratigraphically complex structures to the north of the Guayas River estuary, used for millennia (Stothert 1989). Nothing quite like that has yet been found in the lowlands of El Oro.

Sustaining Potential of Wetlands in the Arenillas Lowlands

Drawing again on research done on the Santa Elena Peninsula, in particular that by Stothert (1981, 1989), there seems little evidence in southwest Ecuador for long-term climatic change during the Holocene. One may assume that the physical environmental constraints and opportunities of today approximate those that faced early humans in this region. We may also assume that the Precolumbian population was "sparse but stable," as has been proposed for the Peninsula (Stothert 1989:4). Their adaptations could have included agricultural as well as foraging and hunting strategies.

Within easy range of the beach ridge on which the Valdivia sites have been found, one may envisage an array of resources: plant foods from both the xerophytic vegetation, various species of the phreatophytic *Prosopis* and the hydrophytes such as those that grow from bulbs in the depressions during the wetter months. Deer are attracted to the *pans* and would have provided an important source of protein, as they do to this day. Lentic and lotic fish would also have been available, as well as aquatic and other birds. These resources would have varied with the seasons and with the arrhythmia of El Niño. The wetland presented an attractive resource concentration for Archaic hunter-gatherer-fishers, complementing the marine resources available nearby.

Moreover, there were the levee tops and wetland margins which might well have permitted incipient cultivation. Agriculture was also possible away from the wetlands in the arid coastal lowlands during the *buenos inviernos* associated with El Niño. The natural conditions for some agricultural elaboration or intensification were present in the floodplain of the Arenillas River and perhaps around some of the *pozas*, especially if their water levels could be manipulated. However, the necessary population concentrations do not seem to be indicated, nor have we yet found vestiges of intensification in the wetlands or in the neighboring hilllands.

The animal and wild plant resources of the foreshore and of the depressions in the coastal plain may also be seen as a complement to agriculture on the floodplain and elsewhere—from the time of early sedentary settlement in this region right through to the present day. As in other places and other times, "It was probably the knowledge of hunter-gatherer resource strategies as alternatives that made horticulture a viable proposition" (Hayden 1981:529).

It is important now to continue the investigation of the role of both the natural and cultural wetlands in the evolution of early coastal agricultural systems. We need to know more about their form, origin, use, and modifications, particularly since there is such an intriguing array of them in this region. We also need to trace the relationships of the wetlands to the remains of settlement and to attempt to sketch out a chronology. And finally, all this needs to be done before commercial food production obliterates the evidence.

Acknowledgments

My thanks to Olaf Holm, director of the Museo Antropológico of the Banco Central del Ecuador, who took an interest in this work and extended his good offices on my behalf, to Jorge Marcos of the Instituto Nacional de Patrimonio Cultural del Ecuador, who provided me with a permit, and particularly to Patricia Netherly, Director of the Proyecto Arqueológico Tahuín, who made the infrastructure of her project and the results of relevant investigations available to me, and put me in contact with important informants in the various relevant governmental offices. Galo Almeida Nieto, Chief of Army Intelligence, furnished a much appreciated document that served as a renewable safe conduct. Alejandro Vera, a soil scientist working in the offices of PREDESUR, kindly discussed various materials relating to the Arenillas Lowlands with me and assisted in the interpretation of the region.

The research on wetlands in Southwestern Ecuador was supported by the Social Science and Humanities Research Council of Canada. I am indebted to John Staller, a graduate student in archaeology at Southern Methodist University, who assisted me in the field, to Gordon Clark, a student in geography at the University of British Columbia, who helped with library research and the production of this paper, as well as to Alastair Robertson, my research assistant at UBC, who marshaled much of the basic data and who participated to very good effect in its interpretation.

This paper is an extensively revised version of a paper published, in Spanish, in the proceedings of a symposium: "Orígines del Hombre Americano," held in Mexico City, June, 1987.

References Cited

Byers, Douglas S. (editor)
1967 *The Prehistory of The Tehuacán Valley, Vol. 1: Environment and Subsistence.* University of Texas Press, Austin.

Consortio Internacional Puyango-Tumbes
n.d. Mapa de Suelos Nos. S-2, S-3.

D'Antoni, H. L. and O. T. Solbrig
1977 *Algarrobos* in South American Cultures Past and Present. In *Mesquite*, edited by B. B. Simpson. Hutchison and Ross, Stroudsburg, Pennsylvania.

Fairbridge, R. W.
1968 *Encyclopedia of the Earth Sciences, Vol. III. Geomorphology.* Reinhold, New York.

Habit, M. A.
1981 Prosopis Tamaruga: *Fodder Tree for Arid Zones.* FAO, Rome.

Hayden, B.
1981 Research and Development in the Stone Age: Technological Transitions among Hunter-Gatherers. *Current Anthropology* 22(5): 519-548.

Instituto Geográfico Militár (IGM)
n.d. *Atlas Geográfico de la República del Ecuador.* Quito, Ecuador.

Lathrap, D. W., D. Collier, and H. Chandra
1975 *Ancient Ecuador: Culture, Clay, and Creativity 3000-300 B.C.* Field Museum of Natural History, Chicago.

Lathrap, D. W., J. G. Marcos, and J. Zeidler
1977 Real Alto: an Ancient Ceremonial Center. *Archaeology* 30(1):2-13.

Meggers, B. J., C. Evans, and E. Estrada
1965 *The Early Formative Period of Coastal Ecuador: The Valdivia and Machalilla Phases.* Smithsonian Contributions to Anthropology. Vol. 1. Smithsonian Institution, Washington, D. C.

Marcos, J. G.
1982 Arqueología de la Península de Santa Elena. *Espejo* 4(5): 94-99.

Netherly, P.
1984 The Management of Prehispanic Irrigation Systems in Northern Peru. *American Antiquity* 49(1):227-254.

Netherly, P., O. Holm, J. Marcos, and R. Marcos
1980 Survey of the Arenillas Valley, El Oro Province. Paper presented at the 45th Annual Meeting of the Society for American Archaeology, Philadelphia.

Niederberger, C.
1979 Early Sedentary Economy in the Basin of Mexico. *Science* 203(4376):131-142.

Orstrom-Francia
1983 *Mapa Morfo-Pedalógico: Machala.* Banco Central del Ecuador, Quito.

Robertson, A.
1980 *The* Chinampas *of the Valley of Mexico.* Unpublished M.A. thesis, Department of Geography, University of British Columbia, Vancouver.

Siemens, A. H.
1978 Karst and the Prehispanic Maya in the Southern Lowlands. In *Prehispanic Maya Agriculture*, edited by P. D. Harrison, and B. L. Turner II, pp. 117-143. University of New Mexico Press, Albuquerque.
1981 Seasonal Flooding and Agriculture in the Southern Gulf Lowlands of Mexico: the Example of El Palmar. Paper presented at the XIII International Botanical Congress, Sydney.
1983 Wetland Agriculture in Pre-hispanic Mesoamerica. *Geographical Review* 73(2):166-181.

Sheppard, G.
1933 The Rainy Season of 1932 in Southwest Ecuador. *Geographical Review* 23(2):210-216.

Staller, J. E.
1993 *Late Valdivia Occupation in Southern Coastal El Oro Province, Ecuador: Excavations at the Early Formative Period (3500-1500 B.C.) Site of La Emerenciana.* Ph. D. Dissertation, Department of Anthropology, Southern Methodist University, Dallas.

Stothert, K. E.
1981 The Guangala Archaeological Project: Results of the 1980 Research Season. Paper presented at the

International Andean Archaeology Colloquium, Austin, Texas.

1989 Traditional Catchment Structures and Water Management in Southwest Ecuador. Ms. on file, Department of Geography, University of British Columbia.

Tichy, F.

1979 Genetische Analyse eines Altsiedellandes im Hochland von Mexico: Das Becken von Puebla-Tlaxcala. *Gefuge der Erdoberflache: Festschrift* 42:339-372. Deutschen Geographentag, Gottingen.

Zevallos M., C., W. C. Galinat, D. W. Lathrap, E. R. Leng, J. G. Marcos, K. M. Klumpp

1977 The San Pablo Corn Kernel and Friends. *Science* 196(4288):385-390.

11

Early Formative Societies in the Tropical Lowlands of Western Ecuador: a View from the Valdivia Valley

J. Scott Raymond

Introduction

Until very recently, Ecuador, like most of the Pacific nations between Mexico and Peru, has been neglected by archaeologists. Following the pathways of the plundering conquistadors, archaeologists concentrated their efforts on the centers of the high civilizations. Situated as it is, adjacent to the Peruvian coast where both organic and inorganic artifacts are conserved in the sands of the dry, cool desert, the moist tropics of coastal Ecuador seemed particularly unattractive for archaeological exploration. In part, the recent attention focused on coastal Ecuador by archaeologists can be understood by demographic changes in the profession, that is, an increase in the number of archaeologists and the dispersal of some of them to lesser known regions (Figure 1). A more significant factor, however, was the discovery in the late fifties of Valdivia (Meggers et al. 1965), a pottery-using culture which, according to radiocarbon dates of ca. 5000 B.P., preceded the appearance of pottery in either Mexico or Peru by at least 1000 years.

The discovery of Valdivia immediately piqued the interest of archaeologists and led to speculation about the early existence of Formative cultures on the Pacific shores of Ecuador. The dearth of research did not discourage the synthesis of cultural models to account for the precocious presence of pottery. The first syntheses of the Ecuadorian Formative stressed the importance of marine resources and attributed cultural development to influences, ideas, and people arriving by sea, some from distant corners of the Pacific (Ford 1969; Meggers et al. 1965; Willey 1971). The new ideas and technologies, in turn, were seen to be exported to other parts of the Americas, some by land, some by sea, via a network of early ceramic-using communities. This synthesis never gained wide acceptance and was criticized by some for its lack of evidence and for failing to account for local cultural processes.

Research in Ecuador during the past two decades has turned away from speculation about the origins of Valdivia and focused on the local culture history and on under

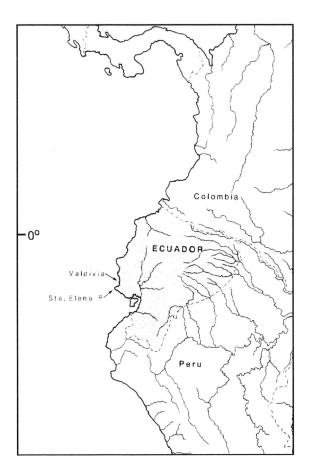

Figure 1. Coastal Ecuador.

standing the economic and social dimensions of the Formative cultures. As research has progressed in other lesser known parts of South and Central America, the Formative sequence in southwestern Ecuador has been shown to be contemporaneous with cultural development elsewhere in the tropical lowlands. The Formative cultures of the moist tropics are no longer regarded as having always been developmentally behind those of the arid lands of Mexico and Peru. In some respects, e.g., plant domestication, they seem to have been precocious (Lathrap et al. 1975).

In 1980 and 1982 research teams from the University of Calgary undertook a complete survey of the Valdivia River valley and carried out excavations at Loma Alta, an early Valdivia period site situated mid-way up the valley (Figure 2). Less intensive surveys were carried out in the neighboring valleys and along adjacent sections of the coast. The main research objectives were to study the subsistence and settlement patterns during the Early Formative period, i.e., to study the first evidence of sedentism.

In our survey of the region we discovered evidence of settlements in all phases of the Formative period. Our excavations provided evidence of dietary, subsistence and residential patterns. In this paper I will summarize the settlement evidence during the Early Formative period and the first part of the Middle Formative period, and discuss the implications of these data for developing models of economic and social patterns.

Chronological Context

In Chapter 12, Pearsall presents an excellent summary of the early cultural periods of the region, so this chapter will be limited to a brief review of the sequence. The record of settlement begins with the preceramic Vegas tradition, which has been identified at 31 sites on the Santa Elena peninsula. Vegas has been dated from 8000 to 4600 B.C.[1] Following an approximate 1000-year hiatus in the record, Vegas is succeeded by Valdivia at ca. 3200 B.C. Valdivia, the first ceramic-producing culture, comprises the Early Formative period. The ceramic styles of Machalilla and Engoroy follow Valdivia and respectively signal the beginnings of the Middle Formative period, ca. 1200 B.C., and the Late Formative period, ca. 800 B.C.[2] All three styles are clearly sequential parts of a ceramic tradition common to a large part of southwestern Ecuador. This sequence was used to temporally order the sites discovered in the survey. Hill's (1975) eight-phase seriation of the Valdivia style was used to divide the Early Formative period into: Early Valdivia (phases 1-2), Middle Valdivia (phases 3-5), and Late Valdivia (phases 6-8). Lippi's (1983) seriation of Machalilla was used to identify Early Machalilla settlements.

Resources and the Environment

Situated at the northern edge of the region known as the

Santa Elena Peninsula, the Valdivia River flows from its headwaters in the Colonche Hills through a narrow valley to the Pacific Ocean. Its course is no more than 50 km long and its source is less than 800 m above sea level. To the east across the divide of the Colonche Hills, lies the vast tropical alluvial basin of the Guayas River, the largest river in the eastern Pacific (Figure 2).

The Santa Elena region is situated in an environmental transition zone, just north of the extremely dry Peruvian desert and south of the extremely wet rainforest of northwest South America. Seasonality is determined by a pattern of equatorial monsoons, with marked wet and dry seasons. The climate is characterized by a sequence of extremely dry years followed by an extremely wet year, a pattern of rainfall governed by the capricious behavior of El Niño, which in recent studies has been shown to affect the climate of a large part of the eastern Pacific (Graham and White 1988). The Humboldt Current bathes the southern shores of the region seasonally, enriching the sea fauna and creating dry conditions along the coastal strip. Humidity is high, 75 to 80 percent even during the dry season (Blandin Landivar 1977). The humid air condenses into a drizzly precipitation as breezes carry the sea air up the valleys.

Most of the peninsular region today is barren. Cacti and other desert plants are the predominant vegetation. It is

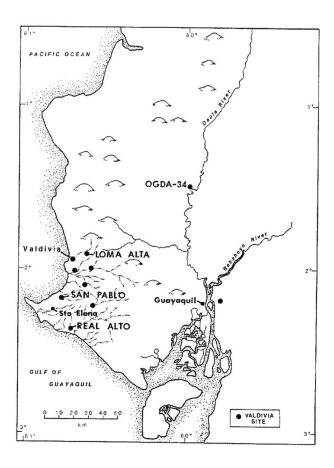

Figure 2. Southwestern Ecuador, Showing Some of the Principal Valdivia Sites.

unlikely, however, that the landscape was as bleak in the past. Accounts of early explorers tell of forests covering much of the land (Marcos 1973). Older residents of the Valdivia River valley can remember when trees lined the banks of the river in the middle part of the valley and forests covered the surrounding hills. Through a meticulous analysis of paleobotanical material and charred bits of wood, Pearsall (1979) has been able to reconstruct characteristics of the ancient forests of the Chanduy River valley, which borders the eastern side of the peninsula. Degradation of the environment in southwestern Ecuador began in colonial times (Marcos 1973) with the logging of the forest to build houses in the treeless desert of Peru and for the construction and repair of Spanish sailing vessels. It accelerated as land was cleared for ranching. The importation of goats and their propensity to eat young seedlings probably sealed the fate of the forests. Today the last remnants of the forest are disappearing as logging for timber and fuel continues in the upper valleys.

Attempts to reconstruct the paleoclimate of the peninsula have been frustrated by a lack of reliable evidence. It seems unlikely that the climate has remained constant over the last 5000 years; however, it seems equally unlikely that there have been dramatic changes. A lessening or an increase in the frequency of wet years may have caused some of the boundaries of plant communities to shift, but it is doubtful that any were eradicated, as they have been in modern times. The area most affected by a change in climate would have been the southwestern point, which is the driest and most barren part today, the least affected would have been the peripheral valleys, such as Valdivia, which in most years have flowing water.

With the assumption that there have been no cataclysmic changes in climate, we can generally reconstruct the different environmental zones of the Valdivia Valley and hence the distribution of resources at the onset of the Formative period 5000 years ago.

Forest probably covered much of the valley, to within 2 km of the sea, or perhaps closer. This was a gallery forest on the valley floor and a semi-deciduous forest on the surrounding uplands. Evergreen species became dominant in the wetter headlands of the valley. Toward the mouth of

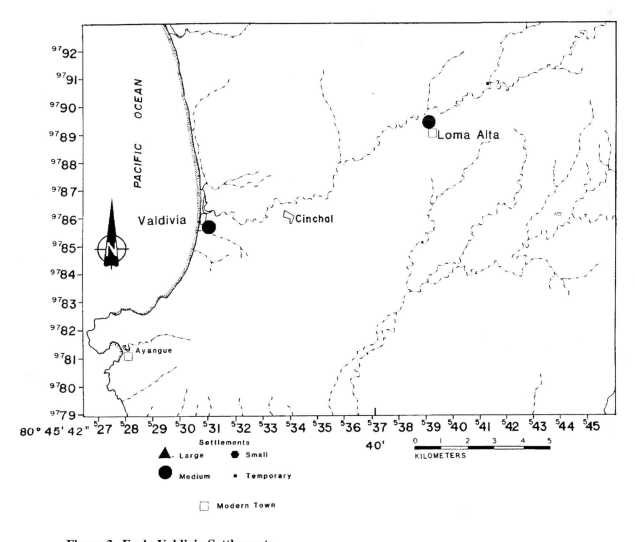

Figure 3. Early Valdivia Settlements.

151

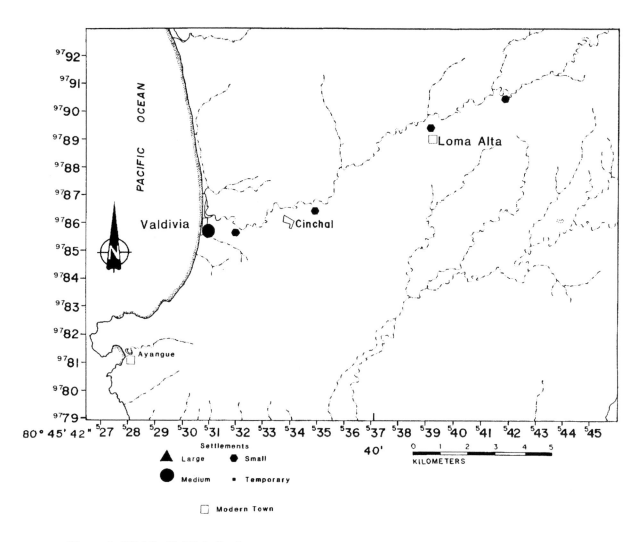

Figure 4. Middle Valdivia Settlements.

the valley the taller tree species of the forest were replaced by shorter, thornier species adapted to the drier conditions of the seaside. This xerophytic formation probably continued south along the coast becoming progressively broader toward the point of the Peninsula.

The forest cover would have provided a habitat for numerous mammals, birds and reptiles, species which have retreated to forested havens in the Colonche Hills in modern times. The more open xerophytic formation along the coast would also have supported small rodents, foxes, anteaters, weasels, opossums and other animals which inhabit semi-arid environments. The forest would also have enhanced the agricultural potential of the valley. Evaporation and runoff would have been reduced significantly from present-day levels, thereby raising the water table and increasing moisture retention in the soil. The decay of leaf-litter insured the continuous renewal of soil nutrients.

The seaside was a sandy beach, partly protected to the south by the headland of Ayangue. Today the village of San Pedro, at the mouth of the valley, is one of several fishing ports along the Ecuadorian coast, taking advantage of the rich sea fauna that thrive in the Humboldt Current. Most of the commercial fishing is done in large vessels well out to sea, but familial subsistence needs can be met much nearer to shore. A wide variety of fish, molluscs, crustaceans, and sea birds can be harvested in the estuary, both along the beach and within a short distance off-shore. Fish are traded up-valley to small land holders in an informal bartering system between farmers and fishermen which probably has ancient beginnings.

Our survey indicates that the relative elevations of sea and coast at the mouth of the valley have changed very little in the past 5000 years. The estuary was a mangrove swamp, providing a habitat for the mangrove oyster and other potential food species. Terraces along the valley bottom attest to the progressive down-cutting of the riverbed and also to extensive periodic flooding and alluviation in some sections. Extensive alluvial bottom lands occur in mid-valley, near Loma Alta, and in the lower valley. A small section of alluvial land also occurs in the upper valley near El Suspiro. These lands have the richest soils and could have been used for floodwater farming in the past.

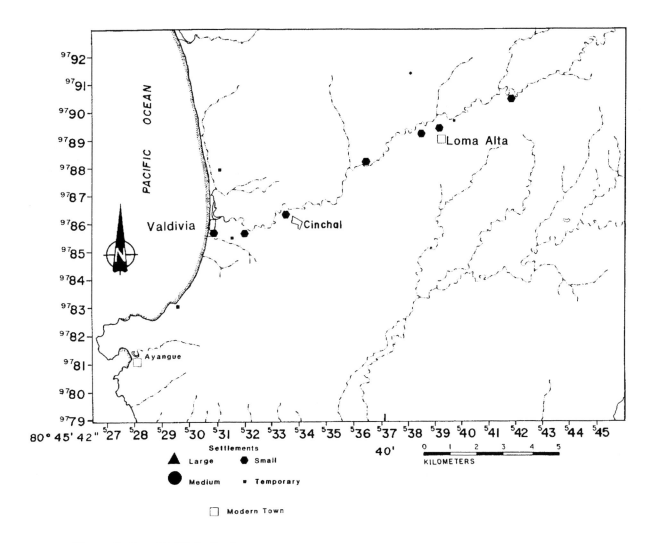

Figure 5. Late Valdivia Settlements.

The distribution of wild plant resources is difficult to reconstruct. Certainly hardwoods, cane, sedges and other materials useful for building and manufacturing tools were readily available within the valley. Wild seeds and fruits were probably also available according to their distributions in the plant formations. Stone for *manos* and *metates*, axe heads and other lithic tools was readily available along the river and in the Colonche Hills.

Settlements and Settlement Patterns

The record of settlement in the Valdivia Valley begins with the earliest occurrence of Valdivia pottery at about 3200 B.C. The only possible evidence of a pre-Valdivia occupation in the valley is an apparent preceramic component which was exposed in the excavations of Bischof and Viteri (1972; Bischof 1979) at the Valdivia type site situated at the valley mouth.[3] The absence of other evidence of Vegas settlements is perplexing, but is consistent with surveys carried out by others in the Chanduy Valley (Zeidler 1986). The only Vegas sites yet identified with certainty are

the 31 mentioned earlier (Stothert 1985) from the extremely dry southwestern corner of the peninsula.

There is no reason to believe that the Vegas people, with their probable use of a wide spectrum of foods, would not have been attracted to the forested valleys of the region, although a pattern of peripatetic settlement in the valleys might be expected in light of the poor suitability of tropical forest environments to hunter-gatherer economies (cf. Lathrap 1968, 1977; Sponsel 1986; Bailey et al. 1989). Evidence of maize from Las Vegas, however, (Stothert 1985; Pearsall, Chapter 12) suggests that there may already have been horticultural accommodation to the scarcity of wild sources of carbohydrates in the tropical lowlands. It seems more probable, then, that absence of Vegas sites from the survey records is a function of the low visibility of preceramic sites, than that the valley was not populated before Valdivia. Unless the Vegas people were bringing quantities of shellfish inland, the only surface evidence of their campsites would be clusters of stone flakes. Such evidence is very likely to have been obscured by more than 5000 years of human settlement.

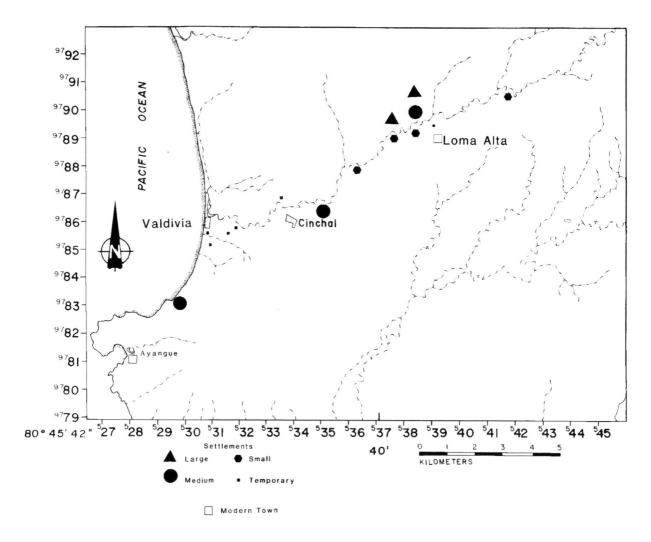

Figure 6. Early Machalilla Settlements.

During Early Valdivia, there were two relatively large settlements in the valley: Loma Alta in the mid-section and the original Valdivia type site at the mouth of the river on the hillside behind the present day towns of Valdivia and San Pedro (Figure 3). There was also a small site, representing perhaps an isolated household, in the upper section of the valley. This pattern of two relatively large, widely separated settlements has been noted in other valleys of the region (Zeidler 1977, 1986; Damp 1984) and seems to be characteristic of Early Valdivia. Loma Alta, the better preserved of the two, is situated on a relict Pleistocene terrace immediately adjacent to a broad expanse of alluvial bottom land. Excavations have shown that the river flowed along one side of the site at the time of occupation. Forested hills were within 1 km to the southeast. The Valdivia type site lies at the seaward edge of the broad alluvial plain in the lower valley, and within .5 km of both the estuary and the beach.

The exact limits of the Early Valdivia component at the valley-mouth site are hard to define since the site continued to be occupied throughout the period and since it is now partly covered by the modern towns. The settlement, however, does seem to have been somewhat smaller than Loma Alta, which covered an area of approximately 2.5 ha. Excavations at Loma Alta also showed that the settlement was organized in a horseshoe shape with a vacant central, probably public, area (Raymond 1988).

During Middle Valdivia, the population of the valley became more dispersed with a slightly greater proportion occupying the lower section of the valley (Figure 4). The Valdivia site at the valley mouth continued to be occupied and perhaps increased slightly in size. Loma Alta, however, decreased in size to a few households. Three new sites, approximately the same size as the reduced Loma Alta settlement, were located along the main axis of the valley: two between Loma Alta and the coast and one up the valley. These sites were spaced at regular intervals of 3-4 km and were built immediately adjacent to alluvial bottom land.

The trend toward dispersal of settlement along the linear course of the river continued in Late Valdivia. Two small settlements, consisting of a few households, were established in the middle section of the valley, one below and the

154

other above Loma Alta (Figure 5). At the same time, the Valdivia site decreased to the same size as the other smaller valley bottom settlements. Five other very small temporary sites of a size comparable to camps or single households occurred at this time as well: two in mid-valley, two near the coast, and one on the sea-cliff 3 km south of the valley mouth. Three of these mark the first time settlements moved away from the alluvial bottoms, and one of these was the first fishing encampment in the area.

In Early Machalilla, the beginning of the Middle Formative period, there was a continuity in the general positioning of sites, but a greater range in their sizes, which can be divided into four size modes, and greater variation in the spacing between them (Figure 6). Of 15 sites identified, two were situated near the alluvial bottom land, following the pattern established in the Valdivia period. Five of the 15, however, were significantly larger than any of the sites known from Late Valdivia, and two of these, 3-6 ha in area, were larger than any previous sites of the area. Furthermore, these two largest sites and one of the next larger (medium) sites were situated in the mid-valley section within 1 km of each other.

Three small sites, equivalent in size to house clusters were also found in the mid-section of the valley. Occupation in the upper valley section, is represented by a small settlement, similar in size and at the same location as the Late Valdivia settlement. In the Lower valley, the three evenly dispersed, small settlements of Late Valdivia were replaced by a single larger (medium) settlement. In addition, three very small temporary sites were found: two in the lower valley and one in the mid-valley section.

The Late Valdivia fishing camp on the sea-cliff south of the valley was replaced by a settlement comparable in size to the second order settlements in the valley. This is the first evidence of a permanent settlement with such an obvious seaside orientation and the first such settlement situated a significant distance from alluvial bottom land.

Analysis of Settlement Data

Throughout the Valdivia period, settlement was concentrated along the margins of the flood plain. At the outset, populations were concentrated in two settlements, both with immediate access to alluvial land: one with greater access to coastal and estuarine resources, the other with access to wild flora and fauna of the tropical forests. Over the course of the succeeding 1500 years, there was a decrease in average settlement size and an increase in number. Settlements were strung out along the course of the river and spaced at regular intervals. There is no evidence of a settlement hierarchy.

Using a population density curve and site area measurements, Schwarz (1987) has calculated relative population by phase (Figure 7). His analysis suggests that there was a significant increase in population from Early to Middle Valdivia and a similar increase in Late Valdivia. In Early

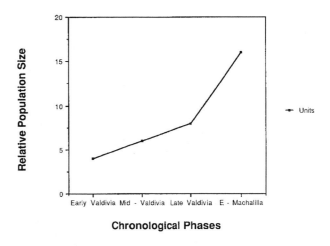

Figure 7. Relative Population Size Changes (after Schwarz 1987, Figure 9.4).

Valdivia times the population was divided between the valley mouth and mid-valley bottom lands, with a slightly greater number in mid-valley. By Middle Valdivia, more people occupied the lower part of the valley near the coast. During Late Valdivia, the population distribution evened out, and there was a close correspondence between population size and available bottom land.

The most notable change from Late Valdivia to Early Machalilla was a near-doubling of the population. This was accompanied by a change in the population distribution within the valley. In contrast to the even spacing between settlements of comparable size in Late Valdivia, nearly two-thirds of the Early Machalilla population was settled in mid-valley. For the first time there was a settlement size hierarchy, ranging from small isolated homesteads to settlements which must have comprised multiple households and which were larger than any known in the Valdivia period. The distribution of the sites shows a continuing strong preference for valley-bottom land, but because of the concentration of settlement in mid-valley a smaller proportion of the population had easy access to the most recent alluvium.

A further change, with both social and economic implications, was the establishment of a large settlement on the sea-shore, removed from potential agricultural land. This suggests an increased reliance on fishing as well as a change in economic and social relations.

Implications

The study of settlement patterns has been a powerful tool for inferring subsistence strategies. An underlying assumption is that there is a close correspondence between the distribution of economically self-sufficient communities and the distribution of potential food resources. Such assumptions are strengthened when there is independent evidence (e.g., macro-botanical remains) of the use of specific foods.

Nevertheless, when using archaeological data, there is always uncertainty about the social and economic boundaries of a community and how they translate into the material residue of settlement on a given landscape—i.e., a single settlement does not necessarily comprise a whole community. Furthermore, as economic and political roles become differentiated in a society, the probability increases that factors other than the proximity to food production determine the locations and sizes of settlements. An additional source of error arises from assuming that at any given time people made rational decisions according to a set of universal principles such as minimization of effort for maximization of return.

There are risks in relying too heavily on the implications of settlement patterns, the greatest of which is assuming what one is setting out to test. Bearing these risks in mind, the settlement data from the Valdivia Valley do have implications which can be weighed against ideas, models, and hypotheses about Early Formative societies in Ecuador offered by various scholars.

Two periods of significant and relatively rapid change are reflected in the settlement data: first, at the beginning of the Formative period with the earliest evidence of Valdivia settlement, and second at the onset of the Middle Formative period with the first Machalilla settlements. Each of these marks a significant change from previous land-use patterns, and each has social and economic implications. One subsistence implication of the Valdivia pattern is that people began to use the rich soils of the lower alluvium which offer the possibility of continuous production of food crops. The residues of domesticated plants, scarce though they may be, (see Pearsall, Chapter 12) support this interpretation. Faunal remains from the sites which have been excavated attest to the trapping and hunting of game from forest and savannah areas of the hinterlands surrounding the settlements (Stahl 1985). Fish and mollusc remains which occurred at sites well removed from the coast indicate that, to some extent, foods were transported up-valley. The species represented were mainly from the estuary and near-shore environments (Byrd 1976).

Fishing was at one time thought to be the main orientation of the Valdivia culture (Meggers et al. 1965:107). However, our settlement data from the Valdivia Valley do not support this hypothesis. With the exception of one small Late Valdivia encampment, no Valdivia sites have been found along the protected shoreline south of the estuary, nor in the excellent nearby fishing harbor of Ayangue; yet both of these locations bear evidence of occupation by the Middle Formative. Further south on the driest part of the Santa Elena Peninsula, however, there were both Early and Middle Valdivia settlements on and near the seashore (Lanning 1967; Hill 1975), suggesting that fishing may have played a more important role in determining site locations in that region.

There was a gradual increase in population throughout the Valdivia period (Schwarz 1987) and continuity in the

settlement locations. The progressive dispersal of small settlements along the flood plain suggests an efficient and intensive use of the best agricultural land. This could be described as a concentration on low-risk resources. As Pearsall (Chapter 12) has mentioned, the Valdivians were probably cultivating a wide range of domesticates, including maize, beans, and root crops, but the data do not allow us to infer which of these were staples.

There is no evidence in the Valdivia settlement data of a social or political hierarchy or of changes in the political-economy. However, this may be in part a function of our focus on a single valley and the presumption that social and economic relations were channeled by the limits of the drainage. In the Chanduy Valley, where similar research has been carried out, there is a contrast between the large Valdivia settlement of Real Alto and a series of smaller settlements distributed along the flood-plain. During Middle and Late Valdivia, the resident population at Real Alto declined, the ceremonial plaza was elaborated, and there was an increase in the number of satellite settlements. Zeidler (1986) has interpreted this to mean that there was a gradual bifurcation of society with a small group involved less and less in food production and dedicated more to politico-religious activities.

During Early Valdivia, Loma Alta and Real Alto had similar settlement plans as evidenced by houses and domestic refuse surrounding a vacant central space. Analogs for this plan are found in the arrangement and organization of many villages which have been recorded ethnographically in the South American tropics (Nimuendaju 1946; Maybury-Lewis 1967). Houses and domestic activities are limited to the outer rim of the village, and the center is reserved as a meeting place for the men and as an arena for ceremonial activities. Such villages are usually politically and economically independent. Social differentiation and political power are usually determined by sex, age and personal charisma.

During Middle Valdivia, while Real Alto became a major center in the Chanduy Valley with its central space transformed into a formalized ceremonial plaza, Loma Alta declined to a small hamlet with no apparent formalized structure. None of the other Valdivia-period settlements in the Valdivia Valley bear evidence of a formalized settlement plan. In the drainages south of the Valdivia Valley, however, we have discovered Middle and Late Valdivia sites much larger than those in the Valdivia drainage. Many of these had vacant centers. This suggests that if we broaden the regional scope of survey and analysis we may find evidence of a settlement hierarchy comparable to that in the Chanduy Valley.

Ironically, the first evidence of settlement size hierarchy in the Valdivia Valley occurred at the beginning of the Early Machalilla period, at a time when site size differences declined in the Chanduy Valley (Zeidler 1986:104-105). There is further contrast between the two valleys at this time in the more even dispersal of settlement in the Chanduy

Valley along the alluvial margins and the concentration of settlement in the mid-section of the Valdivia Valley. These differences underscore the need for a broader regional scale of intensive survey and settlement analysis.

Once established in the Middle Formative period, site-size hierarchies in the Valdivia Valley continued through the Formative and became more marked in post-Formative times (Schwarz 1987). Without more excavation at specific sites, however, we can only speculate on the social and economic implications of such a hierarchy. According to Schwarz's (1987) calculations there were no absolute decreases in population in any sector of the valley, suggesting that there was a continued intensive exploitation of the recent alluvium. The greater degree of nucleation of settlement might indicate that there was a greater degree of co-operative labor with some members of the society becoming economically specialized. Such specialization is most strongly indicated by the establishment of a specialized fishing settlement on the southern shore.

The relative concentration of population in the mid-valley may reflect a diversification of agricultural strategies. The greater potential for swidden agriculture there and in the upper valley in comparison to the drier more fragile environment of the lower valley may partly account for this unequal distribution of the population which continued into later periods.

Summary and Conclusions

In the wider context of early village societies of the New World, the Formative period cultures of Ecuador were precocious both in their early use of ceramic technology and their reliance on domesticated plants. However, as research progresses elsewhere in the moist tropics, most notably Panama, northern Colombia, and the Amazon Basin (Raymond 1989), the sequence of events in Ecuador is but one example of a wide-spread process of intensive settlement alongside tropical rivers. I have side-stepped the question of the immediate origins of the first settlements in the Valdivia Valley. However, the seemingly abrupt appearance of two relatively large sedentary communities is more suggestive of colonization than of the gradual aggregation of local populations. The subsequent population growth and dispersal of settlement is indicative of successful adjustment to the colonized region. A probable source of such colonization is the Guayas Basin where evidence of Early Valdivia settlement has also been discovered (Raymond et al. 1980).

At no time during the Early Formative period in the Valdivia Valley is there evidence which suggests that there was a social, political, or religious hierarchy. In that respect it contrasts with settlement in the Chanduy Valley where hierarchical site differences emerged during the Middle Valdivia period. Such differences, however, may be a function of using valleys rather than broader regions as units of settlement analysis.

In the Middle Formative period, there was an increase in the valley population and the concentration of population near key resources. These changes may have been stimulated by an intensification of agriculture. The site size hierarchy which emerged at the same time suggests a corresponding hierarchy in social and political relations. The concentrations of population also indicate economic specialization and, perhaps, a formalized redistribution network.

Acknowledgments

Research in the Valdivia valley was supported by grants from the Social Science and Humanities Research Council of Canada, and the University of Calgary. Further support in the field came from the Escuela Superior Politécnica del Litoral, Guayaquil; the Programa de Antropología para el Ecuador; and the Museo del Banco Central del Ecuador, Guayaquil.

The research was carried out with the collaboration and support of many colleagues and students. Among these are Jorge Marcos, Presley Norton, Olaf Holm, Peter Stahl, Jonathan Damp, Brian Kooyman, Karen Stothert, Nicholas David, Judy Sterner, Claire Allum, Mary Ann Tisdale, Eric Poplin, John Hoopes, Persis Clarkson, Ann Weiser, Allison Landals, Diane Lyon, James Zeidler, Michael Muse, Judy Kreid, Lisa Valkenier, Coreen Chiswell, George Gumerman, and Frederick Schwarz. For this paper, I am particularly indebted to Frederick Schwarz for his insight on demographic changes in the Valdivia Valley. I am responsible for errors and omissions.

Notes

1. All absolute dates are presented in uncalibrated radiocarbon years

2. Lippi (1983) has suggested that there may be a gap of as much as 300 years between Late Valdivia and Early Machalilla. It is beyond the scope of this paper to assess the reality or possible significance of that gap.

3. Bischof and Viteri (1972; Bischof 1979) also isolated a possible pre-Valdivia ceramic phase, which they called San Pedro, in their excavations at the Valdivia type site. Sherds of a similar style were recovered by Damp (1979) from Real Alto in stratigraphic position above Valdivia I and in association with a Valdivia II assemblage. Radiocarbon dates for San Pedro also fit better with radiocarbon dates of Valdivia II. Since we found no evidence of San Pedro, either in our excavations at Loma Alta or in our survey of the Valdivia Valley and because of the problematic dating, I have ignored it in this analysis of settlement patterns. The reader should be aware, though, that my interpretation of the Early Formative settlement at the mouth of the valley has been simplified both in terms of the possible preceramic antecedents and the earliest

Valdivia presence.

References Cited

Bailey, R. C., G. Head, M. Jenike, B. Owen, R. Rechtman, and E. Zechenter
1989 Hunting and Gathering in Tropical Rain Forest: Is It Possible? *American Anthropologist* 91:59-82.

Bischof, H.
1979 San Pedro und Valdivia—Fruhe Keramickomplexe an der Kuste Sudwest-Ekuadors. *Beitrage zur Allgemeinen und Vergleichenden Archaologie.* Band 1:335-389, German Institute of Archaeology.

Bischof, H., and J. Viteri Gamboa
1972 Pre-Valdivia Occupations on the Southwest Coast of Ecuador. *American Antiquity* 37(4):548-551.

Blandin Landivar, C.
1977 *El Clima y Sus Características en El Ecuador.* XI Asamblea General del Instituto Panamericano de Geografía e Historia, Quito, Ecuador.

Byrd, K. M.
1976 *Changing Animal Utilization Patterns and Their Implications: Southwest Ecuador (6500 B.C. - A.D. 1400).* Unpublished Ph.D. dissertation, Department of Anthropology, University of Florida, Gainesville.

Damp, J.
1979 *Better Homes and Gardens: The Life and Death of the Early Valdivia Community.* Unpublished Ph.D. dissertation, Department of Archaeology, University of Calgary.
1984 Environmental Variation, Agriculture, and Settlement Processes in Coastal Ecuador (3300-1500 B.C.). *Current Anthropology* 25(1):106-111.

Ford. J. A.
1969 *A Comparison of Formative Cultures in the Americas.* Smithsonian Contributions to Anthropology, Vol. 11. Smithsonian Institution, Washington, D.C.

Graham, N. E., and W. B. White
1988 The El Niño: a Natural Oscillator of the Pacific Ocean Atmosphere System. *Science* 240:1293-1302.

Hill, B. D.
1975 A New Chronology of the Valdivia Ceramic Complex from the Coastal Zone of Guayas Province, Ecuador. *Nawpa Pacha* 10-12:1-32.

Lanning, E. P.
1967 Archaeological Investigation on the Santa Elena Peninsula. Report to the National Science Foundation on Research Carried out under Grant GS-402, 1964-1965. Ms. on file, N.S.F., Washington, D.C.

Lathrap, D. W.
1968 The "Hunting" Economies of the Tropical Forest Zone of South America. In *Man the Hunter*, edited by R. B. Lee and I. DeVore, pp. 23-29. Aldine, Chicago.

Lathrap, D. W., D. Collier, and H. Chandra
1975 *Ancient Ecuador: Culture, Clay, and Creativity 3000-300 B.C.* Field Museum of Natural History, Chicago.

Lippi, R. D.
1983 *La Ponga and the Machalilla Phase of Coastal Ecuador.* Unpublished Ph.D. dissertation, Department of Anthropology, University of Wisconsin, Madison.

Marcos, J.
1973 Tejidos Hechos en Telar en un Contexto Valdivia Tardío. *Cuadernos de Historia y Arqueología, XXIII* 40:163-183. Casa de la Cultura Ecuatoriana, Nucleo del Guayas, Guayaquil.

Maybury-Lewis, D.
1967 *Akwe-Shavante Society.* Clarendon Press, Oxford.

Meggers, B. J., C. Evans, and E. Estrada
1965 *Early Formative Period of Coastal Ecuador: The Valdivia and Machalilla Phases.* Smithsonian Contributions to Anthropology, Vol. 1, Smithsonian Institution, Washington, D.C.

Nimuendaju, C.
1946 *The Eastern Timbira*, translated by R. Lowie. University of California Publications in American Archaeology and Ethnology, Vol. 41. University of California Press, Berkeley.

Pearsall, D. M.
1979 *The Application of Ethnobotanical Techniques to the Problem of Subsistence in the Ecuadorian Formative.* Unpublished Ph.D. dissertation, Department of Anthropology, University of Illinois, Champaign-Urbana.

Raymond, J. S.
1988 Subsistence Patterns During the Early Formative in the Valdivia Valley, Ecuador. In *Diet and Subsistence: Current Archaeological Perspectives*, edited by B. V. Kennedy and G. M. LeMoine, pp. 159-164. Archaeological Association of the University of Calgary, Calgary.
1989 Early Settlements in Lowland South America. In *Proceedings of the Plenary Session 11th Congress of the International Union of Prehistoric and Protohistoric Sciences, 1987*, edited by P. Schauer. Romisch-Germanisches Zentralmuseum, Mainz. In press.

Raymond, J. S., J. Marcos, and D. W. Lathrap
1980 Evidence of Early Formative Settlement in the Guayas Basin. *Current Anthropology* 21:700-701.

Schwarz, F. A.
1987 *Prehistoric Settlement Patterns in the Valdivia Valley, Southwest Coastal Ecuador.* Unpublished M.A. thesis. Department of Archaeology, University of Calgary.

Sponsel, L. E.

1986   Amazon Ecology and Adaptation. *Annual Reviews in Anthropology* 15:67-97.

Stahl, P.

1985   The Archaeofaunas of Loma Alta. Ms. on file, Department of Archaeology, University of Calgary, Calgary.

Stothert, K. P.

1985   The Preceramic Las Vegas Culture of Coastal Ecuador. *American Antiquity* 50:613-637.

Willey, G. R.

1971   *An Introduction to American Archaeology. Vol 2: South America.* Prentice Hall, Englewood Cliffs.

Zeidler, J. A.

1977   Early Formative Settlement in the Chanduy Valley, Southwest Ecuador. Paper presented at the 42nd Annual Meetings of the Society for American Archaeology, New Orleans.

1986   La Evolución Local de Asentamientos Formativos en el Litoral Ecuatoriano: El Caso de Real Alto. In *Arqueología de la Costa Ecuatoriana, Nuevos Enfoques*, Vol. 1, edited by J. G. Marcos, pp. 85-127. Biblioteca Ecuatoriana de Arqueología, ESPOL, Guayaquil.

12

Agricultural Evolution and the Emergence of Formative Societies in Ecuador

Deborah M. Pearsall

Introduction

Archaeological research in northwestern South America during the last two decades has documented the occurrence of Formative period village sites with ceramics dating one to two thousand years earlier than such sites occur in Mesoamerica, Central America, or Peru (Figure 1). These early sites, appearing between 3000 and 3500 B.C., occur in western Ecuador and northwestern Colombia (Lathrap et al. 1977; Feldman and Moseley 1983; Damp 1979; Reichel-Dolmatoff 1985). The first early ceramic-producing sites discovered, among them the Valdivia type-site (Meggers et al. 1965), were located adjacent to the coast, leading some archaeologists to propose a coastal adaptation. The Valdivia and Puerto Hormiga traditions were considered part of the northwest littoral tradition, a continuation of an Archaic-type coastal adaptation (Willey 1971).

Research conducted in Ecuador after Meggers, Evans, and Estrada's pioneering work has changed this scenario considerably. Inland Valdivia sites in riverine settings have been documented (Lathrap et al. 1977; Damp 1979; Marcos 1978; Raymond 1988), as has the existence of cultivated plants in both early Formative (Pearsall 1978a, 1979, 1982, 1988) and pre-ceramic (Piperno 1986; Pearsall and Piperno 1990; Stothert 1985) settings. An inland, tropical forest origin for Valdivia and other Formative cultures of northwestern South America is considered likely (Lathrap et al. 1975; Feldman and Moseley 1983).

The nature of these early Formative cultures is incompletely understood, however. Among the unresolved issues are important questions concerning the nature of subsistence and the evolution of agricultural systems during the Formative. Was there a widespread early "Formative adaptation," analogous to Willey's Northwest Littoral Tradition? What role did cultivated plants, such as maize (*Zea mays*) and manioc (*Manihot esculenta*), play in subsistence? How did agricultural systems evolve and when did agriculture come to assume the predominant role in subsistence? Were these ceramic-producing village cultures fully agricultural at 3500 B.C., or was their precocious development limited to ceramic technology?

Although there are no fine-grained answers to these questions, research to date suggests the broad outlines of answers, which can serve as hypotheses for further testing. The remainder of this paper addresses these issues. To place this discussion in theoretical perspective, a review of the nature of domestication and agricultural evolution is presented. Available botanical and archaeological data are then reviewed.[1] A preliminary evaluation of data is made, which suggests that the Late Valdivia period (ca. 2000-1500 B.C.) marks the beginning of the "agricultural" Formative in Ecuador, which by 500 B.C., the traditional end of the Formative (beginning of the Regional Developmental period), had fueled substantial population growth and major technological innovations, among them agricultural land modification.

Domestication and Agriculture

There is a large body of literature on agricultural origins. Flannery (1986) provides a succinct summary of models and theories for domestication, grouping models into five types: climatic change models (e.g., Wright 1977), population pressure models (e.g., Binford 1968; Cohen 1977a, 1977b), broad-spectrum adaption models (e.g., Flannery 1971), the co-evolution model (Rindos 1980, 1984), and multivariate models (e.g., Hassan 1981). For the South American area, general reviews of archaeological and phytogeographical evidence for the evolution of crop plants include those of Harlan (1975), Heiser (1979), Pearsall (1978b, 1992), Pickersgill (1969, 1977, 1984), Pickersgill and Heiser (1977), and Smith (1977).

Crop scientists have long understood that domestication is an evolutionary process, with many stages between the wild and fully domesticated plant which is incapable of self-propagation. This process can occur in a genetically

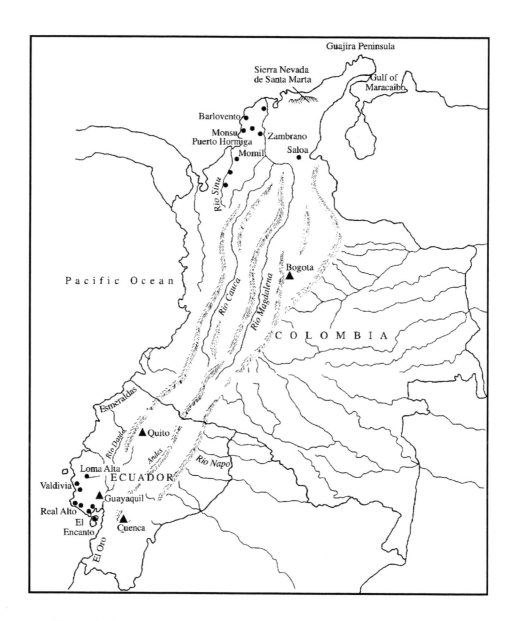

Figure 1. Some Early Formative Period Sites of Northwestern South America (after Lathrap et al. 1975; Reichel-Dolmatoff 1985; Feldman and Moseley 1983).

malleable plant without conscious selection, as long as a cycle of harvesting-planting-harvesting is maintained, whereby a suite of "wild" characteristics are automatically selected against in the population. Anthropologists, such as Bray (1976) and Flannery (1971, 1973), have emphasized the importance of distinguishing between the early stages of domestication, when a domesticated plant is only a minor resource, and the point when the domesticate becomes a dietary staple. The latter stage may occur thousands of years after initial domestication.

The co-evolutionary model of agricultural origins, developed by Rindos (1980, 1984), brings together these perspectives by first distinguishing between domestication and agriculture, then linking these distinctive processes

together into a single model. Domestication is an evolutionary process, the result of predator/prey relationships characterized by mutualism, a relationship in which both predator (human) and prey (plant) populations benefit. As a result of interactions with humans, the plant undergoes morphological changes which increase its productivity. Humans take over as its dispersal agent. Over time, humans reduce their use of non-domesticates, scheduling subsistence activities around the domesticates.

Agriculture is an outgrowth of this relationship, a set of activities which affect the environment inhabited by the domesticated plant. Early agricultural techniques were part of existing subsistence systems (for example, setting fires to drive game can also encourage useful plants). Once stable

Figure 2. Preceramic and Formative Period Sites Discussed in Text.

environments for plant growth (gardens) are created, yields increase, and domesticated plants become more homogeneous. A few domesticated plants assume the primary role in subsistence, which increases instability, since crop failures have a greater impact. Altering the environment to increase yields takes precedence over new domestication. The larger human populations supported by increasing crop yields eventually necessitate increasingly successful techniques of environmental manipulation (i.e., agricultural intensification) to maintain the system. Thus agriculture provides its own impetus for expansion; emigration to seek new planting areas, or in response to crop failures, is seen as a natural outgrowth of the process.

Viewed from the archaeologist's perspective, how does the coevolutionary model of agricultural origins fit the traditional conceptions of the Archaic and Formative stages,

and how would this process appear in the archaeological record?

Based on the coevolutionary model, the early appearance of domesticated plants in non-agricultural settings is a logical evolutionary stage. For example, recovery of squash rind in preceramic middens, mixed with wild plant and faunal resources, would demonstrate that while squash was being grown, it was only part of a system characterized by primary dependence on non-domesticated resources. Morphological changes in a domesticate, or presence of plants outside their native range, would show that harvesting and planting were taking place, but environmental data would reveal little to no modification of the landscape. Even the presence of a crop like maize, which later assumed primary importance in subsistence, in such a setting would not imply agricultural relationships. If species diversity was

163

high and productivity of the domesticate low, the system was in the domesticatory stage.

Evolution of the system may be characterized by increases in the numbers of domesticated plants appearing in the archaeological record. Over time use of wild plants would have declined, especially those whose scheduling conflicted with the increasingly productive domesticates. Morphological changes indicating increased productivity would have begun to appear. Species diversity might have remained high, but the ratio of wild to domestic taxa would have declined. A point may have been reached, however, when productivity of domesticated plants outstriped that of wild resources. When less productive resources were dropped in favor of creating productive environments for domesticates, the agricultural stage had begun.

Archaeologically, this process would be characterized by a decline in species diversity and increasing evidence for agricultural activities. In the tropical forest setting, clearing of forest to increase planting areas may have occurred if early fields were located on naturally renewed, but limited, alluvial soils. Populations may have expanded out from older settlements, founding new settlements near open agricultural lands. While sedentism would not have been necessary to plant and harvest a few incidental domesticated plants, maintaining control over prepared fields of plants important for subsistence would have been. If groups had not already settled in response to other stable resources, one would expect settled village life to have appeared at this point. Societies at this stage of agricultural development would fit the usual conception of "Formative."

The agricultural relationship was an evolving one. With decreasing species diversity and increasing productivity came increasing instability, as the system became more vulnerable to failure. This instability might be indicated by increased stress among the human populations or even abandonment of formerly settled areas if failures led to high mortality or necessitated emigration.

As use of domesticated plants assumed a larger role in subsistence, and population grew, emigration to fill open lands would have accelerated. As available lands filled, or other restraints to emigration occurred, expansion of the system would have taken the form of increasing the productivity of available land, or intensification of the agricultural system. This process may have been characterized by shortening of fallow periods (Boserup 1965) or landscape modification, the creation of new planting areas through irrigation, terracing, ditching, or building raised fields.

Summary of Subsistence Data from the Ecuadorian Formative

Determining the nature of prehistoric subsistence requires recovery and analysis of food remains. Bones, shell, charred seeds, pollen, and phytoliths are the raw data of subsistence reconstruction. Direct data on the diet and health of individuals can also be obtained by study of human skeletal remains. Each data base has its strengths and weakness; integrating more than one line of evidence is the most productive approach.

Recent excavations, using botanical recovery strategies, at early sites in Ecuador have given us limited data on the botanical component of diet during the Preceramic and Formative periods (Figure 2). Because preservation of archaeological plant remains in Ecuador is limited to charred material, we have less detailed information about subsistence than is available from the more arid regions to the south. In Peru, for example, occurrence of chili peppers, squash, gourd, common bean, lima bean, jack bean, potato, manioc, *achira* (*Canna edulis*), cotton, maize, and numerous tree fruits, among others is known by the end of the preceramic (1800-1200 B.C.) (Pearsall 1992). The list of crops documented in contemporary and later Formative sites in Ecuador is much shorter: *achira*, jack bean, coca, cotton, squash, gourd, and maize. It is likely that the diversity of cultivated taxa present in Ecuador was as high as in Peru, but limitations of preservation make documenting this diversity a challenge.

Preceramic Period

Subsistence in the Late Preceramic of Ecuador is known only from sites of the Vegas tradition. Vegas is known from 31 sites located on the Santa Elena Peninsula of southwest coastal Ecuador (Stothert 1985). The Vegas type site, OGSE-80, has been extensively excavated by Stothert, who divided the radiocarbon-dated tradition into Early Las Vegas (8000-6000 B.C.) and Late Las Vegas (6000-4600 B.C.).

Phytolith analysis of soil from Early and Late Las Vegas deposits at OGSE-80, carried out by Piperno (1986) revealed presence of maize in Late Las Vegas strata (i.e., after 6000 B.C.). Recently, Pearsall and Piperno (1990) reexamined their early phytolith analyses at Real Alto (see below) and Vegas, applying Piperno's (1984) three dimensional classification system for maize identification to phytolith samples originally studied using Pearsall's (1978a, 1979, 1982) identification method. Results in both cases reaffirmed the presence of maize: the grain was present in Late Las Vegas, as well as throughout the Valdivia (Formative) sequence at Real Alto. Samples from Early Las Vegas (pre-6000 B.C.) showed *no* indication of maize. However, Piperno (personal communication, 1989) did observe squash (*Cucurbita* sp.) phytoliths throughout the sequence. Whether these represent the remains of wild or domesticated squashes is unknown. Few charred botanical remains were recovered from the Vegas excavations; the only other subsistence data are vertebrate faunal materials, indicating use of both terrestrial and marine (fish) resources, with terrestrial resources the most important by biomass (Byrd 1976), and the common occurrence of the mangrove mollusc *Anadara tuberculosa*.

In summary, the inhabitants of the Santa Elena Peninsula

during the Vegas tradition appear to have practiced diverse subsistence activities, including hunting, fishing, and shellfish-gathering, to which was added cultivation of maize in the period after 6000 B.C. and use of squash throughout the sequence. Given the setting of the sites, it is likely that wild plant foods, such as cactus fruits, small-seeded annuals, and legume tree fruits, were also used, and that squash and other plants were under cultivation. Cultivation of gourd, squash, and chili peppers would not be unexpected, as these plants are reported from this time period in Peru.

Early Formative Period

Valdivia, the first ceramic-producing culture of Ecuador, is also a coastal tradition. Sites date from 3200 B.C. (Valdivia I) to around 1500 B.C. (Valdivia VIII)(see Raymond, Chapter 11, for a summary of Valdivia settlement patterns). The earliest known Valdivia sites occur in southwestern Ecuador (western Guayas, southern Manabí provinces). Botanical data are available from the Real Alto and Loma Alta sites. The Valdivia occupation at Loma Alta ended after Valdivia II, while Real Alto was occupied through Valdivia VII. There are also preliminary data available from the Valdivia VIII occupation at San Isidro (northern Manabí province). Valdivia VIII, dated to 1600 B.C., is the earliest Valdivia in this part of the coast.

Real Alto is a village site located 3 km from the coast in the Chanduy Valley of coastal Guayas province. Its earliest occupation dates to 3200 B.C. (Damp 1979, 1984). The site reached its greatest expanse in Valdivia III times, around 2300 B.C., then declined in size, with a population shift from the center to smaller villages. Occupation ceased with Valdivia VII; no Terminal Valdivia (Valdivia VIII) occupation has been documented. Sites of the subsequent Middle Formative tradition, Machalilla, occur in the area.

Presence of maize at Real Alto is documented by phytolith data. As discussed above, a recent reanalysis (Pearsall and Piperno 1990) of a number of samples from the original study (Pearsall 1978a, 1979) confirmed the presence of maize at the site. Although only a few samples were available from the Valdivia I and II occupations, evidence for maize was found. The much larger body of samples from the Valdivia III village showed wide-spread presence of maize at the site: maize phytoliths were found in 89 percent of the 71 samples tested. The first evidence of achira also dated to Valdivia III; achira phytoliths occurred in 13 percent of samples analyzed. Since wild Canna or related plants did not form part of the floral assemblage of the dry coast, cultivation is implied.

Another cultivated plant present from the beginning of occupation at Real Alto is jack bean (Canavalia plagiosperma) (Damp et al. 1981). Their charred remains are more similar to cultivated than to wild Canavalia. Recent excavations by Damp in the Valdivia I and II sector of the site also resulted in recovery of charred cotton seeds. Although wild cotton occurred on the Ecuadorian Coast,

cultivation has been documented by this time period in Peru (Pearsall 1992).

In addition to cultivated maize, jack bean, achira, and (possibly) cotton, a variety of wild plant foods were recovered during excavation. These included weedy annuals, cactus, and sedge tubers (Cyperaceae). Vertebrate faunal biomass data from Real Alto indicate use of both terrestrial and marine resources, with terrestrial animals having contributed the majority of biomass (Byrd 1976). The mangrove mollusks Anadara tuberculosa and Cerithidea pulchra were also common.

Loma Alta is located in the Valdivia River Valley of southern Manabí province, 12 km inland from the coastal Valdivia type-site (Raymond 1988). Charred botanical materials from the Early Valdivia village (Valdivia I and II) include maize kernels, jackbean fragments, Annona sp. (soursop) rind, and sedge (Cyperaceae) rhizomes (Pearsall 1988). Faunal remains indicated a strong terrestrial orientation. Very few marine fish are present in the samples; terrestrial animals dominated faunal biomass (Byrd 1976). The faunal assemblage recovered from the Valdivia type-site, at the mouth of the river, was similar, but marine animals contributed somewhat more to faunal biomass at that site.

Human skeletal material from Loma Alta is being analyzed for carbon and nitrogen ratios in order to evaluate the importance of maize in the diet (Raymond 1988). This analysis also includes skeletal samples from other Ecuadorian sites, spanning Vegas to late prehistoric times. Preliminary results suggest that maize use increased from early Valdivia through Chorrera (Late Formative) times.

The final Valdivia site with excavated plant materials is San Isidro in northern Manabí province, occupied beginning in Valdivia VIII (1600 B.C.). Presence of jack bean, maize, and gourd has been documented. Remains of wild plants were also present, but have not been identified as yet.

Faunal remains have been analyzed by Byrd (1976) for three Valdivia sites located in the Santa Elena Peninsula, occupied by the preceramic Vegas tradition: OGSE-42, OGSE-62, and OGSE-174. Unlike the faunal record from the Vegas type-site, which showed a mix of marine and terrestrial resources, marine taxa contributed the most biomass to two of the three Valdivia period sites analyzed.

Middle and Late Formative Periods

For the Middle Formative, or Machalilla period (1200-800 B.C.) on the coast, botanical data are available from the La Ponga site, located in the Valdivia River Valley, 15 km inland from the ocean. Only the analysis of maize remains has been reported (Lippi et al. 1984). Charred maize was recovered in all 15 flotation samples taken from the Machalilla component. Presence of two varieties of small-kernelled maize is proposed from detailed analysis of materials.

Faunal data have been reported by Byrd (1976) for two Machalilla sites located in coastal Guayas. Faunal biomass data from OGSE-46, located on the Santa Elena Peninsula, closely resembled the pattern observed at peninsular Valdivia sites, suggesting a strong marine orientation. Remains from OGSE-20, located in the Chanduy Valley near Real Alto, gave biomass figures indicating a more terrestrial orientation.

The only direct data on subsistence from the late coastal Formative (Chorrera or Engoroy) is a cache of maize kernels from a vessel dated by style to around 800 B.C. (Pearsall 1980). The vessel was taken from a tomb in the Río Chico area of central Manabí, near the Chorrera period Chacras site. The maize was a low altitude variant of a narrow, broad kernel line of maize, with distinctive kernels that are wider than they are long, and very narrow.

The earliest Formative cultures of the Ecuadorian Sierra are contemporary with the middle and late coastal Formative. Botanical data are available from two sites, Nueva Era and Cotocollao, both located in the central part of the sierra.

The Formative deposits at Nueva Era span the period from 1100 to 500 B.C. Maize remains, including charred cupules, kernels, and cob fragments, have been recovered from levels dated to 760 B.C. and after (Pearsall 1988). This maize was strikingly similar to that recovered from the coastal La Ponga site (Machalilla period). Sedge (Cyperaceae) tubers were also present in Nueva Era flotation samples. Tuber remains were found in 54 percent of all samples analyzed; maize occurred in 13 percent. A variety of highly fragmented large seeds also occurred.

The Cotocollao site was occupied from about 1500 to 500 B.C. This village, like Nueva Era, was buried by volcanic ash at about 500 B.C. Botanical remains from Cotocollao included maize (phytoliths and charred material), lupine seeds, and sedge tubers. The maize was virtually identical to that recovered from Nueva Era and La Ponga. Ubiquity of occurrence was similar to that at Nueva Era: maize phytoliths in nine percent of samples analyzed; charred maize in 18 percent of samples.

Post-Formative Period

There are very few direct data on subsistence available from sites dating immediately after the Formative (i.e., Regional Developmental period, 500 B.C. to A.D. 500). Phytolith analysis has been conducted at the Peñón del Río site, located on the Guayas River across from the modern city of Guayaquil. This site was occupied from Terminal Valdivia through the Integration period and has a large associated raised field complex. Phytolith analysis of soil from buried field surfaces, dated by associated pottery to the Regional Developmental period, indicated that maize was grown in the complex (Pearsall 1987). Raised fields may be even earlier than this at Peñón del Río, however. Parsons and Shlemon (1987) dated organic material in the soil of a field in another part of the complex to 2000 B.C. That Peñón del Río was occupied by this date or slightly after is shown by occurrence of Late Valdivia (VII, VIII) pottery at

the site (Marcos 1987).

Discussion

The summary presented above of data on subsistence in Ecuador during the Preceramic and Formative periods illustrates how few direct data are available to address the questions of plant domestication and evolution of agricultural systems for one of the earliest Formative cultural traditions in the New World. The information available from Ecuador do suggest some broad patterns of change in the nature of human-plant relationships, however, which may be considered as useful hypotheses for future testing.

The first clear indications of domesticatory relationships occurred in the Late Archaic Vegas tradition. A fully domesticated plant, maize, appeared as a component of a coastal hunting-gathering-fishing subsistence system after 6000 B.C. The presence of one domesticated plant is suggestive: did domesticatory relationships exist between the Vegas population and other plants such as local squash species? This seems likely. Existence of domesticatory relationships with local plants in Early Las Vegas times, for example, would have enhanced the likelihood of later acceptance of introduced domesticates. It can be hypothesized, therefore, that further evidence of local domestication will be found in preceramic contexts dating before the introduction of maize.

Available data from the Early Formative of the coast, the Valdivia ceramic tradition, suggests a second hypothesis: that the nature of the relationship between coastal peoples and both local and introduced plants remained primarily domesticatory until Late Valdivia times, when a transformation occurred. Evidence from Real Alto and Loma Alta documents the continued occurrence of maize in the Early Formative, and the addition of new domesticated plants: jack bean, *achira*, and cotton. Sedge tubers may eventually join this list. Although there is no evidence of morphological change in the limited remains recovered, their common occurrence at the later Nueva Era site is more suggestive of cultivation than gathering. Not only did the number of domesticated plants increase in the Early Formative, but there is evidence that one domesticate, maize, became more important over this time period. For example, maize phytoliths occurred commonly in the Valdivia III deposits at Real Alto.

Both these trends, a rise in the number of domesticates, and an increase in importance of one domesticate, occurred before indications of significant landscape modification to increase yields. In the Chanduy Valley, for instance, after the Valdivia III period, population became less centralized; the Valdivia III center declined in size and smaller settlements appeared nearby. The new settlements were located within the catchment area of the old center, however, indicating that people had not moved in order to open up new agricultural lands. Study of charred wood from the sequence indicates that only by the end of the Valdivia period had cutting of trees in the riverine forest replaced use of coastal xerophytic taxa. This may mark over-exploitation of the hot-burning legume trees of the xerophytic formation. Another interpretation, however, is that a new source of firewood became available in Late Valdivia times, namely, wood cleared from upland cultivation plots under long fallow. The addition of upland swidden plots in Late Valdivia would have brought new land under cultivation.

There are other data suggesting a transformation of subsistence in Late Valdivia times. Peoples producing Terminal Valdivia (VIII) ceramics migrated into previously unoccupied areas of northern Manabí province and coastal El Oro province. The Peñón del Río site, located on the Guayas River in eastern Guayas province, was also initially occupied during this time period. By contrast to this pattern of migration to new territory, some previously long-occupied zones, such as the Chanduy Valley in southwestern Guayas, lacked Terminal Valdivia occupation; a hiatus in the occupation sequence exists. There is no evidence of climate change during this time period (ca. 2000-1500 B.C.) (Pearsall 1979); i.e., there is no evidence that a drying trend in the southeast led to migration to moister, inland zones. An alternative explanation would be that increased reliance on, and labor investment in, domesticated crops by Late Valdivia times resulted in greater instability in the subsistence system and that crop failures (from pests, disease, short-term drought, an El Niño event) led in turn to migration to new agricultural lands. This would mark the beginning of the agricultural stage in human-plant interactions in Ecuador.

If the Terminal Valdivia period can be considered the beginning of the agricultural stage, how did agricultural systems evolve in the subsequent Middle and Late Formative periods? Unfortunately, very few direct data exist to address this issue. Maize cultivation is documented for the first time in the sierra during this time period. A very uniform type of maize was being grown, both in the Andean valleys and on the coast. The role of maize in subsistence, especially in relation to the use of root resources, may have varied between coast and sierra. Detailed data on subsistence and landscape modification are lacking for most of this time period, however, which makes it impossible to document changes in agricultural systems. However, it is clear that by around 500 B.C. dependence on agriculture had reached the point where major earth-moving projects were undertaken to create new cropping areas. The raised field complex at Peñón del Río, under construction by this date, is only one example. If the development and application of innovative technology to increase yields is a characteristic of advanced agricultural systems, then the end of the Formative can be proposed as another point of significant transformation in the system.

Conclusions

The limited data on Formative period subsistence in Ecuador do not permit the drawing of many "final" conclusions on the nature of agricultural evolution and the emergence of fully agricultural societies there. Data are lacking from many regions of the country, and there is a need in all areas to focus on more systematic recovery of biological data. One of the most pressing gaps in our knowledge for coastal Ecuador is the nature of subsistence in the Late Formative and Regional Developmental periods.

Although I have focused on the Ecuadorian Formative in this paper, there is clear evidence that early ceramic-producing villages also occurred in coastal Colombia, perhaps at even earlier dates. There are only hints of what the subsistence bases of these sites might be; exciting information can be expected from this region in the near future.

Research is in progress in the Jama Valley of Manabí province, Ecuador, to document the nature of subsistence from Late Valdivia though Integration period (ca. 1600 B.C.-A.D. 1500), and to test the co-evolutionary model of agricultural evolution. This research will also provide a regional perspective on the nature of agricultural evolution and the development of chiefdom-level societies on the coast.

There is one overall conclusion which I would like to draw. In thinking about the nature of past subsistence systems, it is important to remember that domestication and agriculture are processes, not events. On the one hand, the presence of domesticated plants does not imply fully developed agriculture; on the other, it only takes a few plant remains to signal that the process was underway. Valdivia subsistence was neither fully agricultural, nor exclusively focused on wild resources. It documents an intermediate stage of human-plant interactions on the pathway to agriculture.

Acknowledgments

Laboratory facilities and administrative support for this research were provided by the American Archaeology Division, University of Missouri, Michael J. O'Brien, director. Research in the Jama Valley (San Isidro site) was supported by grants to J. Zeidler and D. Perarsall from the National Science Foundation.

Note

1. This paper was written in 1989. Since that time, new floral and faunal data have become available, adding to our understanding of Formative period subsistence. The greatest growth of information is on Chorrera; there are four new data sets from the Jama River Valley that show maize to be ubiquitous by the Late Formative. In addition, the La Chimba site in the northern sierra contributes data on early potato and *oca* cultivation in that region, and limited information is now available from sites in Esmeraldas Province. Briefly, a rich array of wild, tended, and culti-

vated plant foods was used by Formative peoples in both the coast and sierra. Annual seed crops like maize, jack bean, common bean, and lupine were used in combination with wild or tended tree fruits such as palm, soursop, hackberry, and legume and Sapotaceae trees, among others. Use of root and tuber resources, including sedge, *achira*, arrowroot, potato, and *oca*, is documented. Cotton, gourd, and squash were used. The record remains silent on several important crops, including manioc. While the quality of preservation of macroremains continues to limit quantitative analysis of floral data, phytoliths document continued richness in utilized plant resources throughout the Formative. Root resources are essential elements of coastal and sierran Formative subsistence that predate reliance on maize. A shift to increased maize consumption, in the context of a broad-based agricultural system, appears to be a Late Formative phenomenon (Pearsall 1995; Zeidler and Pearsall 1994).

References Cited

Binford, L. R.
1968   Post-Pleistocene Adaptations. In *New Perspectives in Archeology*, edited by S. R. Binford, and L. R. Binford, pp. 313-341. Aldine, Chicago.

Boserup, E.
1965   *The Conditions of Agricultural Growth.* Aldine, Chicago.

Bray, W.
1976   From Predation to Production: The Nature of Agricultural Evolution in Mexico and Peru. In *Problems in Economic and Social Archaeology*, edited by G. de G. Sieveking, I. H. Longworth, and K. E. Wilson, pp. 73-95. Duckworth, London.

Byrd, K. M.
1976   *Changing Animal Utilization Patterns and Their Implications: Southwest Ecuador (6500 B.C.-A.D 1400).* Unpublished Ph.D. dissertation, Department of Anthropology, University of Florida, Gainesville.

Cohen, M. N.
1977a   Population Pressure and the Origins of Agriculture: An Archaeological Example from the Coast of Peru. In *Origins of Agriculture*, edited by C. A. Reed, pp. 135-177. Mouton Publishers, The Hague.
1977b   *The Food Crisis in Prehistory.* Yale University Press, New Haven.

Damp, J. E.
1979   *Better Homes and Gardens: The Life and Death of the Early Valdivia Community.* Unpublished Ph.D. dissertation, Department of Archaeology, University of Calgary.
1984   Architecture of the Early Valdivia Village. *American Antiquity* 49(3):573-585.

Damp, J. E., D. M. Pearsall, and L. Kaplan
1981   Beans for Valdivia. *Science* 212: 811-812.

Feldman, R. A., and M. E. Moseley
1983   The Northern Andes. In *Ancient South Americans*, edited by J. D. Jennings, pp. 138-177. W. H. Freeman and Co., San Francisco.

Flannery, K. V.
1971   Archeological Systems Theory and Early Mesoamerica. In *Prehistoric Agriculture*, edited by S. Struever, pp. 80-100. The Natural History Press, Garden City, N.Y.
1973   The Origins of Agriculture. *Annual Review of Anthropology* 2:271-310.
1986   The Research Problem. In *Guilá Naquitz: Archaic Foraging and Early Agriculture in Oaxaca, Mexico*, edited by K. V. Flannery, pp.3-18. Academic Press, New York .

Harlan, J. R.
1975   *Crops and Man.* American Society of Agronomy, Madison.

Hassan, F. A.
1981   *Demographic Archaeology.* Academic Press, New York.

Heiser, C. B.
1979   Origins of Some Cultivated New World Plants. *Annual Review of Ecology and Systematics* 10: 309-326.

Lathrap, D. W., D. Collier, and H. Chandra
1975   *Ancient Ecuador: Culture, Clay, and Creativity. 3000-300 B.C.* Field Museum of Natural History, Chicago.

Lathrap, D. W., J. G. Marcos, and J. Zeidler
1977   Real Alto: An Ancient Ceremonial Center. *Archaeology* 30(1):2-13.

Lippi, R. D., R. McK. Bird, and D. M. Stemper
1984   Maize Recovered at La Ponga, an Early Ecuadorian Site. *American Antiquity* 49(1):118-124.

Marcos, J. G.
1978   *The Ceremonial Precinct at Real Alto: Organization of Time and Space in Valdivia Society.* Unpublished Ph.D. dissertation, Department of Anthropology, University of Illinois.
1987   Los campos elevados de la cuenca del Guayas, Ecuador: el proyecto Peñón del Río. In *Pre-Hispanic Agricultural Fields in the Andean Region, Part II*, edited by W. M. Denevan, K. Mathewson, and G. Knapp, pp. 217-224. BAR International Series, 359(ii). British Archaeological Reports, Oxford.

Meggers, B. J., C. Evans, and E. Estrada
1965   *The Early Formative Period on Coastal Ecuador: The Valdivia and Machalilla Phases.* Smithsonian Contributions to Anthropology Vol. 1. Smithsonian Institution, Washington, D. C.

Parsons, J. J., and R. Shlemon
1987   Mapping and Dating the Prehistoric Raised Fields

of the Guayas Basin, Ecuador. In *Pre-Hispanic Agricultural Fields in the Andean Region, Part II*, edited by W. M. Denevan, K. Mathewson, and G. Knapp, pp. 207-216. BAR International Series, 359(ii). British Archaeological Reports, Oxford.

Pearsall, D. M.

1978a Phytolith Analysis of Archeological Soils: Evidence for Maize Cultivation in Formative Ecuador. *Science* 199:177-178.

1978b Paleoethnobotany in Western South America: Progress and Problems. In *The Nature and Status of Ethnobotany*, edited by R. I. Ford, pp. 389-416. Anthropological Papers No. 67. Museum of Anthropology, University of Michigan, Ann Arbor.

1979 *The Application of Ethnobotanical Techniques to the Problem of Subsistence in the Ecuadorian Formative*. Ph.D. dissertation, Department of Anthropology, University of Illinois. University Microfilms, Ann Arbor.

1980 Analysis of an Archaeological Maize Kernel Cache from Manabí Province, Ecuador. *Economic Botany* 34(4): 344-351.

1982 Phytolith Analysis: Applications of a New Paleoethnobotanical Technique in Archeology. *American Anthropologist.* 84(4):862-871.

1987 Evidence for Prehistoric Maize Cultivation on Raised Fields at Peñón del Río, Guayas, Ecuador. In *Prehistoric Agricultural Fields in the Andean Region, Part II*, edited by W. Denevan, K. Mathewson, and G. Knapp, pp. 279-295. BAR International Series, 359(ii). British Archaeological Reports, Oxford.

1988 An Overview of Formative Period Subsistence in Ecuador: Palaeoethnobotanical Data and Perspectives. In *Diet and Subsistence: Current Archaeological Perspectives*, edited by B. V. Kennedy and G. M. Le Moine, pp. 149-158. Proceedings of the 19th Annual Chacmool Conference, Archaeological Association of the University of Calgary, Alberta.

1992 The Origins of Plant Cultivation in South America. In *Origins of Agriculture in World Perspective*, edited by C. W. Cowan and P. J. Watson, pp. 173-205. Smithsonian Institution Press, Washington D.C.

1995 Domestication and Agriculture in the New World Tropics. In Last Hunters—First Farmers: New Perspectives on the Prehistoric Transition to Agriculture, edited by T. Douglas Price and Anne Birgitte Gebauer, pp. 157-192. School of American Research Press, Santa Fe.

Pearsall, D. M., and D. R. Piperno

1990 Antiquity of Maize Cultivation in Ecuador: Summary and Reevaluation of the Evidence. *American Antiquity* 55:324-337.

Pickersgill, B.

1969 The Archeological Record of Chili Peppers (*Capsicum* sp.) and the Sequence of Plant Domestication in Peru. *American Antiquity* 34:54-61.

1977 Taxonomy and the Origin and Evolution of Cultivated Plants in the New World. *Nature* 268:591-595.

1984 Migrations of Chili Peppers, *Capsicum* spp., in the Americas. In *Pre-Columbian Plant Migration*, edited by D. Stone, pp. 105-123. Papers of the Peabody Museum of Archaeology and Ethnology Vol. 76. Harvard University, Cambridge.

Pickersgill, B., and C. B. Heiser, Jr.

1977 Origins and Distribution of Plants Domesticated in the New World Tropics. In *Origins of Agriculture*, edited by C. A. Reed, pp. 803-835. Mouton Publishers, The Hague.

Piperno, D. R.

1984 A Comparison and Differentiation of Phytoliths from Maize and Wild Grasses: Use of Morphological Criteria. *American Antiquity* 49(2):361-383.

1986 The Analysis of Phytoliths from the Vegas Site 0GSE-80, Ecuador. In *The Vegas Culture: Early Prehistory of Southwestern Ecuador*, edited by K. E. Stothert. Museo Antropológico del Banco Central del Ecuador, Guayaquil.

Raymond, J. S.

1988 Subsistence Patterns during the Early Formative in the Valdivia Valley, Ecuador. In *Diet and Subsistence: Current Archaeological Perspectives*, edited by B. V. Kennedy, and G. M. Le Moine, pp. 159-163. Proceedings of the 19th Annual Chacmool Conference, Archaeological Association of the University of Calgary, Alberta.

Reichel-Dolmatoff, G.

1985 *Arqueología de Colombia. Un Texto Introductorio*. Fundación Sequnda Expedición Botánica, Bogotá.

Rindos, D.

1980 Symbiosis, Instability, and the Origins and Spread of Agriculture: A New Model. *Current Anthropology* 21(6): 751-772.

1984 *The Origins of Agriculture*. An Evolutionary Perspective. Academic Press, Orlando.

Smith, C. E., Jr.

1977 Recent Evidence in Support of the Tropical Origin of New World Crops. In *Crop Resources*, edited by D. S. Seigler, pp. 79-95. Academic Press, New York.

Stothert, K. E.

1985 The Preceramic Las Vegas Culture of Coastal Ecuador. *American Antiquity* 50(3):613-637.

Willey, G. R.

1971 *An Introduction to American Archaeology, Volume 2: South America*. Prentice-Hall, Englewood Cliffs, N. J.

Wright, H. E., Jr.
    1977   Environmental Change and the Origin of Agriculture in the Old and New Worlds. In *Origins of Agriculture*, edited by C. A. Reed, pp. 281-318. Mouton Publishers, The Hague.

Zeidler, J. A., and D. M. Pearsall (editors)
    1994   *Regional Archaeology in Northern Manabí, Ecuador, Volume 1. Environment, Cultural Chronology, and Prehistoric Subsistence in the Jama River Valley.* University of Pittsburgh Monographs in Latin American Archaeology, No. 8. Pittsburgh.

13

Andean Coastal Adaptations: Uniformitarianism and Multilinear Evolution

Michael E. Moseley

The longest mountain range in the world forms the Pacific Rim between the antarctic waters of Tierra del Fuego and the tropical Isthmus of Panama. Although narrow, the Andean Cordillera of western South America is also the tallest massif, second only to the Himalayas. For more than 3,500 km the mountain wall splits the continental climate from southern Ecuador (5°00'S) into northern Chile (29°55'S). This results in a juxtaposition of habitats that represent global extremes in environmental conditions. Hypoxic life zones, deficient in oxygen, characterize the upper Cordillera and the Titicaca Basin, which, at 4,000 m above sea level, was the only high altitude cradle of civilization in the ancient world. To the east, the range falls off into the largest of all tropical forests, the Amazon. To the west, mountain flanks descend through the hemisphere's driest desert and into an abyssal ocean trench where upwelling currents support the richest fishery of the Americas.

The proximity of contrasting habitats has fascinated students of evolution ever since Darwin sailed up the coast and pondered the origins of species diversity among its offshore islands. Evolution in Andean South America has been approached in several distinct ways. Darwin and his successors in the natural sciences have pursued a uniformitarian procedure that examines differences among organisms to define species associated with different habitats and to elicit fossil correlations that explain evolution in terms of environmental adaptation. Inquiry into human development in the Cordillera has pursued a different course—one characterized by a unilinear evolutionary approach. Traditionally, archaeologists have assumed that Andean development closely paralleled that in Mesoamerica and other centers of ancient civilizations. They have emphasized similarities among culture-historical sequences by defining recurrent sets of economic conditions and portraying evolution as progression from simple to complex societies. In recent decades, however, some archaeologists working in the Andean region have shifted toward a more uniformitarian approach to the study of economic organization. In this chapter I will review economic continuities linking present, ethnohistoric, and prehistoric populations and then touch upon issues of civil order among early maritime populations. Because perspectives are changing, it is useful to begin with a brief review of evolutionary thinking about Andean societies.

Historical Perspective

Unilinear evolution was cemented into the foundations of American anthropology by Lewis Henry Morgan, one of the discipline's founding fathers. Morgan (1877) presumed that grain agriculture was the economic midwife of indigenous civilization, and that maize-based economies underwrote all complex societies in the New World. This premise has long been contradicted by the fact that in the Andean region, civilizations arose in hypoxic life zones above elevations where maize will grow.

Tiwanaku and other ancient monuments in the Titicaca Basin were explored by Morgan's great correspondent and disciple Adolf Bandelier, but both scholars ignored their economic implications. To defend the agrarian tenants of his theory Morgan had to minimize the importance of complex maritime societies, including the indigenous littoral populations along the Pacific Northwest coast and the Calusa of southwest Florida. He did this by relegating fishing to the most primitive of economic endeavors, and by stereotyping maritime adaptations as an evolutionary stage of "savagery" that was but one step above the primordial invention of speech, and fire. This stereotyping presumed causal linkages between potentially independent cultural variables and correlated types of food with types of social structure and types of political organization.

Although Morgan's theories have undergone refinement, unilinear evolution still assumes correlations among disparate phenomena such as mound building, maize cultivation, and chiefdom-level polities. The occurrence of large preceramic architectural works raises methodological issues about the nature of positive evidence to prove or negative evidence to disprove such correlations. Proponents of the notion that "only maize makes monuments" argue that the architectural monuments could only have been built by maize farmers, while the general absence of plant staples at these sites is explained with accusations of poor excavation and recovery techniques (Wilson 1980; Raymond 1981). Because the hyperarid coast affords the best open site preservation of plant remains in the Western Hemisphere, these accusations underscore an important methodological split among archaeologists who reject or accept negative evidence. The latter often point to an absence of the linkages that unilinear modeling presumes. Those who accept the negative evidence of maize and agricultural staples among early littoral populations reason that the economic premises of unilinear evolution do not work well in the Cordillera because *calories* underwrote what societies did, and it made little difference if energy came packaged in corn husks, potato skins, llama hides or fish scales so long as there were calories.

Presumptions that maize cultivation underwrote the origins of complex societies in South America prevailed through the 1950s. However, the following decade saw a break with old expectations as some scholars in America and in the Soviet Union began, independently, to argue for the early importance of foods other than maize and cereals. These arguments marked a gradual shift from a unilinear to a multilinear evolutionary perspective. This was fostered by the growing realization that different ecological settings fostered different economic adaptations. Because such extremes in aridity, high altitude, and tropical rainfall occur in the Andean region it was reasonable to expect that the diverse environments were associated with distinct ways of making a living. Between 1965 and 1975 "revisionist" models were pioneered for three different adaptive strategies and their associated evolutionary pathways. These depictions may be called: (1) the tropical forest scenario based upon South American root crops, (2) the high mountain scenario emphasizing agro-pastoralism employing domesticated camelids, potatoes and tubers, and (3) the maritime-oasis scenario focused upon fishing and canal-based farming. The mountain and coastal strategies pertain the central Cordillera where the Andes are driest, widest, and loftiest.

Each scenario has environmental, ethnohistorical, and archaeological components. The environmental and ethnohistorical formulations provide economic models that justify reinterpretations of the archaeological record which diverge from traditional unilinear propositions. The maritime component of the maritime-oases scenario was generated exclusively by preceramic archaeological remains that included the biggest architectural works for their time period in the continent. The proposition that marine resources rather than agriculture underwrote the rise of large sedentary societies that built monuments was in print

before ethnohistorians documented the nature of indigenous maritime adaptations, and before the marine and desert ecology were well understood. This prevented the uniformitarian perspective on coastal development that is now made possible by advances in our understanding of the environment and the ethnohistoric record.

Adaptational Perspective

Today fishing and farming along the arid Andean coast are largely mechanized, although traditional forms of both persist. Using present conditions to model the past acknowledges that the Spanish conquest and the current international economy have generated major social transformations. However, these transformations have not changed the inherent nature of coastal resources, nor the basic means of exploiting them. Therefore, present conditions are considered relevant to the past.

Environmental Considerations

In the context of the extremes in environmental conditions found along the Peruvian coast, fishing and coastal farming are subject to very different constraints. Less than 10 percent of the desert can be farmed and even this depends upon irrigation (Robinson 1964). Agriculture requires arable land, water, and domesticated plants. As measured by global standards, plant yields per hectare are exceptionally high. Sugar cane yields are the greatest in the Western Hemisphere, and most other crops exceed world norms. As a consequence of this exceptional productivity, coastal agriculture is intensive, mechanized, geared to the international export marked, and organized as agro-industrial cooperatives which were formerly large plantations. Seasonally inundated river flood-plains and other self-watering terrain accounts for less than one percent of the agricultural land that is in production today (Moseley and Feldman 1984). Canal-based irrigation, derived principally from streams and rivers sustains more than 99 percent of all coastal farming. The majority of large earthbank canals in use today were originally built in prehistoric times.

Normally there is no annual rainfall below elevations of 1,500-2,000 m. Therefore, most irrigation water comes from highland runoff that descends down canyon-like drainages that widen as gradients lessen near the sea. However, where mountains push into the sea, oasis valleys are often deeply incised and topographic limitations on arable land can constrain agriculture. As the Cordillera becomes progressively higher and wider to the south, conditions become dryer and runoff diminishes. Consequently oasis valleys are largest in northern Peru and smallest in northern Chile. The great majority of valley canals are situated well inland. They begin in steep stream gradients and channels can diverge laterally away from rivers to irrigate the maximum amount of land with the shortest possible canal length, thereby minimizing water loss during transport (Moseley et al. 1981). The positioning of canals draws farmers inland. Agriculturalists tend to reside within oases away from the sea, whereas fishers reside at valley mouths and along the desert littoral. This results in T-shaped maritime-oasis settlement patterns with littoral communities strung along the coast and agrarian ones along the perpendicular river courses.

Agrarian yields are very high, but by 1970 Peru generated greater international revenues from near-shore fishing than from coastal farming. This is because little of the desert can be farmed whereas the entire seashore can be fished. Beginning in northern Chile, strong upwelling currents arise and the near-shore fishery stretches up the Andean coast some 2,000 km. This vast, but narrow belt of water has produced annual commercial anchoveta yields on the order of 100 metric tons/km^2. Still richer waters occur around 8°, 11°, and 15° south latitude where there are productivity maxima with annual yields on the order of 1,000 tons/km^2 (Walsh 1981). Such yields made Peru the world's leading fishing nation, and in the early 1970s the fishery supplied one fifth of the sea food consumed by humanity.

High returns are produced using a very simple maritime technology based on netting small schooling fish from small craft employing small crews. Anchoveta are then dried, ground, and turned into meal for storage and shipment. Using modern, yet modest, fishing technology to secure high yields makes near-shore fishing much simpler and more productive than modern irrigation farming. Given the nutritional values for anchovy, and a cropping rate of 50-60 percent of the stock (UNESCO 1980; Walsh 1981), harvests of 10 million metric tons per year could support more than 6,500,000 individuals eating nothing but small fish.

From the perspective of marine biology and known prehistoric fishing technology, there is nothing theoretically untenable about Andean maritime societies achieving social complexity, if the economic mainstay is understood to entail small schooling fish complemented by other sea foods. Assessment of coastal environmental conditions should have suggested that maritime adaptations could precede agrarian adaptations, and that the Andean fishery could sustain very complex societies. However, it was not the environment, but the need to explain large pre-pottery littoral communities with monumental architecture that gave rise to the maritime-oasis scenario. Initially, it was difficult to interpret such early complexes because archaeologists had no models of indigenous coastal life ways dating to the time of Spanish contact.

Ethnohistorical Considerations

Since 1970, ethnohistoric documentation of native coastal economies has been pioneered by Maria Rostworowski de Diez Canseco (1970, 1977, 1981). She defines the nature of late maritime-oasis adaptations and reveals a noteworthy economic division between the production of protein and the production of carbohydrates. Along the central and northern Peruvian coast farmers did not fish and fishermen did not farm. Fishing was a distinct specialization, and in the north fishers spoke their own language or dialect distinct from that of agriculturalists. Furthermore, according to the claims of sixteenth century informants, maritime populations married among themselves, lived in separate littoral communities and were governed by their own *curacas* or hereditary lords.

Why the separation of protein and carbohydrate production? In the present as well as the past, people who attempt to both fish and farm do not produce the same level of yields as professionals who engage in one or the other. Due to constant upwelling currents, fishing goes on year around. Anchoveta can be harvested some 280 days a year, and most other seafoods are perennially available. Farming is also a yeararound occupation. The seasonal nature of highland runoff imparts a seasonal cycle to plant tending which is followed by canal tending. After harvesting, the time and labor of farmers are absorbed by the maintenance of irrigation systems. In addition to occupying people throughout the year, maritime and agrarian pursuits take place in different settings and are associated with either littoral or riparian patterns of residence. Furthermore, the timing of fishing and farming activities often conflict. This is because they are scheduled by very different phenomena and are subject to equally distinct risks. Maritime folk are concerned with lunar cycles, tides, and killer whales, whereas agrarian folk worry about solar cycles, precipitation, and drought. Therefore, the two groups of subsistence specialists pray to different saints and emphasize different holidays.

Ethnohistoric sources indicate that, in the past, fishers and farmers regularly exchanged subsistence commodities. However, coastal polities sought to incorporate both maritime and agrarian populations in order to maintain economic autonomy. Political linkages were expressed as kin linkages. Coastal populations and polities were hierarchically organized as asymmetrical segmentary kinship systems. Social and political formations were divided into moieties by principals of dual organization and then further asymmetrically segmented into four, eight, ten, or twelvefold hierarchical descent groups. Asymmetry was such that one moiety or descent group could draw disproportionately upon the resources of its counterpart. Differential rights and obligations were calculated by descent from founding ancestors, and described in terms of priorities of older versus younger brothers, or older versus younger generations. Segmentary descent characterized both commoners and their hereditary *curaca* rulers at the time of contact. *Curacas* rationalized their rule in terms of closer descent from founding ancestors than commoners.

Ancestors were venerated. Because the deceased defined social position among commoners as well as the *curaca's* right to rule, keeping track of the dead was exceptionally important, and took the form of physically conserving bodies. Although the desert assisted corpse conservation through desiccation, the deceased were often artificially mummified. Mummies were curated in their homes, special quarters or family cemeteries, and dead ancestors consulted on matters of health or well being. Corpses of *curacas* and kings were paraded about on ritual occasions as symbols of hierarchical kin linkages and kin obligations. Because ancestors were the "glue" bonding social and political formations, Andean belief systems emphasized retention of intact corpses. These convictions contrast dramatically with Amazonian beliefs that included mortuary manipulation of skeletal parts, secondary burial, and ossuaries with multiple mixed bodies. It is reasonable to presume that mummification was always associated with ancestor veneration and also, perhaps, hierarchical descent in the Andes. If the association is accepted, then there is very early evidence of asymmetrical segmentary kinship organization on the coast.

Archaeological Perspectives

How did the maritime fishing and oasis farming components of the arid coastal adaptation arise? Apparently it did not take long for early populations colonizing the coast to realize that the richest fishery of the Western Hemisphere offers more to eat than the New World's driest desert. In southern Peru and northern Chile there is early evidence of seafood consumption and early marine exploitation some 8000 to 9000 years ago (Richardson 1989; Dillehay 1989). Thereafter, evidence of economic reliance upon the sea increased in the archaeological record and persisted through ethnohistorical, historical, and recent documentation. This situation is compatible with a uniformitarian proposition that once maritime adaptations were established they endured as an uninterrupted evolutionary pathway that eventually transformed Peru to the world's leading fishing nation.

Although the Andean fishery may feed people, it did not provide fiber for net and line, supply reed or wood for watercraft, nor fuel for fire. Thus, exploiting the sea required an infrastructure based upon terrestrial resources. This added an oasis component to indigenous maritime adaptations. Wild plants of early economic importance occurred along the floodplains of streams and rivers and in *lomas* patches. *Lomas* are island-like plant communities supported by seasonal fog that condenses on isolated hill sides and ground slopes below elevations of 1,000 m. It is evident that floodplain oases and *lomas* provided raw materials of technological importance as well as certain plant foods including seeds from wild grasses and mesquite-like trees (Jones 1981).

In the Pacific sierra of northern Peru there evidence of hunter-gatherers tending domesticated beans and chile peppers more than 8000 years ago (Lynch 1983). By 4000 to 5000 years ago northern maritime societies were growing a wide variety of plants. Cotton, gourd, reed and bulrush served industrial ends while fruit trees provided both wood

and fruit. However, peppers, squash, beans, and some root crops were grown for food as was maize in several locations (Bonavia 1982). Almost all domesticates are inferred to have been tended in river floodplains where planting could take place after inundation by seasonal runoff. Botanical analysis indicates that after harvesting, crops were carried to shore-line fishing settlements where the plants were processed with unusable parts being discarded in middens (Pozorski and Pozorski 1987).

It has been proposed that the presence of domesticated plants at preceramic coastal settlements is indicative of agrarian-based economies rather than maritime ones (Wilson 1981; Raymond 1981). However, desert farming requires more than domesticated plants; there must be land and water to grow them. In the absence of sizable canal systems to irrigate the desert there is very little naturally arable land. River floodplains and other self watering terrain comprises less than one percent of the land that is farmed today. This was certainly very important terrain in the past for people who grew plants but did not construct canals to reclaim the desert. However, farming restricted to self-watering land could not produce as much as fishing, nor sustain such large populations. Thus, it was not a lack of plants, but the dearth of naturally arable terrain that constrained early coastal cultivation.

In the sierra, irrigation presumably began early on among people who both foraged and farmed. The basic technology was not complicated. However, applying it to the coast was demanding, due to the incised nature of the drainages that carry runoff. Floodplains are narrow because rivers flow in deeply down-cut courses. Long lead-off canals must have been built to transport water out of incised drainages before the moisture could be diverted onto desert farm plots. Today, 75 percent or more of the arable terrain in most oases is watered by very long canals, while canals less than 5 km long support relatively little land. The advent of coastal canal agriculture is quite evident in the archaeological record because: (1) major changes in settlement patterns appeared with the rise of large inland populations, (2) marked increases took place in both types and quantities of cultigens consumed, (3) plant processing appeared at inland sites, but disappeared from littoral ones, (4) both ceramics and heddle weaving appeared, and (5) new forms of ceremonial architecture were built within irrigated oases. In some settings inland ceramic-using populations may well have pioneered oasis irrigation while maritime populations continued to pursue conservative preceramic ways of life. Whatever the case, canal irrigation opened a new niche, the desert, to intensive exploitation.

Migration into it was seemingly rapid within individual valleys. However, there were regional differences in the rate of occupation: it began around 1800 B.C. in northern and central Peru, and about 1400 B.C., or later, to the south, in Chile. In all cases an agrarian economy was juxtaposed with a well established fishing economy. Because each way of life could be pursued independently of the other, maritime-oasis adaptations may be thought of as a symbiotic convergence of two evolutionary pathways.

Archaeological Problems and Issues

I will now turn to the maritime pathway and address certain issues and problems pertaining to the organization of littoral societies prior to the advent of irrigation agriculture. Architectural monuments—including the largest known buildings on the continent, for their time period—are the hallmark of early maritime achievement. These works are generally described in terms of "corporate" organization in an attempt to avoid value-laden tags and labels. Corporate construction projects are considered to be undertakings that drew labor from multiple households, coordinating work and focusing it upon a planned outcome. Many corporate activities, such as the business that went on in and around monuments, often elude archaeological detection. Thus, large architectural works, because they survive in tangible form, serve as a barometers for inferring broader conditions. The corporate bodies that executed these projects are inferred to have been kin-based.

Distributions

Preceramic corporate monuments in the form of platform mounds or large masonry buildings have a very limited distribution along some 500 km of the coast between the Río Choa in the north and the Río Chillón in the south. Peripheral to this core, smaller corporate structures expand the range somewhat. In the Río Moche region a circular sunken court of modest size is present at Alto de Salaverry (Pozorski and Pozorski 1979). In the south, the Río Omas site of Asia has a ground level adobe building of probable corporate nature (Engel 1963). It is significant that the distribution of corporate maritime monuments is confined to the northern end of the anchoveta fishery, where productivity maxima are located between 8° and 15° south latitude with annual yields reaching 1,000 tons/km^2. Thus, there is a spatial association between marine productivity and maritime complexity. It is reasonable to postulate that this is not a casual association, but a caloric one.

Origins

Around 3000 B.C. there was a dramatic numerical increase in near-shore sites. At the time the archaeological maritime hypothesis was initially formulated this was thought to represent the "invention" of fishing. It is now understood to be a product of preservation resulting from glacial meltback generating a rapid rise in the ocean that was followed some 5000 years ago by the onset of relative stabilization near modern norms (Richardson 1981). Sea level stabilization provides a convenient geoarchaeological horizon marker for separating the Lithic and Preceramic periods.

The Preceramic period saw construction of large littoral monuments, but probably not the earliest of corporate maritime projects. The preceramic complex of Aspero contains six large platform mounds, two of which were partially explored by Feldman (1980). Excavations, limited to the upper, later construction stages, produced seven ^{14}C dates ranging from 2508±373 to 3145±595 B.P. Basal construction dates would be earlier, and these need not be the first monuments erected by maritime populations. Earlier corporate works may have been erected in near-shore settings later submerged by rising seas.

A case can be made that sea level rise biased the surviving picture of coastal adaptations by inundating shorelines that were the primary focus of economic activity. What survives therefore comes from inland settings that were the focus of secondary activities pertinent to the terrestrial infrastructure of maritime adaptations. With this in mind, it is instructive to mention examples of early and late Lithic period occupations of the north-central Peruvian coast. Distributed between 4° and 11° south latitude, there are lithic remains, known as the Paiján complex, that dated between 7000 and 10,000 years ago. It was well represented by inland quarry and lithic reduction sites, as well as camps with shallow middens yielding mollusks and fish bones, but not large game. Very unusual, thin, elongated projectile points are the hallmark of the complex. Typically, a long, thin shank or stem projected below the basal barbs. Hafting in a hollow socket or in a cane shaft is inferred. The projectiles were characteristically "needle-nosed," with remarkably slim, awl-like points. Indeed, the points rarely survived with their needle-nose in tact, and the tips were initially misidentified as stone awls. On the basis of extensive work with the complex, Chauchat (1988) concluded that the sites were inland manifestations of people who obtained the majority of their protein from the sea, and that the points were used for spearing fish. Harpoons and spears saw persistent use in Chilean maritime economies. However, they did not play to the strengths of the northern fishery. It is not clear if Paiján populations engaged in angling and netting. However, these techniques replaced fish spearing before the end of the Lithic period. The limited number of Paiján burials indicate that the deceased were interred intact.

In northern Chile, evidence of ancestor veneration in the form of elaborate artificial mummification of corpses is associated with the Chinchoros coastal tradition that began some 7000 years ago and endured up to the advent of oasis irrigation (Núñez, Chapter 16). In Peru, concern with the physical conservation of ancestors was evident at the early site of Paloma, where corpses were salted to assist preservation (R. A. Benfer, personal communication, 1989). The diet and health of the mortuary population at Paloma has received intense scrutiny. The settlement was located behind San Bartolo Bay some 15 km north of the Chilca drainage. Situated adjacent to zones of *lomas* vegetation, about 4 km inland, the 15 ha occupation area comprised thin, scattered middens, the largest of which covered 6,500 m², averaged 50 cm in depth, and dated between 6500 and 5000 B.P. The excavators, Engel and Benfer (Benfer 1984), subdivided the occupation into three major phases. Initially Paloma served as a seasonal camp for relatively mobile people, but their descendants became fully sedentary during the two subsequent phases. The local population may have numbered between 30 and 40 individuals who lived in circular dome-shaped houses.

Over the span of one and a half millennia, many people died at Paloma and the largest midden contained an estimated 900 burials. The dead were interred in shallow pits below house floors. Most structures held a number of burials, interpreted to have been family members who lived in the same household. Burying deceased household members in their dwellings represented a minor but persistent coastal mortuary practice. The ancient Palomans salted corpses to prevent deterioration. Typically, individuals were placed on their side with the knees drawn up to the chest and the hands held in the pelvic or facial region. They were usually wrapped in a twined mat of reeds. Other than fragments of twined clothing, burial goods were scarce and normally accompanied men rather than women.

In addition to bone fishhooks, and fragments of fish net, the well-preserved midden constituents included both plant and animal remains. Mollusks, large fish, sea birds and sea mammals were common, but the faunal remains were dominated by the bones of small fish including anchovies and sardines (Reitz 1987). Small fish bones and small seeds from wild grasses were the primary constituents of large quantities of human feces found at the site (Jones 1981).

Although not abundant, cultivated plants, including squash, beans and gourd, occurred in the midden and must have been sown in the Chilca stream bed after its annual flood season. Traces of squash and beans were also present in the stomach contents of some burials.

The excavated mortuary population of more than 200 individuals has been analyzed in detail by Benfer (1984). The intestinal contents of the dead indicated a dietary dominance of small fish. The ear structures of males revealed a high incidence of osseous damage resulting from diving in cold water (Patterson, Chapter 14).

Finally, chemical analysis of human bone showed exceptionally low levels of strontium indicating high protein consumption and pointing to a diet based primarily upon seafood. Initially, males consumed more protein than females, but this difference diminished over time. As the people of Paloma shifted to a sedentary way of life, they came to live longer and enjoy increased life expectancy. The physical stature of adults increased, while the incidence of anemia among children decreased. The community experienced population growth, in spite of attempts to control population numbers by social means. These included marrying and reproducing at a later age, as well as female infanticide. Benfer (1984) also points out that while female protein consumption improved over time, some individuals and some families continued to enjoy better diet than others.

If maritime architectural monuments were products of a minority directing the labor of a majority of people, then the antecedents of this situation should have been reflected in early evidence of status and class distinctions. The Paloma data tell us that gender distinctions existed, with dietary inequities between males and females. Females were also subject to infanticide and adult females were buried with fewer grave goods. The Paloma data also demonstrate inequity among households, with some enjoying both better food and more elaborate treatment of their deceased than others. If we adopt a uniformitarian perspective, then these inequalities were nested in a segmentary kinship system. As in later times, this system allowed some families to accrue more resources than others by using salted mummies to document hierarchical descent that rationalized inequity.

The Chinchoros mortuary complex showed many similar dimensions of burial treatment, compatible with this perspective. There the most elaborate processing of corpses and multifaceted mummification was associated with men, women, and children interred as family groups. Interred individually or in groups, many other corpses received only partial processing or none at all, so we may infer that not all ancestors were equal.

Architectural Expressions

The origins of corporate construction on the coast may be obscure, but late preceramic architectural works were relatively numerous and frequently dramatic. Many reflected sizable work forces, and therefore, large sustaining populations. The majority of monuments were associated with extensive settlements and may be interpreted as community construction projects. Yet some architectural complexes, including El Paraíso the biggest of all, had small residential components and were apparently erected by work forces that did not live nearby.

Due to their size and solid nature, platform mounds are, at present, the most common and conspicuous of preceramic corporate works. Preceramic platform mounds exhibited a number of recurrent canons in both construction and form. Many began as a ground level buildings and rooms that were later filled in to create an artificial eminence. Final size was always a product of "temple interment" entailing multiple construction stages interspersed with periods of maintenance and use. Creating a mound by burying an earlier buildings required substantial quantities of architectural fill. Rather than midden, freshly quarried rock was the preferred construction material. Rocky fill was hauled from quarries in large open mesh satchels. Called *shicra*, and made of coarse sturdy reeds, mesh bags held on the order of 26 kg of stone. Upon reaching the construction site the fill was not dumped. Rather the entire load, satchel and all was deposited within the structure and left intact. This conferred no apparent engineering benefits and used up multitudes of bags.

The practice shows that corporate work was divided into repetitive tasks, perhaps providing a means of accounting for labor obligations and expenditures. The use of *shicra* continued into later times and evolved into "segmentary" construction as adobe building materials came to displace stone fill. In later prehistoric contexts segmentary construction is thought to reflect *mita*-like labor taxation with the subdivision of a project into repetitive tasks defining the work levied upon different communities or kin groups. Segmentary construction persists today in some traditional settings where large building projects, such as church yard and cemetery walls, are divided into long sections. The construction and maintenance of different segments of the project is then undertaken by different *ayllu* kin groups (Urton 1981). Preceramic *shicra* suggest that distinct groups of people contributed labor to corporate projects. Yet, who they were and how they were mobilized is not known.

Preceramic platforms on the coast were rectangular and there were both free-standing examples and those banked against hill slopes. When banked, they could rise as a single eminence, or one structure could be stacked behind another to form a larger terraced platform. Exterior surfaces and inclined sides of mounds were faced with masonry of rounded boulders or angular quarry stone set in mud mortar. The masonry was sometimes tiered or stepped and often plastered with adobe; yet there was little use of adobe bricks in preceramic times.

The most obvious feature of early platform mounds is that they were designed for purposes of ritual display. The apex comprised platform summits occupied by walled structures which included courts and smaller rooms that could accommodate relatively few participants. Summit access was gained via a central flight of stairs or a prominent ramp that very likely served as a stage for display and presentation to audiences assembled in forecourts in front of the mounds. However, those assembled in spacious courts below the platforms were not privy to all the activities which took place on the summit buildings.

On terraced platforms, higher courts were smaller than lower ones and the basal forecourts were biggest of all. It must have taken far more people to build the platforms than could fit upon their terraces and summits, suggesting status differences—although not necessarily permanent or hereditary ones—among the participants.

With few exceptions, there were always two or more platforms of different sizes at a site. This is thought to express pluralism within pantheons and within the social order. Where there were but two mounds, propositions of dual organization are reasonable. The meaning of greater numbers of platforms is open to question, but distinctions in size and elaboration might be interpreted as differences in status.

Platforms were associated with many forms of ancillary architecture. Often a spacious forecourt fronted mounds, and sometimes these rectangular enclosures housed a smaller central sunken court of circular form. As in later times, preceramic corporate architecture was kept scrupulously clean, making their associated activities difficult to infer.

Status Differentiation: Achieved or Ascribed?

Early evidence of mummification suggests coastal populations were kin-based and organized by asymmetrical segmentary descent. Many archaeologists have assumed that erecting platforms and other corporate works entailed a formal chain of command with positions of authority that allowed a minority of individuals to direct activities of the majority. However, it is not clear if positions of leadership were based on an individual's abilities and means, or if offices of authority were inherited, as among the later *curaca* class. *Curacas* were present after 500 B.C.: one of their hallmarks was elaborate ancestor veneration and entombment of the nobility with sumptuary goods that were qualitatively and qualitatively different than those accessible to commoners. Recognizing similar distinctions in preceramic mortuary practices is difficult at best, as the following two examples will demonstrate.

Cloth wraps and textiles were the most ubiquitous of preceramic grave accompaniments. At the site of Asia, 133 cloth items accompanied 28 normal interments (Moseley 1975). Most individuals had two to four textile offerings, but a few individuals received two to three times the norm. The person receiving the most fabrics, 12, also had gourd containers, bone tools, wood tubes, a sling, a slate tablet, a comb, and other goods. This unusually well-furnished grave was that of a young male. He may have achieved high status through personal deeds or he may have been born to a prosperous family that sponsored elaborate interment.

At the Aspero complex Huaca de los Sacrificios is a platform mound that derives its name from two burials, an infant and an adult, found 3.5 m apart on the same floor level of a summit compartment. The poorly preserved adult corpse was tightly flexed and some joints may have been cut to force the body into a cramped position. At one time the individual was either bound or wrapped with cloth and the only accompaniment was a broken gourd. This contrasts with the two-month old flexed infant that wore a cap or hat adorned by 500 shell, plant, and clay beads. Completely wrapped in a large textile, the body and a gourd bowl were placed in a basket that was wrapped in textile then rolled in a mat and tied with strips of white cloth. This was placed on the ground with two large pieces of cotton cloth waded together. The assemblage was then covered with an inverted carved stone basin. The four-legged stone basin is one of the finest preceramic objects ever found, and the burial was obviously one of exceptional importance. Was this the child of a chief with rich grave goods reflecting inherited status, or was the infant a sacrifice with exceptional accompaniments dedicated to the supernatural? The excavator suggests the latter (Feldman 1980). This is in keeping with the fact that numerous preceramic interments have been excavated by many different scholars and no one has argued that there are indications of an inherited elite.

Organizational Models

If the subsistence tenants of unilinear evolution are questionable or inoperative for early littoral adaptations as well as for high altitude adaptations, there is little reason to presume that Andean evolution was necessarily characterized by the types of linkages between economic, social, and political conditions that unilinear development assumes. Unilinear schemes link many different phenomena, including mound building, inherited status differences, and leadership positions. Preceramic maritime societies have been labeled "chiefdoms" on this basis alone, and not because there was reliable archaeological evidence for hereditary rulers. Attention to negative evidence has led some scholars to the conclusion that *curacas* were not present until after spread of Chavín influence during the first centuries B.C. The problem with this seemingly long absence of hereditary status differentiation is that after 1800 B.C. irrigation reclamation of the oasis valleys ushered in an unprecedented spate of monumental construction. By 1200 B.C. oasis populations were erecting the largest architectural complexes in the Western Hemisphere, leading to propositions of state-like political formations (Haas et al. 1989).

The apparent absence of hereditary status distinctions has led to propositions that preceramic and early ceramic societies were "egalitarian." Even so, egalitarian societies can have complex forms of socio-political organization. Two potential models for the organization of egalitarian societies can be drawn from ethnographic and ethnohistoric sources. Both entail chains of command with formal offices that were ranked and endured from one generation to another, but were not inherited.

In one example, hierarchical corporate offices characterize cargo systems of leadership in modern peasant societies. Cargo offices rotate, with individuals moving up and eventually retiring out of the leadership hierarchy. Because cargo posts are associated with the outlay of resources members of wealthy families or kin groups generally suffer the expense of serving in cargo positions. To varying degrees, cargo offices mitigate economic inequities. The suggestion that early maritime polities had cargo-like organization underlies the hypothesis that they were egalitarian.

Turning to an ethnohistoric example, when the Spanish first arrived, oracle cults were common in the Andes, with the most powerful of all based at Pachacamac on the coast near Lima. Drawing pilgrims and devotes from far and wide it was respected by the Inca, and excavations at

Pachacamac suggest it may have been an oracle center for well over a millennium. Ethnohistoric sources are not explicit about the cult's corporate organization but there are no indications that its administration or "priesthood" was vested in inherited offices. An oracle model of organization has been proposed for the Chavín de Huantar and the radiation of its influence after 500 B.C. (Burger 1988). In something of a similar vein, S. Pozorski (1987) argues that still earlier state-like formations on the coast were theocratic in nature. They were indeed associated with an "other worldly" iconography, but not with mortuary practices indicative of inherited rule. Early governance by cargo-like or cult-like principles is not untenable. The Vatican is an apt reminder that state-like formations with non-inherited offices of rule have been present for millennia, and that there were many forms of corporate organization that unilinear evolution fails to acknowledge.

Conclusions

Because the Andean Cordillera juxtaposes contrasting extremes in environmental conditions, it underscores the dissimilarity in how biological and cultural evolution have been approached. Biologists are interested in differences as well as diversity and seek to explain evolution in terms of adaptation. They eschew concepts analogous to the "superorganic" nature of culture that would allow species to float ethereally above the environment, and theories analogous to the "psychic unity" of mankind that would have species always behave in the same way, even in radically different environments. Such concepts ignore the important role of ecological relationships. Focus on variation in these ecological relationships has allowed the study of cultural evolution to pursue a different course from the unilinear one that Morgan outlined long ago. In the case of the Andes, this approach has not been very productive because it is insensitive to alternative adaptations that are common in the Cordillera and require alternative approaches to evolution if they are to be understood.

References Cited

Benfer, R. A.
1984 The Challenges and Rewards of Sedentism: The Preceramic Village of Paloma, Peru. In *Paleopathology at the Origins of Agriculture*, edited by M. N. Cohen and G. J. Armelagos, pp. 531-558. Academic Press, New York.

Bonavia, D.
1982 *Preceramico Peruano—Los Gavilanes—Mar, Desierto, y Oasis en la Historia del Hombre*. Corporación Financiera de Desarrollo S.A. Cofide and Instituto Arqueológico Aleman, Lima.

Burger, R. L.
1988 Unity and Heterogeneity within the Chavín Horizon. In *Peruvian Prehistory*, edited by R. W.

Keatinge, pp. 99-144. Cambridge University Press, Cambridge.

Chauchat, C.
1988   Early Hunter-Gatherers on the Peruvian Coast. In *Peruvian Prehistory*, edited by R. W. Keatinge, pp. 41-66. Cambridge University Press, Cambridge.

Dillehay, T.
1989   Early Peoples in Southern Chile. Paper presented at the Circum-Pacific Prehistory Conference, Seattle. Washington State University Press, Pullman.

Engel, F.
1963   A Preceramic Settlement on the Central Coast of Peru: Asia, Unit 1. *Transactions of the American Philosophical Society* 53(3):3-139. Philadelphia.

Feldman, R. A.
1980   *Aspero, Peru: Architecture, Subsistence Economy, and Other Artifacts of a Preceramic Maritime Chiefdom.* Unpublished Ph.D. dissertation, Department of Anthropology, Harvard University, Cambridge.

Haas, J., S. Pozorski, and T. Pozorski (editors)
1987   *The Origins and Development of the Andean State.* Cambridge University Press, Cambridge.

Jones, D. S.
1981   Annual Growth Increment in Shells of *Spisula Solidissima* Record Marine Temperature Variability. *Science* 211:165-166.

Lynch, T. F.
1983   The Paleo-Indians. In *Ancient South Americans*, edited by J. D. Jennings, pp. 87-137. W. H. Freeman and Co., New York.

Morgan, L. H.
1877   *Ancient Society.* H. Holt and Co., New York.

Moseley, M. E.
1975   Prehistoric Principles of Labor Organization in the Moche Valley, Peru. *American Antiquity* 40:191-195.

Moseley, M. E., and R. A. Feldman
1984   Hydrological Dynamics and the Evolution of Field Form and Use: Resolving the Knapp-Smith Controversy. *American Antiquity* 49:403-408.

Moseley, M. E., R. A. Feldman, and C. R. Ortloff
1981   Living with Crises: Human Perception of Process and Time. In *Biotic Crises in Ecological and Evolutionary Time*, edited by M. Nitecki, pp. 231-267. Academic Press, New York.

Pozorski, S.
1987   Theocracy vs. Militarism: the Significance of the Casma Valley in Understanding Early State Formation. In *The Origins and Development of the Andean State*, edited by J. Haas, S. Pozorski, and T. Pozorski, pp. 15-30. Cambridge University Press, Cambridge.

Pozorski, S., and T. Pozorski
1979   An Early Subsistence Exchange in the Moche Valley, Peru. *Journal of Field Archaeology* 6:413-432.

1987   *Early Settlement and Subsistence in the Casma Valley, Peru.* University of Iowa Press, Iowa City.

Raymond, J. S.
1981   The Maritime Foundations of Andean Civilization: A Reconsideration of the Evidence. *American Antiquity* 46:806-820.

Reitz, E. J.
1987   Preliminary Report on the Vertebrate Fauna from the Ring Site, Peru. Ms. on file, Department of Anthropology, University of Georgia, Athens.

Richardson, J. B. III
1981   Modeling and Development of Sedentary Maritime Economies on the Coast of Peru: A Preliminary Statement. *Annals of the Carnegie Museum* 50:139-150.

1989   Early Peoples on the Coast of Peru. Paper presented at the Circum-Pacific Prehistory Conference, Seattle. Washington State Universiy Press, Pullman.

Robinson, D. A.
1964   *Peru in Four Dimensions.* American Studies Press, S. A., Lima.

Rostworowski de Diez Canseco, M.
1970   Mercaderes del Valle de Chincha en la Epoca Prehispanica: un Documento y Unos Comentarios. *Revista Española de Antropología Americana* 5:135-177.

1977   *Etnía y Sociedad: Costa Peruana Prehispánica.* Instituto de Estudios Peruanos, Lima.

1981   *Recursos Naturales Renovables y Pesca, Siglos XVI y XVII.* Instituto de Estudios Peruanos, Lima.

UNESCO
1980   *Proceedings of the Workshop on the Phenomenon Know as El Niño.* United Nations Educational, Scientific and Cultural Organization, Paris.

Urton, G.
1981   *At the Crossroads of the Earth and the Sky.* University of Texas Press, Austin.

Walsh, J. J.
1981   A Carbon Budget for Overfishing off Peru. *Nature* 290:300-304.

Wilson, D.
1981   Of Maize and Men: A Critique of the Maritime Hypothesis of State Origins on the Coast of Peru. *American Anthropologist* 93:93-120.

14

The Development of Agriculture and the Emergence of Formative Civilization in the Central Andes

Thomas C. Patterson

Since the late 1940s, cultural evolutionism has provided a powerful analytical framework for organizing archaeological evidence. Its central features are (1) a base-superstructure model of society which places final determination in the economic base rather than the political-legal and ideological superstructures, and (2) a purported linear progression of social types or stages from small, loosely organized foraging groups through autonomous, incipient farming villages to class-stratified states and empires with highly developed agricultural economies (Patterson 1987; Willey and Phillips 1958). However, as evidence was collected and evaluated during the 1950s and 1960s, the fit between theory and empirical reality seemed to diminish.

Coastal Peru was one area where what was observed in the archaeological record did not accord with predictions based on the evolutionist analytical categories. This discrepancy provided the foundations for the "maritime foundations of Andean civilization" debate of the last decade. The archaeologists who carried out the research had to struggle with the fact that early communities, only marginally engaged in agricultural food production, built large structures (Patterson and Lanning 1964; Moseley 1975). Their critics claimed that only farming communities produced the quantities of food required to permit large-scale public construction and, therefore, their members must have been farmers (Raymond 1981; Wilson 1981). The large buildings also led some to claim that these incipient farming communities must have been class-stratified and state-based, since, according to the theory, only state-level polities have the capacity to mobilize, or conscript, the labor forces needed to erect monumental architecture (Haas 1987).

During the 1970s, archaeologists introduced the notion of complexity to shore up and salvage the theoretical underpinnings of cultural evolutionism in a way that would allow them to deal with the diverse social and political-economic forms exhibited by anomalous pre-state societies (Price and Brown 1985; van der Leeuw 1981). Ethnographic and historical accounts indicate that their social relations range from egalitarian to chieftainships; their residential patterns from relatively mobile to sedentary; and their economies from broad-based to highly specialized. Since both foraging and farming societies manifest egalitarian and chiefly social relations, the variations in social organization do not mirror the political and economic categories embedded in the "stagist" analytical categories of cultural evolutionist theory (Eggan 1950; Gailey 1987; Lee 1979; Marquardt 1987; Oberg 1973).

There are still unresolved issues concerning how to conceptualize, in theoretical terms, this diversity as well as the transition from an appropriative to a food-producing economy. This paper elaborates earlier efforts to use a Marxist theoretical framework to explore them (Patterson 1983, 1986). I argue that people are organized into social groups and that they satisfy culturally constituted needs through labor. Their labor and productive activity is social and always takes place within definite sets of property relations that grant powers of control and decision-making, that determine what gets produced and who receives it, that structure society, and that create conditions for conflict within and between groups over the control and appropriation of what is produced. The members of each generation are constrained by the pre-existing sets of social relations and conditions and work out their destinies in terms of the range of forms and choices available to them (Neale 1985:xvii-xviii).

More specifically, this essay is concerned with (1) the gradual appearance of food-producing economies in coastal Peru during the third and second millennia B.C., and (2) the social formations and conditions that preceded the apparently sudden crystallization of class-stratified, state-based societies—the rise of civilization—in that area between ca. 400 and 200 B.C. These were chronologically, and conceptually, distinct processes. Thus, the paper examines the historical development of a series of societies, whose economies ranged from foraging and fishing to farming and whose social relations were not based on exploitation. This means that, while there were technical divisions of labor—i.e., culturally constituted differences among those who fished, foraged, or farmed—in these societies, there was no class structure, or social division of labor, in which a group of persons, by virtue of controlling labor power and the means of production, consistently extracted labor or goods from the direct producers to sustain its members (de Ste. Croix 1981:42-45).

Thus, the societies considered here exhibited one or more forms of the communal mode of production. This implies that there was collective control and appropriation of the means of production, that individuals belonged to the community by virtue of their regular participation in activities and practices that gave meaning to their interdependence, and that there were no structural differences between producers and non-producers, since such a distinction describes given individuals in relation to a particular productive activity and disappears when the perspective is broadened to include a number of different events (Leacock 1982:159). The absence of a social division of labor between a class of producers and a class of non-producers implies there was no exploitation. However, this does not mean that these societies necessarily lacked status differences, that social relations were not oppressive on occasions, or even that wealth differentials were absent. In kin-based communal societies, individuals and groups occasionally do withdraw from direct labor and depend for periods of time on the labor of others; however, their ability to appropriate the labor of others is based on the continuing goodwill of the community, since their capacity or authority to do so reflects age, life status, or kin connections rather than force or control over the community's means of production. In kin-based communities, such dependency is fragile and must be continually renegotiated (Clastres 1987:189-218; Gailey 1987).

In all societies, production and consumption are connected processes. They are also continuous and perpetually repeated, since no society can cease to consume. Production is necessary for the maintenance of life. At the same time, the social forms that structure production also reproduce, recreate, or set up the conditions under which production can continue to take place. Thus, regardless of its form, every mode of production is also a mode of social reproduction. This means not only the reproduction of labor power, in the demographic sense, but also the reproduction of the social relations and conditions that organize work and other activities.

The diverse ecological habitats of the Andes and the ocean waters that sweep along their shore provided the raw materials the ancient inhabitants used to satisfy their needs. By extracting materials for use, they transformed the landscape and its raw materials, creating something that had not existed earlier. In the process of creating their world, they also changed themselves. The transformations were not uniform throughout the area but reflected the subtle but significant variations that result when peoples live in a highly diversified environment, have complex historical pasts and varied relations with their neighbors, and emphasize different elements of the forces and relations of production. Even slight differences of emphasis in the forces of production—the raw materials taken from the environment and the implements and labor power employed to transform them into useful items—can yield significant variations in the details of how labor is organized. They can affect the labor processes by introducing different forms of specialization and technical divisions of labor. Differences in the relations of production—whether the producers themselves own or control the means of production and their labor power, or whether these are controlled by another class that extracts goods or labor from them—constitute yet another source of variability.

The Transition from Appropriative to Food-Producing Economies in the Central Andes

The earliest Andean societies for which significant amounts of evidence are available seem to have manifested the communal mode of production. Information from Paloma and other contemporary sites on the central Peruvian coast, spanning a 3000 year-long period from ca. 6000 B.C. to 3250 B.C., can be used to establish a baseline for examining the transition from an appropriative to a food-producing economy in the central Andes (Benfer 1984, 1986; Donnan 1964; Moseley 1978; Patterson 1971; Quilter 1988).

Paloma Society

Excavations in habitation refuse deposits indicate that Paloma society had a subsistence economy that was dominated by fishing, littoral harvesting, hunting, and foraging; however, there is nothing intrinsic in these activities that tells us how work was organized. Analyses of coprolites and intestinal contents, as well as the low strontium content of skeletal remains from Paloma, attest to the dietary importance of marine resources (Benfer 1986:66; Quilter and Stocker 1983; Weir and Dering 1986:38). Some Paloma groups resided in permanent settlements, when the various resources they used were located in close proximity; others moved from place to place as seasonal resources became available. The Paloma site exhibits both residence patterns: an earlier phase characterized by seasonal occupancy and a later one, beginning by about 4400 B.C., with evidence of sedentary habitation (Benfer 1984:536).

The household was the basic unit of production and

consumption in Paloma society, judging by the presence of storage pits near domestic structures and the burials of men, women, and children beneath the floors of occupied houses, and by the presence of storage pits near these structures. The skeletal remains and grave goods indicate that, within households, there was a technical division of labor based on age and gender. The remains of adolescent and adult males frequently exhibit exostoses on the external auditory meatus, while females do not (Quilter 1988:21; Quilter and Stocker 1983:547-548). One circumstance that promotes the growth of these lesions is immersion in water with temperatures below 17.5° C, which are typical of the up-welling ocean-bottom waters along the coast of Peru (Tattersall 1985; Núñez, Chapter 16). This strongly suggests that adolescent boys and young men engaged in deep-water swimming and diving for molluscs, while girls and women did not. The presence of weaving implements in the graves of women and older men indicates that some tasks were age-related rather than gender-specific.

The technical division of labor based on age and gender meant that no individual in the community was able to procure or produce all of the goods essential for life. It necessitated cooperation—sharing the products of one's labor with one or more members of the opposite sex and different generations in return for a portion of the products of their labor. Kinship expresses the linkage between sharing and the division of labor (Siskind 1978). Each item that was acquired or produced—e.g., shellfish or twined mats—potentially moved through a circuit of individuals before it was used or consumed. In Paloma, the circuit through which some subsistence goods moved apparently involved the members of households: their adult men, adult women, and children. Marriage and filiation defined the membership and place of an individual in one of these domestic groups and, given the technical division of labor, determined his or her share of its production.

Households were relatively enduring social groups in Paloma society, judging by the practices of burying the dead beneath the floors of houses that were still in use, re-using old houses, or rebuilding them to conform to the outlines of earlier domestic structures. The durability of households as social units implies they exhibited developmental cycles reflecting changes over time in their size, composition, and organization. It further suggests that there were also long-term connections between the various households or domestic groups of a village or camp.

The small number of people who resided in Paloma settlements—estimated between 25 and 75 individuals—meant that the camps and villages were too small to be autonomous, independent demographic entities. The various bands and villages of the region were linked by matrimonial mobility as men and women moved between groups to find suitable mates, and the composition of the various settlements mirrored this practice. It also means that the relations of production and the relations of reproduction operated at different levels. While the real appro-priation of nature occurred at the level of the household and perhaps the village, neither level was able to ensure demographic replacement and the continuity of the community. Their social and demographic reproduction was underwritten by relations and practices that operated between, rather than within, the communities.

Toward the end of the 4th millennium B.C., the members of various Paloma communities began to cultivate plants—e.g., bottle gourds—that were originally domesticated elsewhere. Thus, land was transformed from an object of labor, provisioned by nature and providing immediate returns, into an instrument of labor—a major means of production—that yielded returns only after a series of labor investments over an extended period of time. The productivity of plant cultivation and agricultural activities was low, judging by the paucity of domesticated plant remains in refuse deposits. Cultivation was merely one of a number of economic practices; it could be adopted because the productivity of other subsistence activities, such as fishing or shellfish harvesting, was sufficient and reliable enough to allow these communities to pursue a marginally productive activity, like cultivation, which involved delayed use or consumption.

Conchas Society

A new form of communal society, called Conchas, emerged on the central Peruvian coast toward the end of the 4th millennium B.C. The economy of Conchas society, which lasted from ca. 3250 to 2350 B.C., was dominated by fishing and shellfish harvesting (Feldman 1980, 1985, 1987; Moseley 1975). The new forms of production which provided the foundations of the economy included: (1) the reorganization and increased productivity of labor processes associated with the extraction of marine resources—i.e., men's work, given the gender division of labor in Paloma society; (2) the development of new labor processes associated with agricultural production—especially of two inedible plants, cotton and gourds; (3) the manufacture of cotton nets, fish line, and textiles, activities associated with women and elderly men in Paloma society; (4) the crystallization of collective labor processes associated with the construction of platform mounds and architectural complexes, whose size placed them beyond the capacity of single households or villages; and (5) the circulation of economically important subsistence and industrial goods between specialized farming and fishing settlements.

Production and its spatial organization were transformed. Permanently occupied villages were established on the coast near rich fishing grounds. However, since agriculture was impossible or only marginally feasible around some of the fishing villages, the cultivation of cotton, gourds, and a few food plants was often carried out at some distance from them. This led to the formation of economically specialized farming and fishing villages. On the central Peruvian coast, it meant that, for at least part of the year, farmers resided and worked in hamlets located 15-20 km from fishing villages, such as Ancón, where agriculture was either marginal or impossible. Farmers grew the gourds that the fishing villagers used as net-floats and the cotton they spun to make fishlines, nets, and clothes. In return, the farmers received fish and marine molluscs from the inhabitants of the fishing villages. Unlike their Paloma predecessors, the economically specialized settlements of Conchas society were not self-sufficient, since neither the farming hamlets nor the fishing villages produced the whole range of goods used and consumed by their inhabitants.

This new territorial organization of production was not merely superimposed on the existing age- and gender-based division of labor characteristic of Paloma society, nor did it completely supplant and transform that arrangement by creating a new technical division of labor between farming and fishing villages. In those localities, where farming and fishing could be carried out by residents of the same village, the traditional division of labor may have persisted. Adolescent boys and men continued to fish and dive for molluscs, while the work of women focused on foraging and cultivation. However, in those communities where the loci of farming and fishing activities were spatially separated, the old gender-based, technical division of labor was transformed. In the new, economically specialized fishing communities, like Huaca Prieta, both men and women engaged in activities centered around the sea, judging by the fact that both sexes suffered from exostoses of the auditory meatus (Tattersall 1985). In inland farming settlements, like La Galgada which is actually somewhat later in time, males and females typically lacked exostoses, presumably since both engaged in farming rather than ocean fishing (Malina 1988:118). Thus, while the labor practices carried out in fishing villages and farming hamlets became more differentiated, the work activities of men and women within the same economically specialized settlement converged.

The relations of production and reproduction that developed in Conchas society did not replicate those that had existed earlier. They involved instead the elaboration of community-level relations and new forms of articulation with the domestic level, which was composed of the households where the real appropriation of raw materials and their transformation into usable goods still occurred. The community-level relations, previously manifested in the practices of matrimonial mobility, came to link economically specialized settlements composed of households, whose members were no longer able to produce all of the materials they consumed given the spatially organized, technical division of labor that had developed in the new kinds of villages. Community-level social relations permitted the inhabitants of the specialized settlements to acquire, on a regular basis, raw materials and goods from distant localities. Such relations were also involved in activities or projects that were beyond the capabilities of a single household or a small number of cooperating domestic groups—e.g., the construction of platform mounds, fish-

drying terraces, and the early stages of the large architectural complex at El Paraíso. The labor required for building each of the handful of platform mounds at Aspero or Río Seco exceeded 60,000 person-days, which was conceivably within the range of a few households with large numbers of productive members; however, the minimum of 1.9 million person-days of labor expended to built the stone structures at El Paraíso clearly surpassed that capacity and must have been raised at the level of the wider community (Feldman 1985, 1987; Patterson 1983). At the same time, community-level social relations apparently continued to function as the relations of reproduction.

La Florida Society

The shift to a truly agrarian economy in coastal Peru, in which the cultivation of food plants rather than fishing played the determinant role in shaping the economic structure, occurred during the time when U-shaped pyramids were built on the central and north-central coasts of Peru, ca. 2350 to 400 B.C. (Burger 1987, 1989; Patterson 1983; Williams 1985). For reference, this can be called La Florida society. Agricultural production, previously concerned mainly with cotton and gourds, was expanded to include greater varieties and quantities of cultivated plant foods. This laid the foundations for new forms of production and appropriation that built on the existing community-level relations and spatially organized, technical division of labor. The reproduction of La Florida society depended on the continued participation of households in community-level institutions and practices—such as the circulation of raw materials and foodstuffs, the construction of platform mounds, and participation in the festivities that occurred at these structures.

In terms of the productive forces, the crystallization of La Florida society involved the formation of additional economically specialized farming hamlets in localities with ecological conditions suited to the production of particular food crops, such as avocados, as well as the construction of water management systems in the mid-valleys and U-shaped platform mounds at inland localities. These pyramids, some of which took 6-7 million person-days of labor to erect, served as the loci for social practices—rituals, predictions, and offerings—that presumably established and maintained the culturally constituted conditions necessary for successful farming (Burger 1987; Patterson 1983; 1985; Ravines and Isbell 1976; Salazar-Burger and Burger 1983). The labor for building projects of this magnitude must have been appropriated at the level of a regional community, since none of the known settlements had populations that were large enough to complete them. The rate at which labor was appropriated for these projects, defined in terms of person-days of labor per year, was two to four times greater than it had been in Conchas society.

Production and the real appropriation of nature continued to occur at the household level. Storage pits and refuse deposits associated with residential structures, as well as toolkits placed in the graves of different individuals, attest to the continued importance of households as production-consumption units in everyday life. There is evidence, however, that the compositions of households, at least in some fishing villages, had changed.[1] The apparent three-fold increase in the size of consumption units at Ancón, from about 5 to 15 individuals, between ca. 2150 and 1400 B.C. suggests that its households were no longer composed simply of nuclear or stem families, even if they had been earlier (Patterson 1984). By contrast, the size of residential structures at Cardal, an inland U-shaped pyramid and village occupied from ca. 1150 to 800 B.C., suggests that its domestic groups may have been nuclear or stem families. Thus, households were apparently organized differently in fishing and farming settlements.

Many of the raw materials and foodstuffs circulated at the level of the regional community. The circulation of these items created the conditions and reproduced the social relations the communities needed to sustain themselves. However, not all of the goods produced by the households in a single village circulated at the level of the regional community. For example, pottery vessels, which were apparently manufactured by a number of individuals in each settlement, only occasionally circulated beyond the limits of their villages.[2]

Like Paloma, the Conchas and La Florida societies were not class-stratified. There is no evidence for inequalities exhibited by artifacts with restricted distributions in the societies; there is no evidence for a class-based distinction between center and countryside, even though economically specialized farming and fishing settlements existed in some localities; and there is no evidence for centralization or for the kinds of settlement hierarchies with multiple levels of decision-making of the kind posited for class-stratified, state-based societies (Patterson 1983; Burger 1987:373). There is also no evidence for a social division of labor in which the members of one social class exploited those of another by permanently appropriating either their labor or products; however, there is evidence from Cardal of differences in status or rank among its inhabitants—i.e., some were interred on the pyramid while others were buried in the residential area (Burger and Salazar-Burger, pers. com., 1990). There is also no evidence from La Florida sites that can be readily cited to support claims of class strug-gle—such as resistance—which is also a defining feature of state-based societies.

This reconstruction and explanation implies that the primary means of production in Conchas and La Florida societies were controlled and appropriated collectively by the community. It also means that each individual was dependent on the group as a whole for his or her continued well-being, and that all members participated directly but differently in the production, distribution, circulation, and consumption of the social product. In other words, like Paloma society, they also manifested the social relations

characteristic of a communal, kin-based mode of produc-tion.

Class and state formation, the expression of exploitation, occurred on the central Peruvian coast at the end of La Florida society rather than in its formative years. The community-level relations of production—which, in Conch-as society, ensured the maintenance and reproduction of a spatially organized economy and mobilized labor for communal construction projects—broke down between 400 and 200 B.C. Labor was no longer appropriated at the community-level for the construction of platform mounds that guaranteed agricultural success of the community as whole. Surplus labor and goods were redirected instead into new channels—the construction of forts, raiding, craft specialization, exchange, and the assertion of class, status, and regional differences. Archaeological evidence from other parts of the central Andes, dating between ca. 400 and 200 B.C. indicate that class-stratified, state-based societies and class struggle crystallized rapidly during this period—in a matter of years or decades rather than centuries or millennia.

Discussion

While the social relations of the Paloma, Conchas, and La Florida societies were continually reconstituted and significant social and economic changes occurred through time, the societies themselves exhibited a stability that must be measured in terms of centuries or even millennia rather than generations. Societies manifesting variants of the communal mode of production have the capacity to incorpo-rate transformations of the productive forces at the same time they resist the formation of hierarchies that permit exploitation (Patterson 1988). There was nothing inherent, in a teleological sense, in the social relations of La Florida society that would necessarily or automatically lead to the development of a class structure, a state apparatus, exploita-tion, and the crystallization of oppositional forces, class struggle, or resistance. Hence, describing the development of La Florida society or the tension between the relations of production and the relations of reproduction is not an entirely adequate account of early class and state formation on the central coast of Peru. It is still necessary to specify how and under what historically contingent conditions the old community-level relations of production and reproduc-tion dissolved and were reconstituted along new lines that facilitated the extortion of labor and/or goods from the members of one group by those of another.

Class and state formation promote uneven development. Ancient states, like modern ones, were characterized by conflicting priorities and continually shifting, unstable configurations of dominant and subordinate groups, whose relations were simultaneously structured by the will to power and by attempts to neutralize the legitimacy of such claims, by intergroup alliances and intragroup conflicts, by ethnogenesis and ethnocide, and by acquiescence and

185

resistance. Class and state formation involve the simultaneous dissolution of the old community-level relations of production and the constitution of new exploitative social relations that were linked to and sustained by the formation of the state, which ensured that bodies were counted for taxation and conscription, that taxes were collected, that internal dissent was suppressed or deflected outward toward other communities, that bureaucrats were selected, that production was reorganized into subsistence and tribute sectors, and that capitals were built.

At issue is how were small numbers of individuals able to transform themselves from being members of kin and residential groupings into masters who were able to dominate their kin and neighbors and appropriate their labor and goods. In Peru during the waning centuries of the 1st millennium B.C. this involved uneven development, and the consolidation of a number of small, regional entities, integrated by tribute extraction, whose attempted exactions were contested or opposed by kin-based communities on their peripheries. In the initial stages, the kin-based communities of the central Peruvian coast were on the margins of early states. What distinguished early Peruvian states from each other were differences in the capacities of their various ruling classes to extract labor and tribute from their own kin and neighbors and to impose their will over the kin-organized communities on their peripheries (Gailey and Patterson 1988).

Acknowledgments

This paper is an adaptation of an earlier, more extensive manuscript. It has profited from the insights and criticism of Barbara Bender, Robert Benfer, Michael Blake, Richard Burger, Stanley Diamond, Christopher Donnan, Robert Feldman, Christine Gailey, Peter Gran, Michael Moseley, Jeffrey Quilter, Peter Rigby, Karen Sacks, Lucy Salazar-Burger, and two anonymous reviewers.

Notes

1. At Ancón, there was steady increase in the volume of cooking vessels during the first five phases of the ceramic sequence, which probably spanned the period from ca. 2150 to 1400 B.C.. This shift was not accompanied by changes in the foods consumed, new culinary practices, or larger portions, since capacities of the plates and bowls remained relatively constant—i.e., about a liter—during this period. Assuming that 1000 cc represents a serving, then the volumes of the *ollas* increased from 9 servings in Ancón to 16 servings in Ancón 2, to 20 servings in Ancón 3-4, and to 30 servings in Ancón 5. If we assign a numerical value of two portions per individual, then the household units expanded from approximately 4-5 individuals in Ancón 1, to 8 individuals in Ancón 2, 10-11 individuals in Ancón 3-4, and 14-15 individuals in Ancón 5-6. The differences in the volumes of the cooking vessels are significant at the .001 level.

2. During the 2nd millennium B.C., there was a great deal of variability in the appearance of pottery vessels, both within and between settlements. The intrasite variability reflected different levels of skill, care in preparation, and concern with the final appearance of the objects. The intersite variations provide information about local village styles, the loci of manufacture, and the circulation of pots and materials they contained (Burger 1987:371).

References Cited

Benfer, R.
1984 The Challenges and Rewards of Sedentism: The Preceramic Village of Paloma, Peru. In *Paleopathology at the Origins of Agriculture*, edited by M. N. Cohen, and G. J. Armelagos, pp. 531-558. Academic Press, New York.
1986 Holocene Coastal Adaptations: Changing Demography and Health at the Fog Oasis of Paloma, Peru, 5000-7800 B.P. In *Andean Archaeology: Papers in Memory of Clifford Evans*, edited by R. M. Matos, S. A. Turpin, and H. H. Eling, Jr., pp. 45-64. Monograph No. 27. Institute of Archaeology, University of California, Los Angeles.

Burger, R. L.
1987 The U-Shaped Pyramid Complex, Cardal, Peru. *National Geographic Research* 3(3):363-375.
1989 Long Before the Inca. *Natural History*, February, pp. 66-73.

Clastres, P.
1987 *Society against the State; Essays in Political Anthropology*. Zone Books, New York.

de Ste. Croix, G. E. M.
1981 *The Class Struggle in the Ancient Greek World*. Cornell University Press, Ithaca.

Donnan, C. B.
1964 An Early House from Chilca, Peru. *American Antiquity* 32(2):137-144.

Eggan, F.
1950 *The Social Organization of the Western Pueblos*. The University of Chicago Press, Chicago.

Feldman, R. A.
1980 *Aspero, Peru: Architecture, Subsistence Economy, and Other Artifacts of a Preceramic Maritime Chiefdom*. Unpublished Ph.D. Dissertation, Department of Anthropology, Harvard University. Cambridge.
1985 Preceramic Corporate Architectural Evidence for the Development of Non-Egalitarian Social Systems in Coastal Peru. In *Early Ceremonial Architecture in the Andes*, edited by C. B. Donnan, pp. 71-92. Dumbarton Oaks Research Library and Collection, Washington, D.C.
1987 Architectural Evidence for the Development of Nonegalitarian Social Systems in Coastal Peru. In

The Origins and Development of the Andean State, edited by J. Haas, S. Pozorski, and T. Pozorski, pp. 9-14. Cambridge University Press, Cambridge.

Gailey, C. W.
1987 *Kinship to Kingship; Gender Hierarchy and State Formation in the Tonga Islands.* University of Texas Press, Austin.

Gailey, C. W., and T. C. Patterson
1988 State Formation and Uneven Development. In *State and Society: The Emergence and Development of Social Hierarchy and Political Centralization*, edited by J. Gledhill, B. Bender, and M. T. Larsen, pp. 77-90. Unwin Hyman, London.

Haas, J.
1987 The Exercise of Power in Early Andean State Development. In *The Origins and Development of the Andean State*, edited by J. Haas, S. Pozorski, and T. Pozorski, pp. 31-35. Cambridge University Press, Cambridge.

Leacock, E. B.
1982 Relations of Production in Band Society. In *Politics and History in Band Societies*, edited by E. Leacock and R. Lee, pp. 159-170. Cambridge University Press, Cambridge.

Lee, R. B.
1979 *The !Kung San: Men, Women, and Work in a Foraging Society.* Cambridge University Press, Cambridge.

Malina, R. M.
1988 Skeletal Materials from La Galgada. In *La Galgada: A Preceramic Culture in Transition*, by T. Grieder, A. Bueno Mendoza, C. Earle Smith, Jr., and R. M. Malina, pp. 103-124. University of Texas Press, Austin.

Marquardt, W.
1987 The Calusa Social Formation in Protohistoric South Florida. In *Power Relations and State Formation*, edited by T. C. Patterson, and C. W. Gailey, pp. 98-116. Archeology Section, American Anthropological Association, Washington.

Moseley, M. E.
1975 *The Maritime Foundations of Andean Civilization.* Cummings, Menlo Park.
1978 *Pre-Agricultural Coastal Civilizations of Peru.* Carolina Biological Supply Company, Burlington.

Neale, R. S.
1985 *Writing Marxist History: British Society, Economy and Culture since 1700.* Basil Blackwell, Oxford.

Oberg, K.
1973 *The Social Economy of the Tlingit Indians.* Monograph 55. American Ethnological Society, Washington, D.C.

Patterson, T. C.
1971 Population and Economy in Central Peru. *Archaeology* 24(4):316-321.
1983 The Historical Development of a Coastal Andean Social Formation in Central Peru, 6000 to 500 B.C. In *Investigations of the Andean Past*, edited by D. H. Sandweiss, pp. 21-37. Latin American Studies Program, Cornell University, Ithaca.
1984 The Ancón Shellmounds and Social Relations on the Central Coast of Peru during the Second Millennium B.C. Paper presented at the annual meeting of the Institute of Andean Studies. Berkeley.
1985 The Huaca La Florida, Rimac Valley, Peru. In *Early Ceremonial Architecture in the Andes*, edited by C. B. Donnan, pp. 59-69. Dumbarton Oaks Research Library and Collection, Washington, D.C.
1986 Class and State Formation: The Case of Pre-Incaic Peru. *Dialectical Anthropology* 10(3-4):275-282.
1987 Development, Ecology, and Marginal Utility in Anthropology. *Dialectical Anthropology* 12(1):15-31.
1988 La creación de la cultura en las formaciones sociales pre-estatales y no-estatales. *Boletín de Antropología Americana* 14:53-62.

Patterson, T. C. and E. P. Lanning
1964 Changing Settlement Patterns on the Central Peruvian Coast. *Nawpa Pacha* 2:113-123.

Price, T. D., and J. A. Brown (editors)
1985 *Prehistoric Hunter-Gatherers: The Emergence of Cultural Complexity.* Academic Press, New York.

Quilter, J.
1988 *Life and Death at Paloma: Society and Mortuary Practices in a Preceramic Peruvian Village.* University of Iowa Press, Iowa City.

Quilter, J., and T. Stocker
1983 Subsistence Economies and the Origins of Andean Complex Societies. *American Anthropologist* 85(3):545-562.

Ravines, R., and W. Isbell
1976 Garagay: un sitio ceremonial temprano en el Valle de Lima. *Revista del Museo Nacional* 41:253-275.

Raymond, J. S.
1981 The Maritime Foundations of Andean Civilization: A Reconsideration of the Evidence. *American Antiquity* 46(4):806-821.

Salazar-Burger, L., and R. L. Burger
1983 La araña en la iconografía del Horizonte Temprano en la costa norte del Perú. *Beitrage zur Allgemeinen und Vergleichenden Archaologie* 4:213-253.

Siskind, J.
1978 Kinship and Mode of Production. *American Anthropologist* 80(4):860-872.

Tattersall, I.
1985 The Human Skeletons from Huaca Prieta, with a Note on Exostoses of the External Auditory Meatus. In *The Preceramic Excavations at the Huaca Prieta, Chicama Valley, Peru*, edited by J. B. Bird, J. Hyslop, and M. D. Skinner, pp. 60-64. Anthro-

pological Papers No. 62. American Museum of Natural History, New York.

van der Leeuw, S. E. (editor)

1981 *Archaeological Approaches to the Study of Complexity*. Universiteit van Amsterdam, Amsterdam.

Weir, G. H., and J. P. Dering

1986 The Lomas of Paloma: Human-Environmental Relations in a Central Peruvian Fog Oasis: Archaeobotany and Palynology. In *Andean Archaeology: Papers in Memory of Clifford Evans*, edited by R. M. Matos, S. A. Turpin, and H. H. Eling, Jr., pp. 18-44. Monograph 27. Institute of Archaeology, University of California, Los Angeles.

Willey, G. R., and P. Phillips

1958 *Method and Theory in American Archaeology*. The University of Chicago Press, Chicago.

Williams, C.

1985 A Scheme for the Early Monumental Architecture of the Central Coast of Peru. In *Early Ceremonial Architecture in the Andes*, edited by C. B. Donnan, pp. 227-240. Dumbarton Oaks Research Library and Collection, Washington, D.C.

Wilson, D. J.

1981 Of Maize and Men: A Critique of the Maritime Hypothesis of State Origins on the Coast of Peru. *American Anthropologist* 83(1):93-120.

15

Archaic Period
Maritime Adaptations in Peru

Karen Wise

Introduction

It has long been known that the preceramic inhabitants of the south-central Andean Coast (Figure 1) relied on maritime resources for many of their subsistence needs. While researchers in the Central Andes found little evidence of coastal occupations that pre-dated 5000 B.P. (Moseley 1975), archaeologists working in Chile found ample evidence of Preceramic coastal occupations. Beginning with the first impressionistic accounts of subsistence remains at preceramic sites in the south-central Andes (Bird 1943, 1946; Uhle 1919) and extending to modern quantitative studies of subsistence remains from both the central and south-central Andes (Sandweiss et al. 1989; Schiappacasse and Niemeyer 1984), studies have provided ample evidence for the use of coastal resources. Models of Archaic period maritime subsistence have been developed by a number of scholars working in the Andes, but have been hampered by: (1) inconsistent chronological terminology (2) a lack of rigor in the identification and evaluation of resources, (3) the lack of a basic theoretical approach to subsistence and subsistence change, (4) regional differences in cultural development, and (5) the general lack of early preceramic sites on the coast of the central Andes. This paper addresses the development of maritime economies in the central and south-central Andes by providing a theoretical basis for the study of subsistence and subsistence change, and by applying it to an analysis of extant data on Archaic peoples in the region. The paper must be considered preliminary, since data relevant to detailed analysis of subsistence practices are few, but it does illuminate several general problems and processes relevant to the study of coastal Andean adaptations.

Theoretical Perspectives

The theoretical issues central to this research include: the potential for intensive maritime exploitation to provide a resource base for large populations; the importance of local environmental variation in influencing economic adaptations to the Andean coastal region; and the pathways that might lead to intensification of maritime exploitation, or

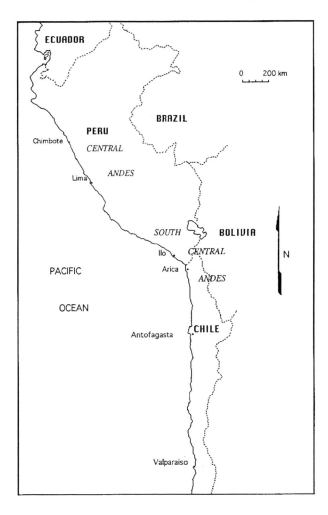

Figure 1. **The Central and South-central Coastal Andean Regions.**

189

other changes in subsistence strategies. In addition, more consideration must be given to the recognition of subsistence change, and accurate evaluation of changes in subsistence strategies as evidenced in the archaeological record.

Although many authors have pointed out the variation in coastal regions around the world, coastal environments often share a number of general characteristics which affect their human inhabitants, including high primary productivity, high resource density and diversity, overall environmental stability, and linear resource distribution (Yesner 1980; Perlman 1980). Perlman (1980) and Yesner (1980) suggest that these characteristics of coastal environments contribute to tendencies toward relatively sedentary communities, technological complexity, high population densities, and territoriality among coastal hunter-gatherers.

In Peru and northern Chile (Figure 1), a rich and diverse coastal environment created by the Peru Current System, is juxtaposed with one of the driest deserts in the world. This environment creates unique constraints for coastal hunter-gatherers, as well as a diverse range of resources. In addition to the linear distribution of marine and coastal resources, the scarcity of water and terrestrial resources is a critical factor in the development of maritime adaptations in this region. Thus, along the Andean Coast, the environmental characteristics suggested in more general studies of coastal regions are even more exaggerated. Archaeologists working in the region have viewed the terrestrial coastal environment, with it's sparse resources, as problematic, and the marine environment as being so rich that it attracted groups of hunter-gatherers to settle there (Llagostera 1979, 1989; Moseley 1975; Núñez 1983, Chapter 16).

In the central Andes, Moseley argues that abundant marine resources, "underwrote the most significant cultural changes that transpired...[and]...fostered a sedentary way of life and supported a marked growth in the size of the coastal population" (Moseley 1975:47). In the south-central Andes, archaeologists have long argued that maritime subsistence was a necessary adaptation to the desertic coast, since terrestrial resources were inadequate to support more than a very few people for short periods of time (Bird 1943, 1946; Núñez 1983), and that the availability and distribution of resources encourage a relatively sedentary lifestyle (Núñez, Chapter 16).

These features can be viewed in terms of characteristics considered important in determining human foraging strategies. Human foragers are expected to concentrate on those resources from which they can collect the most energy relative to the time they spend gathering the resource (Winterhalder 1981; Smith 1983). Resources with higher return rates are expected to be preferred by the forager, and are said to be highly ranked resources. Foragers are expected to concentrate on collecting highly ranked resources, as opposed to lower ranked resources, and they are not expected to utilize lower ranked resources unless encounter rates for higher ranked resources decrease. Thus it is the relative availability of highly ranked resources

which determines diet breadth. In environments with high prey encounter rates (rich environments), foragers are expected to be more selective, while in environments with lower encounter rates (poor or sparse environments), they should be less selective (Smith 1983).

Patches are the particular areas where resources are available. They are also expected to be utilized according to their relative return rates. Patches in use continue to be exploited until their return rates drop below the average return rates of other available patches (Pyke, Pulliam, and Charnov 1977; Winterhalder 1981; Smith 1983). Foragers are expected to concentrate their energies on more productive patches with relatively high return rates.

The juxtaposition of two contrasting ecosystems—one a rich marine environment, the other a dry desert—provides the extraordinary conditions of the central and south-central coastal Andes. The general features of both the marine and terrestrial environments are due largely to the Peru current system, which simultaneously produces the cold rich coastal waters, and creates an extremely arid coast by inhibiting rainfall up to at least 1,500 m in elevation (Bowman 1916; Robinson 1964; Schweigger 1964).

This environment provides a unique set of constraints and opportunities for hunting and gathering peoples. Most importantly, water is a limited resource along the coast, and its distribution determined early settlement locations on the coast. This also affects the distributions of edible plants which are found almost exclusively in the river valleys and *quebradas* (gulleys or washes), and seasonally in the *lomas* (hills with seasonal fog-fed vegetation). Terrestrial animals, especially the larger species, are also limited in distribution. Although birds and some smaller animals may be found year-round in and around river valleys, as well as on the coast, the most abundant locales would have been the *lomas*, but only seasonally. Thus marine resources, which are available year-round, and have high return-rates, are expected to have played an important role in Archaic subsistence practices.

These marine resources are dispersed, stable, abundant, predictable, and evenly distributed along the coastal strip. The year-round abundance of mollusks and fish provides a continuous source of animal resources (Fiedler 1944). Fish and mollusks are generally found in great numbers along the Peruvian coast, and many sea mammals inhabit the region seasonally. Birds, such as cormorants, pelicans, gulls, and gannets are found all along the coast. Foraging strategies directed toward these marine resources are expected to have had important influences on Archaic settlement systems.

Terrestrial resources are generally less abundant and possibly less predictable. Water is scarce but predictable, and was probably an important limiting factor in Archaic settlement. Edible plants may also have been a limiting resource. They too, would have been relatively scarce, but predictable, since they are found where there is water. Terrestrial fauna are scarce and unpredictable, but possibly less so during the late winter, when vegetation on the *lomas* is in bloom. They are, therefore, expected to have been exploited, especially since the return-rates of large terrestrial mammals should be higher than those of most coastal resources. However, they may not necessarily have determined settlement locations.

While there are several important general features of the Andean coastal environment, there is also significant variation at a local level. Local variation in environmental characteristics would have had varying impacts on maritime adaptations depending on the extent to which such variation affected the structure of resource distribution and/or the distribution of high return and other favorable (i.e., easily exploitable or low risk) resources. The abundance and reliability of coastal resources, especially in relation to nearby inland resources, would have affected local adaptations throughout the Andean coastal region.

The Andean Coast, along a narrow band from Chimbote in Peru to Valparaíso in Chile (Figure 1), is one of the driest deserts in the world. The desert becomes increasingly arid, moving from north to south, with considerable variation in the size and importance of river valleys (Robinson 1964). The south-central Andean region is the driest section of this coast.

The argument that the environmental structure of the Andean Coast led to maritime subsistence strategies has been made by a number of researchers (Bird 1943; Llagostera 1979; Moseley, Chapter 13; Núñez 1983, Chapter 16), but this argument alone cannot explain the processes of change that occurred during the Archaic period. A theoretical framework is necessary for understanding the processes of subsistence and cultural change that took place in the area, and to address such questions as why the changes took place?, and why was there so much variation from region to region? To develop this theoretical perspective, it is helpful to borrow from studies of hunter-gatherers that have been conducted in other areas.

Earle (1980) outlines two subsistence strategies that human groups follow as population pressure increases. These are "intensification," defined as increasing specialization on utilized resources, particularly those with high yields, and "diversification," the addition of new resources to those already being exploited. Christensen (1980) suggests that both processes will occur under conditions of population pressure, although there is a limit to the degree of diversification possible in almost any environment. When that limit is reached, intensification and specialization on resources with high potential yields is more likely to occur.

This perspective proves useful for studies of adaptations in the Andean coastal region, where the wide range of marine and coastal resources could be exploited through a variety of strategies. Although there has been little discussion of why population increased, the increasing number and size of coastal sites found in both the central and south-central Andes has often been cited as evidence of significant

population increase during this period (Moseley 1975; Núñez 1983). There is most certainly an increase in the exploitation of maritime resources through time, and this has often been described as a process of "maritime specialization" (Llagostera 1989; Moseley 1975; Núñez 1983). However, the process often described as specialization is not necessarily that. In fact, the expansion of the number of resources used is best described as a process of diversification. Llagostera (1989), building on the work of others (Craig 1982; Muñoz 1982), defines the diversification process that occurred on the south-central Andean Coast in terms of expansion of the range of areas exploited by Archaic peoples. He defines three phases of coastal exploitation, which appear successively throughout the Archaic period. These are: (1) "longitudinal" exploitation, where resources along the seashore can be hunted with harpoons, (2) "bathytudinal" exploitation, where marine fish are caught using hooks, and (3) "latitudinal" exploitation, where marine resources are hunted or fished using boats. Llagostera argues that subsistence remains from a number of sites in northern Chile suggest this successive pattern of expanding exploitation. This general process was one of diversification through technological innovation and changing subsistence strategies, not one of intensification.

Time Frame

The time period before the advent of ceramics has been variously referred to as the Archaic period (Núñez 1983, Chapter 16; Aldenderfer 1989, Chapter 17), the Preceramic period (Moseley 1975; Keatinge 1988), and the Lithic period (Lumbreras 1974). Variable and inconsistent use of these terms to describe a variety of cultural phenomena has led to a lack of consensus as to what to call this time period, and the cultural traits which define it. While Chilean scholars tend to follow North American usage, employing the terms Paleoindian and Archaic, many Peruvianists distinguish among three periods, the Lithic period, followed by the Archaic period, and finally the Cotton Preceramic period. Most archaeologists are in agreement that what is being discussed is the period before the use of ceramics. The other cultural characteristics of this time period, however, are regionally variable, and descriptions of this period are not universal enough to account for the variation. Most notably, sequences for northern Chile and for Peru have been developed virtually independently of one another.

The most extensive divisions were elaborated by Lanning (1967), who defined a coastal sequence extending from 12,000 B.C. to 2000 B.C. based upon seriation of lithic artifacts, many of which come from surface contexts. I will follow Chauchat (1988) in discarding this sequence, since it is more detailed than the evidence supports.

Lumbreras (1974) divides the Preceramic period into two cultural periods: the Lithic and the Archaic. These are distinguished from each other based on the presence or absence of agriculture. The Lithic period (21,000-4000

B.C.) refers to the era before full-scale use of agriculture, and the Archaic period (1300-500 B.C.) refers to the time when people became more dependent on domesticated plants and animals and more sedentary. Núñez (1983) divides the Preceramic period into Paleoindian and Archaic periods. The Paleoindian period is defined on the basis of the environment and subsistence adaptations. Paleoindians lived during the terminal Pleistocene-Early Holocene and generally subsisted on animals that are now extinct. Núñez defines the Archaic period as being a transitional period of experimentation with the resources that were to become the important Andean domesticates.

For the purposes of this paper, the Archaic period is defined as extending up to the beginning of large, aggregated settlement, about 2500 B.C. in Peru, and to the advent of pottery and agriculture in Chile around 1000 B.C. The focus is on hunting and gathering adaptations to the diverse environmental zones of the Andes. While this is a very broad definition of a diverse period in the cultural history of the Andes, it is hoped that a broad approach will allow comparisons across the Chile-Peru border, a focus on overall regional patterns of coastal subsistence and settlement, and an examination of local variations in the context of these broad cultural patterns.

Trends in Archaic Period Prehistory

In attempting to formulate an overall view of the coastal Andean Archaic period, it is necessary to take into account broad Andean cultural patterns as well as regional variation which is often very fine-grained. This is difficult given the dearth of coastal Archaic sites from central and northern Peru, and the resulting difficulty of studying subsistence and settlement systems in the central Andes. For this reason, coastal adaptations during the Archaic period are discussed from a southern perspective, with data from the north used wherever possible. Some of the features that are common to the coastal region throughout the central and south-central Andes are: (1) moderate reliance on fish and other maritime resources, beginning in the Early Archaic period or possibly the Late Paleoindian period (Chauchat 1988; Núñez, Varela, and Casamiquela 1983), (2) increasing reliance on maritime resources through the Middle Archaic period, with intensive exploitation of the ocean through the use of a highly specialized technology by the Late to Terminal Preceramic periods (Bird 1946; Núñez 1983; Weir, Benfer, and Jones 1988), (3) seasonal or relatively short-term occupation of base camps and habitational sites during the Early Archaic period, followed by increasingly permanent and substantial settlements by the Middle to Late Archaic periods (Núñez 1983, 1989), (4) experimentation with domestication of both plants and animals by the Middle to Late Archaic periods (Lynch 1983; Núñez 1983), (5) the development of sophisticated mortuary practices indicating the significance of a maritime focus by the Middle to Late Archaic periods (Bittmann 1982; Quilter 1989).

There are, however, distinct differences between the cultural patterns seen in central Peru and those seen in northern Chile, especially during the period after 3000 B.C. In Peru, numerous sites have been found which indicate increasing cultural complexity, including evidence of complex religious practices and centralized political entities between 2500 and 1800 B.C. (Feldman 1987; Fung 1988; Moseley 1975). In northern Chile, the period between 3000 and 1000 B.C. is one of aggregated settlements, intensive exploitation of resources, and complex religious practices including elaborate mummification of the dead (Núñez 1983, Chapter 16; Bittmann 1982), however population density was lower than it was in Peru, and political entities were smaller and less centralized.

Archaeological Evidence

Recent research throughout the Andean coastal zone has expanded greatly our knowledge of Preceramic period adaptations. The volume of recent work, combined with the increasing use of modern techniques of excavation and processing, such as the use of column samples and flotation, promise to make important contributions to an emerging picture of long-term coastal adaptations in the Andean region. To date, quantitative studies are rare, and the discussion that follows is based on the few data that are available. Figure 2 shows the locations of sites mentioned in the following discussion.

The earliest evidence of coastal occupations in the Andes comes from both the central and south-central Andes. Paleoindians and Early Archaic peoples appear to have inhabited the coast of the central Andes beginning around 13,000 B.P. (Chauchat 1988), as is indicated at such sites as Quirihuac Shelter, La Cumbre, and Paiján complex sites in the Cupisnique Desert that date roughly between 13,000 and 8000 B.P. (Chauchat 1988). Although these sites lie 20 to 100 km inland from what was the coastline 10,000 years ago (Richardson 1981), they do provide evidence of some use of the coastal region by early inhabitants of the Andes. The presence of mastodon at La Cumbre and lizards, fox, and vizcacha at Cupisnique sites indicate reliance on terrestrial fauna. The presence of fish remains at Paiján sites in the Cupisnique area leads Chauchat (1988:58) to suggest that Paiján projectile points might have been used for fishing. Unfortunately, coastal sites in the central Andes generally do not contain deep middens or substantial remains of marine resources. One reason for this is that many truly coastal sites,. those that were located within several kilometers of the ocean itself, have probably been lost due to post-Pleistocene sea level rise (Richardson 1981).

The Paleoindian occupation of Quereo, in northern Chile (Núñez et al. 1983, 1994) appears to have been intensive and long-term, with subsistence remains indicating heavy reliance on Pleistocene mammals, with some supplemental exploitation of fish. Radiocarbon dates for the Paleoindian levels at this site extend from 11,600 to 10,925 B.P.

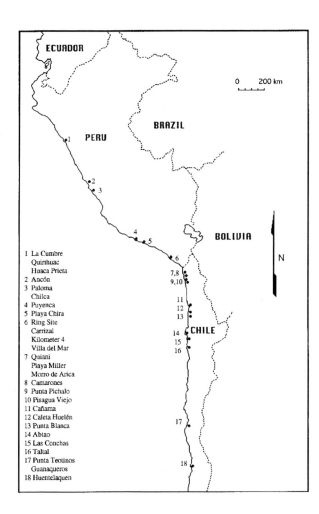

1 La Cumbre
  Quirihuac
  Huaca Prieta
2 Ancón
3 Paloma
  Chilca
4 Puyenca
5 Playa Chira
6 Ring Site
  Carrizal
  Kilometer 4
  Villa del Mar
7 Quiani
  Playa Miller
  Morro de Arica
8 Camarones
9 Punta Pichalo
10 Pisagua Viejo
11 Cañama
12 Caleta Huelén
13 Punta Blanca
14 Abtao
15 Las Conchas
16 Taltal
17 Punta Teotinos
  Guanaqueros
18 Huentelaquen

Figure 2.   **Archaic Period Sites in the Central and South-central Coastal Andean Regions.**

Early Archaic sites are relatively scarce, compared with later sites, although they are more common than Paleo-indian sites. In northern and central Peru, Paiján and other early lithic traditions extend well into the Archaic period, since Paiján tools were found in association with modern fauna (Chauchat 1988; Malpass 1983). In southern Peru, Ravines (1972) recorded several preceramic coastal sites which yielded evidence of Early Archaic habitation. These include Puyenca, with dates of 7855±150 B.P. and 8070±145 B.P., and Playa Chira I, with a single date of 8765 B.P. Although Ravines did not specifically discuss subsistence remains, he did mention that several of these sites were shell-middens. Early Archaic projectile points were found in the *lomas* of Ilo (Ravines 1972; Wise 1989), and radiocarbon dating of shell from the Ring Site suggests an Early Archaic occupation, where most of the subsistence remains were marine (Sandweiss et al. 1989). Early Archaic sites from northern coastal Chile include Las Conchas, Huentelauquén, and the earliest levels of Camarones 14 (see Núñez, Chapter 16). These sites provide evidence of the exploitation of both marine and terrestrial

resources, but there is little else known about them. Fish and shellfish were found at Huentelauquén (Núñez 1983), although there are few details available. At Las Conchas (Llagostera 1979) 24 marine species were recovered, including various mollusks, marine mammals, and coastal birds, as well as guanaco and some hallucinogenic seeds from inland plants. It is clear that these sites represent a substantial commitment to the exploitation of marine resources by Early Archaic peoples. The presence of coastal resources at inland sites such as Tiliviche (Núñez and Moragas 1978) supports this. The presence of artifacts similar in form and materials to those found inland is generally interpreted as reflecting a transhumant population which was only partially reliant on the coastal region or on coastal resources for subsistence (Aldenderfer 1989, Chapter 17; Núñez 1983, Chapter 16).

Middle Archaic sites from central and northern Peru are represented by lithic scatters in numerous areas. The Luz complex Ancón area sites discussed by Lanning (1963, 1967) date between 6000 and 7300 B.P. The best studied Middle and Late Archaic site is La Paloma in central Peru (Benfer 1986; Weir and Dering 1986; Reitz 1988; Weir et al. 1988; Quilter 1989). Research at this *lomas* site indicates long (7800-5000 B.P.) and intensive occupation by a group of hunter-gatherers who exploited marine fauna intensively, and also used *lomas* flora and fauna (Reitz 1988; Weir and Dering 1986).

Middle Archaic sites in the south-central Andes include many sites that indicate increasing reliance on marine resources combined with increasing specialization and diversification of technology devoted to the exploitation of the marine environment. Coastal sites providing these data include the Ring Site, in southern Peru, and Quiani, Camarones 14, and Punta Pichalo in northern Chile, as well as numerous other sites, such as Cerro Colorado, Punta Blanca, and Morada which are not yet well studied.

Quiani is a well-known shell-midden which is the type site for Bird's (1943;1946) "Shell Fish-hook Culture" and "Cactus Thorn Fish-hook Culture." The midden contained abundant fish remains, shellfish, sea mammals, and birds (Bird 1943). The only terrestrial fauna found were guanaco bones used for artifacts (Bird 1943; Dauelsberg 1974; Llagostera 1979).

At Camarones 14, a shell-midden on the south side of the Río Camarones, remains of 9 species of fish were found, along with sea mammals, 19 species of shellfish, and 6 species of birds (Schiappacasse and Niemeyer 1984). Guanaco, vizcacha, and vicuña were also found in this richer terrestrial environment. Maritime subsistence is also indicated at the other probable Middle Archaic sites.

Although there are few data for the Middle Archaic period from the central Andes, research at Paloma suggests that the exploitation of maritime resources was an important component of the Middle Archaic coastal economy. Coastal subsistence seems to have been based on a mix of marine and terrestrial resources. Maritime fishing and hunting were clearly culturally significant, as indicated by the presence of fishing gear and sea mammal bones in human graves at Paloma (Quilter 1989). Research in the south-central Andes indicates a substantial cultural importance of the ocean environment as evidenced by the complex and sophisticated practices of the Chinchorro complex (Bittmann 1982).

Late Archaic (Late Preceramic) coastal sites are much more common in both Peru and Chile than Early and Middle Archaic sites. They provide evidence of nucleated settlements, the development of substantial architecture, and artificial mummification as well as the inclusion of rich grave goods in burials (Llagostera 1989; Núñez 1983; Bittmann 1982).

In the Central Andes, 5000 B.P. has long been considered the initial date for the appearance of coastal adaptations. The scenario developed in the Maritime Hypothesis for the development of Andean Civilization posits intensive occupation of the coast beginning about 5000 B.P., accompanied by intensive exploitation of the marine and coastal environment for subsistence. Lanning's (1963) survey of the Ancón region defined the Encanto phase, characterized by maritime and terrestrial resource exploitation. The type site, Encanto, revealed large quantities of fish bone, as well as mollusk shell, cervid bone, and terrestrial plant remains (Moseley 1975). Lanning (1967) dates the Encanto phase at 3600-2500 B.C., based on dates obtained from a site in the Chilca region which contained the remains of ocean resources.

This phase is contemporaneous with sites such as Huaca Prieta de Chicama (Bird 1948), Chilca (Donnan 1964), and probably Asia (Engel 1963). At Chilca, which dates to about 5000 B.P., fish and shellfish were found, along with the remains of sea-lions, which Donnan suggests were a main source of meat. Whale bone was used to support the houses. In addition, Donnan illustrates a cactus-spine fish-hook and shell beads. The house sat atop a substantial shell-midden, indicating some time depth for maritime adaptations at the site.

In the south-central Andes, ongoing work at the sites of Kilometer 4 and Carrizal suggest heavy reliance on ocean resources even in spring-fed areas that might be expected to produce substantial quantities of terrestrial resources.[1] At Carrizal, a Late Archaic shell-midden with dates of 4390 ± 110 B.P. (Beta-18920) and 4690 ± 120 (Beta-27417) and at Kilometer 4, a similar site where a sample from one of the deepest strata yielded a date of 4620 ± 90 (Beta-27416), preliminary analysis revealed large percentages of fish bone, as well as sea mammal bone and shells, and some bird bone. Flotation of column samples produced significant samples of seeds and other plant remains, but there was very little evidence of terrestrial fauna from either site. Research at the Late Archaic site of Villa del Mar produced the remains of at least one harpoon (Torres et al. 1986) and this site contained ample but as yet unstudied remains of marine organisms (Watanabe, personal communication, 1989).

Farther south, desert coast sites, including Abtao-1, Cáñamo, and La Herradura, contained marine resources almost exclusively. The sites found near river valleys, such as Caleta Huelén 42, Guanaqueros, and Punta Teotinos, tend to have a greater range of terrestrial plants and animals as well as fish, shellfish, and marine mammals. They also tend to be more substantial, containing houses and cemeteries. This suggests a pattern of habitation in favorable areas, and specialized use of other coastal areas.

Inland sites (up to 80 km from the shore) along four *quebradas*: Camarones, Tiliviche, and Tarapacá, have also produced substantial evidence of coastal exploitation from their Early and Middle Archaic components (Núñez 1983). Depending on the environment in which the sites are located, there were also remains of local terrestrial resources. At Tiliviche, 950 m in elevation, Núñez (1983; Núñez and Zlatar 1978) found plant remains representing items immediately available in the vicinity of the *quebrada*. The faunal remains included guinea pig and other rodents as well as camelids, and relatively large amounts of marine animals, including shellfish, seals, and ocean birds. At Aragón, located 34 km from the ocean at an elevation of 1,100 m, most of the faunal remains were marine fish (Núñez and Zlatar 1978).

Evaluating Changes in Subsistence Strategies

It should be clear from the foregoing discussion that coastal sites from the central and south-central Andes contain substantial remains of marine resources and evidence of ocean-oriented technology. The trend appears to be one of increasing elaboration of ocean-oriented technology, and expansion of exploitation of ocean resources. Llagostera (1989) has presented a framework for analysis of marine niches by defining littoral resource patches in terms of increasing difficulty of access, and increasing technological requirements. An examination of species exploited from the few sites with quantitative data should also prove illuminating.

As noted above, in spite of the relatively large number of Archaic period sites that have been studied, especially in the south-central Andes, there are few quantitative data available on Archaic subsistence remains. This makes it difficult to evaluate subsistence strategies of Archaic peoples. What data are available, however, suggest that coastal peoples focused increasingly on marine resources throughout the Archaic period.

Table 1 lists the number of identified taxa from the seven Archaic coastal sites from which these data are available. These sites are not from comparable environmental areas, nor are the samples from each site the same. The data do not show any strong temporal trends. This is not to say that comparisons cannot be useful, but that they need to be made using comparable units, and preferably among sites from similar environmental settings. In addition, evaluation of subsistence strategies must be based on detailed information

Table 1. Number of Identified Taxa from Seven Archaic Period Sites.

Site	Terrestrial Mammals	Marine Mammals	Birds	Fish	Shellfish
Paloma	3	1	4	13	13
Ring Site	2	3	9	12	23
Camarones-14	5	3	6	9	19
Carrizal	2	1	5	17	20
Las Conchas	1	2	?	24	?
Abtao-1	?	2	?	9	?
Punta Blanca	?	?	?	9	?

about species present, including knowledge of behavior that could be used to discuss the methods of capture.

The presence of marine resources was discovered at sites dating as early as the Paleoindian period. These remains are sparse, but they do indicate knowledge and exploitation of the marine environment by early inhabitants of the Andean Coast. Beginning during the Archaic period, exploitation of marine resources grew in significance. There is little evidence of specialized technology geared toward the exploitation of the marine environment at this time. Subsistence strategies were based on shoreline collecting and harpooning: Llagostera's longitudinal exploitation strategy.

By the Middle Archaic period, maritime subsistence practices are represented both in the faunal remains and in the fishing technology (i.e., Bird's Shell Fish-hook and Cactus Fish-hook stages). During this period, there exists clear evidence of fish-hooks and lines, technology which extends both the range of species and areas that can be exploited. The use of nets is also implied by this kind of exploitation, although we have little direct evidence for them. It is not until the Late Archaic period that the presence of numerous small fish, such as anchovy, indicates the regular use of nets.

In Llagostera's scheme, the advent of rafts or boats allows the expansion of areas exploited to include those previously unavailable, even by the use of lines and nets from shore.

Although the quantitative data are not conclusive, research to date suggests an continual expansion of the range of marine patches that were exploited. Also, technology became more specialized, with an increasing number of tools and implements that were useful only for the exploitation of ocean resources. This process is best described, in general terms, as one of diversification, the addition of new resources to the repertoire of those already exploited.

Conclusions

As a habitat for hunter-gatherers, the Andean littoral zone is a coastal desert with access to rich and varied maritime resources. The course of earlier Andean prehistory reflects a pattern of adaptation to this environment based on increasingly intensive exploitation of the marine and coastal resources by groups of increasingly sedentary hunter-gatherers. In spite of years of research on Preceramic coastal adaptations, much remains unknown about subsistence patterns due to the general lack of systematic studies on subsistence remains, and to the late arrival of such techniques as flotation and nutritional analysis of human remains. It is only within the last five to ten years that Andean archaeologists working on the coast have begun to employ these techniques, which have greatly increased our ability to understand prehistoric subsistence patterns in the Andes. Such studies as those conducted at Quereo (Núñez et al. 1983) and at Paloma (Benfer 1986; Reitz 1988; Weir et al. 1988; Weir and Dering 1986) are providing crucial quantitative and qualitative data on prehistoric subsistence that will allow archaeologists to further refine their studies of the Andean Preceramic.

As a preliminary model, I would suggest a pattern, common throughout the central and south-central Andes, of coastal population increase, leading to diversification and expansion of resources exploited, until the period of approximately 5000 B.P., when such diversification was no longer possible. Specialization and intensification of exploitation of particular high-yield resources–possibly including anchovy–then became important. Along with this change in subsistence and economic strategies came aggregated settlements, leading to more complex social, political, and religious forms throughout the Andes, but particularly in the central Andes.

Testing this as a general model will require continued and expanded use of modern techniques of subsistence and settlement studies, as well as demographic analysis. In addition, future studies should be informed by the ever-increasing body of theory on hunter-gatherer subsistence and settlement (Price and Brown 1985; Christensen 1980; Jochim 1981; Winterhalder 1981), as well as the more specialized studies on coastal archaeology (Braun 1974; Perlman 1980; Yesner 1980). Discussions of technological specialization should be guided by studies such as those of Oswalt (1976), Torrence (1983) and others (Torrence 1989). By applying theory and methodologies that have proven useful elsewhere to regional studies in the Andes we should be able to move beyond general and untestable theories of "maritization," and begin to understand the cultural processes involved in the development of distinctly Andean economic, social, and political forms along the coast.

Acknowledgments

The ideas expressed in this paper are the product of

195

several years of working in the south-central Andes. Mark Aldenderfer first provided me with the opportunity to work there in 1984, and his continued support has allowed me to pursue my interest in the coastal region. The work done in Moquegua was supported by Northwestern University Research Grants and by NSF grant BNS-8822261 to him and by a Northwestern University Dissertation Year Grant to me. The Southern Peru Copper Corporation also supported the work through Programa Contisuyo. I am indebted to Michael Moseley, Robert Feldman, and Garth Bawden for sharing data and ideas with me at all stages of my research. Guillermo Rodríguez both worked with me in the field and provided invaluable information on the natural history and environment of southern Peru. Students and volunteers who participated in the field and laboratory work included Gladys Bareto, Mary Bareto, Augusto Cardona, Gerardo Felipe Carpio, Cecilia Chavez, Elaine Huebner, Simon Krause, Marina Lungstrom, Shawn Penman, Marcela Rodriguez, Gisela Swartz, David Swartz, and Carlos Vela. Elizabeth Reitz analyzed the vertebrate fauna from Carrizal and has discussed the faunal remains and their implications with me on numerous occasions. Finally, Mark Aldenderfer, Michael Blake, and Lawrence Kuznar read drafts of this paper at various stages and provided very useful comments and criticism.

Note

1. See Wise(1990) and Wise et al. (1994) for a recent summary of work at these sites.

References Cited

Aldenderfer, M. S.
1989 The Archaic Period in the South-Central Andes. *Journal of World Prehistory* 3(2):117-158.
Benfer, R. A.
1986 Holocene Coastal Adaptations: Changing Demography and Health at the Fog Oasis of Paloma, Peru 5,000-7,800 B.P. In *Andean Archaeology*, edited by R. Matos M., S. A. Turpin, and H. H. Eling, pp. 45-64. Monograph No. 27. Institute of Archaeology, University of California, Los Angeles.
Bird, J.
1943 Excavations in Northern Chile. *Anthropological Papers of the American Museum of Natural History* 38:171-318.
1946 The Cultural Sequence in the Northern Chilean Coast. In *Handbook of South American Indians* vol. 2, edited by J. Steward, pp. 587-594. Bureau of American Ethnology, Washington, D.C.
1948 Preceramic Cultures in Chicama and Virú. In *A Reappraisal of Peruvian Archaeology*, edited by W. C. Bennett, pp. 21-28. SAA Memoirs No. 4. Society for American Archaeology, Washington, D.C.

Bittmann, B.
1982 Revisión del Problema Chinchorro. *Chungará* 9: 46-79.
Bowman, I.
1916 *The Andes of Southern Peru.* Henry Holt and Company, New York.
Braun, D. P.
1974 Explanatory Models for the Evolution of Coastal Adaptation in Prehistoric Eastern New England. *American Antiquity* 39(4):582-596.
Chauchat, C.
1988 Early Hunter-Gatherers on the Peruvian Coast. In *Peruvian Prehistory*, edited by R. W. Keatinge, pp. 41-66. Cambridge University Press, Cambridge.
Christensen, A. L.
1980 Change in the Human Food Niche in Response to Population Growth. In *Modeling Change in Prehistoric Subsistence Economies*, edited by T. K. Earle and A. L. Christensen, pp. 31-72. Academic Press, New York.
Craig, A. K.
1982 Ambiente Costero del Norte de Chile. *Chungará* 9:4-21.
Dauelsberg, H. P.
1974 Excavaciones Arqueológicos en Quiani, Provincia de Tarapacá, Departamento de Arica, Chile. *Chungará* 4:7-38.
Donnan, C.B.
1964 An Early House from Chilca, Peru. *American Antiquity* 30:137-144.
Earle, T. K.
1980 A Model of Subsistence Change. In *Modeling Change in Prehistoric Subsistence Economies*, edited by T. K. Earle and A. L. Christensen, pp. 1-29. Academic Press, New York.
Engel, F.
1963 A Preceramic Settlement on the Central Coast of Peru: Asia, Unit 1. *Transactions of the American Philosophical Society* 53(3):3-139. Philadelphia.
Feldman, R.
1987 Architectural Evidence for the Development of Nonegalitarian Social Systems in Coastal Peru. In *The Origins and Development of the Andean State*, edited by J. Haas, S. Pozorski, and T. Pozorski, pp.9-14. Cambridge University Press, Cambridge.
Fiedler, R.
1944 The Peruvian Fisheries. *The Geographical Review* 34:96-119.
Fung., R.
1988 The Late Preceramic and Initial Period. In *Peruvian Prehistory*, edited by R. W. Keatinge, pp. 67-96. Cambridge University Press, Cambridge.
Jochim, M. A.
1981 *Strategies for Survival.* Academic Press, New York.

Keatinge, R.W. (editor)
1988 *Peruvian Prehistory.* Cambridge University Press, Cambridge.

Lanning, E. P.
1963 A Pre-Agricultural Occupation on the Central Coast of Peru. *American Antiquity* 28:360-371.
1967 *Peru before the Incas.* Prentice-Hall, Englewood Cliffs, New Jersey.

Llagostera, A.
1979 9,700 Years of Maritime Subsistence on the Pacific; an Analysis by Means of Bioindicators in the North of Chile. *American Antiquity* 44:309-324.
1989 Caza y Pesca Maritima. In *Culturas de Chile, Prehistória*, edited by J. Hidalgo, V. Schiappacasse, H. Niemeyer, C. Aldunate, and I. Solomano, pp. 57-79. Editorial Andrés Bello, Santiago.

Lumbreras, L.
1974 *The Peoples and Cultures of Ancient Peru.* Translated by B. J. Meggers. Smithsonian Institution Press, Washington, D.C.

Lynch, T. F.
1983 The Paleo-Indians. In *Ancient South Americans*, edited by J. D. Jennings, pp. 87-137. W. H. Freeman and Co., New York.

Malpass, M. A.
1983 The Preceramic Occupations of the Casma Valley, Peru. In *Investigations of the Andean Past*, edited by D. H. Sandweiss, pp. 1-20. Latin American Studies Program, Cornell University, New York.

Moseley, M. E.
1975 *The Maritime Foundations of Andean Civilization.* Cummings, Menlo Park.

Muñoz, I.
1982 Las Sociedades Costeras en el Litoral de Arica Durante el Período Arcáico Tardío y sus Vinculaciones con la Costa Peruana. *Chungará* 9:124-151.

Núñez, L.
1983 Paleoindian and Archaic Cultural Periods in the Arid and Semiarid Regions of Northern Chile. In *Advances in World Archeology,* vol. 2, edited by F. Wendorf and A. Close, pp. 161-203. Academic Press, New York.
1989 Hacia la Producción de Alimentos y la Vida Sedentaria. In *Culturas de Chile, Prehistoria*, edited by J. Hidalgo, V. Schippacasse, H. Niemeyer, C. Aldunate and, I. Solomano R., pp. 81-105. Editorial Andrés Bello, Santiago.

Núñez, L., and C. Moragas
1978 Occupación Arcáica Temprana en Tiliviche, Norte de Chile (I Region). *Boletín del Museo Arqueológico de La Serena* 16:53-76.

Núñez, L., J. Varela, and R. Casamiquela
1983 *Ocupación Paleoindio en Quereo (IV región): Reconstrución Multidisciplinária en el território semiárido de Chile.* Univ. del Norte, Antofagasta.

Núñez, L., J. Varela, R. Casamiquela, and C. Villagrán
1994 Reconstrucción multidisciplinaria de la ocupación prehistórica de Quereo, centro de Chile. *Latin American Antiquity* 5(2):99-118.

Núñez, P., and V. Zlatar
1978 Actividades en la Communidad de Pisagua (Período Preceramico). *Boletín del Museo Arqueológico de La Serena* 16:42-52.

Oswalt, W.
1976 *An Anthropological Analysis of Food-Getting Technology.* Wiley Interscience, New York.

Perlman, S. M.
1980 An Optimum Diet Model, Coastal Variability, and Hunter-Gatherer Behavior. In *Advances in Archaeological Method and Theory*, vol. *3*, edited by M. B. Schiffer, pp. 257-310. Academic Press, New York.

Price, T. D., and J. A. Brown (editors)
1985 *Prehistoric Hunter-Gatherers.* Academic Press, New York.

Pyke, G. H., H. R. Pulliam, and E. L. Charnov
1977 Optimal Foraging: a Selective Review of Theory and Tests. *Quarterly Review of Biology* 52:137-154.

Quilter, J.
1989 *Life and Death at Paloma.* University of Iowa Press, Iowa City.

Ravines, R.
1972 Secuéncia y Cambios en los Artifactos Líticos del Sur del Peru. *Revista del Museo Nacional* 38:133-184.

Reitz, E. J.
1988 Faunal Remains from Paloma, an Archaic Site in Peru. *American Anthropologist* 90:310-322.

Richardson, J. B. III
1981 Modeling the Development of Sedentary Maritime Economies on the Coast of Peru: A Preliminary Statement. *Annals of the Carnegie Museum* 50:139-150.

Robinson, D. A.
1964 *Peru in Four Directions.* American Studies Press, Lima.

Sandweiss, D. H., J. B. Richardson III, E. J. Reitz, J. T. Hsu, and R. A. Feldman
1989 Early Maritime Adaptations in the Andes: Preliminary Studies at the Ring Site, Peru. In *Ecology, Settlement, and History in the Osmore Drainage, Peru,* edited by D. S. Rice, C. Stanish, and P. R. Scarr, pp. 35-84. BAR International Series 545. British Archaeological Reports, Oxford.

Schiappacasse, V., and H. Niemeyer
1984 *Descripción y Análisis Interpretivo de un Sitio Arcáico Temprano en la Quebrada de Camarones.* Publicación Ocasional Nm. 41. Museo Nacional de História Natural, Universidad de Tarapacá.

Schweigger, E.

1964 *El Litoral Peruano*. Universidad Nacional Frederico Villareal, Lima.

Smith, E. A.

1983 Anthropological Applications of Optimal Foraging Theory: A Critical Review. *Current Anthropology* 24:625-651.

Torrence, R.

1983 Time Budgeting and Hunter-Gatherer Technology. In *Hunter-Gatherer Economy in Prehistory: A European Perspective*, edited by B. Bailey, pp. 11-22. Cambridge University Press, Cambridge.

Torrence, R. (editor)

1989 *Time, Energy, and Stone Tools*. Cambridge University Press, Cambridge.

Torres, E., C. O. Clement, N. R. Clark, and J. C. Tello**

1986 Informe Preliminar de un Entierro Precerámico Doble en Viña del Mar. *Resumen* I. Encuentro Arqueología Regional, Ilo, Peru.

Uhle, M.

1919 La Arqueología de Arica y Tacna. *Boletín de la Sociedad Ecuatoriana de Estudios Históricos Americanos* 7-8. Quito.

Weir, G. H., R. A. Benfer, and J. G. Jones

1988 Preceramic to Early Formative Subsistence on the Central Coast. In *Economic Prehistory of the Central Andes*, edited by E. S. Wing and J. C. Wheeler, pp. 56-94. BAR International Series 427. British Archaeological Reports, Oxford.

Weir, G. H. and J. P. Dering

1986 The *lomas* of Paloma: Human-Environmental Relations in a Central Peruvian Fog Oasis: Archaeobotany and Palynology. In *Andean Archaeology*, edited by R. Matos M., S. A. Turpin, and H. H. Eling, pp. 18-44. Monograph No. 27. Institute of Archaeology, University of California, Los Angeles.

Winterhalder, B.

1981 Optimal Foraging Strategies and Hunter-Gatherer Research in Anthropology: Theory and Models. In *Hunter-Gatherer Foraging Strategies*, edited by B. Winterhalder, and E. A. Smith,. pp. 13-35. University of Chicago Press, Chicago.

Wise, K.

1989 Archaic Period Research in the Lower Osmore Drainage. In *Ecology, Settlement, and History in the Osmore Drainage, Peru,* edited by D. S. Rice, C. Stanish, and P. R. Scarr, pp. 85-100. BAR International Series 545. British Archaeological Reports, Oxford.

1990 *Late Archaic Period Maritime Subsistence Strategies in the South-Central Andes.* Unpublished Ph.D. dissertation, Department of Anthropology, Northwestern University, Evanston.

Wise, K., N. R. Clark, and S. R. Williams

1994 A Late Archaic Period Burial from the South-Central Andean Coast. *Latin American Antiquity* 5(3):212-227.

Yesner, D. R.

1980 Maritime Hunter-Gatherers: Ecology and Prehistory. *Current Anthropology* 21:727-750.

16

Archaic Adaptation on the South-Central Andean Coast

Lautaro Núñez

Introduction

The Archaic populations of the coast of the south-central Andean area (Figure 1) present a cultural sequence lasting from the 9th to the 4th millennium B.P. in one of the world's most arid regions between Ilo, Peru and Taltal, Chile. Using a stratigraphic approach, this chapter will describe a series of cultural stages defined on the basis of diverse adaptive, cultural, and ideological factors. These stages constitute a distinctive cultural and productive process of increasing reliance on maritime resources, a process quite distinct from that of agricultural evolution found in other parts of the New World. The ancient fisher-gatherer-hunters of the Pacific Coast gradually adapted to the maritime resources, becoming highly efficient in their exploitation and eventually becoming semi-sedentary (Yesner 1980; Núñez 1983; Llagostera 1979a, 1979b). The nature of this process, in relation to the characteristics of the coastal environment in the south-central Andean area, will be reviewed below.[1]

Environmental Considerations and the Exploitation of Resources

The South-Central Andean coast, characterized by the flow of cold, nutrient-rich, sub-antarctic water, known as the Humboldt Current, provides easy access to abundant food resources for fisher-hunter-gatherers (Moseley, Chapter 13). This pattern, which exhibits less seasonal variation compared to that of inland or mediterranean environments, occurs both near-shore as well as in deeper waters off-shore (Perlman 1980; True 1975).

Species diversity has remained stable during the Pleistocene and Holocene, and oceanographic characteristics did not vary greatly from those of today (Herm 1969; Craig 1982). Nevertheless, at least from the beginning of the Holocene, there is evidence of thermal fluctuations or intermittent incursions of currents of warm water which disrupted the cold Humboldt Current (see also Moseley, Chapter 13; Wise, Chapter 15). This produced a detrimental, temporary, disequilibrium of the ecosystem by displacing marine fauna: the so-called "El Niño." These thermal fluctuations also generate a true "desertification" or critical loss of resources along the south-central coast (Llagostera 1989; Núñez 1983). However, even during El Niño events, these variations only affected restricted localities, leaving large expanses of the coast productive.

It has been proposed that marine resources were more reliable than terrestrial resources because they exhibited less seasonality (Perlman 1980). This is partly because the sea provides such a diverse range of foodstuffs, some of which were obtained with sophisticated and clever fishing technologies (i.e., hooks and nets) and others of which were harvested using simpler techniques such as shellfish gathering (Núñez 1986; Meehan 1977). This notion of the availability and reliability of marine resources has provoked considerable debate concerning the hypothesis that, in the central Andean coastal area, non-agricultural civilizations arose during Late Archaic times (Moseley 1975; Raymond 1981). Nevertheless, the technological developments of the central Andean coastal peoples did not surpass similar developments along the south-central coast. Although the Late Archaic populations of the south-central coast did not achieve as high a degree of stratification and social complexity as their neighbors to the north, they did develop a remarkably high degree of technological efficiency in exploiting marine resources.

During the early post-glacial period the climate along this section of coast seems to have been more moist than at present. This may have helped increase the vegetation cover on the *lomas* (low hills) in southern Peru, and may also have led to an increase in the extent of the "fog oasis" vegetation in the western foothills of the coastal *cordillera* in northern Chile. For Archaic period hunter-gatherers, these conditions improved the quantities of economically important terrestrial plant resources, including cacti,

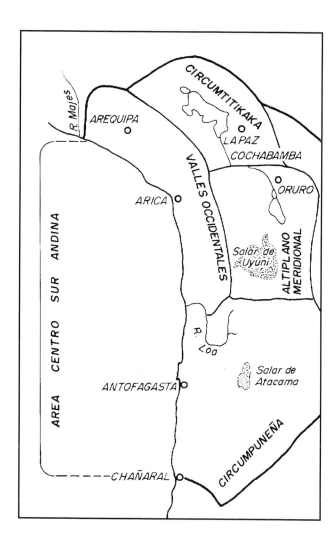

Figure 1. Location of the South-Central Andean Coast.

of inland sites, they were only occupied seasonally, probably by small groups or "work parties" who set up temporary camps, and then returned to the larger settlements on the coast (True et al. 1970; Núñez and Moragas 1978; Núñez and Hall 1982; Núñez and Zlatar 1976).

The marine resources of the south-central coast were exploited by two successive modes (Núñez 1973; Llagostera 1989; Bailey 1981). The first was the opportunistic exploitation of areas rich in resources close to the shore using simple fishing and gathering technology. The second was a more direct and conscious exploitation of resources beyond the inter-tidal zone. This second mode required the use of more sophisticated hunting and fishing skills and tools such as harpoons, fish-hooks, rafts, and nets. These skills and tools were added gradually over the millennia: each technological innovation depending on local ecological and cultural conditions. For example, by the 5th millennium B.P. on the Arid Coast of Abtao, fisher-folk were highly skilled in the use of fish-hooks (Llagostera 1982); while during the same period, the fisher-folk of the Fertile Coastal site of Morro 1 (Arica) were expert harpoonists and rarely included offerings of fish-hooks in their burials (V. Standen, pers. comm., 1989). By the end of the Archaic period people were undoubtedly using complex combinations of technologies and exploitative practices depending on local availability of resources and differences in environmental conditions along the coast.

In comparison to the inland zones, the sea offered more abundant food supplies so that the coastal populations were larger and achieved greater residential stability than inland peoples. Coastal estuaries had the highest population densities. Semi-tropical valleys in southern Peru were more productive north of the Río Majes and resources gradually diminished to the south of the river. To the south of the Río Camina (Pisagua) lies the Atacama Desert with a coast-line that is absolutely arid, except for the zone around the mouth of the Río Loa. Archaic occupation of this area was sparse because there was so little available drinking water. Precisely because of this, settlements tended to be located near the mouths of rivers and springs.

The distribution of archaeological sites along the more productive coast (south of Ilo, Arica, Camarones, and Pisagua) as well as the distribution along the Arid Coast (south of Iquique, Cobija, Abtao, and Taltal) suggests that these populations were semi-sedentary (Bird 1943, 1946, 1967; Núñez 1986), not sedentary as some have suggested (Bittman 1986). Little is known yet about biological, technical and cultural necessities which prompted a subsistence-settlement system combining both mobility and residential stability (Richardson 1981). However, archaeological, ethnohistoric, and ethnographic evidence all indicate a pattern of high mobility along the coast because the supply of resources available near the base-camp sites was not always continuous and plentiful. The coastal biomass is by nature an essentially dynamic and fluctuating resource which could not be domesticated (i.e., fish-farm-

succulent roots, fibers, and many others. An additional source of vegetal resources was found in the valleys and neighboring *quebradas* with gallery forests and shrub formations. Also important were inter-montane river basins near the coast which contained stands of *algarrobo* (*Prosopis juliflora* and *P. tamarugo*). This plant was doubly useful: it provided hardwood, both for fuel and for tool hafts, and fruit-pods high in sugar (glucose) (Núñez 1983; Siemens, Chapter 10). Although extremely important in this hyper-arid environment, these plant resources were not on their own sufficient for a reliable diet. Archaic peoples had to balance their subsistence regimes between the resources from the sea and those found in the inland valleys and river basins.

Throughout the Archaic period, marine resources were probably more important than terrestrial resources. Plant and animal resources from the warm valleys, fog oases, and *quebradas*, were probably perceived of as complementary to those from the sea. Judging from the size and distribution

ing), nor allow fully sedentary lifestyles, unlike some of the resources found inland and in the highlands (i.e., potatoes, maize, camelids).

One may consider the nature of Archaic period settlement and, in particular, the degree of settlement stability in relation to the appearance of various subsistence modes: opportunistic or mobile as well as fixed and localized. In general, highly mobile and opportunistic subsistence modes were encouraged by the unpredictability and capriciousness of the coastal environment. Indeed, even though a sector of the coast can be rich in resources throughout a given time-span, at the same time it can be poor in food potential due to natural causes beyond all human control (Núñez 1986). Periods of shortage were common during the following sets of circumstances: (1) during El Niño events, (2) when red tides (*irihue*) approached the shore, (3) with the collapse of marine beaches, and (4) during prolonged sea-storms. In contrast, periods of abundance were recurrent when (1) deep sea shoals were stranded or beached, (2) colonies of seals and sea birds congregated, (3) deep sea shoals of fish approached the coast within reach of rafts, and (4) fish and mollusks were unexpectedly concentrated for short periods of time along temporary beaches near shore.

During initial settlement of a stretch of coast, the diverse resources neighboring base-camp sites could have supported local communities at optimum levels of self-sufficiency. Gradually, though, the catchment areas of most base-camps would have become over-exploited, offering fewer resources and supporting fewer people. At this point, smaller "work parties" of adults and youths would have gone farther afield to locate richer, unexploited, patches of resources, returning to the base-camp with any surplus they may have collected.

These semi-nomadic movements to temporarily rich coastal localities included neighboring valleys and oases which could have been settled regularly throughout the year or in certain seasons (e.g., the oases of Tiliviche and Conan-oxa). It is known that sea storms are common during winter, the beaches drift and shoals of sardines and their accompanying predators withdraw to deeper waters. In addition, cold winters and rare periods of full low-tide make gathering difficult. In contrast, during the warmest summer months, the sea provides great wealth of transitory resources, such as the concentrations of mollusks on drift beaches, and the arrival of the *guanayes* (*Phalacrocorax boungainvillii*) from the north.

The two contrasting seasons, summer (October to March) and winter (April to September) had a profound effect on the coastal settlement-subsistence system. More work activity took place during summer, due to the increased availability along the shore-line of sardines and larger fish, mollusks, and seals. During winter as these species became scarce, people began to look for other resources beyond the inter-tidal zone using more complex fishing technologies such as fish-hooks, *chispas*, nets, rafts, and other tools. At the same time, complementary species would be hunted and gathered, such as birds, which were always resident on the

coast. Perhaps during this season when marine resource were not so plentiful, people would undertake hunting trips to valleys, *quebradas* and oases within a one or two day's journey from the coast.

Another question that has arisen is the degree to which the reliability and availability of marine resources prevented or buffered against periodic food shortages (Osborn 1977; Schiappacasse and Niemeyer 1984). One of the strategies for buffering against periodic shortages is the use of storage techniques and facilities, but these are difficult to detect archaeologically. If food resources were generally available through storage and natural abundance, then nutritionally-related health stress would have diminished. However, it is still a matter for debate whether during the Archaic period there was less biological or health stress among coastal peoples compared with inland populations (Allison et al. 1981). At present, inland Archaic period cemeteries have not been found which would provide skeletal samples allowing comparisons with coastal populations.

At any rate, It is probable that Archaic period coastal and inland people had contact with one another. People may have traveled or migrated from the coast into the higher valleys and the highlands or *altiplano*, or vice-versa. If they did not interact directly, they may have established networks of exchange contacts between the coastal zones and the Andean highlands. Archaeological evidence indicates that shells and dogfish teeth appear in highland Archaic rock shelters dating to the beginning of the Postglacial period (Santoro and Núñez 1987). Additionally, the high frequency on the coast of highland obsidian, camelid hides, Andean *rhea* skin, and the remains of highland birds, are unequivocal indications that direct and/or indirect contacts existed during the Archaic period. Even so, the nature of those interactions remains to be clarified.

The use by Archaic period coastal peoples of Fertile inland *quebradas* and oases, at altitudes of not greater than 1,200 m, has been well documented at sites such as Tili-viche. In these riverine zones, there is much evidence for imported marine shells and fish before the 5th millennium B.P. (True et al. 1970; Núñez and Hall 1982). These imports may have been crucial in trading for other exotic goods such as domesticated guinea pigs (*Cavia* sp.), maize, *totora* roots (*Scirpus* sp.), and workable fibers, all of which have been found in Archaic contexts at Tiliviche. To this list we can add maize and chenopod (*Chenopodium* sp.) pollen found in other Archaic period sites in the Tarapacá *quebrada* (Núñez 1986; Williams 1980). The presence of vicuña (*Vicugna vicugna*) skins in Archaic period coastal settlements, dating from the 8th millennium B.P., suggests significant early contacts with the highest altitude inland regions. The presence of vizcacha (*Lagidium* sp.) and chinchilla (*Chinchilla* sp.) remains (two animals that come from near the inland *quebradas* and oases) at the coastal site of Camarones suggests that these coastal people may have procured for themselves mammal protein and traded for still other more exotic materials that had been imported from the distant highlands.

In summary, coastal resource exploitation included fishing, gathering, and hunting, including maize and *quinoa* (*Chenopodium quinoa*) horticulture, and raising guinea pigs. Even though the coastal zone is hyper-arid and lacks most plant resources, the marine resources, including mollusks, sea mammals, and fish, succeeded in providing greater nutritional value, in terms of quantity and quality, than the resources found in the Fertile ecozones inland. In spite of this, there is some evidence that Archaic period coastal peoples occasionally suffered times of food shortage and nutritional stress. For example, mortuary remains from cemeteries on the Camarones Coast as well as in the Tiliviche Oasis which show high rates of infant mortality (Standen and Núñez 1984; Schiappacasse and Niemeyer 1984).

The Early Archaic Period (10,000-8000 B.P.)

The origin of the first people who occupied the coast of the south-central Andes has not yet been identified. On the one hand, people may have migrated along the coast from northern and central Andean areas during the early Holocene. On the other hand, during the early Post-glacial period, there may have been movement to the coast by waves of Andean hunters displaced from upland valleys and plains by sudden food shortages and by desertification (Ochsenius 1985; Núñez and Varela 1963). By about 10,000 B.P., these hunters may have begun to use coastal resources, quickly resulting in the growth of populations dependent on the sea (Núñez and Santoro 1989).

The occupation of the coast seems to have taken place some two millennia later than the earliest rock shelters identified on the highland *puna*. If older sites existed on the coast, they must lie beneath the present day sea level or be situated at higher elevations, unaltered by rockfall or by marine transgressions. The only coastal site that dates prior to the 10th millennium B.P. is the Anillo site (also known as the Ring site) in southern Peru. Thus, there is evidence for a long early Archaic cultural sequence that can be broken into various stages defined on the basis of radiocarbon dates.[2] The sequence has been recognized both on the relatively Fertile stretch of coast from Ilo to Pisagua, as well as on the more arid stretch of coast from Pisagua to Taltal.[3]

Tiliviche, Anillo and Las Conchas Stages

Sites of this period have been found on the south Peruvian coast between the mouth of the Río Moquegua and the neighboring southern coast. The sites are located along remnant fossil beaches, as is the case, for example, with the Anillo site (Ring site) which has an initial occupation dated at 10,575 B.P. (but the reliability of this ^{14}C date is uncertain since it was made using marine shell). The accumulation of the shell mound continued until the beginning of the Middle Archaic period (Richardson 1987). Another early occupation was discovered in a campsite situated in the Tiliviche Oasis, near the coast of Pisagua. The first evidence of human activity at the site dates to 9710 B.P. and includes seafood refuse, grinding stones, projectile points, and lanceolate knives (Figure 2a-c). The abundance of foodstuffs brought in from the coast link this population to the settlements at the shell mound sites of Pisagua and Camarones. By this stage in Tiliviche, there began an agglutinated residence pattern of small semicircular houses, hollowed out floors, and posts for light roofs, surrounded by small heaps of coastal refuse associated with concentrations of lithic debris from flaking stone tools (Núñez and Moragas 1978; Núñez and Hall 1982). The Archaic occupation of Tiliviche lasted until 3810 B.P. when there appeared a cemetery, exceedingly rare for inland sites near the coast, whose occupants showed traits similar to those found in coastal cemeteries.

These camps were semi-sedentary, and their inhabitants incorporated coastal resources as dietary complements to the terrestrial resources found locally. The residents also used a range of local lithic materials for stone tools, and fibers and wood for making hafts and other artifacts. Occupations similar to the Tiliviche sequence occurred in other oases and *quebradas* along the coast. For example, at Aragón, located near Tiliviche and 32 km inland from the coast, there was a camp site dating to 8650 B.P. The occupants of this site ate Pacific mollusks and fish, gathered vegetal matter including the roots of aquatic plants, and used grinding stones with a conically-shaped hollow depression, similar to ones found at Tiliviche. A later occupation of the site, dating to 5170 B.P., shows evidence for a greater consumption of shellfish and fish, caught with cactus thorn fish-hooks (P. Núñez and Zlatar 1976, 1977).

During the Tiliviche period (during the 9th millennium B.P.), discoidal shell fish-hooks were common on the coast (e.g., in early deposits at Camarones 14) as well as the oasis sites (e.g., Tiliviche 1). Also during this period, grinding stones and projectile points or leaf-shaped knives were common in camp-sites. Posthole patterns and other features at these sites indicate that people built roofed semi-circular dwellings.

Further south along the Arid Coast near Antofagasta, there developed a culture contemporary with, but distinct from, Tiliviche. It is called the Las Conchas stage, after the Las Conchas site, a small camp-site consisting of a badly eroded shell midden, dating to 9680 B.P. (Llagostera 1979a). This occupation is characterized by the presence of geometric sandstone objects (cog stones), polished discs, tanged points, anvils, and *manos* (Carevich 1978; Núñez 1983: Fig. 4.11). The polygonal-shaped stones are similar to those recorded for the Huentelauquén Culture, located further to the south along the coast. As a result, a northward migration from Huentelauquén has been proposed, with the site of Las Conchas being the northernmost extent of the distribution. The use of sinkers and nets, as well as the evidence for sub-adult mollusks, and the juvenile nature of the fish caught, suggest beach fishing and gathering.

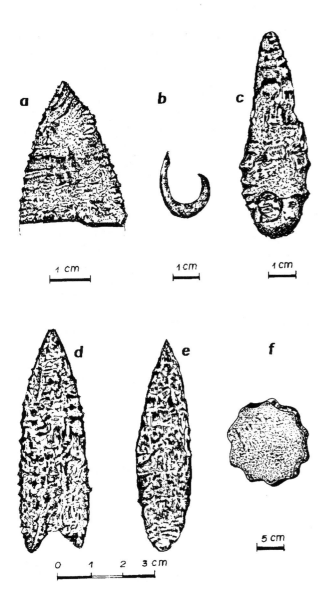

Figure 2. Early and Middle Archaic Period Artifacts: (*a*) Bifacial Knife, (*b*) Shell Fishhook, (*c*) Leaf-shaped Point, all from Tiliviche (Núñez 1983); (*d*) Concave-base Point, and (*e*) Leaf-shaped *hoja de sauce* Point, both from Camarones 14 (Shiappacasse and Niemeyer 1984); (*f*) Cog Stone from Las Conchas/Huentelauquén (Llagostera 1989).

Some of the species caught were from warmer waters, suggesting that they may have come close to shore during periodic El Niño events. The location of the site, 1 km inland, adjacent to an intermittent stream, suggests that it was more important to locate sites near drinking water than along the ocean shore where food resources could be more easily obtained. Sea foods were brought the 1 km to the site and then prepared and cooked in hearths. Surrounding the

hearths are concentrations of stone flakes, and large numbers of polygonal-shaped stones (Llagostera 1979a).

To sum up, the Anillo and Las Conchas components are, at present, isolated segments of cultural traditions situated at the extremes of the south-central area, the former linked with some little known period in the south of Peru and the latter linked with the southern area (Huentelauquén period). The Tiliviche and Aragón components constitute a single period and persisted, like Anillo, into later times. In all of these locations, people of this period were involved in the exploitation of fish, mollusks, the hunting of mammals and birds. The absence of fish-hooks in the earliest deposits of this period, if proved, would demonstrate an opportunistic use of resources along the shore, with little evidence of deep-water fishing. Later during this period, shell fish-hooks as well as harpoons came into use. Based on the kinds of artifacts recovered, it is likely that during these early periods the exploitation of marine mammals, camelids, birds, and certain fish would have been the most important staples. This diet was supplemented by the gathering of mollusks and wild plants.

Middle Archaic Period (8000-6000 B.P.)

After 8000 B.P., there is no evidence for the Las Conchas stage on the Arid Coast. However, the numbers of sites grew in the river estuary zones, giving rise to dense coastal populations. This pattern is most clearly seen during the Tiliviche stage at the mouth of the Río Camarones where the type site of Camarones 14 is located. The increase in the number of sites is also apparent further inland in zones such as the Tiliviche Oasis.

Camarones Stage

There is a great deal of continuity from the previous Tiliviche stage: Camarones stage people used base camps with similar dwellings, harpoons, lanceolate projectile points (Figure 2d-e), discoidal shell fish-hooks, and grinding implements. There were also new developments. Camarones 14, a semi-sedentary settlement, had the first cemetery which contained bodies prepared using artificial mummification. This initiated a "cult of the dead," possibly reflecting a regional or ethnic identity and represents an increasing ideological cohesion within the region (Schiappacasse and Niemeyer 1984). The mortuary population was biologically homogeneous with high rates of fertility and infant mortality. The high infant mortality suggests that people still underwent times of periodic food stress in this coastal environment.

Some family groups may have traveled from the coast inland to oases, such as Tiliviche, where they set up temporary camps. There they provisioned themselves with lithic blanks, *algarrobo* wood, camelids, rodents, edible plants, and plants materials for making basketry, cordage, and other items.

Most of the mortuary information for this stage comes from the site of Camarones 14. Burials of both adults and subadults were laid out in an extended position and covered with mats and camelid skins. Neonates and unweaned babies were mummified using Chinchorro techniques. It is likely that mortuary ceremonies typical of later fishing peoples were first developed during this stage.

Quiani Stage

By the 6th millennium B.P., the descendants of Camarones stage peoples had settled other Fertile river mouth zones and expanded towards the Arid Coast. This new period is called the Quiani stage, represented by a complex of coastal settlements which stretch from the Fertile Coast at Arica to the southernmost Arid Coast at Taltal. During this stage, there was an increase in specialized coastal resource procurement technologies (Bird 1943). The combination of shore-line and off-shore hunting and fishing was more balanced than earlier, due to increased skills and better technologies for deep-sea fishing. This trend is seen in the tools and faunal remains found in the densely packed shell mounds of Arica (e.g., Quiani 1, dating to 6170 B.P., and Punta Pichalo, Pisagua, and North Camarones, dating to 6200 B.P.), the climax of which has been dated to the latter part of the 6th millennium B.P. Common items include: simple fish-hooks of mussel shell, composite fish-hooks, some with an added sinker, harpoons with detachable heads and bone barbs, lanceolate and double-ended projectile points, bone punches, lava grinding stones, and a varied lithic industry with both hard-hammer and pressure flaking, net bags, cordage of vegetal fiber and wool, as well as the traditional technique of twining (Figure 3). Judging from the interment of artificially mummified human remains in the Quiani shell mound near Arica, this mortuary ritual persisted into the Quiani stage (Bird 1943).

We still know very little about the dwellings used during this period along the Fertile Coast. Nevertheless, at Quiani 9, near Arica, Muñoz (1981, 1982) reports the discovery of some hollowed-out floors with raised posts, suggesting windbreaks or simple shelters, that date to between 6370 and 6115 B.P. The neighboring shell mounds were used until about 5250 B.P.

The Quiani stage people extended their hunting, fishing, and gathering activities along the Fertile Coast. They created densely packed and deep shell mounds in the vicinity of Arica, Camarones and Pisagua (Pichalo and Pisagua Viejo), North Camarones (6220-4950 B.P.), and South Camarones (5640 B.P.), where the beginnings of occupation include discoidal fish-hooks and complex technological equipment.

As the Quiani stage people migrated to the Arid Coast from the Fertile Coast, they may have eased the demographic pressure on the sheltered northern beaches (e.g., Caramucho, dating to 5980 B.P.). By the 6th millennium B.P. this expansion, which had continually progressed

southwards, finally reached the most protected bays of Cobija and Taltal. The earliest layers of the sites along these bays contain shell fish-hooks which are typical of the Quiani stage. These southernmost communities were geographically isolated around the small fresh-water springs that emerge from the narrow terrace next to the western slopes of the coastal cordillera (Núñez 1983; Sanhueza 1980; Bittman 1982, 1984; Llagostera 1989).

It is probable that some of these groups reached the coast of the southern Andean area near Coquimbo, since typical Quiani stage artifacts, such as shell fish-hooks and large lanceolate, Taltal-like, projectile points were found at the site of Guanaqueros.

During this period, coastal communities, such as Pisagua and Camarones, continued using complementary goods from the nearby inland oases. Between 6830 and 6430 B.P. coastal people traveled up the Tarapacá Valley to the site of Tarapacá 14(A), and, at the end of the period, to the site of Tarapacá 2(A). In all of these inland sites there were marine fish and mollusk remains and evidence of grinding maize and *quinoa*, judging from the quantitative analysis of coprolites and pollen (True et al. 1970; True 1975; Williams 1980; Núñez and Hall 1982). It is quite possible that the remains of camelids and rodents came from local hunts

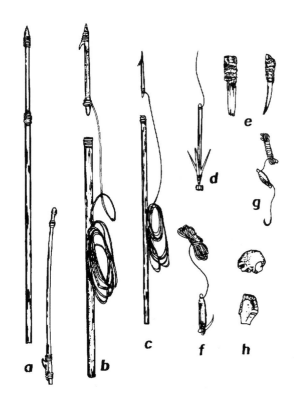

Figure 3. Archaic Period Hunting and Fishing Equipment: (*a*) Dart and Spear Thrower; (*b*) Sea Mammal Harpoon; (*c*) Fish Harpoon; (*d-g*) Fish-hooks and Fishing Tools; (*h*) Lithics for Processing Mammals and Fish (after Llagostera 1989).

of valley and *quebrada* species, and the traces of *totora* were from plants gathered locally for making cordage, mats, and other items, as well as for the edible root. In addition, the lithic industry is similar to that found in coastal sites during this period (True et al. 1970; Bird 1943).

In summary, the Quiani stage is characterized by expansion along the Fertile Coast (particularly at the mouths of rivers) as well as into the Arid Coast to the south of Pisagua. These components are marked by their most diagnostic artifact: the discoidal shell fish-hook.

Late Archaic Period (6000-4000 B.P.)

By the Late Archaic period, the populations had achieved a high degree of cultural and technological uniformity, both along the Fertile and Arid Coasts. All locations near water sources had settlements and most of these contained cemeteries. Moreover, they practiced a wide range of techniques for exploiting coastal resources, eventually including the use of floating devices such as simple rafts. These must have been early precursors for the well-constructed rafts, common in post-Archaic periods, that made regular access to deep sea shoals possible.

Cultural and technological traits show a marked continuity with adaptive and productive achievements of previous periods. Nevertheless, the full development of this coastal Archaic life style was eventually disrupted by the immigration of highland populations. These peoples brought innovations in agricultural production, including both plants and livestock, and craft production such as ceramics. These influences and changes resonated throughout the area. Outlined below are the most representative stages of the Late Archaic period.

Chinchorro Stage

The Chinchorro stage, with many traits derived from the earlier periods, spread all along the Fertile Coast. It is characterized by continued use of artificial mummification, large leaf-shaped and tanged projectile points, spear-throwers, cactus thorn fish-hooks, crude clay figurines, and textile production using wool and other fibers. We know little about the camps of this stage, but the cemetery sites are more frequent and densely populated. This wide-spread mortuary practice may define a regional cultural tradition stretching from the coast of Ilo to the mouth of the Río Loa between 5000 and 3800 B.P. The most characteristic sites of this stage are located near Arica and include: Chinchorro, Morro 1, and Aborígenes de Arica.

Studies of Chinchorro stage human remains from Morro 1, dating between 5300 and 3800 B.P., show trauma caused by work-related accidents, pathologies in women caused by a calcium deficiency, and high fertility rates. At the same time, the absence of trauma caused by acts of violence suggests that these societies were not involved in raiding or warfare. In some individuals, evidence of aural osteomas,

Figure 4. Artificially Mummified Burial from the El Morro Site, Showing Details of Preparation below the Layer of Modeled Clay (after Allison et al. 1985).

caused by repeated and prolonged deep sea diving, suggests work specialization. These people may have made up a social stratum of mollusk divers and submarine harpoonists of fish such as sole, conger eel, and *torroyo* (see Patterson, Chapter 14). Other specialists may have included marine hunters using harpoons and spear-throwers; fishers with cactus thorn fish-hooks; and of course experts in mummification and associated funeral rituals (Standen et al. 1984, 1985; Allison et al. 1984). The Chinchorro funerary complex is one of the earliest cases of the use of mummification in mortuary ritual in the world, however, it lacks many of the specialized embalming techniques used by the ancient Egyptians.

The coastal mortuary tradition involves an unusual technique consisting of the skinning, de-fleshing and evisceration of both adults and juveniles. The body cavities were then dried over a fire and rubbed with ashes. Afterwards they were filled with vegetal fiber, ash and clay and subsequently the skin was replaced to reform the body. This operation involved the stuffing of wood between the skin and bones, from the ankles to the skull, through the foramen magnum. Then the exterior was modeled with clay, including facial features, genitals and breasts; sometimes a wig and layers of paint in the manner of a mask were

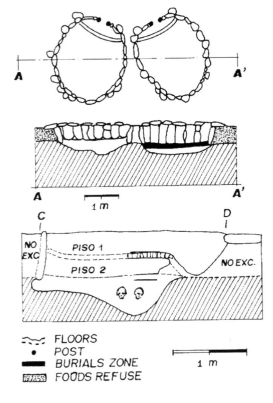

Figure 5. Extended Burials Beneath Floor of Structure at Caleta Huelén 42 (after Núñez et al. 1975 and Llagostera 1989).

FLOORS
POST
BURIALS ZONE
FOODS REFUSE

1 m

1 m

A   A'
C   D
NO EXC   PISO 1   NO EXC.
PISO 2

applied. A twined wrapping gave the impression of a compact and rigid package for ceremonial effect. The mummification or modeling with clay over the remains of birds, fish, human fetuses and dogs, indicates that this practice was widely used (Figure 4). Mummified human bodies have also been found associated with untreated corpses (Uhle 1917; Allison et al. 1984; Standen et al. 1984).

It has been proposed that these funerary customs were brought by immigrants from the tropical forests (Rivera and Rothhammer 1986), but the presence of vicuña skins among these burials might equally suggest an auspicious connection with the highlands. Most likely, though, because the coastal sequence was of such long duration, this funerary ritual arose as a local phenomenon. In any case, the question of its origin continues to be debated.

The occupation of the Fertile Coast during this period continued, with seasonal movements inland to obtain complementary goods from the nearby oases. For example, fishers, using cactus thorn fish-hooks, occupied the *quebrada* of Aragón between 5170 and 4480 B.P. (Núñez and Zlatar 1976). Tiliviche Oasis was also occupied during this period and included the construction of a cemetery around 3900 B.P. (Standen and Núñez 1984). In the valley of Tarapacá the campsite of Tarapacá 14(A) was reoccupied at

4780 B.P., Tarapacá 12 at 4690 B.P. and Tarapacá 18 at 3910 B.P. (True et al. 1970).

Other groups went up the Camarones valley, no more than two days' journey from the coast, creating camps in Conanoxa, which dated between 4020 and 3740 B.P. (Niemeyer and Schiappacasse 1963). In all of these sites, located beside permanent streams, people carried out activities such as grinding seeds, gathering and consuming *algarrobo* fruits, hunting camelids and rodents, and gathering wood, fibers, and the roots of aquatic plants. They may also have practiced some horticulture including plants such as maize and *quinoa*.

The southern extreme of the Chinchorro stage, along the Arid Coast, had a typical pattern of semi-sedentary settlements. For example, at the mouth of the Río Loa, the site of Huelén 42, dating to 4780 B.P., was characterized by camp-sites with agglutinated but not contiguous circular rooms. The buildings were constructed with vertical blocks joined with ash mortar and hollowed out dwelling floors (Núñez et al. 1975). Extended burials were placed beneath the compacted floors of the dwellings (Figure 5). Some of the burials had clay masks and accumulations of ochre, but artificial mummification was not used. Other Chinchorro stage components are known from Canastos 3 (3490 B.P.), Cobija 13 (5060 B.P.), and southwards to Chacaya 2, Abtao 4, and other similar sites near sheltered beaches approaching the bay of Taltal (Llagostera 1989; Bittman 1982; Zlatar 1983; Núñez et al. 1975).

This settlement pattern is distributed along the Arid Coast (Loa-Taltal), but it is not observed on the Fertile Coast of Tarapaqueña. It also coincides with a complex of contemporary and formally homologous camp-sites situated along the western slopes of the Puna de Atacama (hunters of the Tulan stage). At Huelén 42 were recovered rare feathers of the cordilleran parrot, obsidian, lanceolate projectile points, and grinding stones, all similar to artifacts found in the camps of the hunters of the Puna de Atacama. The similarity of these coastal and inland components, all precisely dated between the 5th and 4th millennium B.P., suggests that the pattern of construction at Huelén 42 could have derived from contacts between Archaic coastal and highland populations, but the exact nature of this interaction remains to be clarified (Núñez et al. 1975; Núñez 1983).

The terminal Archaic cultures typified by the sites of Abtao (second occupation) and Cáñamo (first occupation), and dating from 3500 to 2800 B.P., maintained an essentially coastal lifestyle, but without the typical dwellings and without links to other more complex societies. The first significant changes in this pattern occurred at the end of the Archaic period, appearing first at Cáñamo by about 2800 B.P. There we see the first ceramics associated with maize, possibly originating from Formative period communities in distant valleys (Llagostera 1989; Núñez and Moragas 1977).

On the Arid Coast, between Río Loa and Río Taltal there were more radical cultural innovations in two distinct and distant localities. At Cobija 10, near the north end of the Arid Coast, burial tumuli similar to ones found in the Tarapacá Valley, and associated with ceramics and cultigens dating between 2270 and 1600 B.P., have been reported (Moragas 1982). At Abtao, near Antofagasta on the south end of the Arid Coast, ceramics and cultigens, dating to about 2450 B.P., may have initially come from the inland San Pedro de Atacama culture (Núñez 1984).

Farther to the south, on Fertile Coast, the characteristics of the terminal Chinchorro stage are not well known. It is possible that some populations became isolated, such as the fishers at Camarones 15, who continued to use facial masks as part of their mortuary customs until about 3000 B.P. This suggests that, from the 4th millennium B.P., the terminal Archaic populations of the Fertile Coast came increasingly into contact with farming immigrants who cultivated the rich lands in the warm valleys along the Pacific Coast.

Capilla Stage

This stage, dating approximately to the fourth millennium B.P., falls within what has been called the Initial period and represents a transition between the Late Archaic and Formative periods. The earliest component of this stage was found in the rock shelter site of Capilla 1. Muñoz (1982) reports finding various plant remains, including sweet potato (*Hipomoeba batata*), gourd (*Lagenaria* sp.), manioc (*Manihot utilissima*), squash (*Cucurbita* sp.) and cotton (*Gossypium barbadense*), dating between 3670 and 2790 B.P. The nature of these contacts between the coastal fisher-folk and the inland farmers is not yet known. Another Capilla stage component was discovered at the site of Quiani 7 (3590 B.P.), near Arica. It is particularly interesting because of the sophisticated wool and cotton textiles that were recovered. Further progress in textile manufacturing is evident at Camarones 15 (3060 B.P.), where funerary offerings include textiles produced on a waist loom. Some of these textiles had been dyed (Dauelsberg 1982). Towards the end of the Capilla stage, Late Archaic traits began disappearing as a result of contacts with inland farming populations. Mortuary patterns changed most noticeably: a range of new burial patterns, including flexing of the legs became common, while the older, extended burial style gradually disappeared.

It seems certain that Capilla stage coastal fishing people began to merge both biologically and culturally with farming immigrants from the inland valleys, giving rise to the first coastal populations that experimented with cultivated crops while at the same time maintaining a staple seafood diet. During this stage, the first fully sedentary villages would have begun in the lower reaches of the valleys, next to permanent springs. Sites near Ilo (e.g., Viña del Mar) contain textiles such as turbans, dyed cotton fabrics, and textiles with stepped designs (Torres et al. 1990). Some of these sites also have evidence of domesticated camelids (Aldenderfer 1989).

This pattern suggests that, during the Capilla stage, there emerged a mixed economy that included fishing, hunting, gathering, and horticulture. For the coastal villagers, though, marine resources still provided the corner-stone of the subsistence economy. This is clearly demonstrated at the site of Acha 2 in the Azapa Valley, where fishing people left behind composite-sinker and cactus thorn fish-hooks. Although both rhomboid and leaf-shaped projectile points have also been found, there were fewer remains from hunting and cultivation than there were from fishing activities (Muñoz 1982). While the last Archaic peoples of the Fertile Coast were able to maintain horticultural plots in the nearby valleys, they were not able to prevent the colonization of the coastal valleys by immigrant farmers, as will be seen below.

Early Formative Period (3200-1800 B.P.)

Although beyond the scope of this paper, it is useful to briefly discuss the beginning of the Formative period, particularly as it is manifested in the Azapa stage, and its successor, the Alto Ramírez stage. These stages represent the full disappearance of Archaic patterns and traditions, and the adaptation of coastal peoples to farming, including the rearing of animals and the cultivation of plants. By way of a conclusion, I will now briefly discuss the main characteristics of these stages of the Formative period, showing how clearly they contrast with the preceding stages of the Archaic period.

Azapa and Alto Ramírez Stages

By about 3250 B.P., in the Azapa Valley, farmers began herding domesticated llamas and cultivating various plants. For the first time resources other than seafood became dietary staples. Formative period coastal villagers also began producing ceramics, sophisticated textiles, and they carried out metal working (Santoro 1980). The origin and evolution of the Azapa stage is still not well known, however, during the subsequent Alto Ramírez stage, beginning about 2350 B.P., we see the expansion of maize agriculture, full-blown sedentism, and the use of burial tumuli. At the beginning of the Formative period there must have been a great deal of biological, cultural, and economic overlap and interaction between the terminal Late Archaic coastal populations and groups arriving from the highlands. These latter folk who brought new economic and cultural patterns, including agricultural and livestock-rearing, may have been people of the Pakara culture originating in the Titicaca Basin (Mujica 1978).

While these Formative period components occurred in the valleys of the Fertile Coast, adjacent to the Pacific shore, it is probable that remnants of coastal Archaic populations would have maintained their unrestricted dependence on the sea. Nevertheless, they imported some of the new material goods produced by their Formative neighbors: ceramics, wool, and metal goods, among others. The site of Faldas del Morro provides an example of this pattern of interaction. Even though the site's inhabitants had a robust and clearly coastal pattern of technology, researchers have discovered ceramics of an experimental nature, and metal objects (e.g., a spoon with a double handle), but no cultivated plant remains other than squash (Dauelsberg 1982).

Formative period inhabitants of the Pacific coast continued to exploit coastal resources with extreme skill, but as participants in a mixed coastal-agrarian economy. Nevertheless, on the Arid Coast, far from the semitropical valleys, the sea remained the principal source of subsistence. Archaic technology survived and even improved in efficiency until it reached the capacity to obtain surpluses which were then traded to the farming communities in the inland valleys and in the highlands. Thus evolved the use of llama caravans led by specialized traders from the valleys and highlands, who traveled to both the Fertile and Arid Coasts exchanging highland goods for preserved seafood.

Patterns of resource exploitation and exchange which were initiated early in the Archaic period continued and evolved until the arrival of the first Europeans in the early sixteenth century. At the time of the conquest, there were communities of Changos Indians who specialized exclusively in marine resource harvesting along the Arid Coast. They traded these marine resources to inland communities in exchange for resources that their Archaic ancestors had once traveled inland to obtain for themselves.

Acknowledgments

I wish to thank Penny Dransart for her kindness in translating this paper. In addition, I would like to thank V. Standen and C. Santoro for their assistance and discussions of the ideas presented in this chapter.

Notes

1. This paper was written in 1991-1992. Since then, substantial results concerning both the Archaic period and the Archaic-Formative transition have appeared in print. This period continues to receive attention from archaeologists who are undertaking superb multidisciplinary analyses—an approach that was largely missing in the work prior to the 1990s [e.g., Arriaza (1994, 1995); Aufderheide et al. (1993); Cervellino (1994); Guillen (1992, 1994); Llagostera (1992, 1994); Monenegro (1994); Muñoz (1994); Muñoz et al. (1991); Standen (1991, 1994)].

2. All of the dates presented in this chapter are uncalibrated and based on ^{14}C determinations detailed in the various cited sources.

3. For practical reasons I am using three Archaic periods which subdivided into "stages" that are more or less equivalent to archaeological phases in the traditional terminology. These stages are characterized by diagnostic traits within a restricted time span and constitute sequential phases in the process of maritime adaptation. Each stage is arbitrarily named after the most typical site, or the site where the assemblage was first discovered. In turn, each stage is comprised of well-documented sites which constitute components of occupation.

References Cited

Aldenderfer, M. S.
1989 Archaic Period "Complementarity" in the Osmore Basin. In *Ecology, History, and Settlement in the Osmore Drainage, Peru*, edited by D. S. Rice, C. Stanish, and P. R. Scarr, pp. 101-128. BAR International Series 545. British Archaeological Reports, Oxford.

Allison, M. J., G. Focacci, C. Santoro, and J. Munizaga
1981 Estudio radiográfico y demográfico de morbilidad y mortalidad de pueblos precolombinos del Perú y Chile. *Chungará* 8:265-274.

Allison, M. J., G. Focacci, B. Arriaza, V. Standen, M. Rivera, and J. M. Lowenstein
1984 Chinchorro, momias de preparación complicada: métodos de momificación. *Chungará* 13:155-174.

Arriaza, B.
1994 Tipología de las momias Chinchorro y evolución de las prácticas de momificación. *Chungará* 26(1)11-24.
1995 Chinchorro Bioarchaeology: Chronology and Mummy Seriation. *Latin American Antiquity* 6(1)35-55.

Aufderheide, A., L Muñoz, and B. Arriaza
1993 Seven Chinchorro Mummies and the Prehistory of Northern Chile. *American Journal of Physical Anthropology* 91(2):189-201.

Bailey, G. N.
1981 Concepts of Resource Exploitation: Continuity and Discontinuity in Paleoeconomy. *World Archaeology* 13:1-15.

Bird, J.
1943 Excavations in Northern Chile. *Anthropological Papers* No. 38:171-318. American Museum of Natural History, New York.
1946 The Cultural Sequence in the Northern Chilean Coast. In *Handbook of South American Indians,* vol. 2, edited by J. Steward, pp.587-594. Bureau of American Ethnology, Washington, D.C.
1967 Muestras de radiocarbón de un basurero precerámico de Quiani. *Boletín de la Sociedad Arqueológica de Santiago* 4:13-14.

Bittman, B.
1982 El proyecto Cobija: Investigaciones antropológicas en la costa del desierto de Atacama (Chile). *Simposio Culturas Atacameñas*, pp. 99-146. Instituto de Investigaciones Arqueológicas, Universidad del Norte, Antofagasta, Chile.

1984 Arqueología de Cobija, fechas radicarbónicas: un comentario. *Occasional Papers in Anthropology-Archaeology* No. 19, pp. 97-115. University of Northern Colorado.

1986 Los pescadores-cazadores-recolectores de la costa árida chilena: un modelo arqueológico. *Chungará* 16-17:59-65.

Carevich, A.

1978 *Proyecto arqueológico Quebrada Las Conchas; un asentamiento temprano en la costa de Antofagasta.* Unpublished Thesis, Departamento de Historia y Arqueología, Universidad del Norte, Antofagasta, Chile.

Cervellino, M.

1994 Breve análisis del desarrollo cultural prehistórico de la costa de la región de Atacama a la luz de viejas y nuevas evidencias. *Resumen de Ponencia*, XIII Congreso Nacional de Arqueología Chilena, Antofagasta.

Craig, A. K.

1982 Ambiente costero del norte de Chile. *Chungará* 9:4-20.

Dauelsberg, P.

1982 Prehistória de Arica. *Diálogo Andino*, No. 1. Universidad de Tarapacá, Arica, Chile.

Guillen, S.

1992 *The Chinchorro Culture: Mummies and Crania in the Reconstruction of Coastal Adaptations in the South Central Andes.* Ph.D. Dissertation, Department of Anthropology, University of Michigan, Ann Arbor.

1994 Morro 5 (Arica): momias y cráneos para discutir el origen y naturaleza de la cultura Chinchorro. *Resumen de Ponencia*, XIII Congreso Nacional de Arqueología Chilena, Antofagasta.

Herm, D.

1969 Marines pliozän und pleistozän in hord-und-mitte Chile under besander beruck e chtigung der entiwoklung der Molluskenfauney. *Zitteliana* 2. Germany.

Llagostera, A.

1979a Ocupación humana en la costa norte de Chile asociada a peces local-extintos y a litos geométricos: 9680±160 a.C. *Actas del VII Congreso de Arqueología Chilena.* Editorial Kultrun, Santiago de Chile.

1979b 9.700 Years of Maritime Subsistence on the Pacific: An Analysis by Means of Bioindicators in the North of Chile. *American Antiquity* 44:309-324.

1982 Tres dimensiones en la conquista prehistórica del mar, un aporte para el estudio de las formaciones pescadoras de la costa Sur Andina. *Actas del VIII Congreso de Arqueología Chilena*, pp. 217-245.

1989 Caza y pesca marítima. In *Culturas de Chile, Prehistória*, edited by J. Hidalgo, V. Schiappacasse, H. Niemeyer, C. Aldunate, and I. Solimano,

pp. 57-79, Editorial Andrés Bello, Santiago de Chile.

1992 Early Occupations and the Emergence of Fishermen on the Pacific Coast of South America. *Andean Past* 3:87-109.

1994 Secuencia cultural en Abtao-1. *Resumen de Ponencia*, XIII Congreso Nacional de Arqueología Chilena, Antofagasta.

Meehan, B.

1977 Man Does Not Live by Calories Alone: The Role of Shellfish in a Coastal Cuisine. In *Sunda and Sahul*, edited by J. G. J. Allen, and R. Jones, pp. 439-532. Academic Press, New York.

Montenegro, N.

1994 Un aporte a la cronología de la costa desertica del norte de Chile. *Resumen de Ponencia*, XIII Congreso Nacional de Arqueología Chilena, Antofagasta.

Moragas, C.

1982 Túmulos funerarios en la costa de Tocopilla (Cobija) II Región (Chile). *Chungará* 9:152-173.

Moseley, M.

1975 *The Maritime Foundations of Andean Civilization.* Cummings, Menlo Park.

Muñoz, I.

1981 Antecedentes sobre patrones habitacionales en el norte de Chile y sur del Perú. *Chungará* 8:3-32.

1982 Las sociedades costeras en el litoral de Arica durante el período arcaico tardío y sus vinculaciones con la costa peruana. *Chungará* 9:124-151.

1994 El poblamiento costero prehistórico en la costa de Arica y desembocadura del Camarones. *Resumen de Ponencia*, XIII Congreso Nacional de Arqueología Chilena, Antofagasta.

Muñoz, I, J. Rocha, and S. Chacon

1991 Camarones 15: asentamiento de pobladores correspondiente al período arcaico y formativo en el extremo norte de Chile. *Actas X. Congreso de Arqueología Chilena 11.* Santiago, Chile.

Mujica, E.

1978 Nueva hipótesis sobre el desarrollo temprano del altiplano, del Titicaca y de sus áreas de interacción. *Arte y Arqueología* 5-6:285-308. La Paz, Bolivia.

Niemeyer, H., and V. Schiappacasse

1963 Investigaciones arqueológicas en las terrazas de Conanoxa, valle de Camarones (Provincia de Tarapacá). *Revista Universitaria* 26:101-166. Universidad Católica de Chile, Santiago de Chile

Núñez, L.

1973 Verticalidad por atracción marítima en el Norte de Chile. *Resúmen del Primer Congreso del Hombre Andino.* Universidad del Norte, Antofagasta, Chile

1983 Paleoindian and Archaic Cultural Periods in the Arid and Semiarid Regions of Northern Chile. In *Advances in World Archaeology*, vol. 2, edited by

F. Wendorf and A. Close, pp. 161-203. Academic Press, New York.

1984   Secuencia de asentamientos prehistóricos en el área de Taltal. *Revista Futuro* 8:28-76. Taltal, Chile.

1986   Evidencias arcaicas de maíces y cuyes en Tiliviche: hacia el semisedentarismo en el litoral fértiI y quebradas del norte de Chile. *Chungará* 16-17:25-47.

Núñez, L., and H. Hall
1982   Análisis de dieta y movilidad en un campamento arcaico del Norte de Chile. *Boletín del Instituto Francés de Estudios Andinos* 11(3):91-113.

Núñez, L., and C. Moragas
1977   Una ocupación con cerámica temprana en la secuencia del distrito de Cáñamo (costa desértica del Norte de Chile). *Estudios Atacameños* 5:21-49. Universidad del Norte, San Pedro de Atacama, Chile.

1978   Ocupación arcaica temprana en Tiliviche, Norte de Chile (I Región). *Boletín del Museo Arqueológico de La Serena* 16:53-78.

Núñez, L., and C. Santoro
1989   Cazadores de la puna seca y salada. *Estudios Atacameños* 9. Universidad del Norte, San Pedro de Atacama, Chile.

Núñez, L., and J. Varela
1963   Un complejo pre-agrícola en el Salar del Soronal (Provincia de Tarapacá). *Revista del Instituto de Antropología*, vol. 2. Universidad Nacional de Córdoba, Argentina.

Núñez, L., V. Zlatar, and P. Núñez
1975   Caleta Huelén-42: Una aldea temprana en el Norte de Chile (Nota preliminar). *Hombre y Cultura*, pp. 1-37. Universidad de Panamá.

Núñez, P., and V. Zlatar
1976   Radiometría de Aragón-1 y sus implicancias en el precerámico costero del Norte de Chile. *Actas y Memorias del IX Congreso Nacional de Arqueología Argentina*, Parte 1. Mendoza, Argentina.

1977   Tiliviche 1b y Aragón-I (estrato V) dos comunidades precerámicos coexistentes en Pampa del Tamarugal, Pisagua, Norte de Chile. *Actas y Trabajos III, Congreso Peruano "El Hombre y la Cultura Andina"* 2:734-736. Lima, Perú.

Ochsenius, C.
1985   Pleniglacial Desertization, Large Animal Mass Extinctions and Pleistocene-Holocene Boundary in South America. *Revista Norte Grande* 12:35-47. Santiago de Chile.

Osborn, A. J.
1977   Strandloopers, Mermaids, and Other Fairy Tales: Ecological Determinants of Marine Resource Utilization: the Peruvian Case. In *For Theory Building in Archaeology*, edited by L. R. Binford, pp. 157-197. Academic Press, New York.

Perlman, S. M.
1980   An Optimum Diet Model, Coastal Variability and Hunter-Gatherer Behavior. In *Advances in Archaeological Method and Theory*, vol. 3, edited by M. B. Schiffer, pp. 257-310. Academic Press, NY.

Raymond, J. S.
1981   The Maritime Foundations of Andean Civilization: a Reconsideration of the Evidence. *American Antiquity* 46:806-821.

Richardson, J.
1981   Modeling the Development of Sedentary Maritime Economies on the Coast of Peru: a Preliminary Statement. *Annals of Carnegie Museum* 50:139-150.

1987   Archaeology at the Shellring Site. *Willay* 26-27:27-29.

Rivera, M., and F. Rothhammer
1986   Evaluación biológica y cultural de poblaciones Chinchorro: Nuevos elementos para la hipótesis de contactos trans-altiplánicos, Cuenca Amazónica—Costa Pacífico. *Chungará* 16-17:295-306.

Sanhueza, J.
1980   Asentamiento precerámico en la costa desértica de interfluvio: Caramucho-3 (Provincia de Iquique, I Region, Norte de Chile). *Memoria de Titulo*. Universidad del Norte, Antofagasta, Chile.

Santoro, C.
1980   Estratigrafía y secuencia cultural funeraria: fases Azapa, Alto Ramírez y Tiwanaku (Arica, Chile). *Chungará* 6:24-45..

Santoro, C., and L. Núñez
1987   Hunters of the Dry *puna* and Salt *puna* in Northern Chile. *Andean Past* 1:57-110.

Schiappacasse, V., and H. Niemeyer (editors)
1984   *Descripción y análisis interpretativo de un sitio arcaico temprano en la Quebrada de Camarones*. Publicación ocasional No. 41. Museo Nacional de Historia Natural, Santiago de Chile.

Standen, V.
1991   *El cementerio Morro 1: nuevas evidencias de la tradición funeraria Chinchorro (período arcaico, norte de Chile)*. Unpublished Master's Thesis, Department of Archaeology, Pontificia Universidad de Chile, Lima.

1994   Secuencia cronológica y momificación artificial en el norte de Chile: 7000-3600 A.P. *Resumen de Ponencia*, XIII Congreso Nacional de Arqueología Chilena, Antofagasta.

Standen, V., and L. Núñez
1984   Indicadores antropológicos-físicos y culturales del cementerio precerámico Tiliviche-2 (Norte de Chile). *Chungará* 12:135-154.

Standen, V., M. Allison, and B. Arriaza
1984   Patologías óseas de la población Morro-I asociada al Complejo Chinchorro: Norte de Chile. *Chungará* 13:175-185.

1985 Osteoma del conducto auditivo externo: hipótesis en torno a una posible patología laboral prehispánica. *Chungará* 15:197-210.

Torres, E., C. O. Clement, N. R. Clark, and J. C. Tello

1990 De un entierro precerámico doble en Viña del Mar, Ilo, Perú: reporte preliminar. In *Trabajos arqueológicos en Moquegua, Perú*, vol. 1, edited by L. Watanabe, M. Moseley, and F. Cabiezas, pp. 177-183. Lima.

True, D.

1975 Early Maritime Cultural Orientation in Prehistoric Chile. In *Maritime Adaptations of the Pacific*, edited by R. W. Casteel, and G. I. Quimby, pp. 89-143. Mouton, The Hague.

True, D., L. Núñez, and P. Núñez

1970 Archaeological Investigations in Northern Chile: Project Tarapacá. *American Antiquity* 35(2):170-184.

Uhle, M.

1917 Los aborígenes de Arica. *Publicaciones del Museo de Etnología y Antropología de Chile* 4-5:15-176. Santiago de Chile.

Williams, L. R.

1980 Analysis of Coprolites Recovered from Six Sites in Northern Chile. In *Prehistoric Trails of Atacama: Archaeology of Northern Chile*, edited by C. Meighan, and D. L. True, pp. 195-228. University of California Press.

Yesner, D. R.

1980 Maritime Hunter-gatherers: Ecology and Prehistory. *Current Anthropology* 21:727-735.

Zlatar, V.

1983 Replanteamiento sobre el problema Caleta Huelén 42. *Chungará* 10:21-28.

17

The Late Preceramic-Early Formative Transition on the South-Central Andean Littoral

Mark S. Aldenderfer

Introduction

Despite more than 20 years of intensive research, relatively little is known of the crucial Late Preceramic-Early Formative transition (5000-2500 B.P.) on the south-central Andean littoral. At 5000 B.P., subsistence was focused upon the intensive and specialized exploitation of marine resources (Aldenderfer 1989a; Wise 1989, 1990). Settlement patterns were either fully sedentary (Muñoz 1982b) or seasonally mobile between the littoral and the fertile oases of the low intermediate valleys (Núñez 1986, 1989). Sites consisted of groupings of light circular or semi-circular structures (Muñoz 1982a). Mortuary patterns, while characterized by complex treatment of the dead and their placement in cemeteries, nevertheless reflect an egalitarian social system (Bittman 1982; Llagostera 1989).

By 2800 B.P., while marine resources remained important, subsistence was augmented by various cultigens, including *camote*, *Legenaria* sp., mandioca, and *zapallo*, and, at least in the low intermediate valleys, maize (Núñez 1974, 1986; Muñoz 1982b). Quinoa, a highland seed crop, has been commonly found at some coastal sites (Muñoz 1982b) and cotton, an industrial cultigen, occurs in sites on the littoral. During this period, settlement patterns were fully sedentary, and although villages or dense groupings of structures were not yet present, the archaeological remains of structures are described as more permanent (Muñoz 1982a, 1989; Santoro 1982; Núñez 1989). Mortuary practices are suggestive of increased sociopolitical complexity, and some burials of the Faldas del Morro phase (ca. 2800 B.P.) contain small decorative objects of gold and copper, and cloth and clothing made of camelid wool (probably llama) (Dauelsberg 1985). Basketry and both grit-tempered and fiber-tempered ceramics have been commonly encountered in sites of this period (Santoro 1982;

Dauelsberg 1985).

What factors caused this significant transition? Most explanations center upon some combination of population movement and stimulus diffusion. Rivera (1984), for example, has argued that aspects of the Alto Ramirez I phase (ca. 3000-2500 B.P.), are derived directly from altiplano sources. While the mechanisms of this derivation remain unclear, a close reading of Rivera's work suggests that they are somehow tied to the appearance of "classic" vertical complementarity (as defined by Murra [1972]) with an emphasis on "reciprocity" and "complementarity." He has also postulated that aspects of the Chinchorro complex (7000-2500 B.P.) were brought by populations from the Amazonian lowlands to the western littoral of the Andes (Rivera 1984:147), and has further attempted to bolster this position with biometrical data on skull form (Rivera and Rothhammer 1986). A similar hypothesis has been offered by Muñoz (1982b), who has argued that early cultigens such as yuca, *camote*, *Legenaria*, and cotton were either diffused or carried by maritime foragers down the central coast of Peru to northern Chile during the period 4000-3000 B.P. Similarly, metals, woolen textiles, and quinoa are thought to have diffused to the coast from the Titicaca Basin.

There is no question that both artifacts and subsistence resources from other parts of the continent begin to be found on the littoral in greater frequency throughout the period 5000-2500 B.P., but the mechanisms, and most importantly, the societal context into which these materials appeared, remain generally unexplored and unexplained. It has been documented repeatedly that "diffusion" is a complex socio-cultural process, and that a satisfactory explanation of the presence of a "foreign" trait in a new cultural setting cannot be based simply upon this assertion.

Instead of focusing on an asocial process of diffusion, it may be more profitable to explore the causal force and consequences of two social processes of considerable antiquity in the south-central Andes: regional packing and ecological complementarity. By unraveling the trajectory of these complex social processes and their mutual interaction, it may prove possible to create the social context required to explain the successful diffusion and adoption of "foreign" domesticates and artifact types on the south-central Andean littoral. This paper has two parts: a discussion of our theoretical understanding of regional packing and ecological complementarity followed by a review of the archaeological data from the region that can be used to evaluate and examine the mutual interaction of these processes. Much of this paper is speculative, in hopes that it might stimulate new and critical discussion on the emergence of social complexity in this region as well as new archaeological work in areas that are crucial to testing the power of this approach.

Regional Packing and Ecological Complementarity

Regional packing, a form of social circumscription, has long been identified as a causative force in the sedentarization process of mobile foragers. It has also been implicated as a factor in the emergence of cultural complexity in foraging societies undergoing sedentarization. An early form of the argument was outlined by Binford (1968) in his attempt to explain the origins if sedentary communities of foragers in the ancient Middle East. Since that time the "packing" argument has undergone a number of significant transformations and modifications (Brown 1985; Cohen 1985), and has endured substantial criticism as well (Hayden 1990). Despite controversy about its place in the causal chain, it is clear that all foraging societies that eventually emerged as socially "complex" were situated within densely-packed regions of neighboring groups. The question is not whether or not packing "caused" food production, but instead, to what degree did packing provide an economic and social context for the eventual appearance of food production? The question of how important a role regional packing played in this transformation is particularly relevant to the example of the south-central Andes.

Regional packing is ultimately driven by population growth in circumscribed environments. Circumscription, either environmental or social, inhibits group mobility as a means of dealing with temporary resource shortfalls, thereby increasing "stress," either perceived or actual, in nutritional deficiencies, retarded growth rates in children, increased disease load, or depressed female fecundity. Circumscription also has social implications, including increasing levels of scalar stress (Johnson 1982), and the potential for greater levels of inter- and intra-group conflict (Brown 1985). Short- term resource shortfalls probably did not produce significant levels of stress in foraging groups, but as both local and regional-scale population densities increased, and thus as mobility further declined, the incidence of significant levels of stress undoubtedly increased.

These effects can be exacerbated under conditions of environmental degradation.

Foragers are known to have responded to packing through a number of technological and social mechanisms, including intensification of resource utilization by widening niche breadth (Christenson 1980) focusing on **r**-selected species (Hayden 1981), creating storage technologies for these and other storable products (Testart 1982), the intensification of trade or other social ties between neighboring groups, such as the substitution of balanced for generalized reciprocity (Hitchcock 1982), increasing dependence upon ritual to mediate emerging social conflict (Cohen 1985; Aldenderfer 1993b), territorial bounding and maintenance (Dyson-Hudson and Smith 1978), and outright intergroup conflict. Which or how many of these alternatives are selected and in what temporal order remains a subject of intense study, but two constraints on the selection of these options seem clear: the rate of population growth within a region, and the availability, stability, and productivity of suitable secondary resources or **r**-selected species. I have argued elsewhere (Aldenderfer 1993b) that under conditions of relatively slow population growth but perceived stress, which I believe characterized the south-central Andes from 5000-2800 B.P., social ties will be intensified through increased or transformed ritual practice either before or at the same time as significant changes in subsistence technology or significant changes in social interaction. The social condition which makes this claim feasible is the long tradition of ecological complementarity between the foraging groups of this portion of the south-central Andes.

As originally conceived by Murra (1972), complementarity is a form of land-use characterized by direct, central control of vertically-stratified resource producing zones: "vertical archipelagoes." Puna-based societies reliant upon tuber production and pastoralism would attempt to control sierra valley production of maize and cotton through state-supported mechanisms of centralized redistribution. Early debate centered around the mode of control: establishment of colonies, conquest, or state-controlled exchange. Independent inter-zonal trade and exchange were deemed unimportant. From an ecological perspective, the system operated to buffer risk for puna polities by increasing their access to a wide variety of resources.

Since its publication, other forms of Andean complementarity have been recognized, and attempts have been made to generalize their salient characteristics across a number of environmental and social parameters (Salomon 1985). Two dimensions of variability are important: 1) decentralized or reciprocity-based systems versus centralized, redistributive systems, and 2) systems based on direct access to resources versus those based on indirect access, primarily different modes of trade, exchange, and barter. This dimension also includes the number of external contacts a group must maintain in order to obtain access to desired resources (Salomon 1985:513-516). Seasonal residential mobility (direct access by foragers to multiple resource zones without an exchange medium) could be considered to be a very simple form of ecological complementarity (Lynch 1971, 1981). A modification of direct access through unhindered mobility is buffering (Spielmann 1986), in which periodic resource shortages faced by a group are countered by movement of that group, with permission, into the territory of another group. More complex forms of reciprocity-based complementarity, that increase the number of external contacts, include the formation of exchange relationships between groups in different resource zones, such as mutualism (Spielmann 1986), a strategy based upon the regular exchange of subsistence resources between groups able to produce surpluses, home-base or boundary reciprocity, and down-the-line trading (Renfrew 1975:41-43; Shimada 1985:382; Salomon 1985).

Viewed from an evolutionary perspective, residential mobility as a means of ecological complementarity is a least-cost means of buffering a population against short-term resource shortfalls. The virtues of mobility and group fissioning as a means of solving intra-group conflict, avoiding inter-group conflict, and obtaining critical information on resource abundance and location are also well understood (Lee 1979). Residential mobility would have been the method of choice for dealing with either risk or resource shortfall as long as it was feasible. This implies that other, more complex and expensive forms of complementarity, such as buffering and mutualism, would not have appeared until residential mobility had been sufficiently constrained.

Modern Ecology and Late Holocene Environments in the South-Central Andes

Although the western valleys of the south-central Andes are characterized by a mosaic of different habitats, each of them can be described by three primary features: 1) ecological zones that vary with changes in altitude, creating a vertical banding of habitats from the coast to the puna; 2) pervasive aridity leading to low primary plant productivity and the clustering of resources around permanent water sources; and 3) high variance and unpredictability in the availability of resources in most habitats (Molina and Little 1981). Climate and ecology are strongly affected by the geographical massiveness and high altitude of the Andes, and the interplay between latitude and altitude (Winterhalder and Thomas 1978:12). Rainfall tends to decrease from northwest to southeast and from northeast to southwest across the two cordilleras of the Andes. The Atacama desert extends over all elevation gradients, and some areas, such as the littoral, receive virtually no rainfall over the year. Rainfall has a generally seasonal distribution, with a wet season from December to April, but its predictability in amount and frequency decreases from north to south.

Four distinct habitats can be defined: 1) fertile coast and

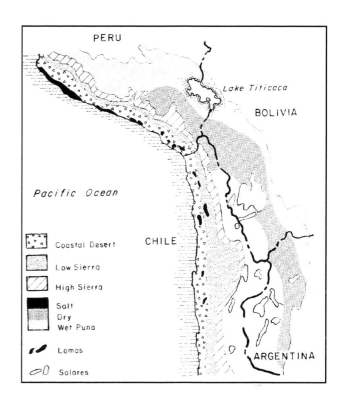

Figure 1. Major Habitats in the South-Central Andes.

littoral, 2) interfluvial desert coast, 3) low transverse valleys and basins (also known as the mid-valleys), 4) high transverse valleys and basins (or high sierra), and 5) puna, or altiplano, which includes two sub-types: dry, and *suni* (Figure 1). These habitats differ primarily in temperature and precipitation, variations in vegetation communities, and presence of special features, such as *lomas*, salt lakes and pans, small freshwater lakes, and *bofedales*, bogs which are highly productive pasturage for camelids in high elevation zones of the region.

While quantitative comparisons of the productivity of each habitat are not possible, relative rankings of their importance for foraging peoples can be made based on two criteria: productivity and uncertainty (Aldenderfer 1989b:Table 1). Clearly, the fertile coast and dry puna are the most productive habitats, followed by the low intermediate valleys and high sierra. Importantly, both the littoral and puna have **r**-selected species available: anchovies and shellfish on the littoral and *Chenopodium* spp., or quinoa and various species of lupines like *tarwi* on the puna. While *Chenopodium* spp. is available in the high sierra, resource patches are very small, and this, combined with the highest uncertainty in rainfall abundance and periodicity, limit the utility of the sierra to humans. The most important valley resource is *Prosopis* ssp., (*algorobbo*), a South American version of mesquite which takes from five to seven years to mature.

The most uncertain environments, as measured by the predictability of rainfall abundance and periodicity (Colwell

215

1974), are the high sierra and puna. In contrast, the littoral and valleys are highly predictable since they almost never experience rainfall. Both the high sierra and puna are subject to frosts and extreme low temperatures over much of the year, with some parts of the puna experiencing frost over 250 days in each year (Murra 1984:122). However, Murra (1984:120-121) also notes that because of elaborate storage strategies, as well as maintenance of complementary relationships, famine and general ecological catastrophies were rare.

Although there have been few paleoenvironmental studies of this portion of the south-central Andes, enough has been accomplished by researchers in northern Chile, southeastern Bolivia, and southern Peru to offer a tentative reconstruction of environmental conditions. The Middle Holocene (ca. 8000-5000 B.P.) has been described as a period of increased aridity and decreased temperature that would have significantly reduced the both plant and animal populations available to foragers in the region (Aldenderfer 1989a; Santoro and Núñez 1987). However, it is becoming increasingly clear that there is considerable regional variability in both the onset and the termination of these harsh climatic conditions in the south-central Andes. Palynological evidence from Sajima on the dry puna of Bolivia (Ybert and Miranda 1984) suggests that climate from 7500-6000 B.P. was a characterized by increased aridity and cold. This was followed by a period (6000-3500 B.P.) of continued cold but increased moisture. Modern climate was established after 3500 B.P.. In contrast, Graf-Meier (1981) has argued that on the basis of data obtained from Escona, approximately 50 km northeast of Lake Titicaca near the Peru-Bolivia border, the dry puna was cold and dry until ca. 6500 B.P., when a transitional period that featured increased temperature and moisture appeared. This transition lasted until 5500 B.P., when modern puna conditions were established.

While these studies are difficult to reconcile fully, it is clear that there was a period of environmental flux that lasted from ca. 5500-3500 B.P. On the puna, this may have led to the increased abundance, then relative decline, of resource patches such as quinoa, *tarwi*, and possibly tubers. A process of relatively rapid population growth could have been initiated as early as 5500 B.P. The effect of this changing environment on the high sierra and mid-valley are less clear, but if moisture increased even marginally after 6000 B.P., it would have led to the expansion of existing resource patches. This in turn could have provided stimulus for population expansion.

On the littoral, recent studies in coastal geomorphology have provided significant insights into two processes that may have affected the stability of the coastal environment: coastal uplift and inundation, and the retraction of coastal springs. Richardson (1981) has demonstrated that prior to ca. 5000 B.P., the Peruvian coast was relatively unstable due to the combined effects of tectonic uplift and inundation of the continental shelf due to glacial melting in the highlands.

The coastal environment stabilized just after this date. While the effect of these processes on fish and shellfish populations is currently under study, the implication is clear that a stabilization of the ocean floor and water temperature would have positively affected the abundance and predictability of major fish and shellfish species. Associated with the tectonic uplift of the coast is the retraction of the water table in a number of valley systems both north and south of Ilo. Clement and Moseley (1986), in a detailed examination of the hydrology of the Quebrada Carizal, have traced this retraction through the late prehistoric and colonial periods, and are beginning to extend their results to earlier periods. Their research suggests water availability may have been greater in the past.

Taken together, the 5000 B.P. environment, while subject to some regional as well as habitat-specific variability, had stabilized to a significant degree, and in addition, was relatively benevolent. Resource patches of all major subsistence species were probably larger and denser than before 5000 B.P. or in modern times. Henry (1989) has argued, against fashion, that such environmental changes for the good were significant causal factors in the sedentarization, and thus eventual population growth, of groups of Levantine foragers after 12,000 B.P. A similar process seems underway in the post-5000 B.P. south-central Andes.

The Archaeological Evidence for Regional Packing and Complementarity

Regional Packing

There are two major lines of evidence for regional packing in the western valleys of the south-central Andes beginning around 5000 B.P. First, there are at least three distinct groups of foragers that occupy different habitats in these valley systems: littoral, mid-valley, and high sierra/puna foragers, and second, there is limited evidence for population growth at the regional and habitat scale when compared to earlier time periods.

I have shown elsewhere (Aldenderfer 1989a:129-132) that at least two distinct groups of foragers—littoral and highland peoples—were present just after the initial occupation of the region. By 5000 B.P., the evidence for three groups is significant. As in most regions where differential preservation makes the direct observation of social differences or ethnicity difficult, the data that support this position are based on subsistence characteristics. Since the initial occupation of the region, foragers of the littoral focused their subsistence efforts almost exclusively on marine products. In the Osmore basin, Sandweiss et al. (1989) have shown that through the Early and Middle Preceramic, diet at the Ring Site was almost exclusively composed of marine species, and that the terrestrial component to the diet, in terms of the range of species and the percent contribution to the diet, was very small. This trend continues through the Late Preceramic after 5000 B.P., although the proportion of terrestrial species, such as locally-available camelids, increases slightly (Wise 1990). Artifact inventories reflect marine subsistence, and include a variety of harpoon points, fishhooks, net sinkers, and other artifacts used in fishing or shellfish collecting. The data from northern Chile corroborate these general trends (Llagostera 1989).

Mid-valley foragers are known from a single site in northern Chile: Tiliviche (Núñez 1986). Núñez sees Tiliviche as a wet-season residential base in a "semi-sedentary" settlement pattern. Resources at the site include shellfish, fish, and marine mammals as well as plants common to the oasis environment such as *totora*, carob (*Prosopis tamarugo*), algorrobo (*Prosopis chilensis*), and local rhizomes. Very small amounts of maize have been recovered from levels dating before 7000 B.P., but the majority of maize finds from secure archaeological contexts are found in levels dating from 6700-5200 B.P., with many more finds dating to 5200-3800 B.P. (Núñez 1986:40-44). The material culture includes fishhooks, lanceolate points, grinding stones, and shell knives. Núñez explains the existence of marine products at Tiliviche by suggesting a pattern of residential mobility, which has mid-valley foragers moving seasonally to the littoral, and having a form of "co-residence" (Núñez 1986:38) with littoral foragers living at sites such as Camarones-14. While this pattern may be possible, I prefer to see these products as a measure of complementarity relationships between these two distinct ethnic groups.

High-elevation foragers utilized both the high sierra (2800-4000 m) and dry puna (4000-4500 m) zones throughout the Archaic period. Puna lithic raw materials are commonly found at high sierra sites, and projectile points made of puna raw materials are found as stray finds and at low-density lithic scatters at strategic locations (Aldenderfer 1989b). Subsistence focused upon the hunting of deer and camelids, and probably the collection of small amounts of *Chenopodium* spp., and sites like Asana were probably wet-season temporary camps occupied by the entire co-residential group (Aldenderfer 1990, 1993a). Base camps of longer duration were probably located beyond the rim of the puna.

Although the data are tentative, population growth appears to increase significantly around 5000 B.P. (Aldenderfer 1989a). Evidence is in the form of larger numbers of known sites dating to the early portions of the Late Preceramic. The evidence for this is best seen on the littoral and in the high sierra, the two environmental zones most comprehensively surveyed in the region. On the littoral, north of the Osmore River (Aldenderfer 1986; Wise 1989, 1990), a number of large sites were found that date to the period just after 5000 B.P., and the situation is similar on the north Chilean littoral in the Lluta, Azapa, and Camarones drainages (Llagostera 1989). In the high sierra of the Osmore basin, site numbers increased five-fold, and a number of smaller rockshelters and caves were occupied

for the first time (Aldenderfer 1989a: 144). Finally, Kuznar (1989) has shown that the numbers of sites in the interior region of the dry puna increase dramatically after 6000 B.P.

Taken together, it seems clear that while there are flaws and inadequacies in the data, they nevertheless demonstrate that ethnic differentiation was in place by 5000 B.P., and that in each of these areas, population appeared to have been growing rapidly.

Complementarity Relationships

There is evidence of social interrelationships (complementarity) between: (1) littoral and mid-valley foragers, (2) mid-valley foragers and high sierra/puna foragers, and to a more limited extent, (3) littoral foragers and high sierra/puna foragers. Interrelationships between the different habitats of the region are based on the presence of artifacts and subsistence products in areas where it is unlikely or impossible they could have been produced. For instance, some form of high sierra-puna relationship is inferred because finished projectile points made of puna raw materials have been found in the sierra. At the same time, there is no evidence for puna raw material reduction debris at sierra sites, suggesting the finished points were brought or traded into the region from the puna. Smaller numbers of points made of sierra raw materials are found at puna sites. Similarly, there is some evidence of littoral products, such as marine shells, shark's teeth, and other marine products found in sierra and puna sites (Aldenderfer 1989a) and at mid-valley sites such as Tiliviche (Núñez 1986, 1989). Also, some projectile points made of high sierra and puna raw materials have been found on the littoral. There exists scant evidence of mid-valley and high sierra-puna interaction, but some lithic raw material types, probably abundant in the mid-valley regions, have been found at high sierra sites. These interrelationships began almost with the initial occupation of the region, ca. 9000 B.P. (Aldenderfer 1989a).

As I have argued elsewhere (Aldenderfer 1989a, 1989b, 1990), complementarity relationships can be seen the archaeological record of the earliest foragers of the region, who first occupied the Osmore basin around 10,000 B.P. During the Early, and most of the Middle Preceramic (10,000-6000 B.P.), access to critical subsistence resources was maintained through residential mobility and possibly a buffering relationship. In the case of foraging societies, as long as residential mobility remained an option for dealing with resource shortfalls, more complex forms of complementarity relationships were unlikely to have developed. Interregional relationships, be they buffering or trade, were symbolized by "tokens," objects of little intrinsic value such as projectile points or shark's teeth that nevertheless represented a significant social relationship between individuals in different groups. Through the Middle Archaic period, the numbers and kinds of tokens remains limited. However, around 5000 B.P., not only were more tokens beginning to be exchanged throughout the region, but also, subsistence goods, such as quinoa and vicuña began to appear in small quantities in coastal sites. Because of limited excavations, it is difficult to tell whether or not significant quantities of these materials are present. However, I believe the appearance of these goods marks a major change in the form of the relationship between high sierra-puna foragers and those at lower elevations and may possibly signal the origins of a more mutualistic relationship. There is also clear evidence of interaction between mid-valley foragers and littoral foragers, and although regional-scale mobility may have declined, marine products are still found at mid-valley sites. In addition, maize has been found in secure archaeological contexts on littoral sites after 5000 B.P.

Because of limited data, it is difficult to assess the intensity of these complementarity relationships. However, it is clear that the tokens of generalized reciprocity were being replaced by foodstuffs that bespeak a form of balanced reciprocity and further argue for a transformation of the structure of complementarity relationships in the region. The scale, and probably the frequency, of residential mobility declined at least in part as a result of the problems associated with regional packing, but populations in all habitats continued to grow.

The Emergence of Food Production and Social Complexity on the South-Central Andean Littoral

With this background, we are now in a position to model the emergence of food production and more complex societies on the south-central Andean littoral. The following comments are offered more as guidelines to research rather than fully-formed or explicated hypotheses.

Shortly after 5000 B.P., all three distinct groups of foraging societies began either to intensify social mechanisms that enhanced or transformed existing complementarity relationships or to intensify subsistence practices. To date, we only know of social transformation in the ecotone between mid-valley foragers and high sierra-puna foragers at Asana (Aldenderfer 1990, 1993a). Shortly after 5000 B.P., a series of ritual structures was constructed and elaborated prior to the obvious intensification of subsistence (Aldenderfer 1991). By ca. 4500 B.P., after ritual practice had been transformed, people began to intensify Chenopodium spp. exploitation. Both ritual practice and seed plant utilization were replaced by ca. 4300 B.P., and possibly earlier, by guanaco pastoralists (Kuznar 1990), who initiated the process of camelid domestication in the high sierra-puna rim.

Although little is known about the intensification of tubers, we know more about the intensification of Andean seed crops such as quinoa and cañihua. In the south-central Andes, the earliest known specimens of quinoa appear in coastal assemblages dating to 4780 B.P. at Caleta Huelen-42 (Núñez 1983) and at other Chinchorro complex sites

possibly as early as 5000 B.P. (Núñez 1974). Browman (1986) reports heavy use of both Chenopodium spp. and Amaranthus in Phase 1A (3300-2950 B.P.) at Chiripa, but since seed sizes are small, it is probable that wild plants were being harvested. It is likely that the plant was fully domesticated by 2550-2250 B.P. (Browman 1986). In the absence of direct indicators, it once again becomes necessary to rely upon indirect measures of the intensification of seed use. It is reasonable to conclude that intensification of these r-selected species began shortly after 5000 B.P.

Post-5000 B.P. foragers on the littoral had also begun the process of subsistence intensification by increasingly exploiting smaller fish such as anchoveta that can be taken by nets. They also increased the breadth of their food niche by taking a wider range of both fish and shellfish, and exploited a number of new off-shore habitats (Aldenderfer 1989a; Wise 1990). There were limits to this intensification, however. None of these species are domesticable, and although they are present in large numbers, they cannot be artificially manipulated. Their productivity remains grounded wholly in nature, and further, there are no indigenous r-selected species available in the habitat. Continued population growth was not sustainable on this mix of species and strategies.

This situation also has implications for the structure of existing complementarity relationships. As I suggested earlier, generalized reciprocity was replaced by balanced reciprocity in the high elevation habitats of the western valleys. In the mid-valley and high sierra-puna rim, it is probable that a mutualistic system involving the exchange of foodstuffs emerged. While other social forms of relationship probably existed, such as intermarriage, these have left no trace in the archaeological record. In fact, it is clear that in both the mid-valley and high sierra-puna rim, groups could have produced food surpluses, one of the major conditions for the emergence of mutualistic complementarity relationships. In the littoral, people would have been unable to sustain surplus production relying strictly on marine resources, and therefore, it would have been difficult to compete socially in emerging systems of mutualistic complementarity. Littoral groups faced both subsistence and social "shortfalls."

The appearance of already domesticated species from the coast further to the north, such as zapallo, other gourds, and especially the important industrial domesticate cotton would have filled in this potential subsistence and social shortfall. Cotton would have been the most important of these species, in that its successful adoption would have provided littoral foragers with a new means of creating a "surplus" that could have been used to participate in an emerging system of balanced reciprocity based on mutualism. Enterprising individuals, or "accumulators" (Hayden 1990), could have "cornered the market" on cotton production, and could have entered into lucrative trade partnerships with highlanders. Controlling cotton would have been, at least in the short run, more attractive to accumulators than adopting maize because it was a product of high social value, similar to high-quality animal wools. This process may explain why maize did not appear in large quantities in littoral assemblages until after 3500 B.P. The control of cotton could also have provided the basis for social differentiation. The appearance of highland products such as gold, silver, camelid wool clothing, and similar luxury items in mortuary contexts on the littoral may reflect the success of local accumulators, rather than the movement of highland groups into low elevation habitats.

Thus the region-wide transformation of complementary relationships combined with regional packing created a social climate of ready acceptance of "foreign" cultigens. It also laid the basis for the local development of social differentiation that began to emerge after 3000 B.P. In relation to highland groups, especially the puna-based foragers that eventually became the complex societies of the altiplano and that controlled much of the low elevation production in later times, littoral foragers were always in "reactive" position. However, I believe that this socially driven model of the Late Preceramic to Early Formative transition is more parsimonious and realistic than models driven either by long-distance population movements or vaguely defined social notions.

Acknowledgments

An earlier, very different version of this paper was read at the Circum-Pacific Prehistory Conference in Seattle in August 1989. I thank both Michael Blake and Dale Croes for their patience and understanding in waiting for the somewhat difficult birth of this incarnation of this paper. Karen Aldenderfer drafted the Figure 1, and I thank her beyond measure for her contribution to our research.

References Cited

Aldenderfer, M.

1986   Archaic Period Settlement Patterns in the Sierra of the Osmore Drainage, Southern Peru. Preliminary Report of the 1985 field season of the Northwestern University Archaic Project (NUAP). *Northwestern Archaeological Reports* 7.

1989a   The Archaic Period in the South-central Andes. *Journal of World Prehistory* 3(2):117-158.

1989b   Archaic Period "Complementarity" in the Osmore Basin. In *Ecology, History, and Settlement in the Osmore Drainage*, edited by D. S. Rice, C. Stanish, and P. R. Scarr, pp. 101-128. BAR International Series 545. British Archaeological Reports, Oxford.

1990   Late Preceramic Ceremonial Architecture at Asana, Southern Peru. *Antiquity* 64(244):479-493.

1991   Continuity and Change in Ceremonial Structures at Late Preceramic Asana, Southern Peru. *Latin Amer-ican Antiquity* 2(3):227-258

1993a   Domestic Space, Residential Mobility, and Ecological Complementarity: the View from Asana. In *Domestic Architecture, Ethnicity, and Ecological Complementarity in the South-Central Andes*, edited by M. Aldenderfer, pp. 13-24. University of Iowa Press, Iowa City.

1993b   Ritual, Hierarchy, and Change in Foraging Societies. *Journal of Anthropological Archaeology* 12:1-40.

Binford, L.

1968   Post-Pleistocene Adapatations. In *New Perspectives in Archaeology*, edited by S. Binford and L. Binford, pp.318-341. Aldine, Chicago.

Bittmann, B.

1982   Revisión del problema Chinchorro. *Chungará* 9: 46-79.

Browman, D.

1986   *Chenopodium* Cultivation, Lacustrine Resources, and Fuel Usage at Chiripa, Bolivia. Ms. on file, Department of Anthropology, Washington University, St. Louis.

Brown, J. A.

1985   Long-term Trends to Sedentism and the Emergence of Cultural Complexity in the American Midwest. In *Prehistoric Hunter-Gatherers: The Emergence of Cultural Complexity*, edited by T. D. Price and J. A. Brown, pp.201-234. Academic Press, Orlando.

Christenson, A.

1980   Change in the Human Food Niche in Response to Population Growth. In *Modeling Change in Prehistoric Subsistence Economies*, edited by T. Earle and A. Christenson, pp. 31-72. Academic Press, New York.

Clement, C., and M. Moseley

1986   Agrarian Contraction of Coastal Spring-fed Irrigation Systems at Ilo, Peru. Paper Presented at the 51st Annual Meeting of the Society for American Archaeology, New Orleans.

Cohen, M.

1985   Prehistoric Hunter-Gatherers: The Meaning of Social Complexity. In *Prehistoric Hunter-Gatherers: The Emergence of Cultural Complexity*, edited by T. D. Price and J. A. Brown, pp. 99-119. Academic Press, Orlando.

Colwell, R.

1974   Predictability, Constancy, and Contingency of Periodic Phenomena. *Ecology* 55:1148-1153.

Dauelsberg, P.

1985   Faldas del Morro: fase cultural agroalfarería Temprana. *Chungará* 14:7-44.

Dyson-Hudson, R. and E. Smith

1978   Human Territoriality: an Ecological Reassessment. *American Anthropologist* 80:21-41.

Graf-Meier, K.

1981   Palynological Investigations of Two Post-Glacial

Peat Bogs Near the Boundary of Bolivia and Peru. *Journal of Biogeography* 8:353-368.

Hayden, B.
1981   Subsistence and Ecological Adaptations of Modern Hunter-Gatherers.   In *Omnivorous Primates*, edited by R. Harding and G. Teleki, pp. 344-421. Columbia University Press, New York.
1990   Nimrods, Piscators, Pluckers, and Planters: The Emergence of Food Production. *Journal of Anthropological Archaeology* 9:31-69.

Henry, D.
1989   *From Foraging to Agiculture.* University of Pennsylvania Press, Philadelphia.

Hitchcock, R.
1982   Patterns of Sedentism Among the Basarwa of Eastern Botswana. In *Politics and History in Band Societies*, edited by E. Leacock and R. Lee, pp. 223-267. Cambridge University Press, Cambridge.

Johnson, G.
1982   Organizational Structure and Scalar stress.   In *Theory and Explanation in Archaeology*, edited by C. Renfrew, M. Rowlands, and B. Seagraves, pp. 389-421. Academic Press, New York.

Kuznar, L.
1989   The Domestication of Camelids in Southern Peru: Models and Evidence. In *Ecology, Settlement, and History in the Osmore Basin, Peru*, edited by D. Rice, C. Stanish, and P. Scarr, pp. 167-182. BAR International Series S545. British Archaeological Reports, Oxford.
1990   *Economic Models, Ethnoarchaeology, and Early Pastoralism in the High Sierra of the South-Central Andes.*   Ph.D dissertation, Department of Anthropology, Northwestern University. University Microfilms, Ann Arbor.

Lee, R.
1979   *The !Kung San: Men, Women, and Work in a Foraging Society.* Cambridge University Press, Cambridge.

Llagostera, A.
1989   Caza y pesca maritima. In *Culturas de Chile: Prehistoria desde sus Orígenes Hasta los Albores de la Conquista*, edited by J. Hidalgo, V. Schiappacasse, H. Niemeyer, C. Aldunate, and I. Solimano, pp. 57-80. Editorial Andrés Bello, Santiago.

Lynch, T.F.
1971   Prehistoric Transhumance in the Callejon de Huaylas, Peru. *American Antiquity* 38:139-48.
1981   Zonal Complementarity in the Andes: a History of the Concept. In *Networks of the Past*, edited by P. Francis, F. Kense, and P. Duke, pp. 221-31. Proceedings of the 12th Annual Chacmool Conference, Archaeological Association of the University of Calgary, Alberta.

Molina, E., and A. Little
1981   Geoecology of the Andes: the Natural Science Basis for Research Planning. *Mountain Research and Development* 1:115-44.

Muñoz, I.
1982a   Dinámica de las estructuras habitacionales del extremo norte de Chile (Valle-Costa). *Chungará* 8:3-32.
1982b   Las sociedades costeras en el litoral de Arica durante el periodo arcaico tardío y sus vinculaciones con la costa Peruana. *Chungará* 9:124-151.
1989   El período formativo en el norte grande (1000 a.C. a 500 d.C.) In *Culturas de Chile: Prehistoria Desde sus Orígenes Hasta los Albores de la Conquista*, edited by J. Hidalgo, V. Schiappacasse, H. Niemeyer, C. Aldunate, and I. Solimano, pp. 107-128. Editorial Andrés Bello, Santiago.

Murra, J.
1972   El control "vertical" de un máximo de pisos ecológicos en la economía de las sociedades andinas. In *Visita de la Provencia de León de Huánuco en 1562*, pp. 429-476. Universidad Nacional Hermilio Valdizán, Huánuco, Perú.
1984   Andean Societies. *Annual Review of Anthropology* 14: 119-141.

Núñez, L.
1974   *La Agricultura Prehistórica en los Andes Meridonales.* Editorial Orbe, Santiago.
1983   Paleoindian and Archaic Cultural Periods in the Arid and Semiarid Regions of Northern Chile. *Advances in World Archaeology* 2:161-203.
1986   Evidencias arcaicas de maices y cuyes en Tiliviche: hacia el semisedentarismo en el litoral fértil y quebradas del norte de Chile. *Chungará* 16/17:25-47.
1989   Hacia la producción de alimentos y la vida sedentaria. In *Culturas de Chile: Prehistoria Desde sus Orígenes Hasta los Albores de la Conquista*, edited by J. Hidalgo, V. Schiappacasse, H. Niemeyer, C. Aldunate, and I. Solimano, pp. 81-106. Editorial Andrés Bello, Santiago.

Renfrew, C.
1975   Trade as Action at a Distance: Questions of Integration and Communication. In *Ancient Civilization and Trade*, edited by J. Sabloff and C. Lamberg-Karlovsky, pp. 3-95. University of New Mexico Press, Albuquerque.

Richardson, J. III
1981   Modeling the Development of Sedentary Maritime Economies on the Coast of Peru. *Annals of the Carnegie Museum* 50:139-150.

Rivera, M.
1984   Altiplano and Tropical Lowlands Contacts in Northern Chilean Prehistory: Chinchorro and Alto Ramirez Revisited.   In *Social and Economic Organization in the Prehispanic Americas*, edited

by D. Browman, R. Burger, and M. Rivera, pp. 143-161. BAR International Series 194. British Archaeological Reports, Oxford.

Rivera, M., and F. Rothhammer
1986   Evaluación biología y cultural de poblaciones Chinchorro: nuevos elementos para la hipótesis de contactos transaltiplánicos, cuenca amazonas-costa pacífico. *Chungará* 16-17:295-306.

Salomon, F.
1985   The Dynamic Potential of the Complementarity Concept. In *Andean Ecology and Civilization*, edited S. Masuda, I. Shimada, and C. Morris, pp. 511-531. University of Tokyo Press, Tokyo.

Sandweiss, D., J. Richardson III, E. Reitz, J. Hsu, and R. Feldman
1989   Early Maritime Adaptations in the Andes: Preliminary Studies at the Ring Site, Peru. In *Ecology, Settlement, and History in the Osmore Drainage Peru*, edited by D. S. Rice, C. Stanish, and P. R. Scarr, pp. 35-84. BAR International Series 545. British Archaeological Reports, Oxford.

Santoro, C.
1982   Formativo temprano en el extremo norte de Chile. *Chungará* 8:33-62.

Santoro, C., and L. Núñez
1987   Hunters of the Dry Puna and Salt Puna in Northern Chile. *Andean Past* 1:57-110.

Shimada, I.
1985   Perception, Procurement, and Management of Resources: Archaeological Perspective. In *Andean Ecology and Civilization*, edited by S. Masuda, I. Shimada, and C. Morris, pp. 357-400. University of Tokyo Press, Tokyo.

Spielmann, K.
1986   Interdepedence in Egalitarian Societies. *Journal of Anthropological Archaeology* 5:279-312.

Testart, A.
1982   The Significance of Food Storage Among Hunter-Gatherers: Residence Patterns, Population Densities, and Social Inequality. *Current Anthropology* 23:523-38.

Winterhalder, B., and B. Thomas
1978   *Geoecology of Southern Highland Peru.* Occasional Paper No. 27. Institute of Arctic and Alpine Research, Boulder.

Wise, K.
1989   Archaic Period Research in the Lower Osmore Drainage. In *Ecology, Settlement and History in the Osmore Drainage, Peru*, edited by D. S. Rice, C. Stanish, and P. R. Scarr, pp. 85-100. BAR International Series 545. British Archaeological Reports, Oxford.
1990   *Late Archaic Maritime Subsistence Strategies in Southern Peru.* Ph.D dissertation, Department of Anthropology, Northwestern University. University Microfilms, Ann Arbor.

Ybert, J., and P. Miranda
1984   Análisis palinológico de un corte del Sajima. *Actas Segundo Congreso Geológico de Bolivia*, pp.691-695. La Paz.

Contributors

Mark S. Aldenderfer
Department of Anthropology
University of California
Santa Barbara, California, U.S.A.

Barbara Arroyo
Universidad del Valle de Guatemala
Guatemala

Bruce F. Benz
Texas Wesleyan University
Fort Worth, Texas, U.S.A.

Michael Blake
Department of Anthropology and Sociology
University of British Columbia
Vancouver, British Columbia, Canada

John E. Clark
New World Archaeological Foundation
Brigham Young University
Provo, Utah, U.S.A.

Richard G. Cooke
Smithsonian Tropical Research Institute
Balboa, Panamá, República de Panamá

Arthur A. Demarest
Department of Anthropology
Vanderbilt University
Nashville, Tennessee, U.S.A.

Michael W. Love
Institute for Social, Behavioral and Economic Research
University of California, Santa Barbara
Santa Barbara, California, U.S.A.

George H. Michaels
Office of Instructional Consulting
University of California, Santa Barbara
Santa Barbara, California, U.S.A.

Michael E. Moseley
Department of Anthropology
University of Florida
Gainesville, Florida, U.S.A.

Lautaro Núñez
Instituto de Investigaciones Arqueológicas
Universidad Católica del Norte
San Pedro de Atacama, Chile

Thomas C. Patterson
Department of Anthropology
Temple University
Philadelphia, Pennsylvania, U.S.A.

Deborah M. Pearsall
Department of Anthropology
University of Missouri
Columbia, Missouri, U.S.A.

Dolores R. Piperno
Smithsonian Tropical Research Institute
Balboa, Panamá, República de Panamá

Mary E. Pye
The Spanish Institute
New York, New York, U.S.A.

Anthony J. Ranere
Department of Anthropology
Temple University
Philadelphia, Pennsylvania, U.S.A.

J. Scott Raymond
Department of Archaeology
University of Calgary
Calgary, Alberta, Canada

Stuart D. Scott
Department of Anthropology
State University of New York
Buffalo, New York, U.S.A.

Alfred H. Siemens
Department of Geography
University of British Columbia
Vancouver, British Columbia, Canada

Barbara Voorhies
Department of Anthropology
University of Colorado
Boulder, Colorado, U.S.A.

Karen Wise
Department of Anthropology
L A County Museum of Natural History
Los Angeles, California, U.S.A.